Colony to Empire

Colony to Empire

Episodes in American Legal History

George Dargo

The Lawbook Exchange, Ltd.
Clark, New Jersey

ISBN 9781616191443 (hardcover)
ISBN 9781616191450 (paperback)
Lawbook Exchange edition 2012

Religious Tolerance and its Limits in Early America, reprinted with permission, vol. 16 *Northern Illinois University Law Review*, p. 341–370, (Spring 1996).

The Sarah Roberts Case and the Origins of "Separate But Equal" originally published *as The Sarah Roberts Case in Historical Perspective* reprinted from *Massachusetts Legal History*, Vol. 3 (1997) permission of Supreme Judicial Court Historical Society, Boston Mass.

Steamboats and Tugboats on the Mississippi originally published as *Steamboats, Towboats and Legal Historiography: The Law in Louisiana and the New Nation* reprinted, by permission, from *Louisiana's Legal Heritage*, edited by Edward F. Haas, published for the Louisiana State Museum by The Perdido Bay Press, 1983.

THE LAWBOOK EXCHANGE, LTD.
33 Terminal Avenue
Clark, New Jersey 07066-1321

Please see our website for a selection of our other publications and fine facsimile reprints of classic works of legal history:
www.lawbookexchange.com

Library of Congress Cataloging-in-Publication Data

Dargo, George.
Colony to empire : episodes in American legal history / by George Dargo.
p. cm.
Includes bibliographical references and index.
ISBN-13: 978-1-61619-144-3 (hardcover : alk. paper)
ISBN-10: 1-61619-144-9 (hardcover : alk. paper)
ISBN-13: 978-1-61619-145-0 (pbk. : alk. paper)
ISBN-10: 1-61619-145-7 (pbk. : alk. paper)
1. Law--United States--History. 2. United States--History--Colonial period, ca. 1600-1775. I. Title.
KF361.D375 2011
349.73--dc23

2011032350

Printed in the United States of America on acid-free paper

For Jessica, Jody, Stephen, Lois, Sarah and Ethan

“. . . a page of history is worth a volume of logic.”

Oliver Wendell Holmes, Jr., 1921

Contents

Twentieth Century Episodes

Foreword

My father, George Dargo, passed away on January 5, 2012, a few short weeks after he finished writing this book. He had spent his last couple of months battling his illness in hospitals and rehabilitation facilities. Folders that contained the manuscripts for this book had sat on his hospital room bureau for quite some time before he was strong enough to work on them. Or, perhaps it was the presence of those pages in the hospital room that gave him the strength to finish editing, since it was his dedication to writing and teaching, to history and the law, that defined his extraordinary professional career.

It was the same passion that drove my father to complete his dissertation on his manual Smith Corona typewriter when I was just a toddler in 1974. He had mentioned me in his acknowledgements, thanking me for leaving him enough typing paper to finish the book, which I thought was rather gracious of him (and of me, for that matter). His dissertation was published by Harvard University Press and was titled *Jefferson's Louisiana: Politics and the Clash of Legal Traditions.* The book sat on our living room bookshelf throughout my childhood, and I would open it once in a while to see my name in print, mostly oblivious to its contents (except for my part in the acknowledgements). I loved the retro 1970's font on the cover with its bold red, white and blue graphics, and I loved the fact that my father had written it. But it was not until over 35 years later that I was given the opportunity to experience firsthand what an impact this book had on the written history of Louisiana and the United States.

My father had always assumed that his dissertation would most likely gather dust in law and history libraries around the country. But *Jefferson's Louisiana* turned out to be a monument to the history of the Louisiana Purchase and one of the definitive texts on the subject. The book was in great demand decades after its modest first printing, and it delighted my father to no end when Georgia Chadwick, Director of the Law Library of Louisiana, approached Greg Talbot at the Lawbook Exchange with the idea of publishing a revised edition.

My father added a new introduction and performed "surgery" on the first chapter (he loved using that term). He enlisted Stanley N. Katz to write a new preface, and carefully selected maps and illustrations that were not able to be included in the original edition. Though the subject matter was the same, the changes brought the historical and legal scholarship of Louisiana history up to date, relating the importance and relevance of the subject to the present day.

And so the stage was set for the book's re-launch—in New Orleans in January 2010. There would be a luncheon reception at Antoine's, the famous New Orleans restaurant, to celebrate the book's re-publication (as well as the introduction of a new series on the foundations of civil law by the Lawbook Exchange). My father would also be the keynote speaker at the Louisiana Historical Society's Annual Banquet, which has been held every year on January 8 since 1815 to commemorate the United States' victory over the British in the Battle of New Orleans, which concluded the War of 1812.

I bought a plane ticket to New Orleans.

I had never been to New Orleans, and I was excited to visit this unique city for this auspicious occasion. I knew I was there for something special, not for Mardi Gras, not for Jazz-Fest, not for the food. But it wasn't until my mother Lois and I accompanied my father to the luncheon in the historic "Rex Room" at Antoine's that it became clear that I was there to see him in a way I had never seen him before. As soon as his editor, Valerie Horowitz, introduced him to the room, my father turned into . . . a rock star.

My father was lauded for his accomplishments and for his contribution to the history of New Orleans, as he was the following night at the banquet. He posed for pictures. He went to book signings. He was thrilled.

And so was I. I had always known my father to be an academic, to be my personal editor of high school papers and college essays and the in-house scholar of our family. We even presented a paper together in April 2001 at the Joint Annual Conference of the Popular Culture Association and the American Culture Association titled "Bartleby: The House of a Fool." (My father taught the Melville short story *Bartleby the Scrivener* in his "Law and Literature" class, and I had designed a conceptual house for the character in architecture school.) He collaborated with my sister Jessica too, and it was as a result of her helping him in his hospital room that he was able to complete this volume.

I may have sometimes failed to appreciate that my father had both a PhD in History as well as a JD, but his colleagues never did. The attention he received in New Orleans showed me how respected he really was in his field.

I have already forgotten parts of the speeches he gave that weekend, but I will never forget how our experience in New Orleans permanently fixed my father's legacy in my mind's eye. So in the same way that those days in New Orleans were a personal affirmation of my father's impact in the field of American History, my hope is that this book, *Colony to Empire: Episodes in American Legal History,* will affirm his professional legacy to his colleagues, students and peers.

Stephen Dargo
Brooklyn, 2012

Preface

We used to say that Herodotus was "the Father of History," but we now understand that History has "mothers" as well as "fathers." Equally numerous are characterizations as to the nature of historical writing itself. Henry Ford said that "history is one damned thing after another." Somewhat more reflective was William Faulkner who said that "the past is never dead; it is not even past." Still, perhaps the best known of these short and catchy aphorisms was that of the philosopher George Santayana who opined that "those who cannot remember the past are condemned to repeat it." Such admonitions abound, but they usually are of little concern to working historians. They are more the stuff of philosophy than of history itself. Historians try to "do" history rather than theorize about it. Historians leave the theories of history—technical issues such as the conflict between objectivity and relativity, the hazards of present-mindedness, the nature of historical fact, and the role of causation—to philosophers and students of epistemology.

Nonetheless, for our purposes, Henry Ford's famous quip is not a bad place to begin. "One damned thing after another" is the way most of us see the past—and the way we try to understand it—as a sequence of events as they happen in chronological time. Time is the essential gravitational force in history—both for the past "as it happened" and for our understanding of the past as reported in the works of historical writing. Time is what binds history together. To quote Cicero, "history bears witness to the passage of time." Sensitivity to time and how events, personalities, forces, and ideas fit within the arc of time is essential to historical comprehension. This, in turn, directs our attention to narrative, the most time-honored and tested form of historical writing as we have come to know it. After all, the greatest histories in our literary tradition were narrative histories. These include the Hebrew Bible, the Gospels, the classical works of Homer, Herodotus, Thucydides, Josephus, Tacitus, Livy and Polybius, the medieval chroniclers, and modernists from Francis Parkman and Leo Tolstoy to George M. Trevelyan, Thomas B. Macaulay, Jules Michelet and Henry Adams all the way to such gifted popular historians as David McCullough and Doris Kearns Goodwin. Narrative history is the kind of history that we think about when we think at all about history.

Colony to Empire is not that kind of history. The book assumes a basic knowledge of the essential facts and events which trace the historical growth and development of the United States. Here is the familiar summary: the country began as a group of colonial settlements bound to the British Crown and Empire; these colonies fought a War of Independence; then, as separate sovereign states, these former colonies created a federal union under a written constitution; the country expanded westward and fought a civil war over the issue of racial slavery as it affected that expansion, a war which led to the abolition of the slave system; the nation then went on to develop its economy, expand the basis of its democracy, admit millions of immigrants, and become a great industrial, political, and military power in the world; the United States also participated in the "great game" of 19th century imperialism thereby acquiring colonial possessions, most notably the Island of Puerto Rico; in the 20th century, the nation fought in two world wars, suffered through a great depression, fought a cold war with the Soviet Union and became the only remaining super-power in the post-cold war world. The essence of this narrative has been told, in whole or in part, many times over and in many different ways and with different, often conflicting, interpretations.

This book is different. It is bound together by a fundamental chronological sequence, but the elements of that sequence are intersections or "*inflection points*"—which either highlight something unique or which point to a moment when history came to a fork in the road, when historical development could go either way. These "*inflection points*," in what might be called a "*pointillist*" approach to history, interrupt the continuity of narrative and force us to recognize that history is neither purposeful nor logical nor necessarily steady in its march toward some inexorable goal. The trajectory of history is not the product of a single *cause* or a multiplicity of *causes* but of *contingencies* which point to the vagaries of the unpredictable in human affairs. Because it is *contingent*, history can go in any direction, up or down, backwards as well as forwards. *Inflection points* are innumerable, but some are more consequential than others. A few such episodes have been selected for this book.

The other common feature of *Colony to Empire* is that almost all of the essays selected for inclusion are related to law in some way. The marriage of law and history is not always a happy one. While historians and lawyers both deal with the past, their perspectives are profoundly different. The focus of historians is the past, that of lawyers the present. Historians are trained to observe events, institutions, ideas, cultures, and personalities through past lenses. The objective of the historian is to understand the past on its own terms and, if possible, to reconstruct it. In contrast, lawyers use the past in response to the needs of the present. The past is mined for materials that inform present issues or illuminate evolving legal principles as they are needed to solve present problems. The scope of general historical investigation tends toward breadth while the legal researcher seeks to narrow the focus of inquiry. The historian's definition of relevant evidence and proof is broader than that of the lawyer. Nevertheless, the two disciplines—history and law—often intersect, and, for our purposes, these points of intersection can also be thought of as historical *inflection points*.

Some of the episodes included in this collection are broad in scope. They describe general conditions and common circumstances which provide a template against which specific events can be measured. This is true of the very first series of essays on the American colonial period. The essays on legal rights, the place of religion, the condition of the press, and the character of politics in colonial America all provide a broad basis for an understanding of American legal and constitutional development in the decades that followed. Similarly, the chapter on law in the new republic—a period historians call the early national period—provides a broad survey of fundamental legal ideas in the early 19th century. Together this group of essays serves as a reminder of just how important these formative periods of United States history were in establishing the basis of the American legal and constitutional order.

The essays which follow are more specific in nature as they address particular events, issues, or controversies. This is certainly true of the essays on Louisiana. The first of these, on Louisiana's first civil law digest, provides a broad background for understanding the unique character of Louisiana's "mixed legal system." Louisiana's decision to adopt a civil law digest in the first decade of the 19th century was surely a significant *inflection point*. Against that background, the essay on the New Orleans *Batture* can be better understood. The litigation over the right to possession of this most valuable piece of real estate proved to be one of the most hotly fought legal issues of the 19th century.

The Louisiana Purchase itself was the underlying reality behind the issues discussed in the several essays on Louisiana history. The Purchase, which doubled the geographic size of the United States, is still celebrated as a great achievement—certainly one of the signal accomplishments of the early Jefferson Administration. While Jefferson himself tried to justify the acquisition of all of Louisiana—he called it "an empire for liberty"—there is no doubt that the Louisiana Purchase reoriented the very nature of the young American republic. Thus, we can think of the Louisiana Purchase as the beginning of American imperialism—an imperialism which began in 1803, the year of the Purchase and which reached its first high point in 1898 with the Spanish American War and the acquisition of territories beyond our shores, Puerto Rico being one of them. The final essay with a particular focus on Louisiana attempts to show how early technological change—in this case, the first use of steam-powered vessels on inland waterways—was addressed in Louisiana as compared with the approach taken in neighboring common law states. In short, the essays on Louisiana and the final essay on Puerto Rico, discussed below, can be thought of not only as *inflection points* but also as brackets for the title—*Colony to Empire*.

The other essay on a 19th century subject is the essay on the case of *Sarah Roberts* v. *City of Boston*, a legal controversy that dealt with the question of racial segregation in public schools in Massachusetts nearly fifty years before *Plessy* v. *Ferguson*. *Plessy* was the 1896 Supreme Court decision that upheld racial segregation in places of public accommodation and thereby supplied the imprimatur of legality to the Jim Crow system. That system of enforced racial segregation lasted until *Brown* v. *Board of Education* and the civil rights revolution of the mid-20th century. The Supreme Judicial Court of Massachusetts, the high court that decided *Sarah Roberts* v. *City of Boston* in 1849, was one of the most influential courts in the United States during the 19th century. Courts in other states as well as the federal courts—including the United States Supreme Court—looked to Massachusetts for legal guidance. This episode in American legal history should be more widely known. The *Sarah Roberts* case demonstrated that legal segregation by race began in the North—in this case in the city of Boston, the "Cradle of Liberty" itself.

The last three essays are drawn from different episodes in American legal history during the 20th century. The first deals with the Red Scare that followed soon after the end of the First World War. That episode has faded from memory because it has been superceded by more recent "red scares" such as the McCarthy era of the 1950s. But the Red Scare of 1919/1920 was important not only because it was the very first "red scare" in modern America, but because it also gave rise to important groups such as the American Civil Liberties Union and the Federal Bureau of Investigation. As recounted in this episode, the story of the Red Scare also created the legal basis for modern American principles of "due process of law" and important ideas in administrative law and practice.

The next chapter explores the application of the ancient "blue laws" of Massachusetts to a religious group that was not in North America at the time of their enactment in the Colonial Period. The "blue laws" were originally designed to ensure proper Sunday Sabbath observance by wayward Puritans, but in the 20th century the group that was found most often to be in violation of those laws were observant Jews and other "Sabbatarians" whose Sabbath came on Saturday, not Sunday. The essay is largely based upon archival materials. It is an example of a case-specific historical study and details the claims of religious people who believed the "blue laws" were being unfairly applied.

The last episode brings us back to the main theme of the underlying narrative suggested by the title—*Colony to Empire.* Like the previous essay, it draws heavily upon the personal papers of Judge Calvert Magruder, chief judge of the United States Court of Appeals for the First Circuit (1939–1959). This essay explores the relationship between the United States and the Island of Puerto Rico, which the United States acquired as a result of the Spanish American War at the very end of the 19th century. The legal status of Puerto Rico is a vestige of the age of colonialism. The colonial status of Puerto Rico is a relic of that era. Puerto Rico remains tied to the United States not only politically, but also juridically. It is this latter connection that is explored in some detail in this final episode of the book.

These chapters have all been previously published, but the occasion of their publication was different in each case. They first appeared either as book chapters or as separate articles. The present volume used either the intrinsic interest of the subject, or the episode's relationship to other essays as determining factors in the selection process. All have been significantly edited, revised and, where necessary, updated. All are illustrative of an approach to legal history which emphasizes the strong relationship between legal development and general historical change. This is the methodology that binds these seemingly disparate historical materials together.

In his great book about America, Alexis De Tocqueville wrote that "there is hardly a political question in the United States which does not sooner or later turn into a judicial one." De Tocqueville's *Democracy in America* was an extraordinary chronicle of the institutions, the culture, and the character of the United States and its people, but this particular insight throws into sharp relief the importance of law in American history. That should not be surprising given the fact that awareness of the interface of law and general history is probably essential for a complete understanding of America and its colorful past. But legal history need not be technical or off-putting, and the materials included in this collection are meant to be accessible to the general reader.

History, then, is surely more than just "one thing after another." What we can learn from history including legal history—what it does have to teach—is that history is not just a narrative but an account of how points in time—"*inflection points*"—are reached and choices made. Almost by definition, law provides a mechanism for decision-making. Accordingly, legal writing may be the pragmatic example of "inflection points" in action.

George Dargo
2011

Acknowledgments

I wish to express my appreciation to students and colleagues at New England Law|Boston for their assistance in bringing this book to completion. Julie Anne Franklin did an enormous amount of work in getting the print editions of these essays into digitalized format. In addition, Julie did a remarkable job in assembling the footnote documentation for three of the four essays on the colonial period. Cheryl Ann Parker did excellent work on the essay dealing with religious toleration. The original published version of that essay required a good deal of surgery as well as adjustments in the footnote documentation, and Cheryl proved to be up to the task. Grace Cary Roessler helped iron out some issues in the Preface and transcribed several essays into digital format. Robert P. McGovern, Jr., did excellent editorial work on several essays and footnote checking in a number of others. Petia Lukova-Iannicelli assisted with checking the documentation of the last three essays.

As always, the Library Staff at New England Law|Boston assisted in various ways including the assemblage of 17th and 18th century published documents. In particular, Brian Flaherty was enormously helpful in doing work on the documentation of several of the early chapters and was indispensable in putting the index together. The faculty support staff performed numerous tasks that contributed to this publication. Angela Cheung was extremely generous with her time in formatting all of the chapters into the "hybrid" format we used that combined the *Chicago Manual of Style* for most citations with *Bluebook* legal format for strictly legal sources such as cases and statutes. Jennifer W. Kain, Shalane Reeves-Torkelson and Sarah E. Wysocki did excellent proofreading work. Faculty colleagues provided useful insights particularly with respect to some of the ideas and issues raised in the Preface.

I want to take this opportunity to express very special appreciation to Dean John F. O'Brien of New England Law|Boston. Dean O'Brien has committed his office to supporting the publication of numerous works of serious legal scholarship by his faculty at New England. Dean O'Brien has consistently supported my own work including this project. For his confidence, and enthusiasm I am delighted to acknowledge the generous support Dean O'Brien has given so graciously over many years.

My good friend, Professor Neil S. Hecht of the Boston University School of Law shared his broad knowledge and deep insight for which I am most grateful. Neil's enthusiasm was a driving force behind the publication of this book.

Finally, I want to thank Valerie Horowitz, Greg Talbot and the rest of the staff of the Lawbook Exchange for their hard work and encouragement. Valerie's enthusiasm and thoughtful suggestions as editor contributed greatly to the final product. I also want to thank Valerie for finding such a dramatic Currier and Ives print for the jacket cover and Kati Fahey Moody used for its design.

My wife, Lois, provided indispensable support during the many, many weeks during which this book was readied for publication.

Needless to say, any errors or mistakes that remain in the text (hopefully they are few in number) are my responsibility alone.

Colonial Foundations

Episode 1

The Legal Rights of Early Americans

> No man's life shall be taken away, no man's honour or good name shall be stayned, no mans person shall be arrested, restrained, banished, dismembred, nor any wayes punished, no man shall be deprived of his wife or children, no man's goods or estaite shall be taken away from him, nor any way indammaged under colour of law or Countenance of Authoritie, unlesse it be by virtue or equitie of some expresse law of the Country warranting the same, established by a generall Court and sufficiently published.
>
> *Body of Liberties*, Massachusetts Bay Colony, 1641[1]

Legal historians have measured the degree to which early American law either diverged from or duplicated English law. The pioneer scholars in this field, deeply influenced by Frederick Jackson Turner's themes of frontier nationalism and American exceptionalism, emphasized the wide disparities between English and American law in the colonial period, but others have pointed to the parallels and similarities between American law and English common law or local law. Some have even spoken of a process of legal "Anglicization," particularly when referring to the eighteenth century.[2]

A corollary concern of more immediate interest is whether the English Government intended to transfer English law to the colonies and the related issue of what the understanding of the colonists was on this matter. Confusion continued to surround these

---

* Source: Chapter 3 ("The Legal Rights of Early Americans") in George Dargo, *Roots of the Republic: A New Perspective on Early American Constitutionalism* (New York: Praeger, 1974.)

1. John Cotton, "Massachusetts Body of Liberties," in *Puritan Political Ideas, 1558–1794*, E. S. Morgan, ed. (Indianapolis, IN: Bobbs-Merrill Company, Inc., 1965), 179 (reprint of the "Massachusetts Body of Liberties," co-authored by Nathaniel Ward and Reverend John Cotton).
2. Hendrik Hartog, "The Public Law of a County Court: Judicial Government in Eighteenth Century Massachusetts," *American Journal of Legal History*, Vol. 20 no. 4 (1976) 297.

issues right up until the American Revolution. Indeed, the misunderstandings that prevailed on opposite sides of the Atlantic contributed to the Revolution itself. Americans demanded the legal "rights and liberties of Englishmen," but the English resisted this demand.[3]

The key to the problem lies in the so-called conformity clauses of colony charters and royal commission to provincial governors. For example, the Virginia Charter of 1612 stipulated that the Virginia Company was to have full power to pass laws and ordinances for the good and welfare of the colony "*so always*, as the same be not contrary to the Laws and Statutes of this our Realm of *England*." With only minor variations in wording, this formula was repeated in every subsequent grant of authority issued by the Crown. Did it imply the transfer of English law? If so, which laws and which statutes? Did it mean local customary law as well as the common law of the central royal courts? General statutes in which the plantations were not named as well as particular ones in which they were? Statutes passed before the settlement of America as well as those enacted afterward?

There were no clear-cut answers to these questions. The Privy Council, the Crown's principal agency with final authority over colonial affairs, never settled the issue of the extension of English law as a matter of legal doctrine. However, what is clear is that the English interpreted the conformity clauses as restrictive, with the Crown having final authority to decide when the restrictions had been exceeded. In essence, the Crown could and did use the conformity clauses as a convenient instrument for striking down colonial laws found to be administratively or otherwise objectionable. On the other hand, the colonists viewed these conformity clauses as the basis for a wholesale reception of the common law, with all its attendant procedural checks on royal prerogative and discretion. The colonists claimed the full range of English common-law liberties, limited only by parliamentary statutes in which the colonies were specifically named.

The closest approximation to settled law on this whole matter was *Calvin's Case* (also referred to as the *Case of the Postnati*),

---

3. David S. Lovejoy, "Equality and Empire: The New York Charter of Liberties, 1683," *William and Mary Quarterly* 3rd Ser., Vol. 21 (1964): 496 (discussing the advanced definition of the "rights of Englishmen" reflected in New York's *Charter of Liberties*).

decided in the Court of Exchequer Chamber in 1608, at the very outset of English colonization.[4] The case of one Robert Calvin, an infant born in Scotland in 1606, after the accession of James I, was entered in the courts of King's Bench and Chancery and then removed for hearing by a panel of the most distinguished judges of the realm. The court held that Scots born after the personal union of Scotland and England in 1603 were not aliens and thus could inherit real property like other subjects of the English King. But with regard to the new American colonies, the most relevant portion of the decision, as rendered by Sir Edward Coke, was the following:

> . . . there is a Diversity between a Conquest of a Kingdom of a Christian King, and the Conquest of a Kingdom by an infidel; for if a King come to a Christian Kingdom by Conquest . . . he may at his Pleasure alter and change the Laws of that Kingdom, but until he doth make an Alteration of those Laws, the ancient Laws of that Kingdom remain. But if a Christian King should conquer a Kingdom of an infidel, and bring them under his subjections, then...the Laws of the infidel are abrogated, for that they be not only against Christianity, but against the Law of God and of Nature, contained in the Decalogue, and in that Case, until certain Laws be established amongst them, the King by himself, and such Judges as he shall appoint, shall judge them and their Causes according to natural Equity. . . . But if a King hath a Kingdom by Title of Descent . . . he cannot change those Laws of himself, without Consent of Parliament.[5]

According to this decision, lands outside the realm acquired by the King fell into three categories: (1) in lands seized by conquest from a Christian king, existing law remained in force until altered by the new sovereign; (2) in lands taken from infidels, local law was automatically abrogated by the fact of conquest, and the territory came under direct royal governance; and, (3) in lands acquired by descent, local law could not be changed without the consent of Parliament.

But none of these three conditions of territorial acquisition described the circumstances under which England settled America. For the most part, the early settlements were established by the peaceful "plantation" of regions that had been sparsely inhabited

---

4. (1608) 77 Eng. Rep. 377 (K.B.) (*Calvin's Case*).
5. Ibid., 397–398.

or, in the case of occupied lands, by purchase from the Indians. Only rarely did acquisition occur through conquest and treaty. Moreover, the automatic application of royal authority to lands acquired by conquest from infidels, as set forth in *Calvin's Case*, hardly pertained to America, since here the question was not what law would govern the native people but what law would govern migrating Englishmen. Nevertheless, for purposes that suited the English imperial authority, the fiction was maintained that America had been conquered from infidels and, as such, was subject to the royal prerogative. Charter grants, such as that given to Massachusetts, merely affirmed familiar powers customarily extended to local corporate bodies in England; they in no way diminished the absolute sovereignty of the Crown to govern its overseas plantations.

The use to which the Crown later put *Calvin's Case* is even more curious in view of the fact that, from the early seventeenth century, it was becoming fairly clear that Englishmen in "settled territories" outside the realm (in Northern Ireland, for example), were subject to the jurisdiction of Parliament and, by inference, possessed all the constitutional rights of English citizens. *Calvin's Case* itself suggested that once English law had been introduced, as in Ireland, "[The King] can no longer alter those laws without the consent of parliament"—dictum that was later applied to settled colonies in general.[6] In settled (as opposed to conquered) territories, English law was in force because English subjects did not surrender their common-law birthright by migrating to lands outside the realm. Parliamentary statutes specifically provided that subjects born or living abroad (that is, in land outside the English realm and its dominions) were entitled to all the rights of Englishmen living in the realm. Accordingly, to American colonists, it was strange doctrine indeed that gave to English subjects living in foreign countries more rights in English law than subjects living in colonies to which they had migrated for the greater glory of King and country.

By the middle of the eighteenth century, the distinction between conquered and settled colonies was clarified in *Campbell* v. *Hall*, when the great Lord Mansfield held that Englishmen in

---

6. William F. Holdsworth, *A History of English Law*, Vol. XI (London: Metheun & Co. Ltd., 1966), 234 (discussing the issues involved in *Calvin's Case*).

settlements outside the realm had all the rights of English subjects.[7] As Blackstone put it in his influential *Commentaries*:

> . . . if an uninhabited country be discovered and planted by English subjects, all the English laws are immediately there in force. For as the law is the birthright of every subject, so wherever they go they carry their laws with them. But in conquered or ceded countries, that have already laws of their own, the king may indeed alter and change those laws.[8]

Yet, although reality begged for recognition that the American settlements fell more into the category of uninhabited territories to which Englishmen had migrated bearing English law and English rights, the conquered-territory doctrine continued to be applied to America in one of the most interesting and consequential fictions of Anglo-American legal history. Blackstone, citing *Calvin's Case*, continued:

> Our American plantations are principally of this latter sort, being obtained in the last century either by right of conquest and driving out the natives . . . or by treaties. And therefore the common law of England as such has no allowances or authority there; they being no part of the mother country, but distinct (though independent) dominions.[9]

To this view of things the American colonists demurred. They resisted the implications of *Calvin's Case*, their subjugation to unimpaired royal prerogative, the non-applicability of many parliamentary statutes to them, and the prevalent English doctrine that the common law had not been transferred across the sea either by charter grant or by the fact of settlement. Where they could, the Americans disregarded these limits on their legal competence. In civil and criminal litigation not subject to Privy Council review, the Americans simply drew their law from the deep well of English common and statutory law. Colonial legislatures adopted parliamentary statutes in name or in substance as needed without

---

7. (1774) *Campbell* v. *Hall*, 98 Eng. Rep. 1045 (K.B.).
8. William Blackstone, *Commentaries on the Laws of England* (Philadelphia, PA: Robert Bell, Union Library Press, 1781), 106–107 (discussing the decision in *Calvin's Case* as it relates to English subjects in the new Americas).
9. Ibid., 106.

worrying about their legal authority to do so, even though such legislative acts were, potentially at least, subject to royal disallowance. By the time of the Revolution, it was still not clear which elements of English law applied to America. The colonists claimed that American courts and legislatures, not Parliament, the Board of Trade, or the Privy Council, should decide which parts of common and statute law were received in the colonies. England's refusal to accede to these demands and to modify its legal posture contributed to the polarization that led to independence.

As transplanted Englishmen, colonial Americans had a keen sense of those constitutional liberties that were England's pride in the seventeenth and eighteenth centuries. England's legal and constitutional development was living history for Americans. Substantive and procedural guarantees of personal freedom dating back to the *Magna Carta* were standards by which government performance was measured in colonial and Revolutionary America. The transplantation of many of those guarantees can be noted both in formal constitutional documents and in the everyday administration of justice. Indeed, one of the more remarkable achievements of colonial Americans was the significant process of refinement that some of those guarantees underwent in the course of their migration across the Atlantic. Such guarantees were part of the written law of every colony in America by 1701. New England, the Middle Atlantic provinces, and the South—royal, proprietary, and charter colonies alike—all reflected a lively appreciation of the English constitutional tradition. This formal recognition can easily be documented, but for purposes of illustration it is necessary only to point to a few leading examples.

In 1638, the first Maryland General Assembly passed an act "for the liberties of the people" (one year before the enactment of the even more famous *Maryland Act of Religious Toleration*) stating that the individual safeguards embedded in the English common law were to be the rights of Marylanders as well as Englishmen:

> . . . that all the Inhabitants of this Province being Christians (slaves excepted) shall have and enjoy all such rights liberties immunities privileges and free customs within this Province as any naturall born subject of England hath or ought to have or enjoy in the Realm of England by force or vertue of the common law of Statute Law of England . . . And shall not be imprisoned

> nor disseissed or dispossessed of their freehold goods or Chattels or be out Lawed Exiled or otherwise destroyed fore judged or punished than according to the Laws of this province.[10]

Maryland's freemen clearly desired to establish basic common-law protections thereby creating in Maryland a legal environment attractive to prospective settlers. Indeed, despite its dubious legal authority, such references to the "liberties, franchises and immunities" of freeborn English subjects, with only minor modifications, were included in nearly every colonial charter. Such general references to rights served to advertise the attractiveness of overseas adventure, colonization, and settlement.[11]

Perhaps the leading example of the effort to establish basic rights in the early colonial period occurred in Massachusetts. The *Body of Liberties* of 1641 was enacted in response to growing fears that the magistracy of the Bay Colony was becoming a domineering oligarchy. More a "compilation of constitutional provisions" than a written code of laws, the *Body of Liberties* was designed to keep the tendency toward arbitrary rule in check.[12] Nathaniel Ward, the principal draftsman of this historic document, was one of the few men in Massachusetts with legal training. While the code contained Mosaic provisions responsive to the colony's religious orientation, its detailed enumerations of civil liberties reflects Ward's substantial common-law background as well as English legal culture in general.

There are numerous concordances between the *Body of Liberties* and English common law. In fact, to answer complaints that local law did not conform sufficiently to English law, the General Court later issued the *Declaration of 1646*—a parallel listing of the "common lawes and customes of England, beginning with Magna Carta," on one side, and, on the other, the "summe of such lawes

---

10. John Leeds Bozman, *The History of Maryland, from its First Settlement in 1633 to the Restoration in 1660, with a Copious Introduction and Notes and Illustrations*, Vol. 2 (Baltimore, MD: James Lucas and E.K. Deaver, 1837), 116.
11. Dick A.E. Howard, *The Road From Runnymede: Magna Carta and Constitutionalism in America* (Charlottesville, VA: The University Press of Virginia, 1968), 15.
12. Cotton, *Puritan Political Ideas, 1558–1794,* 178.

and customes as are in force and use in this jurisdiction."[13] For its own political purposes, the General Court exaggerated the degree of concordance between the two bodies of law. Without doubt, many were clearly rooted in the English tradition. Of none was this more true than Liberty One:

> No man's life shall be taken away, no man's honour or good name shall be stayned, no man's person shall be arrested, restrained, banished, dismembred, nor any wayes punished, no man shall be deprived of his wife or children, no man's goods or estaite shall be taken away from him, nor any way indammaged under colour of law or Countenance of Authoritie, unlesse it be by virtue or equitie of some expresse law of the Country warranting the same, established by a generall Court and sufficiently published.[14]

While the phrase "due process of law" does not appear in this first and most important provision of the *Body of Liberties*, it was close enough to the famous "law of the land" in section 39 of the Magna Carta to demonstrate a conscious effort at duplication: "No free man shall be taken, imprisoned, disseised, outlawed, banished, or in any way destroyed, nor will We proceed against or prosecute him, except by the lawful judgment of his peers and by the law of the land."[15]

Other provisions of the *Body of Liberties* also reflected English common law: the right to equal justice, the right to fair trial by jury, and the guarantees against the use of cruel and barbarous punishments. But more significant than these rough approximations between the *Body of Liberties* and the fundamentals of the common law were the refinements, improvements, and innovations with which the Puritans worked over their legal heritage. Thus, aliens as well as inhabitants were to enjoy equal justice; bail was less restrictive than in England; jurors were free to follow their consciences in reaching a just verdict and were not to be intimidated by

---

13. Howard, *The Road from Runnymede*, Appendix C, 401–411. *See also* Richard B. Morris, "Massachusetts and the Common Law: The Declaration of 1646," *American Historical Review* Vol. 31, No. 3 (1925–26): 443–453.
14. John Cotton, "Body of Liberties," in *Puritan Political Ideas, 1558–1794* (Indianapolis, IN: Bobbs-Merrill Company, Inc., 1965), 179.
15. Howard, *The Road from Runnymede*, Appendix A, 388 (quoting an excerpt from the *Magna Carta*, Ch. 39 (1215)).

threats of fine or imprisonment by the court as jurors often were in England itself; an appeal was granted as of right in capital cases and was not restricted to review of trial-court procedural errors; double jeopardy extended to civil and criminal cases alike and was not, as in England, limited to capital offenses; and, finally, the right to confront witnesses and accusers was, in Massachusetts, absolute in capital cases and more extensive in noncapital cases than it was in England, where written depositions were normally accepted in evidence in felony trials.[16] In addition, no man was required to fight in offensive wars but only in defensive wars; all inhabitants—freeman and foreigner alike—were able to participate in public deliberations such as town meetings; the right to travel freely was recognized; the right to counsel was guaranteed without restriction as to the nature of the offense; a minimum of two witnesses was required for conviction in capital cases (a Biblical concordance); and jurors were to be chosen by the freemen of the town.[17] All of these provisions of the *Body of Liberties* added up to a program of genuine legal reform.

The experiment in written constitutionalism that began with the Bay Colony's charter itself and continued with the *Body of Liberties*—a kind of early *Bill of Rights*—reached its culmination with the *Laws and Liberties* of 1648: the "first modern code of the Western world."[18] It was a model for legal draftsmen in other colonies, and the basic law of Massachusetts until the abrogation of the original charter in 1684. The *Laws and Liberties* carried forward the tradition of reform already established in the early legislation of the 1640s in the *Body of Liberties*. The basic freedoms outlined in the *Body of Liberties* were detailed at greater length. Moreover, as a code of fundamental law, the *Laws and*

---

16. Howard, *The Road from Runnymede*, 34–41. For an incisive review of the trends in historical writing in the hybrid historic legal field, see Stanley N. Katz, "Looking Backward: The Early History of American Law," *University of Chicago Law Review* Vol. 33, No.1 (1966): 867–884.
17. Ibid.
18. *The Laws and Liberties of Massachusetts* (San Marino, CA: The Huntington Library, 1998) (introduction by Richard S. Dunn), v. For more on colonial and legal history, see Thorpe L. Wolford's "The Laws of Liberties of 1648," in *Essays in the History of Early American Law*, David Flaherty, ed. (Chapel Hill, NC: The University of North Carolina Press, 1969), 147–185 and George Lee Haskins' *Law and Authority in Early Massachusetts: A Study in Tradition and Design* (New York, NY: The MacMillan Company, 1960).

Liberties was designed to limit the discretion of legislators and magistrates to fixed principles—an idea that was to reach fulfillment and conceptual clarity only in the constitutional period in the latter part of the eighteenth century. The basic rights that formed so essential a part of this legislation raised them to a higher level of constitutional significance. In that respect, the Massachusetts code of 1648 sounded the note that was to be struck repeatedly in the seventeenth century, one that would resonate many years later in the Antifederalist claim that a constitution without basic liberties was not a constitution at all.[19]

Both the Maryland law of 1638, which projected a reception of English liberties by general reference, and the Massachusetts legislation of the 1640s with a more detailed enumeration of basic rights, represent initiatives taken by freemen and their deputies to establish popular safeguards against arbitrary rule. A very similar regard for "constitutional rights" came, somewhat surprisingly, at the hands not of those "below" but of those "above."[20] The *Concessions and Agreements of West New Jersey* (1677) was authored by Edward Byllynge, the purchaser of the Berkeley proprietary interest in West Jersey, with the collaboration of William Penn, one of the managers of Byllynge's affairs[21]. Like the earlier *Concessions and Agreements* of 1665, issued by Berkeley and Carteret, the original grantees of the Province of New Jersey, the Byllynge-Penn version was designed to promote settlement by offering generous conditions to immigrants. But unlike the Berkeley-Carteret *Concessions*, the fundamental laws of 1677 were animated by the same spirit of liberalism that would generate William Penn's *Frame of Government* for Pennsylvania in 1683. In both instances—that of West New Jersey and that of Pennsylvania—we find the establishment of a standard of what already can be called "constitutionalism" as

---

19. For more on the formal enactment, codification, and adoption of legal guarantees of personal liberty, see Robert A. Rutland's *The Birth of The Bill of Rights* (Chapel Hill, NC: University of North Carolina Press, 1955), 23–32.
20. Julian P. Boyd, "Concessions and Agreements of West New Jersey," in *Fundamental Laws and Constitutions of New Jersey, 1664–1964* (Princeton, NJ: Princeton University Press, 1964), 71–104.
21. For more on Byllynge, see John E. Pomfret's "The Problem of the West Jersey Concessions of 1676–77," *William and Mary Quarterly,* 3rd Ser., Vol. 5, No. 1 (1948): 99–102 (Pomfret discusses whether Edward Byllynge was the author, based on his *A Mite of Affection Manifested in 31 Proposals* written in 1659, which contained many items similar to those in the Concessions [101]).

measured by guarantees of personal liberty resulting from the convictions of a small group of high-minded leaders determined to establish in America a home for English liberties that was impossible to achieve in England itself.

The *Concessions and Agreements of West New Jersey* was a precedent for later American constitutionalism in three important respects: First, it vested the power of self-government in the inhabitants of the province through the establishment of a general assembly of deputies chosen in free elections and exercising full legislative competence.[22] Second, it secured basic guarantees of civil liberty: freedom of conscience and of worship; no deprivation of life, liberty, or estate but by lawful judgment of twelve jurymen, with the accused having an absolute right to thirty-five peremptory challenges and an unlimited right to challenge for cause; in all offenses excepting felony and treason, every inhabitant was entitled to notice by official summons stating the cause, the identity of the accusers, and the court of hearing at least fourteen days prior to appearance, such notification to precede any subsequent process for arrest, attachment, or imprisonment; the judgment of the jury was not subject to court reversal; two witnesses were required for conviction in civil and criminal causes; no person was obliged to employ counsel but could plead his own cause; and all trials were to be public "that Justice may not be done in a corner nor in any Covert manner [and] that all and every person and persons Inhabiting the said Province shall as far as in us lies be free from oppression and slavery."[23] Third, the *Concessions and Agreements* set forth the principle of the fundamentality of a written constitution as opposed to ordinary statutory legislation, a distinction implied in the Massachusetts codes but articulated with philosophic and stylistic precision in West New Jersey. Chapter 13 spelled out this understanding with remarkable clarity:

> That the common Law or fundamental Rights and priviledges of West New Jersey are Individually agreed upon by the Proprietors

---

22. Boyd, "Concessions and Agreements of West New Jersey," 95–100.
23. Ibid. (quoting original *Concessions and Agreements of West New Jersey*, Ch. XIII (1677)). For a detailed study of crime and punishment focusing on the available methods of criminal procedure in various settlements of New Jersey, see H.B. and W.B. Weiss, *An Introduction to Crime and Punishment in Colonial New Jersey* (Trenton, NJ: Past Times Press, 1960).

> and freeholders thereof to be the foundation of the Government which is not to be altered by the Legislative Authority or Free Assembly hereafter mentioned and constituted[.] But that the said Legislative Authority is constituted according to these fundamentalls to make such Laws as agree with and maintaine the said fundamentalls and to make no Laws that in the least contrast differ or vary from the said fundamentals under what pretence or allegation soever.[24]

Members of the Assembly who willfully attempted to "move or excite any to move" legislation subversive of these fundamentals were to be proceeded against as "traitors to the said Government."[25] Additionally, this "great Charter of fundamentals" was to be read at the opening and at the dissolution of every General Assembly and four times a year in the courts of justice.[26]

A century later, at the time of the American Revolution, the distinction between fundamental and statutory law would achieve institutional expression in the "convention," an assembly of the representatives of the "people out of doors," organized for the sole purpose of devising a framework of government and a list of constitutional rights untouchable by ordinary lawmakers.[27] The *West New Jersey Concessions and Agreements* anticipated this development. Although it was drafted by the chief proprietor and his agent, it was adopted by the mutual consent and agreement of proprietors, freeholders, and inhabitants.[28] It lodged genuine sovereign power in the people's representatives, limited only by the guarantees of the basic charter itself. "In every sense [it] was a true constitution."[29]

There were other examples of charter rights in early America. Some approached the elaboration of the Massachusetts codes and the New Jersey charter. Such was the case in Pennsylvania, where the "Laws agreed upon in England," adopted in May, 1682, provided for the full panoply of civil liberties—one of the hall-

---

24. Boyd, "Concessions and Agreements of West New Jersey," 83 (referencing the original text of the *Concessions and Agreements*, Ch. XIII (1677)).
25. Ibid., 84.
26. Ibid., 85.
27. Gordon S. Wood, *The Creation of the American Republic, 1776–1787* (Chapel Hill, NC: University of North Carolina Press, 1969), 308–309.
28. Boyd, "Concessions and Agreements of West New Jersey," 71.
29. Ibid.

marks of William Penn's "Holy Experiment."[30] Technically not a part of Pennsylvania's "frame of government," this early legislation was considered as fundamental as the charter itself and survived subsequent modifications in the Pennsylvania constitution in 1701. Elsewhere, particular concerns received special emphasis. For example, the Rhode Island royal charter of 1663 secured the "free exercise and enjoyment of all civil and religious rights" and to that end guaranteed "that noe person within the sayd colony . . . shall bee any wise molested, punished, disquieted, or called in question, for any differences in opinione in matters of religion."[31] Other civil liberties received the customary scanty formulaic assurance of the "libertyes and immunityes of free and naturall subjects . . . of England."[32] New York's *Charter of Libertyes,* enacted by the first General Assembly of that province in 1683 (but subsequently repudiated by the Privy Council), claimed rights and privileges that no other English colony possessed: not only jury trial, bail, and the other element of due process, but freedom from taxation without representation, liberty of conscience, protection against the quartering of troops or the imposition of martial law, and, finally, the establishment of a provincial legislature virtually equal in sovereign power to Parliament itself.[33] Such local pretensions to independence and civil liberty invited disallowance, particularly at a time when the last of the Stuart monarchs was attempting to consolidate England's imperial dominions while increasing the power of the royal prerogative in the colonial sphere. Still, the *Charter of Liberties* is a paradigmatic case illustrating colonial claims to English liberty. While the charter itself did not remain in

---

30. E.B. Bronner, *William Penn's "Holy Experiment": The Founding of Pennsylvania, 1681–1701* (New York, NY: Greenwood Press, 1962).
31. Roger Williams, "Rhode Island Royal Charter of 1663," in *The Federal and State Constitutions, Colonial Charters, and Other Organic Laws of the States, Territories, and Colonies, Now or Heretofore Forming the United States of America,* v. 5 (Washington, DC: Government Printing Office, 1909), 3212.
32. Ibid., 3221.
33. Julius Goebel, Jr., "Courts and Law in Colonial New York," in *Essays in the History of Early American Law*, David Flaherty, ed. (Chapel Hill, NC: The University of North Carolina Press, 1969), 248. For more on the research conducted regarding the work of the Privy Council in controlling American legislative enactments and court decisions, see Joseph H. Smith, "Administrative Control of the Courts of the American Plantations," in *Essays in the History of Early American Law*, David Flaherty, ed. (Chapel Hill, NC: The University of North Carolina Press, 1969), 281–335.

force for very long, its civil-libertarian provisions, especially those regarding criminal process, were re-enacted in subsequent legislation and were adopted as standards for the administration of justice.

Finally, at the opening of the eighteenth century, one of the greatest expressions of the colonial mind—*Pennsylvania's Charter of Privileges of 1701*—implanted a system of government and a standard of official performance unsurpassed for its constitutional liberalism either in England or even in America.[34] Not as detailed as the Massachusetts *Laws and Liberties* of 1648 nor even as extensive as the New Jersey *Concessions and Agreements* of 1677, the Pennsylvania charter had the simplicity and economy of later state constitutions. It extended the detailed legal guarantees of 1683 in several important respects: for example, in guaranteeing to the accused in criminal trials the right to counsel and to summon witnesses and to have them testify under oath. Moreover, Article VIII clearly established the fundamentality of the charter by providing that "no Act, Law or Ordinance whatsoever, shall at any time hereafter, be made or done, to alter, change or diminish the Form or Effect of this charter . . . without the Consent of the Governor . . . and Six Parts of Seven of the Assembly."[35] Any laws passed contrary to its provisions were to be of no force or effect.

Despite variations in emphasis, elaboration, or philosophical clarity, by the end of the seventeenth century, the American constitutional experience—as reflected in royal charters and concessions handed down by the Crown or by the proprietors of royal grants as well as in legislation initiated from below by the people's deputies—recognized the central importance of legal guarantees of personal liberty secured by some kind of written enactment whose authority was beyond ordinary statutory control. A diverse assortment of civil liberties, from the ancient right to a jury trial to the new recognition of freedom of conscience, had won formal endorsement in many of the mainland colonies that would later become the United States. The Pennsylvania *Charter of Privileges* was the basis of government in that province until the Revolution, but it may also be interpreted as a kind of summary

---

34. Bronner, *William Penn's "Holy Experiment."*
35. William Penn, "Charter of Privileges, (Pennsylvania, 1701)," in *The Federal and State Constitutions, Colonial Charters, and Other Organic Laws of the States, Territories, and Colonies, Now or Heretofore Forming the United States of America*, v. 5 (Washington, DC: Government Printing Office, 1909), 3079.

statement of the seventeenth-century American colonial mind and experience. That experience had seen the adoption of written instruments containing minimal standards for local and imperial authorities to follow. This in itself was a remarkable achievement. It meant that, at their very inception, American political societies gave recognition to the more liberal and forward-looking elements in the English legal tradition.

But the American colonial experience went even further. Not only in form, but in substance and practice as well, the American colonies endeavored to achieve, and in many places did achieve, a record of performance that legitimized, perpetuated, and advanced the English constitutional tradition more than basic legislative enactments and even corporate charters could ever do. The record of this performance is to be found not only in the acts of colonial legislatures loftily claiming the rights of Englishmen but in the everyday workings of the judicial system, particularly in the sphere of criminal-law enforcement. It is in this area—where the individual confronts the weight and power of the state—that the true measure of early American constitutionalism can be taken.

The record of the American colonies is not uniform. From one province to another and even within a single colony, the pattern of judicial administration varied from the frontier counties, where legal knowledge was thin, to the capital city, where the trained bar congregated. Even so, recent studies of county courts in colonial America show surprisingly high levels of judicial administration in fairly remote settlements, with procedures comparable in efficiency and sophistication to more established regions and to local law enforcement in England itself. The higher the degree of judicial refinement, the greater the likelihood that Americans enjoyed the benefits of "due process of law."

The phrase "due process of law" has had a long and honored career in Anglo-American legal history. Its reservoirs of 'residual meaning" have given it renewed life in every major era of constitutional development, so that it defies easy definition. It implies that all authority must act according to law "that there is no sovereign unless he conforms to the principles of legality" which is a general definition with wide ramifications.[36] However, at the very minimum, "due process of law," particularly in the colonial period,

---

36. Rodney L. Mott, *Due Process of Law* (New York: De Capo Press, 1973), 589.

meant the employment of proper forms of indictment, notice, hearing, and trial. In America, due process did not become a great rallying principle until the Revolution, but the colonists did expect courts of law and law officers to follow appropriate procedures. This was the basic standard governing the administration of justice—a standard, interestingly enough, that judges, lawyers, and prosecutors upheld as a matter of professional obligation as much as laymen demanded it as a matter of high principle.

The legal history of colonial New York illustrates the extent to which due process of law was recognized in pre-Revolutionary America. In some ways, New York equaled contemporary English procedures in safeguarding the rights of individuals caught up in the machinery of criminal justice. This was particularly true in the field of "summary process," the trial of persons accused of crimes before judges without juries. Both in England and in America, social conditions necessitated summary procedures. The problem of vagabondage and petty crime was serious and growing in the eighteenth century. Faced with the costs of detaining and trying the vagrant poor, legislatures resorted to the expedient of increasing the number of offenses that were subject to summary process. The result was that, while great constitutional importance was attached to the formal procedures of accusation by grand jury and trial by petit jury, the bulk of criminal offenders were, in effect, dealt with administratively before a magistrate or a justice of the peace.

The wide use of summary process was probably inevitable given the growth of social unrest in the late colonial period, but it certainly vitiated the high-sounding claims to constitutional liberty—in particular the inviolability of the jury—that colonial New Yorkers continued to assert right up to the Revolution. The precedents for the use of summary procedures were well established in England, where justices of the peace and local committing magistrates traditionally exercised such powers in criminal-law enforcement. The colonists insisted that magistrates adhere to regular procedures as set forth in the leading handbooks, such as Dalton's *Countrey Justice*. Accordingly, in this important area of law enforcement, the Americans did not progress much beyond administrative practices customary in England.

However, in other ways, Americans did improve on English practice in protecting individual liberties. In English common law, defendants were not permitted the benefit of counsel in felony cases. Counsel, if present, could not cross-examine witnesses or address the jury but could only raise legal points for the consideration of the court. Given the low state of development of the law of evidence, however, this was of little consequence in most trials, even when defendants could afford legal counsel.

Some mainland colonies followed English practice in this way. For example, the very fact that New York nearly duplicated English practice than most other provinces meant that the less desirable features of common law—such as the deprivation of counsel—were in force there. Elsewhere, however, this was not the case. In 1669, Rhode Island permitted the employment of defense counsel in all cases. In Connecticut, it is not altogether clear when the received law was reformed, but in the 1790s Zephaniah Swift, an early court reporter, noted that "we have never admitted [in Connecticut] that cruel and illiberal principle of the common law of England that when less a man is on trial for his life, he shall be refused counsel, and denied those means of defence, which are allowed, when the most trifling pittance of property is in question."[37] The Pennsylvania *Charter of Privileges* of 1701 (also in force in Delaware) specifically provided that "all criminals shall have the same Privileges of Witnesses and Council as their Prosecutors," and a 1718 Pennsylvania statute required the assignment of counsel in capital cases as well as witness process for those accused of crime.[38] In 1701, the Massachusetts General Court provided for counsel in criminal as well as civil cases. In general, Massachusetts courts assigned counsel for needy defendants in murder cases. A Virginia law of 1734 allowed defense counsel in capital cases but did not permit cross-examination or address to the jury. South Carolina in 1731 provided for the assignment of counsel at the request of the accused, since, in the words of the statute, many innocent persons under criminal prosecutions, may suffer for: "want of knowledge in the laws, how to make a just defence . . . for which reasons [they] ought to have proper assistance, and all just

---

37. Felix Rackow, "The Right to Counsel: English and American Precedents," *William and Mary Quarterly* Vol. 11 (1954): 15.
38. See *Charter of Privileges*, http://www.ushistory.org/documents/charter.htm. For more studies on colonial Pennsylvania's crime and punishment trends, see H.W.K. Fitzroy, "The Punishment of Crime in Provincial Pennsylvania," *Pennsylvania Magazine of History and Biography* Vol. LX (1936): 242–269.

and equal means allowed them to defend their innocencies."[39] In short, in about half of the original Thirteen Colonies, counsel was permitted in felony cases long before the Revolution, though in all probability most criminal defendants could not afford a trained attorney, and only in Massachusetts, Pennsylvania, and South Carolina was counsel assigned. But by the time of the formation of the federal Constitution, the right to counsel was established in the fundamental law of nearly every state, including New York—a significant advance over the English practice, where the right to a full defense by legal counsel in felony trials was not recognized by statute until 1836.[40]

Innovations on English practice occurred in other areas as well. The grand jury of accusation began as an instrument of royal justice in the days of the Norman kings, but in the course of its evolution it had become a popular check upon the royal prerogative. The grand jury protected the citizen from unfounded accusation. However, by the seventeenth century the English grand jury was becoming more an arm of the state and less a popular defense against arbitrary power—similar in some ways to the American grand jury today.

In colonial America, the grand jury—when it was used—achieved much greater independence and autonomy than its English counterpart. The absence of a regular constabulary meant that individual grand jurors assumed responsibility for presenting criminal offenders. There are instances of colonial grand juries hearing evidence for the defense, whereas in England only King's evidence was admissible. Jurymen were not always chosen by the county sheriff, as in England, but sometimes by local bodies, such as the courts or town meetings. Property qualifications for grand-jury service were not high (except in the Carolinas), so that grand jurymen were drawn from a wider social group, and jury duty was not strictly confined to the wealthy few. In New England towns, grand-jury service was rotated among the free inhabitants. Grand juries took on many local administrative functions: they reported on road conditions, investigated official performance, passed local ordinances. It was, in fact, a representative institution of local government, a kind of county parliament.

---

39. Rackow, "The Right to Counsel: English and American Precedents," 20 (reference to original South Carolina text).
40. Ibid.

In the field of criminal-law enforcement, there was a widespread belief that accusation by grand jury was the only acceptable means of initiating proceedings against criminal offenders. In 1715, Maryland prohibited accusation by any other means, and in 1727 a committee of the South Carolina legislature opposed the *information,* a method of accusation by the prosecutor acting alone.[41] Also in 1727, in an act subsequently disallowed by the Privy Council, New York barred accusations by information.[42] Moreover, except in the South, grand juries were reluctant to approve the *bill of indictment* customarily prepared in advance by the prosecution; preferring the *presentment,* a formal accusation initiated and drawn by the grand jury itself. This preference was evidence of the tendency of some American grand juries to revert to medieval English practice, in which the grand jury was a genuine investigatory body, or "inquest," of citizens. The New York experience illustrates an attitude widespread in colonial America, that the grand jury was an important defense of individual liberty and a check on Crown officers, prosecuting attorneys in particular. Through the grand jury, the power to prosecute was curbed, and this had a major impact on the government's ability to enforce seditious-libel laws or violations of the Navigation Acts.

As a consequence, the Crown resorted to the information in proceeding against law violators, although the records indicate that, even in New York, it was used less frequently than in England. In addition, the *qui tam* action—a civil action brought by a private informer suing for a breach of some statute who then shares the penalties with the government—was a device employed by the Crown to enforce the provisions of the Navigation Acts without having to go before the local grand jury for an indictment. Oddly enough, there seems to have been less objection on constitutional grounds to *qui tam* proceedings—often employed in summary process—than there was to the Crown information.

In other ways, American legal practice achieved a level of performance comparable to English procedure. The right against

---

41. Richard D. Younger, *The People's Panel: The Grand Jury in the United States, 1634–1941* (Providence, RI: Brown University, 1963), 25. For a detailed study of crime and punishment focusing on criminal procedure in various settlements of Maryland, see Raphael Semmes, *Crime and Punishment in Early Maryland* (Baltimore, MD: The Johns Hopkins University Press, 1938).
42. Ibid.

compulsory self-incrimination—one of the focal points of the constitutional debates of the Stuart period—was recognized in England by the middle of the seventeenth century. It emerged out of the struggle between the state and individuals accused of public crimes such as treason, sedition, and heresy, but, by the end of the seventeenth century, it was being applied to defendants in ordinary criminal proceedings. However, like other common-law liberties, this right was not automatically transferred to the American colonies. It was a right that "had to win its way to recognition in every colony."[43] While the record indicates that America lagged behind England on the right against self-incrimination in the early period, by the time of the Revolution it had achieved nearly universal acceptance in the colonies. The right of a defendant not to be compelled to give evidence against himself was manifested in a number of ways: The accused could be questioned but not under oath during preliminary examination; witnesses could not be compelled to incriminate themselves when giving evidence against others; and oaths of purgation, in which a failure to swear one's innocence of a statutory violation was prima facie evidence of guilt, were gradually abandoned.

To be sure, the right against self-incrimination was not, in the eighteenth century, what it was to become in the twentieth century. Nowadays, the accused must be apprised of his right to say nothing to the police, and coerced confessions are inadmissible in evidence. But in the colonial period, the right not to incriminate oneself had to be claimed. The state had no obligation to advise the prisoner to remain silent. Confessions, usually elicited by intimidation ("close examination"), though unsworn, were admitted in evidence at trial. If the accused challenged pretrial admissions, he opened himself to questioning by the court and comment by the prosecutor. In fact, the admissibility of confessions often led to conviction in a summary proceeding, and this in itself denied the most important

---

43. Leonard W. Levy, *Origins of the Fifth Amendment: The Right Against Self-Incrimination* (New York: Oxford University Press, 1968), 334 (discussing civil liberties encompassed within the Fifth Amendment and its origins). For a balanced scholarly debate on whether colonial New York recognized the privilege of not being forced to incriminate oneself under oath, and to what extent, see the work of Leonard Levy and Lawrence H. Leder, "*Exotic Fruit: The Right Against Compulsory Self-Incrimination in Colonial New York*," *William and Mary Quarterly,* 3d Ser., Vol. 20, No.1 (1963): 3–32.

element of due process—the right to a jury trial. For the poor and ignorant offender, unaided by legal counsel, the right against compulsory self-incrimination was often an empty and meaningless constitutional liberty. Still, to the extent that it was available for those who were knowledgeable enough to demand it, the right against compulsory self-incrimination was a part of American liberty in the late colonial period.

So was the privilege of *habeas corpus ad subjiciendum*—the right of an individual confined by the authorities to a court inquiry into the cause of his confinement. Whether or not the privilege of the writ of habeas corpus, the "most celebrated writ in English Law,"[44] was in force in the colonies involved the larger question of the transference of parliamentary statutes—in particular, the *Habeas Corpus Act* of 1679. The Act itself did not establish the privilege; it merely regulated and improved the procedures governing its enforcement in England. The accepted doctrine was that, since the colonies were not named in the Act, it did not apply. Efforts by individual colonies to adopt the 1679 statute in name or in substance by legislative enactment met disallowance by the King in Council. Nevertheless, the right to habeas corpus was widely recognized in fact by colonial courts. The writ was part of the common law to which the colonists believed they were entitled. In most provinces, the threat of royal disallowance or suspension prevented formal reception of the *Habeas Corpus Act*, but the privilege was known and implemented in most of the colonies and was allowed to exist with only intermittent interference from royal authorities. [45]

---

44. Blackstone, *Commentaries on the Laws of England, III*, 129; A.H. Carpenter, "Habeas Corpus in the Colonies," *American Historical Review* Vol. 8, No. 1 (1902): 18–27; Paul D. Halliday, *Habeas Corpus: From England to Empire* (Cambridge, MA: Harvard University Press; 2010), 256–257 ("Habeas corpus went to new imperial dominions by common law. But colonial subjects in such dominions generally clamored for a habeas corpus act of their own. . . . In the Caribbean and North America, one colonial legislature after another passed an act in imitation, though in each case, it required approval of the Privy Council, through the Board of Trade and Plantations, to take effect. . . . [S]uch approval was not always forthcoming; sometimes it came decades after the effort began.").

[45] "[C]olonists had little doubt that the famous Habeas Corpus Act of 1679 applied to them." Justin J. Wert, *Habeas Corpus in America* (Univ. of Kansas; Lawrence, Kan., 2011), 33.

As late as the eighteenth century, the English common-law criminal trial was but a dim foreshadowing of modern trial procedure. The criminal defendant could not see the indictment. There was no pretrial discovery of the prosecution's evidence. Counsel was barred in felony cases, on the theory that innocence needed no defense and that the criminal law was simple enough to comprehend, so that the average defendant needed no technical legal knowledge in order to prove his defense. The jury trial was, in concept at least, a kind of gladiatorial combat between equal contestants, with the court sitting as a neutral referee, alert to infringements of the legal rights of the accused.

In fact, however, the whole procedure was weighted in favor of the prosecution. Rules of evidence were rudimentary and little was excluded on grounds of inadmissibility. Written depositions could be read in evidence without the chance for rebuttal or cross-examination of absent witnesses. Defendant confessions, exacted by intimidation or duress in pretrial proceedings, were admissible at trial. Finally, juries were deprived of creature comforts during deliberation and were virtually coerced into rendering guilty verdicts.

In general, New York followed English trial practices. In felony cases, counsel could intercede only on points of law, although—again as in England—in misdemeanor and treason trials, counsel could conduct a full defense. Jury panels were selected impartially. The right to challenge for cause was recognized, although, in the absence of defense counsel, it was seldom used. Juries resisted directed verdicts and found special or general verdicts as their consciences—not the court—dictated. For the most part, jury trials, when conducted, were fair. The sanctity and finality of the trial jury's verdict were upheld as a basic constitutional principle, and this was recognized by the government and the courts. When Lieutenant Governor Cadwallader Colden challenged this well-established tradition in the mid-1760s, he raised a clamor as loud as the protest against the Stamp Act itself.[46] Trials were

46. Raymond T. Naughton and Julius Goebel, *Law Enforcement in Colonial New York: A Study in Criminal Procedure, 1664–1776* (Montclair, NJ: Patterson Smith, 1970), 248. For further important discussion of available legal rights in colonial New York, refer to the work of Milton M. Klein, "Prelude to Revolution in New York: Jury Trials and Judicial Tenure," *William and Mary Quarterly,* 3d Ser., Vol. 17, No. 4 (1960): 439–462.

speedy because of the likelihood that defendants in custody would escape, and also because it was costly for all concerned to drag out the proceedings. In the eighteenth century there was a growing recognition of defendants' right to postponement—part of the general expansion of the rights of the accused in the Age of Enlightenment.

Defendants in felony cases were hurt by limited subpoena privileges, arbitrary court decisions on whether or not defense witnesses could be sworn, the admissibility of hearsay evidence, secrecy surrounding the indictment, and defendants' inability to confront their accusers at preliminary hearings. On the other hand, juries often sided with the accused when the prosecution was upholding Crown interests; the burden of proof was on the shoulders of the state; written depositions were allowed only in misdemeanor trials after 1750; and at summary trials defendants were allowed to cross-examine.[47] Thus, despite the English standard, and despite all the impediments strewn in the path of the accused, the records indicate a large number of acquittals in jury trials. In the end, the conduct of trials was no more oppressive in New York than in contemporary England and probably much less so, given the greater independence of juries plus the popular hostility to the Crown, which New York juries both reflected and represented.

Measured by court practices, the precise meaning of "due process of law" varied considerably from one colony to another. Even within a single province, judicial practice went through marked transformations from the seventeenth to the eighteenth century. As a result, it is difficult to make accurate generalizations regarding the colonial experience as a whole. Nevertheless, certain tendencies are apparent in the development of colonial law. There was a decided movement toward the "Anglicization" of American law as the colonial period advanced.[48] As the bench and the bar became better trained and more knowledgeable, and as the written sources of law became more available, colonial law moved closer to the English model. The result was a growing attention to procedural

47. Julius Goebel, Jr., "Law Enforcement in Colonial New York," in *Essays in the History of Early American Law*, David Flaherty, ed. (Chapel Hill, NC: The University of North Carolina Press, 1969), 380.

48. William E. Nelson, *Americanization of the Common Law: The Impact of Legal Change on Massachusetts Society, 1760–1830* (Cambridge, MA: Harvard University Press, 1975).

exactitude and increasing awareness of the importance of proper form. Moreover, the tension between English common law and seventeenth-century colonial law gave American law a certain dynamic thrust that pushed it in the direction of change. Indeed, while the English standard was the goal, where American procedure had improved upon it—as in the early recognition and widespread implementation of the right to counsel in felony cases or the somewhat greater emphasis upon oral evidence at trial—those advances were preserved, thus imparting to the American legal tradition a reformist character that was one of the singular and lasting achievements of the colonial period.

Thus, the legal experience of early America suggests that the attempt to establish English law and the "rights and liberties of Englishmen" was constant from the first settlements to the Revolution. There were, of course, important exceptions. Everywhere in America, slaves were treated differently. Special courts were set up to deal with crimes committed by slaves. Grand-jury presentment was usually abandoned where slaves were concerned, and trial by a panel of judges took the place of trial by a jury of laymen. On the other hand, out of solicitude for their masters, slaves were sometimes permitted, in felony cases, to have an attorney—usually their owner—in places where legal counsel was normally barred. In addition, although statutory penalties for black slaves were usually more severe than for whites convicted of the same crime, since slaves were valued as property, mitigation of sentence was fairly frequent. Finally, while regular due process was dispensed with, there was a feeling that, even in cases involving slaves, some regularity of procedure should prevail.

Bonded servants also received modified treatment in court. In Virginia, for example, the jury panel in cases involving indentured servants could be drawn entirely from the bystanders at court rather than from residents of the vicinity of the crime.[49] When servants

---

49. Arthur P. Scott, *Criminal Law in Colonial Virginia* (Chicago, IL: University of Chicago Press, 1930). For another colorful study of colonial Virginia criminal procedure, see Hugh F. Rankin's *Criminal Trial Proceedings in the General Court of Colonial Virginia* (Williamsburg, VA: Colonial Williamsburg Press, 1965). For a comprehensive treatment of both criminal and civil process in colonial (particularly 17th century Virginia, see, Warren M. Billings, *Magistrates and Pioneers: Essays in the History of American Law* (Clark, NJ: The Lawbook Exchange, Ltd.,

petitioned the court, their complaints were usually handled informally rather than by regular process. They were also excluded from jury service, a proscription that seriously impaired their ability to achieve equal justice. But bonded servants also possessed certain rights in law: the terms of their contracts were enforceable in the courts; statutes protected them from cruel and inhuman treatment; and servant testimony was accepted in evidence even in cases between master and servant.[50]

In general, the bias inherent in a judicial system in which local magistrates and judges were recruited from the propertied classes while the poor, the vagabond, the semi-free and the slave were all subject to summary or informal process undercut the chances of equal treatment for all before the law. The legal disabilities facing these groups defined the limits of civil liberty in colonial America. Nevertheless, measured by the eighteenth century rather than the twentieth, colonial Americans were in the forefront of legal reform and in the process of broadening and redefining the meaning of due process of law. English common law was thought to be the closest approximation to justice that mankind had ever achieved. The colonists resented the accepted English doctrine, which withheld that law from them; they disregarded it where they could; and after 1760, they resisted, even to revolution, imperial attempts to enforce it. Above all, the Americans were determined to create a system of law that was responsive to their needs and experience as well as to their English heritage. The results, while uneven, point to a consistent effort to implement in fact what early charters, codes, and basic statutes of fundamental law had set forth with simple clarity and liberal zeal. Constitutional guarantees of personal liberty were at least as secure in colonial America as in England and in some respects even more so.

2011) Essay 9: "Pleading, Procedure and Practice: the Meaning of Due Process of Law in Seventeenth Century Virginia."
50. Ibid.

Episode 2

Religious Toleration and its Limits in Early America

> Religious indifference is imperceptibly disseminated from one end of the continent to the other . . . zeal in Europe is confined . . . here it burns away in the open air and consumes without effect.
>
> J. Hector St. Jean De Crevecoeure
> *Letters from an American Farmer, 1782*

Provincial recognition of religious freedom was widespread in early America. Of all the written guarantees of individual freedom codified in the charters, organic laws, patents, agreements, and constitutions of early America, religious toleration and freedom of conscience were the provisions most frequently encountered. From New Hampshire to the Carolinas, principles of religious liberty were adopted in nearly every English mainland settlement either by royal instruction, proprietary grant, or provincial self-enactment. But religious liberty was not universal, nor was the regime of liberty uniformly distributed in place or in time. Differences in religious culture were present from region to region throughout early America. Religious dissent was tolerated in some colonies, but not others, and both the growth of a tolerant spirit and the advance of liberty were not inexorably progressive.

Maryland, for example, offers an early example of religious toleration. Founded by Roman Catholics, Maryland was initially hospitable to Catholics until Anglicanism became established early in the eighteenth century. Thereafter, Maryland Catholics were reduced to second-class status, and by the time of the American Revolution there was only one free-standing Roman Catholic church in the entire province. Similarly, in colonial Virginia, the church establishment became more entrenched in the eighteenth century than it had ever been in the seventeenth century.

American colonial society was the most liberal in the western world for its toleration of religious minorities. But religious freedom in early America was not rooted in a theory or philosophy of religious toleration. Rather, early Americans promoted religious freedom to the extent that a tolerant, liberal policy comported with the immediate needs of settlement.

Why did colonial America become the scene for the realization of a tolerant ideology in matters of religious policy, and what was the scope and extent of that tolerance once it had been achieved? Religious toleration in early America was a product of social circumstance and historical necessity. But lofty philosophical principles gave way to societal needs whenever the two were in conflict. The development of toleration reflected the demands and necessities of colonial society. "[T]oleration in practice . . . owe[d] more to circumstances, or to religious indifference, than to the promptings of the religious conscience itself."[1] Social reality, rather than philosophic principles, was the engine behind the development of religious freedom in colonial society. A multiplicity of factors supplied the momentum for this unique regime—religious pluralism, geographic spaciousness, and historical development explain the emergence of a limited regime of religious liberalism in early America.

The overwhelming reality of colonial religious life was the presence of religious pluralism. The rich assortment of religious groups, the proliferation of communities with distinct religious histories, and the increasing number and variety of Dissenter (or Nonconforming) faiths created a climate of religious tolerance that nurtured the idea of freedom of conscience. Where no single sect predominated, it was difficult to maintain notions or institutions based upon religious uniformity. This was particularly evident in the middle colonies such as Pennsylvania. Eighteenth century Pennsylvania was home not only to its Quaker founders but also to Mennonites, Dunkers, Moravians, Schwenkfelders, Lutherans, Dutch Reformed, Presbyterians, Baptists, Anglicans, Jews, and Roman Catholics. The Anglican missionary Charles Woodmanson declared, "Africk [sic] never more abounded with New Monsters,

---

* Source: "Religious Toleration and its Limits in Early America" in *Northern Illionois University Law Review*, Vol. 16, Spring 1996, No. 2, 341–370 (by George Dargo).

1. Edwin S. Gaustad, *Historical Atlas of Religion in America* (rev. ed., New York: Harper & Row, 1976), 3.

than Pennsylvania does with new sects . . . ."[2] The same was true in New York. As the English governor Sir Edmund Andros observed of New York in 1686, "there are Religions of all sorts, one Church of England, several Presbyterians, and Independents, Quakers and Anabaptists of several sects, [and] some Jews . . . ."[3] But where uniformity of religion was more prevalent, religious freedom was less secure and toleration was the exception rather than the rule.[4]

The single-church establishment was the familiar cultural mold that shaped the thinking and set the course for the first European settlers in America. Under this system of close church-state cooperation, a single religious body, usually encompassing a majority of the population, enjoyed special legal privileges and protections. Competing religious institutions and doctrines were suppressed, either directly or indirectly. Tax monies for the support of the predominant church and minister were collected by the authorities. The official church ran the schools. Church officials administered welfare and charity. The crucial events of family life—birth, marriage, divorce, and death—were regulated by the deeds and punctuated by the ceremonies of the standing order.

---

2. Ibid., at 2. See also Sydney E. Ahlstrom, *A Religious History of the American People* (New Haven: Yale University Press, 1972), chaps. 13–16. On the complexity of the American religious experience in the Colonial era, see John M. Murrin, "Religion and Politics in America from the First Settlements to the Civil War," in *Religion and American Politics: From the Colonial Period to the 1980s*, ed. Mark A. Noll (New York: Oxford University Press, 1990), chap. 1 ("Religion in the Middle Atlantic Colonies marked the most striking departure from the European norm of an established church.").

3. For conflicting interpretations of the early American religious experience, compare Jon Butler, "Coercion, Miracle, Reason: Rethinking the American Religious Experience in the Revolutionary Age," with Patricia U. Bonomi, "Religious Dissent and the Case for American Exceptionalism," in *Religion in a Revolutionary Age*, eds. Ronald Hoffman and Peter J. Albert, (Charlottesville: University Press of Virginia, 1994). Bonomi emphasizes the growth of dissent after 1680, which contributed to the separation of America from England. In contrast, John Murrin concludes that by the middle of the eighteenth century dissent "was stagnant or declining. (. . .) More than a century after the first settlements, most of the people in British America lived within a narrower band of religious choices than fellow subjects enjoyed in England." Murrin, "Religion and Politics," 21.

4. "[H]owever varied their experiences, Americans of the Revolutionary age usually encountered Christianity in a state-supported church, which provided the most readily available minister, services, and places of worship." Butler, "Coercion, Miracle, Reason," 6.

Above all, an orthodox constellation of beliefs was enforced by the vigorous application of criminal statutes against heresy, blasphemy, and idolatry.[5]

Governmental power was the major instrument for achieving uniformity of faith and worship. Religious uniformity could not be sustained without governmental coercion. True religion, said attorney Nathaniel Ward in 1645, "strictly binds every Conscience to contend earnestly for the Truth: to preserve unity of spirit, Faith and Ordinances, to be all like minded, of one accord; every man to take his Brother into his Christian care, to stand fast with one spirit, with one mind striving together for the faith of the Gospel; and by no means to permit Heresies or Erroneous Opinions."[6] Church and state were allied institutions in the common struggle to recreate well-ordered polities in a wilderness environment.

But while the single-church establishment was the model, the American environment was hostile to traditional patterns of church-state relations. The geography of North America, the conditions of American life, the necessities of settlement, and the character of the immigrant population eroded established traditions and replaced them with attitudes and practices that pointed in new directions. The idea that church and state best served society when they rotated in separate and distinct spheres was not widely accepted until after the American Revolution, but tendencies in that direction were in motion at the very outset of American colonial life. There was the brute fact of sheer size. Religious liberty in early American history was a function of geographic spaciousness. Provincial America's greatest problem was its need for people—to fill the land, to supply labor, to develop the country—in order to increase the wealth and power of the English empire and the various corporate entities to which the Crown had delegated governing authority. Religious exclusivity did not square with such goals. As an example, Catholic Maryland quickly accepted the need to tolerate English Protestants. The colony had been established by Roman Catholic proprietors, but since Catholics did not emigrate to America in large numbers, Maryland had to be hospitable to the greater number of Protestants who would. Consequently, the *Maryland Toleration Act of 1649*, a

---

5. Nathaniel Ward, *The Simple Cobbler of Aggawam*, (n. p., 1645).
6. Jon Butler, "Protestant Pluralism," in *Encyclopedia of the North American Colonies*, ed. Jacob Earnest Cooke (vol. 3, New York: Charles Scribner's Sons, 1993), 619–620.

great moment in the early history of American religious liberty, was neither a Catholic nor Protestant measure, nor was it a product of the liberalism theory. Rather, the *Toleration Act* was a practical device for making Maryland more attractive to settlers of diverse religious persuasions. Similarly, in the case of Quaker Pennsylvania, William Penn's liberalism happened to coincide with the needs of settlement. Penn's easy land-grant policy, the liberality of his frames of government, and his toleration of non-Quakers made Pennsylvania the home of a motley assortment of religious groups who contributed to the peopling of that province.[7]

Indeed, when individual colonies became too zealous in their pursuit of spiritual uniformity, they were subject to rebuke from the English government for discouraging settlement. Thus, when South Carolina excluded dissenters from sitting in the provincial assembly and tried to establish an Anglican ecclesiastical court, the Privy Council objected because such a policy was likely to depopulate the province. Again, in 1750, when the Virginia Council tried to limit the activities of dissenter preachers, the Lords of Trade[8] advised that a "free Exercise of Religion is so valuable a branch of true liberty, and so essential to the enriching and improving of a Trading Nation, it should ever be held sacred in His Majesty's Colonies."[9]

Geographic spaciousness had other consequences for traditional religious establishments. The openness of the land weakened the hold that churches could exercise through customary procedures of discipline and control. Government was weak. Social hierarchy was fragile. American society "was an institutional void."[10] Any attempt to impose strict orthodoxy led to seepage at

---

7. The English Privy Council was the most powerful legal and political institution close to the Crown.

8. Dargo, *Roots of the Republic*, 79.

9. Murrin, "Religion and Politics," 23.

10. Virginia DeJohn Anderson, "British Settlements: New England," in *Encyclopedia of the North American Colonies*, ed. Jacob Earnest Cooke (vol. 1, New York: Charles Scribner's Sons, 1993), 160, 162. Although Roger Williams is credited as the founder of Rhode Island, it is Doctor John Clarke who persuaded King Charles II in 1663 to grant Rhode Island a charter that recognized religious toleration. On July 15, 1663 Clarke convinced King Charles II to grant him a charter for Rhode Island that established religious freedom and separation of church and state. The charter states in part "that it is much on their hearts (if they may be permitted), to hold forth a livlie experiment . . . with a full libertie in

the edges—of those for whom the prevailing orthodoxy was too conservative, and of others for whom it was too easy-going. In England, the seepage was "vertical;" the heterodox went underground into secret "gatherings" and "conventicles." But in America, the seepage was "horizontal;" dissenters moved away in voluntary exile or through a process of punitive banishment. Rhode Island, on the one hand, and the towns of the Connecticut Valley, on the other, were spin-offs from the orthodoxy of Massachusetts, which was too narrow for the followers of Roger Williams, founder of Rhode Island, and too broad for the likes of Thomas Hooker, founder of Connecticut.[11] Thus, with the establishments of the Rhode Island and Connecticut colonies, the American pattern of "horizontal" exit from orthodoxy created competing religious communities that, in time, would shorten the reach of the standing order.

Similarly, the distances between the colonial branches and the European stock also had an impact upon religious freedom. Such distance made provincial churches separate in fact if not in faith, made discipline from the center impossible to enforce, made kindred churches within provinces into semi-autonomous bodies, and made loose interprovincial denominational associations the norm in church governance. Such spatial relations had a revolutionary impact upon the traditional association of church and state and pointed toward greater religious freedom.[12]

Other factors deepened the gulf between the old doctrine of a uniform faith within a single-church establishment and the emerging condition of American religious diversity. The whole spirit of the eighteenth century was against coerced belief, organized religious establishments, and even religion itself. Deism and philosophical rationalism pushed orthodoxy into a defensive posture. The religious enthusiasm that we associate with the itinerant preachers of the Great Awakening also challenged the status quo and the cold and lifeless orthodoxy of the established ministry.[13] Beset by these threatening forces, the Protestant churches, which in the sixteenth and seventeenth centuries had

---

religious concernements . . . ." See James Wermuth, "The Forgotten Patriot," Op Ed., *Boston Globe*, April 28, 2011.

11. Bonomi, "Religious Dissent," 34–45.

12. The Great Awakening of the 1730s and 1740s, closely identified with the Evangelical ministers Jonathan Edwards and George Whitefield.

13. Butler, "Coercion, Miracle, Reason," 20–24; Murrin, "Religion and Politics," 25–26.

divided over fine points of ecclesiology, now faced new enemies—the Enlightenment on one side and religious fundamentalism on the other. Established churches found that they had more to lose than to gain by alienating dissenting churches that otherwise remained traditional in the fundamentals of belief and practice.[14]

Still other agents contributed to the breakup of ancient attitudes governing church-state relations. Commerce, politics, and war remained serious competitors for attention in the eighteenth century. The need for population was another factor, particularly on the frontier. Colonial authorities preferred to encourage immigrants, who were often members of left-wing Dissenter or German Pietist groups, to settle in exposed borderlands. And still another fact to be reckoned with was plain indifference. In addition to moving away from one church and toward another, many colonists had the additional option of abandoning organized religion altogether. Here again, the spatial dimensions of America played a critical role in altering the position of the church in society. Even after the embers of the Great Awakening had cooled in coastal regions, the frontier simmered with religious fundamentalism. The only ministers available for service in such places were itinerants, each with a different sectarian persuasion. But sectarian distinctions were a matter of indifference as long as preachers could exhort, extol, exhalt, and declaim. On the frontier, the learned clergy were as rare as lawyers, judges, doctors, and teachers. Consequently, religious communities often found themselves to be "sheep without shepherds."[15]

In 1766, Charles Woodmanson, the Anglican missionary, made the following observation regarding the absence of religion in the colony of North Carolina:

> As to North Carolina, the State of Religion therein is greatly to be lamented . . . . The manners of the North Carolinians in General are Vile and Corrupt. The whole Country is in a Stage of

---

14. Bonomi, "Religious Dissent," 36.
15. Gaustad, *Historical Atlas of Religion*, 3–4. What one Congregationalist clergyman observed about Baptist preachers could be applied more generally to the situation that prevailed on the western frontier: "Many people are so ignorant, as to be charmed more with sound than sense. And to them, the want of knowledge in a teacher . . . may easily be made up, and overbalanced, by great zeal, an affecting tone of voice, and a perpetual motion of the tongue." Ibid., 132.

> Debauchery, Dissoluteness and Corruption—and how can it be otherwise? The People are compos'd of the Out Casts of all the other Colonies who take Refuge there . . . Marriages (thro' want of Clergy) are perform'd by ev'ry ordinary Magistrate—Polygamy is very common—Celibacy, much more—Bastardy, no Disrepute—Concubinage General—When will this Augean Stable be cleans'd![16]

Such was the result of the paucity of clergy. Moreover, a religious establishment was always a costly legal obligation. Few frontier or breakaway communities could afford to build a church or keep a minister even if one were available. If the settlers were not homogeneous in faith, several churches would have to be maintained, a capital expenditure far beyond ordinary means. Indifference to fine points of doctrine, therefore, was for some a matter not of choice but of circumstance.[17]

The widespread recognition of principles of religious liberty was reflected in the documentary record very early in colonial times. Rhode Island's charter of 1663 declared that "everye person and persons may, from tyme to tyme, and at all tymes hereafter, freelye and fullye have and enjoy his and theire owne judgments and consciences, in matters of religious concernments."[18] Rhode Island was the most liberal of all the early colonies. By the end of the seventeenth century, Newport, Rhode Island, was home to a number of important religious minorities—Quakers, Baptists, Jews, and Roman Catholics all located within one square-mile area. It was as if Newport had been zoned for religious freedom.[19]

---

16. "[R]eligious indifference is imperceptibly disseminated from one end of the continent to the other. . . . zeal in Europe is confined . . . here it burns away in the open air, and consumes without effect." J. Hector St. Jean, *Letters from an American Farmer* (Philadelphia, 1782) 47.
17. *Charter of Rhode Island and Providence Plantations* (1663), reprinted in *The Federal and State Constitutions, Colonial Charters, and Other Organic Laws of the States, Territories, and Colonies Now or Heretofore Forming the United States of America*, ed. Francis Newton Thorpe, (6th ed., Washington, D.C.: Government Printing Office, 1909), 3211, 3213 [hereafter *The Federal and State Constitutions*].
18. As several Dutch Reformed ministers once observed: "Rhode Island . . . is the receptacle of all sorts of riff-raff people, and is nothing less than the sewer of New England." Gaustad, 1.
19. *Charter of Carolina* (1663), reprinted in *The Federal and State Constitutions*, (5th ed.), 2743, 2752–2753.

In 1663, the royal charter to the Anglican proprietors of Carolina recognized freedom of conscience when it stipulated that:

> because it may happen that some of the people and inhabitants of the said province, cannot in their private opinions, conform to the publick exercise of religion, according to the liturgy, form and ceremonies of the church of England . . . and for that the same, by reason of the remote distances of these places, will, we hope, be no breach of the unity and uniformity established in this nation; our will and pleasure therefore is, and we do by these presents, . . . give and grant . . . (for conscience sake) . . . [the liberty not to follow the] liturgy and ceremonies, . . . the oaths and articles [of the Anglican establishment, provided only that the behavior of religious dissenters] . . . do not disturb in any wise the peace and safety thereof, or scandalize or reproach the said liturgy, forms and ceremonies.[20]

In 1676, the proprietors of West New Jersey, in *Concessions and Agreements*, asserted that:

> no men, nor number of men upon earth, hath power or authority to rule over men's consciences in religious matters . . . [and, therefore, that] no person or persons whatsoever within the said Province . . . shall be . . . upon any pretence whatsoever, called in question, or in the least punished or hurt, either in person, estate, or privilege, for the sake of his opinion, judgment, faith or worship towards God in matters of religion.[21]

In New Hampshire, the Commission of John Cutt, to establish a government separate from that of Massachusetts, provided that:

> for [the] greater ease & satisfacon of [our] s[aid] loving subjects in matters of Religion We do hereby will, require & com'and [that] liberty of conscience shall be allowed unto all protestants; [and that those who conformed to the rites of the church of Eng-

---

20. *Charter of Fundamental Laws of West New Jersey Agreed Upon* (1676), reprinted in *The Federal and State Constitutions* (5th ed.), 2548–2549.
21. *Commission of John Cutt* (1680), reprinted in *The Federal and State Constitutions* (4th ed.), 2446, 2448.

land] shall be particularly countenanced & encouraged.[22]

The *New York Charter of Liberties and Privileges*, adopted in 1683 by the first assembly of deputies to convene in that colony, confirmed the existence of several Christian churches (Dutch Reformed, Congregational, Presbyterian, and Anglican), and established these as "privileged Churches," guaranteeing the same rights to all Christian churches that were to be settled thereafter.[23] In addition, the charter stated that no person professing belief in Christ "shall at any time be any ways molested punished disquieted or called in Question for any Difference in opinion or Matter of Religious Concernment."[24] The *New York Charter of Liberties and Privileges* was never ratified by the Privy Council, but legislation passed in the 1690s confirmed many of its provisions, including liberty of conscience.

Even Virginia, the province where Anglicanism was first established and where it enjoyed the most substantial popular support of any of the Church of England colonies, eventually gave way to the winds of change sweeping across British America. As early as 1679, a royal instruction to the Virginia governor required that, in order "to give all possible encouragement to persons of different persuasions in matters of religion to transport themselves thither with their stocks, you are not to suffer any man to be molested or disquieted in the exercise of his religion." Roman Catholics were subsequently excluded from this imperial directive, which was later applied to all the royal provinces.

In 1682, the *Frame of Government of Pennsylvania* decreed that no persons shall be "molested or prejudiced for their religious persuasion, or practice, in matters of faith and worship."[25] This same concept of religious freedom was also echoed in the 1701 *Charter of Privileges* granted by William Penn to the inhabitants of Pennsylvania and Delaware.[26] The *Charter* stated that "no People

---

22. *Charter of Liberties and Privileges* (1683), reprinted in *Sources and Documents of United States Constitutions*, ed. William Finley Swindler (7th ed.), 164, 167.
23. Ibid., 166.
24. *Frame of Government of Pennsylvania* (1682), reprinted in *The Federal and State Constitutions* (5th ed.), 3052, 3063.
25. *Charter of Privileges Granted by William Penn, Esq. to the Inhabitants of Pennsylvania and Territories* (1701), reprinted in *The Federal and State Constitutions* (5th ed.), 3076–3077.
26. Ibid.

can be truly happy . . . if abridged of the Freedom of their Consciences."[27]

Even in New England, religious orthodoxy began to collapse. In 1691, the *Charter of Massachusetts Bay* granted to its people a "liberty of conscience."[28] In this case, such liberty of conscience was limited to all Christian inhabitants excepting "papists." In Connecticut, where a Congregational religious establishment would outlast all others save that of Massachusetts, religious tolerance was accepted as early as 1669, when deviants from strict orthodoxy who were otherwise sound in faith were given "allowance of their persuasion and profession in church ways or assemblies without disturbance."[29] In the first decade of the eighteenth century, the entrenched Connecticut establishment granted dissenters the right to worship in public, provided that they were prepared to continue to give tax support to the Congregational Church. In approving the *Saybrook Platform of Church Discipline* (1708), a form of "presbyterial Congregationalism," the Connecticut Assembly provided that:

> nothing herein shall be intended and construed to hinder or prevent any society or church that is or shall be allowed by the laws of this government, who soberly differ or dissent from the united churches hereby established, from exercising worship and discipline in their own way, according to their consciences.[30]

This provision referenced a law passed earlier in the year which applied the *English Act of Toleration* "granting liberties of worshipping God in a way separate from that which is by law established . . . without any let, hindrance and molestation whatsoever." Connecticut's "little statute of toleration" was more an effort to appease the English and deflect a move against the colony by the imperial authorities than a measured response to local demands for religious liberalism. Even so, it fit the pattern of a loosening church establishment.

To be sure, liberty of conscience was circumscribed by laws against Quakers, Jews, Catholics, Unitarians, freethinkers, and

---

27. *Charter of Massachusetts Bay* (1691), reprinted in *The Federal and State Constitutions*, at 942, 950.
28. Ibid.
29. Dargo, *Roots of the Republic*, 83.
30. Ibid., 83–84.

Atheists and by laws establishing religious tests for office. Nevertheless, provincial recognition of the principle of toleration, restricted though it was, represented a significant modification of the traditional pattern of church-state relations. The results of this widespread recognition of freedom of conscience early in our colonial history can best be measured by the dramatic increase in the number, variety, and distribution of churches from the mid-seventeenth to the mid-eighteenth century. In 1650, only four colonies—Rhode Island, New York, Maryland, and Delaware—had two or more denominations. The rest of the colonies had but one. The Congregational establishment in most of New England and the Anglican establishment of Virginia enjoyed undisputed ecclesiastical hegemony. But in Rhode Island and Maryland, the two colonies that openly espoused a policy of toleration, there was a mixture of churches. Three of Catholic Maryland's four Anglican churches were set up in 1650, one year after the *Maryland Toleration Act*. What would later be the English colony of New York was already showing its characteristic religious diversity, with New England's Puritan overflow of Congregationalists and Presbyterians competing with New York's dominant Dutch Reformed Church. A century later, by 1750, there was a "mixture" of churches in every colony, ranging from three separate churches in New Hampshire, to seven in South Carolina, New Jersey, and Pennsylvania, and eight in New York. No denomination was found in fewer than five colonies, and two (Presbyterians and Baptists) could be found in as many as eleven. There were five settled Jewish communities in five different colonies from Rhode Island in the northeast to Georgia in the south. Predictably, the Anglican Church had a presence in all of the original Thirteen Colonies. In provinces that had supported a single-church establishment, the pattern of uniformity had been broken; where diversity existed from the start, it intensified. The policy of toleration, widespread by 1700 and even broader by 1750, had had the effect of encouraging the proliferation of churches, measured in terms of their overall distribution throughout British America.

Protestant Christianity was dominant everywhere but Atheists were beyond the pale even in the most liberal colonies. Atheists represented a challenge to the standing order, whether the structure of that standing order was rigidly orthodox or tolerant of dissent. Atheists undermined true belief and thus interfered with religious practice. Freedom of conscience did not include the freedom to disbelieve, nor was the government neutral toward disbelief. Even dissenter groups expected the authorities to be active against Atheists. To question the truth of religion was "to dissolve all those obligations whereby . . . civil societies are preserved."[31] Unlike other marginal groups, however, Atheists were individualists. Their religious beliefs—or lack of such beliefs—did not require communal expression. While atheism was abhorrent as a philosophical position, it represented no serious threat to social stability in real terms.

Quakers were more suspect. Their presence was strongest in Pennsylvania, a Quaker colony. But elsewhere, Quakers were reviled. One North Carolinian observed that "[t]he Quakers in this precinct are very numerous, extremely ignorant, insufferably proud and ambitious, and consequently ungovernable."[32] Quakers were considered to be radical and given to excess in their political as well as in their religious beliefs. Quakers believed that revelation came through an "inner light" and that a trained ministry was not required for personal salvation. But the doctrine of the "inner light" was viewed by the Anglican establishment and dissenter groups alike as highly subversive of authority. Quaker pacifism and refusal to pay taxes, plus their stubborn adherence to the principles of their faith, led to persecutions both in England and in most of the American colonies, particularly in the early period of settlement. Nevertheless, Quakers did have settled communities in Rhode Island as well as in the colonies of New Jersey and New York even before William Penn received his grant to establish Quakerism's "Holy Experiment" in Pennsylvania.[33]

Prejudice toward Roman Catholics was deep-seated and widespread. Only in Pennsylvania and Rhode Island did Catholics find a mildly hospitable reception. "Anti-popery" was a term of profound opprobrium, and it reflected a deep-seated and widespread animus toward Catholics and the Roman Catholic Church that was pervasive in American colonial society. "Anti-popery proved to be a

———

31. Gaustad, *Historical Atlas of Religion*, 3.
32. Clarence L. Ver Steeg, *The Formative Years: 1607–1763* (New York: Hill & Wang, 1964), 118–19. See also Joseph E. Illick, "Quakerism," in *Encyclopedia of the North American Colonies*, ed. Jacob Earnest Cooke, vol. 3 (New York: Charles Scribner's Sons, 1993), 595.
33. Francis D. Cogliano, *No King, No Popery: Anti-Popery and Revolution in New England, 1745–1791*, (unpub. Ph.D. Dissertation, Boston University, 1993), viii.

remarkably durable cultural system."[34] It was a major source of unity amidst the clamor of disparate voices in American colonial society. The general tendency of colonial history was toward church disestablishment, but Roman Catholicism had a strong establishment tradition. Moreover, England's major imperial rivals were the Catholic countries of France and Spain. "Papists" were thought to have an affinity toward England's enemies, a fear that was reinforced by the Seven Years War. American Protestants viewed Roman Catholicism as cruel, superstitious, idolatrous and conspiratorial.

Anti-popery was rooted in English culture and was part of the cultural baggage of British America. In the seventeenth-century, for example, John Foxe's *Book of Martyrs*, a sixteenth century chronicle of Catholic atrocities against Protestants, was, along with the Bible, the most commonly used book in New England.[35] By 1750, only five colonies had any Roman Catholics to speak of. Most of these were located in New York and Maryland. Anti-Catholic laws remained ubiquitous, and few Catholics settled in colonies where such laws existed. Anti-Catholic attitudes only began to diminish when independence was declared and the Continental Congress forged alliances with the major Catholic countries. In the Revolution, "anti-popery proved an impediment to the rebel cause."[36] Americans redirected their political hatred toward the English monarchy and all things English, thus allowing anti-Catholicism to subside. Although anti-popery did not disappear from American life, it would never occupy the central position it held for so long, with such virulence, in the cultural ideology of Colonial America.

Jews were yet another suspect class. Jews were concentrated in the largest commercial cities (New York, Newport, Philadelphia, and Charleston), but their numbers were few. Jews were usually part of the merchant class with some of the most successful Jews assimilating into the larger culture through intermarriage. Jewish religious institutions were very weak, and there were no ordained rabbis in the colonies. Rather, religious questions had to be referred to the London rabbinate. Since Jewish identity was attenuated, it represented no threat to the dominant culture. This may explain

---

34. Ibid., 19.
35. Ibid.
36. Leo Hershkowitz, "Judaism" in *Encyclopedia of the North American Colonies*, ed. Jacob Earnest Cooke, vol. 3 (New York: Charles Scribner's Sons, 1993), 638.

why Jews were tolerated wherever they settled. There were no Jewish ghettos, no "Jew codes," and no official anti-Semitism; however, Jews could not vote, even in tolerant Rhode Island, despite the fact that Parliament enacted a statute in 1740 conferring the rights of British subjects on Jews and Quakers living in the American colonies. Colonial America was an open society relative to what Jews had experienced at other times in their history. Thus, while Jews were not full participants in colonial American life, America did offer to those who settled here a safe haven and the chance to develop their separate communities. Still, even the liberal Newport minister, Ezra Stiles, predicted that "Jews will never become incorporated with the people of America."[37]

What of the other principal "minorities" in Colonial America—"minorities" not by virtue of their religious views but "minorities" by virtue of race, principally African-Americans, both slave and free, and Native Americans? What was the religious experience of these groups amid the growing pluralism of American religious life? Did African-Americans and American Indians find American religion coercive or liberating?

African-Americans did not have their own separate churches until late in the Colonial period. As traditional African religions did not survive the Atlantic crossing, many African-Americans practiced some form of Christianity. Nevertheless, conversion to Christianity was a slow process since owners were reluctant to convert their slaves. One English minister who visited the Virginia colony late in the seventeenth century observed that African slaves had not been converted to Christianity because "[t]rade [was] preferred before Religion and Christ made to give place to Mammon."[38] Another minister observed that:

> Christians in America . . . especially Protestants . . . take very little care to have their slaves instructed . . . as if it were not a positive duty incumbent on them, by the precepts of Christianity . . . . There, provided that the slaves can multiply, and work hard for the benefit of their masters, most men are well satisfied with-

---

37. Albert J. Raboteau, *Slave Religion: The 'Invisible Institution' in the Antebellum South* (New York: Oxford University Press, 1978), 98.
38. Ibid.

out the least thoughts of using their authority and endeavors to promote the good of the souls of those poor wretches.[39]

The reasons for this deliberate aversion toward converting Africans were several. First, conversion required teaching, and slave owners refused to provide the necessary time for the instruction of slaves. Second, owners feared that baptism would make slaves ungovernable by fostering dangerous notions of personal emancipation. Third, the equality implicit in Christianity would make it difficult to maintain discipline and subordination. Additionally, many slaves resisted Christianity because it was the religion of their oppressors. In order to encourage the conversion of slaves by their reluctant masters, a number of colonies enacted legislation specifically providing that manumission would not automatically follow upon conversion, and these enactments were upheld by the Crown after appeal. Indeed, to justify racial slavery, Christian evangelists began to argue that conversion enhanced docility and contributed to slave control because it constructed "a stout wall between spiritual and temporal equality."[40]

Even by the middle of the eighteenth century, Christianized slaves were still a minority in the African-American population, and those who did convert were not treated as equals by their white co-religionists. There were no separate black churches even in the Southern colonies where most African-Americans lived. African-American preachers had not yet emerged as a leadership class within the African-American community. For the most part, worship took place in the presence of whites. Slaves either accompanied their owners to services or sat in segregated back pews. Increasingly, however, slaves were drawn to the more emotional strains of American Protestantism—Baptism, Methodism, New Side Presbyterianism and New Light Congregationalism. "[T]here were enough similarities [between evangelical Protestantism and the African spiritual heritage] to make it possible for slaves to find some common ground between the beliefs of their ancestors and those of the white Christians."

The Great Awakening caused profound change in the religious orientation of many African-Americans who went through personal

---

39. Ibid., 103.
40. Ibid., 133 (quoting John Thompson, *The Life of John Thompson, A Fugitive Slave* (Worcester: J. Thompson, 1856).

conversion experiences in increasing numbers. The egalitarianism of religious revival meetings, particularly those conducted by Baptist and Methodist preachers, had great emotional appeal for African-Americans. The personal account of a former slave, written many years later and recounting childhood experiences, reflects the power that evangelicals had in the rural South in the early nineteenth century:

> My mistress and her family were all Episcopalians. The nearest church was five miles from our plantation, and there was no Methodist church nearer than ten miles. So we went to the Episcopal church, but always came home as we went, for the preaching was above our comprehension, so that we could understand but little that was said. But soon the Methodist religion was brought among us, and preached in a manner so plain that the way faring man, though a fool, could not err therein. This new doctrine produced great consternation among the slaveholders. It was something which they could not understand. It brought glad tidings to the poor bondman; it bound up the broken-hearted; it opened the prison doors to them that were bound, and let the captive go free. As soon as it got among the slaves, it spread from plantation to plantation, until it reached ours, where there were but few who did not experience religion.[41]

Such religious conversion put less emphasis upon religious instruction and more on religious feeling. African-Americans with a talent for preaching appeared in Southern communities and often preached to people of both races. The fervor of religious enthusiasm among whites led to a relaxation of the strictures against the conversion of African-Americans. Racially-mixed congregations developed as the number of African-American congregants increased. This led to racial splits in some congregations and to the emergence of all-African-American churches. The first such all-African-American church was established at Silver Bluff, South Carolina, one year before independence.

For many African-Americans, religion changed from a coercive to a liberating experience. For free African-Americans as well as for the slave population, religion created an enclave of freedom in an otherwise oppressive and racist world. The egalitarianism of the

---

41. Ibid., 139.

more evangelical forms of Protestantism even caused what one historian has called "religious reciprocity" between African-Americans and whites: through a shared religious experience some whites came to recognize the essential humanity of a people once thought to be inferior in every way.[42]

Phyllis Wheatley, the African-American poet who had been abducted from Africa at the age of eight, and whose *Poems on Various Subjects Religious and Moral*[43] was the first full-length book by an African-American, merged "the memory of African sun worship . . . with the language of evangelical Christianity and the language of Revolutionary freedom to produce a poetics of ascent and liberation."[44] In one of her poems, Wheatley wrote:

> Soaring through air to find the bright abode
> Th'empyreal palace of the thund'ring God,
> We on the pinions can surpass the wind,
> And leave the rolling universe behind:
> From star to star the mental optics rove,
> Measure the skies, and range the realms above.
> There in one view we grasp the mighty whole,
> Or with new worlds amaze th'unbounded soul.[45]

In short, African-Americans, slave as well as free, were able to find within the Christian evangelical experience, an idiom for the expression of their most profound yearnings for freedom, personal salvation and at least a partial re-identification with their African past.

But the great exception to the regime of religious liberty was the posture of American colonial society toward the American

---

42. Phyllis Wheatley, *Poems on Various Subjects Religious and Moral* (London, 1773).
43. Betsy Erkkila, "Phyllis Wheatley and the Black American Revolution," in *A Mixed Race: Ethnicity in Early America*, ed. Frank Shuffleton (New York: Oxford University Press, 1993), 236 [hereinafter *A Mixed Race*].
44. Ibid.
45. The terms "Native American Church" and "Native American Religion" have been used by a leading modern scholar of the subject. See, Joseph Epes Brown, *The Spiritual Legacy of the American Indian* (Indiana: World Wisdom, 1993), 12–14. ("It has now become abundantly clear that it is a fundamental and universal characteristic of Native American cultures . . . that religion . . . is not a separate category of activity or experience that is divorced from culture or society").

Indian and what has been called the Native American Church.[46] One student of Native American religion has referred to "the illusion of religious freedom for indigenous Americans."[47] The Supreme Court of the United States has "continued the destruction of Indian religions by the Courts' restrictive interpretation of the Constitution's free exercise clause in Indian litigation."[48] Thus "the suppression of [N]ative American religion has a long history."[49] Since the beginning of the conquest of North America by Europeans, Native Americans "have learned over generations of bitter experiences to preserve their sacred traditions underground."[50] Unable to find a place in American society the Native American faced not only military conquest, loss of land, and loss of hope, but cultural extinction as well. An integral part of this process of extinction was the destruction of the diverse legacy of Native American spiritualism. Thus, the failure of American colonial society to accommodate the Native American Church represented the outer limit of religious toleration in an otherwise benign regime of religious freedom. There was little room in the understanding of the early colonists for the traditional spiritual practices of the American Indian or for African slaves. Both Native Americans and African slaves were converted to Christianity. But while conversion for Africans became a source of liberation, for Native Americans, it was a matter of pure survival.

For Native Americans, conversion to Christianity was more a matter of survival than of liberation. Assimilation to European culture on European terms was the only alternative to physical annihilation. "Any Christianity they espoused either lay very lightly on the surface of their lives or was deeply syncretized with native

---

46. Russell Lawrence Barsh, "The Illusion of Religious Freedom for Indigenous Americans," 65 *Oregon Law Review* 363 (1986).
47. Ibid. 363. See also *Employment Division* v. *Smith*, which held that the first amendment of the United States Constitution does not protect Native Americans who use peyote during traditional Native American religious ceremonies. 494 U.S. 872 (1990). In response to *Employment Division* v. *Smith*, Congress, in 1996, passed a statute regulating the "Traditional Indian Religious Use of Peyote." 42 U.S.C. § 1996a, which provides that the use of peyote by Native Americans for religious purposes is lawful, subject to various exceptions.
48. Barsh, 369.
49. Brown, 48.
50. James Axtell, *The European and the Indian: Essays in the Ethnohistory of Colonial North America* (New York: Oxford University Press, 1981), 270.

elements; in whatever degree its acceptance was calculated to ensure their tribal independence and ethnic identity."[51] Native American spiritualism did have some impact upon the Christianity that Native Americans came to practice, but the growing isolation of Native American communities and their rapidly declining numbers in relation to the dominant white population were more important factors in Native American history than conversion to Christianity. Conversion itself was a very different experience for Native Americans than it had been for African-American slaves. For Native Americans, Christian conversion blended into well-established indigenous practices and articles of faith, a process referred to by one student of the subject as "nonexclusive cumulative adhesion."[52]

The first Bible published in British America was a translation of the Old and New Testaments into one of the Algonquian languages by the Massachusetts missionary, John Eliot. Eliot

---

51. Brown, *The Spiritual Legacy of the American Indian*, 26–27.

> The pervasive force of historical Christian ministries has probably had some impact upon all American Indian peoples. The gradations of Indian affiliation with Roman Catholicism and Protestant denominations span two extremes: there are those who have fully accepted the new faith, accompanied by conscious rejection of their own religious traditions and even of their own languages, and those who have been exposed to elements of Christianity, or who even may once have totally accepted Christianity, but have since returned to an often intensified participation in their own sacred ways. Incomplete evidence suggests that these two groups constitute minorities in relation to those who are situated in [a] unique manner between the two extremes. A key element in the evaluation of Indian affiliation with Christianity, to which sufficient attention has not been given in either scholarly literature or in church documents, lies in [the] special meaning of conversion for most American Indians . . . . When, therefore, the Christian message came to the peoples through dedicated missionaries who led exemplary and sacrificial lives, the people easily understood the truths of message and example due to the profundity of their own beliefs; it was not difficult for them to adopt and adapt new expressions of values into the sacred fabric of their own religious culture. The historical phenomenon is thus not conversion as understood in exclusivistic manner by the bearers of Christianity, but rather a continuation of the people's ancient and traditional facility for what may be termed nonexclusive cumulative adhesion.

Ibid.

52. Gary B. Nash, *Red, White, and Black: The Peoples of Early America* (Englewood Cliffs, NJ: Prentice-Hall, 1974), 311.

converted more than one thousand Native Americans to Christianity. By 1676, Eliot's "praying Indians" lived in nearly two dozen separate Native American villages with their own ordained ministers, but the bloody encounters that took place during King Philip's War (1675–1676) left only four of these Christian villages intact despite the fact that these "praying Indians" sided with the English settlers. The English made "[o]nly minimal efforts . . . to instruct Indian tribes in Christian doctrine and most of the efforts were inspired by the hope that conversion would go hand in hand with pacification and political control."[53]

For political and economic reasons, American Indians and African-Americans were treated as inassimilable by the colonists, but African-Americans eventually found a subordinate niche in colonial American society through the institution of slavery. Christianization became very much a part of the system of racial domination. The unique African-American forms of Protestant observance were tolerated as part of the broadening base of American religious practice. But American Indians had no such position in American society. Consequently, the Indian way of life, including Native American spirituality, remained outside the boundaries of tolerable religious experience.[54] As far as the assimilation of Native Americans was concerned, "nothing could have been less desirable to European settlers, who coveted Indian land but not land with Indians on it. Nor did Indians seek entry into white society, for there was little they wanted from Europeans that they could not obtain through bartering skins and furs."[55]

One measure of the contrast in the position of these two groups—African Americans and Native Americans—was their divergent demographic histories. Even though black mortality was higher than that of whites during the colonial period, the African-American population continued to grow. But the Native American population declined dramatically because of epidemic disease, war,

---

53. Doreen A. Saar, "The Heritage of American Ethnicity in Crevecoeur's Letters from an American Farmer," in *A Mixed Race*, 253. "While Africans, against their will, were implicated in the system of society that enable[d] the white immigrant to become an American and so, as slaves, . . . occupy a peculiar place within the system, the Native American st[ood] outside the system entirely". Ibid.
54. Nash, 311.
55. Axtell, 306.

and physical displacement from their lands.[56] Alcohol "was distributed among Indian tribes in order to create not only dependency but addiction. Rum . . . was intended to sustain life among blacks while destroying life among Indians."[57] The American colonists sought to increase the population of African Americans while decreasing the population of Native Americans.

The widespread experience of religious freedom in early America did not exist in a philosophical vacuum. A growing body of thought advocating toleration of religious dissent, or even absolute liberty of conscience, created a climate that was conducive to progressive development. Chief among these theoretical writings, and surely the outstanding American contributor to the debate on religious freedom, was Roger Williams, the founder of Rhode Island. Because of his numerous writings published both in England and America, and because of his prominence as a Puritan minister, political statesman and student of Native Americans, Roger Williams' position as early America's strongest advocate of toleration, freedom of conscience, and separation of church and state was well known. As one historian has observed, "No one was indifferent to what Roger Williams had to say."[58] Williams, however, did not derive his liberal position on religious freedom solely on the basis of theological or doctrinal postulates. On the contrary, Williams drew much of his argument from historical experience. He defended Catholics, Jews, Turks, and even anti-Christians as "peaceable and quiet subjects, loving and helpful neighbors, fair and just dealers . . . ."[59] Williams pointed to examples in history where whole kingdoms flourished despite the presence of these groups because they were loyal to the civil

---

56. Nash, 315.
57. Irwin H. Polishook, *Roger Williams, John Cotton and Religious Freedom: A Controversy in New and Old England* (New Jersey: Prentice-Hall, 1967), 24. Williams' continuing battles over matters of religious doctrine and church governance with John Cotton, orthodoxy's spiritual leader in the Massachusetts Bay Colony, were well publicized. The running controversy between Williams and Cotton constituted "a transatlantic debate over church-state relations." Ibid.
58. Roger Williams, *Bloudy Tenent of Persecution for Cause of Conscience Discussed in a Conference Between Truth and Peace*, (rev. ed., London, 1948).
59. Ibid.

government. For Williams, "reason and experience," not the dictates of philosophy, pointed in the direction of liberty.[60]

In 1644, while in London trying to secure a charter for Rhode Island, Williams hastily composed his principal work on the theory of religious toleration and freedom of conscience. In the *Bloudy Tenent of Persecution*, Williams set forth a radical critique of the established religious order and pleaded for the total separation of what he elsewhere identified as the "garden" of the church from the "wilderness" of the world. In the *Bloudy Tenent of Persecution*, Williams proposed an extremely liberal view of freedom of conscience articulated in the introduction in which Williams offered an overview of his philosophical position in one of the book's few clear passages:

> The doctrine of persecution for cause of conscience, is proved guilty of all the blood of the souls crying for vengeance under the alter .... It is the will and command of God, that ... permission of the most Paganish, Jewish, Turkish, or anti-Christian consciences and worships be granted to all men in all nations and countries .... The permission of other consciences and worships than a state professeth, only can, according to God, procure a firm and lasting peace.[61]

---

60. *Bloudy Tenent* was "a messy book." In structure and style the work was unusually prolix, yet the main themes of Williams' philosophy of religious freedom were contained within its many complex pages. Edwin S. Gaustad, *Liberty of Conscience: Roger Williams in America*, (Grand Rapids: W. B. Eerdmans, 1991), 69.

61. *Letter from Roger Williams to the Town of Providence* (1655), in *Letters of Roger Williams, 1632–1682*, ed. John R. Bartlett, (Providence: Printed for the Naragansett Club, 1874), 278–279.

> That ever I should speak or write a title, that tends to such an infinite liberty of conscience, is a mistake, and which I have ever disclaimed and abhorred. To prevent such mistakes, I shall at present only propose this case: There goes many a ship to sea, with many hundred souls in one ship, whose weal and woe is common, and is a true picture of a commonwealth, or a human combination or society. It hath fallen out sometime, that both papists and protestants, Jews and Turks, may be embarked in one ship; upon which supposal I affirm, that all the liberty of conscience, that ever I pleaded for, turns upon these two hinges— that none of the papists, protestants, Jews, or Turks, be forced to come to the ship's prayers or worship, nor compelled from their own particular prayers or worship, if they practice any. I further add, that I never denied, that notwithstanding this liberty, the commander of this ship ought to command the ship's course,

Some years later, Williams modified his approach to religious liberty, probably because he had gained a position of some political authority with attendant responsibilities. Soon after he was elected to the presidency of Rhode Island, Williams wrote a letter of political advice to the people of the town of Providence. Now in the role of a government official, Williams had to justify the legitimate claims of civil government thereby modifying and refining what some perceived as his extreme philosophy of religious freedom. Without abandoning any of the central principles he had formulated as a religious outsider, Williams acknowledged that there were limits to freedom of conscience imposed by the responsibilities of citizenship.[62] Written as a reply to a seditious paper then circulating in Providence, Williams denied ever having sanctioned principles of religious liberty that would subvert civil peace. He disavowed any adherence to "an infinite liberty of conscience" as he had implied in the *Bloudy Tenent of Persecution,* and he acknowledged that there were limits to freedom of conscience and limits imposed by the responsibilities of good citizenship. Analogizing civil government with a ship at sea, Williams stated that Catholics as well as Protestants, Jews as well as Turks, were equally bound to the ordinary duties and responsibilities that every ship's commander had the power and right to impose upon passengers and crew alike. While permitted to absent themselves from the ship's religious observances in order to follow their own, as members of the ship's company all were required "to obey the common laws and orders . . . concerning their common peace or preservation."[63]

> yea, and also command that justice, peace and sobriety, be kept and practiced, both among the seamen and all the passengers. If any of the seamen refuse to perform their services, or passengers to pay their freight; if any refuse to help, in person or purse, towards the common charges or defence; if any refuse to obey the common laws and orders of the ship, concerning their common peace or preservation; if any shall mutiny and rise up against their commanders and officers; if any should preach or write that there ought to be no commanders or officers, because all are equal in Christ, therefore no masters nor officers, no laws nor orders, nor corrections nor punishments; — I say, I never denied, but in such cases, whatever is pretended the commander or commanders may judge, resist, compel and punish such transgressors, according to their deserts and merits.

Ibid.

62. Ibid., 279.

63. Gaustad, *Liberty of Conscience*, 28.

However, Roger Williams did not share the same beliefs about American Indians held by other early Americans. Williams managed to establish a rapport with and understanding of the native population unmatched by any of his countrymen in the New World.[64] Williams' first published book, *A Key into the Language of America*, was a careful and extensive study of the Native Americans of New England.[65] The book was based upon Williams' contacts with native people, which he undertook soon after his arrival in Massachusetts in 1631.[66] Ostensibly a language study, when finally printed in London in 1643, the book proved to be the first serious anthropological investigation of Native American culture in British America.[67]

"Nature knows no difference," Williams wrote, "between Europeans and Americans in blood, birth, bodies, etc., God having of one blood made all mankind."[68] It was an extraordinary statement, for it meant that, at least for Roger Williams, Native Americans and English Christians were on the same level. As a consequence, Williams made no effort to convert the Rhode Island Narragansetts to the Gospel not only because of his opposition to forced conversion, but also because of his profound respect for the Native American's spiritual integrity. Williams summarized this idea in his book on Native American language:

> Boast not proud English, of thy birth & blood,
> Thy brother Indian is by birth as Good.

---

64. Roger Williams, *A Key into the Language of America* (4 ed., New York: Russell & Russell, 1973).
65. "During his stay [in Plymouth] Williams made the most of his contact with the natives of the region. His bold respect for the Indians' dignity as men and his willingness to deal with them on a basis of equality won their lasting friendship." Polishook, *Roger Williams, John Cotton and Religious Freedom*, 8.
66. In Chapter XXI of the work, *Of Their Religion*, Williams detailed Native American religious beliefs and practices. As he observed on the first page of the chapter: "He that questions whether God made the World, the Indians will teach him. I must acknowledge I have received in my converse with them many Confirmations of those two great points. 1. That God is [and] 2. That He is a rewarder of all them that diligently seek Him."
67. Gaustad, *Liberty of Conscience*, 28.
68. Williams, *Bloudy Tenent of Persecution*, at 81. More than a century later, "An American Farmer" echoed Roger Williams' appreciation of the Native American when he wrote that Indians were as "stout and well made as Europeans [and] are in many instances superior to us." St. Jean De Crevecouer, 209–210.

Of one blood God made Him and Thee, & All,
As wise, as fair, as strong, as personall.[69]

By his actions and his attitudes, Williams manifested a deep appreciation of the Native American and explicitly recognized the rights of native people to their own system of religious belief.

Prejudice toward Native Americans is rooted in a long tradition of intolerance that goes back to America's earliest times. While the most liberal contemporary writers on the subject of religious toleration in early America—Roger Williams being the exemplary case—were prepared to include the American Indian within the ambit of religious freedom, the religion of America's indigenous people was subjected to systematic suppression. This occurred while European settlers were establishing the foundations of religious liberty in North America, both in practice as well as in legal formulations. Religious toleration in early America was widespread as long as it did not interfere with the necessities of settlement. While African-Americans were able to define a place for themselves in the colorful spectrum of American religious diversity, in part because they occupied an important niche in the exploitive slave system, the Native American faced the most formidable obstacles. Unable to establish a permanent status for themselves in their own land, native people found that the religious pluralism of white America had no place for them. The heritage of oppression, established early in our history, marked the limits of religious liberty in America's historical experience, and it continues to haunt the efforts of native people to fully enjoy religious recognition.

---

69. Roger Williams, *A Key into the Language of America*, 81.

Episode 3

The Condition of the Colonial Press

> Printers are educated in the Belief, that when Men differ in Opinion, both sides ought equally to have the Advantage of being heard by the publick; and that when Truth and Error have fair Play, the former is always an overmatch for the later.[1]
>
> Benjamin Franklin, 1731

Not too long ago, some influential historians were reporting that government instrumentalities of one kind or another severely restricted the freedom of the press in colonial America. Royal governors acting under the authority of their instructions continued to issue licenses to printers, thereby exercising control over newspapers, until about 1730—a generation after prior censorship died in England, in 1695, with the expiration of the Licensing Act.[2] In the seventeenth and eighteenth centuries, laws against blasphemy and heresy were still used to punish anticlerical or antireligious publications, but increasingly the more common challenges to the established order were criticisms of the state rather than of the church.[3] Libel and sedition were now the major offenses that invited suppression of the press. At first, the court trial was the most likely forum in which the government could proceed against troublesome authors, editors, and printers. Then in the middle decades of the eighteenth century, the scene shifted from

---

* Source: Chapter 5 ("The Condition of the Press") in George Dargo, *Roots of the Republic: A New Perspective on Early American Constitutionalism* (New York: Praeger, 1974.)

1. Franklin, Benjamin, "Apology for Printers," in *The Pennsylvania Gazette*, (May 27, 1731).
2. Nelson, Harold, "Seditious Libel in Colonial America," in *American Journal of Legal History,* Vol. III (1959), 161 (providing an early statement of the interpretative trend that emphasized the role of the legislature in press suppression).
3. Levy, Leonard W., *Legacy of Suppression: Freedom of Speech and Press in Early American History*, (Cambridge, MA: Harvard University Press, 1960), 9–11.

the courtroom to the assembly hall. Colonial legislatures became the major menace to a free press. The threat—and often the reality—of legislative process rather than the criminal trial against individuals stifled press freedom.[4]

The pivotal episode in the story of colonial journalism was the celebrated case of John Peter Zenger, whose trial and acquittal in 1735 has been looked upon for generations as the real beginning of a free press in America.[5] Zenger was originally from Germany, and emigrated with his family to America as a child. His mother apprenticed him to William Bradford, New York's public printer and the founder of the one of the great colonial printing families. In 1726, Zenger went into business for himself. His *Weekly Journal* began publication in 1733, as the political organ of the most powerful opposition faction to the governor of New York, William Cosby. From the fall of 1733 until Zenger's arrest, the *Journal* was involved in a hot "paper war" against the Cosby regime.[6] Zenger published the libertarian essays of Thomas Gordon and John Trenchard (known as *Cato's Letters* which attacked the corruption and immorality then pervasive in British politics), personal attacks upon the governor himself, and fake advertisements ridiculing the governor's close associates. On the other side, Bradford's *New-York Gazette* defended the Cosby regime.[7] Cosby was determined to suppress public criticism and felt impelled to act. In November, 1734, the governor had Zenger arrested for seditious libel.

When Zenger's two attorneys, James Alexander and William Smith, were disbarred for calling into question the commissions of the two Supreme Court justices before whom the case was to be tried, Zenger's supporters managed to recruit Andrew Hamilton of

---

4. For a complete catalogue of cases of press repression in the eighteenth century, see L.R. Schuyler's *The Liberty of the Press in the American Colonies Before the Revolutionary War. With Particular Reference to Conditions in the Royal Colony of New York*, (New York: Whittaker, 1905).
5. Levy, Leonard W., *Freedom of the Press from Zenger to Jefferson*, (New York: The Bobbs-Merrill Company, Inc., 1966), xix.
6. For a concise, lucid account of essential facts and legal points of the *Zenger* case, refer to the work of James Alexander, *A Brief Narrative of the Case and Trial of John Peter Zenger: Printer of the New York Weekly Journal*, ed. Stanley Katz, (Cambridge, MA: Harvard University Press, 1963), 10–17.
7. Buranelli, Vincent, "Peter Zenger's Editor" in *American Quarterly*, Vol. VII, (1955), 74–81. This author provides an important discussion on the role of James Alexander and the importance of Zenger's *journal* as opposed to Zenger's *trial*.

Philadelphia, reputed to be the best trial lawyer in the colonies.[8] Hamilton's defense rested on bad law, but his argument won an acquittal from the jury. Hamilton argues that in seditious-libel cases the jury should have the power to decide not only whether the accused had published the material in question but whether that material was true or false. The accepted legal doctrine was that writings or publications that defamed a public official and had the effect of provoking hatred, contempt, or ridicule breached the public peace, whether the allegations were true or not. The provocation and not its truth or falsehood was the offense that was subject to criminal penalty. According to the prevailing view, this in no way impaired the freedom of the press, which consisted, as Blackstone would later put it, "in laying no *previous* restraints upon publication, and not in freedom from censure for criminal matter when published."[9]

In contrast, Hamilton argued that truth should be a defense in any prosecution for seditious libel and that only false criticism of the government ought to be punishable. Freedom of the press meant, among other things, freedom to criticize wrongdoing. This was the best protection for popular liberties and constitutional government. Hamilton canonized the role of the jury who, as guardians of liberty, had to review not merely the fact of publication but its content as well. Thus, his position was more of a constitutional argument than a strictly legal defense of Zenger. The law was clearly on the government's side. Nevertheless, the jury disregarded the law and, in perhaps the most famous example of "jury nullification," Zenger was acquitted of all charges.

Although Zenger was set free on the strength of Hamilton's impassioned appeal to constitutional liberty and the obligations of juries, the Zenger case had little immediate effect on the common law of seditious libel either in England or in the American colonies. Legal doctrine did not change for more than half a century.[10] At

---

8. Alexander, *A Brief Narrative of the Case and Trial of John Peter Zenger*, 21.
9. Blackstone, Sir William and Sprague, William C., *Blackstone's Commentaries*, 9th ed., (Chicago: Callaghan and Company, 1915), 463.
10. For an argument against Levy, resting on the fundamental assumption that the colonial press reflected a wide range of opinions on basic political and constitutional issues, see Leder, Lawrence H., *Liberty and Authority: Early American Political Ideology, 1689–1763*, (Chicago, IL: Quadrangle Books, 1968). For further discussion on whether freedom of the press existed in society prior to being written into law, also refer to the work of Lawrence H. Leder, "The Role of

best, the Zenger case showed that juries were an unreliable support for prosecutions by unpopular colonial governors. As a result, court trial of seditious-libel cases soon diminished, not only because of the reluctance of trial juries to convict but also because grand juries refused to indict.

But if judges acting under royal commissions were no longer the chief inquisitors of printers and editors, houses of assembly and governors' councils quickly filled the void. The major cases occurring between Zenger in 1735 and the outbreak of the Revolution all involved actions brought by legislative bodies on grounds of either libel or breach of legislative privilege.[11] In 1742, the Massachusetts Council brought an action against Thomas Fleet of the *Boston Evening Post* for libeling the administration of Sir Robert Walpole.[12] At about this time, William Parks, publisher of the *Virginia Gazette*, was accused by the Virginia House of Burgesses of libeling one of its members. In 1753, Hugh Gaine of the *New York Mercury* was summoned to the Assembly to explain why he had published its official proceedings without permission.[13] Three years later, James Parker, Gaine's competitor, was jailed for one week by order of the House for reporting distress among the people of Orange and Ulster counties, which the legislature interpreted as a negative reflection on government policy.[14] Between 1756 and 1758, William Smith, provost of the College of Philadelphia, was called to the bar and twice jailed for his printed criticisms of the Assembly, which were considered a breach of

---

Newspapers in Early America: 'In Defense of Their Own Liberty'" in *Huntington Library Quarterly*, Vol. XXX, (1966), 11–16.

11. For more on the role of the press in the crisis of the Revolution, see Phillip Davidson's *Propaganda and the American Revolution, 1763–783*, (Chapel Hill, NC: University of North Carolina Press, 1941).

12. Nelson, "Seditious Libel in Colonial America," 168.

13. *The Journals of Hugh Gaine, Printer*, Vol. 1, ed. Paul L. Ford, (New York: Dodd, Mead & Company, 1902), 5–7.

14. For a comprehensive encyclopedia of press and news-gathering actors and mechanisms, see McMurtrie, Douglas C., *A History of Printing in the United States: The Story of the Introduction of the Press and of its History and Influence during the Pioneer Period in Each State of the Union*, Vol. II, (New York: R. R. Bowker Company, 1936). Additional reference should be made to McMurtie's *History of Printing in the United States'* predecessor, the original encyclopedia of the press and printing written by Isaiah Thomas, titled *History of Printing in America*, Vol. 2, (New York: Burt Franklin, 1874).

privilege.[15] In 1770, Alexander McDougall was jailed for publishing a broadside attacking the New York legislature for voting supplies to provision the local English garrison. Released when the government's principal witness, James Parker, died, McDougall was summoned for examination by the House.[16] When he refused to respond to interrogation, a vote was taken, and he was recommitted to confinement. In 1773, a governor's council in South Carolina summoned Thomas Powell, printer of the *South Carolina Gazette*, to appear before it for publishing a protest authored by William Drayton and William Henry Drayton, two dissenting councilmen who were later to become leading South Carolina patriots. Powell was charged with contempt and breach of privilege.[17] He was released at the trial of his habeas corpus petition on the ground that the council was not a true legislative body but more in the nature of a privy council and, therefore, without the punitive powers it claimed. In short, as Leonard W. Levy[18] has argued:

> The *Zenger* case at best gave the press the freedom to print the "truth," but only if the truth were directed away from the assembly. The power of the assembly to punish nonmembers, as well as members, for breach of privilege, enabled it to control the press.

From this perspective a rather bleak picture of the condition of the colonial press emerges. Daniel Boorstin,[19] describing the "conservative" press of the era, says that, in Philadelphia, "libel trials and suppression of the opposition press were common . . . until the eve of the Revolution." Boorstin conveys the impression of a press that was the handmaiden of government, lackluster in

---

15. Mott, Frank L., *American Journalism: A History, 1690–1960*, 3rd ed. (New York: The Macmillan Company, 1962), 30 (describing colonial reflections on the problem of news-gathering in America).
16. Ibid.
17. Cohen, Hennig, *The South Carolina Gazette, 1732–1775*, (Columbia, SC: The University of South Carolina Press, 1953), 13.
18. Levy, Leonard W., "Did the *Zenger* Case Really Matter? Freedom of the Press in Colonial New York," in *William and Mary Quarterly,* 3rd Ser., Vol. XVII, (1960), 39–40 (referencing the importance of documentation and the legislature in press suppression).
19. Boorstin, Daniel, *The Americans: The Colonial Experience*, (New York: Random House, 1958), Chap. 51, 333.

content, and devoid of vigor. From his extensive work in the field, Leonard Levy concluded that:

> The persistent image of colonial America as a society in which freedom of expression was cherished is an hallucination of sentiment that ignores history.... In colonial America, as in England, the common law of criminal libel was strung out like a chicken wire of constraint . . . making the open discussion of public issues hazardous, if not impossible. . . .[20]

One wonders, however, whether the case has not been overstated, and whether historians have not gone beyond their evidence in arriving at such conclusions. Granted that the common law of seditious libel continued to be good law down to the end of the century, that the *Zenger* case had little immediate impact upon legal doctrine, and that legislatures used their newly won independence and power to suppress offensive material—does this mean that a vigorous press was absent from American life in the late colonial period? The answer must be that, on the basis of the kind of evidence recent writers have uncovered, we cannot tell. We have learned much about attitudes toward freedom of the press and the legal parameters of press freedom in the eighteenth century, but we need to know more about the actual condition of the press during this period of judicial and legislative restriction. For example, the emphasis on the law of seditious libel has obscured the real importance of Zenger's *Journal* as opposed to Zenger's trial.[21] Unlike most newspapers of the period, the *Weekly Journal* was avowedly political. Politics was its reason for being. In this respect, it was a major journalistic innovation, the real foundation of the tradition of political journalism in America. If Zenger's case really did not matter, the *New York Weekly Journal* certainly did.

The concentrated attention to examples of legislative suppression and the ferreting out of every last case of supposed intimidation distort the image. The mere citation of cases does not make it clear whether they were the rule or the exception. In those cases where editors or printers were condemned to jail or fined for costs, the sentences were short and the penalties minimal. The victims were amply compensated by increased publicity, which

---

20. Levy, *Legacy of Suppression: Freedom of Speech and Press,* 18–19.
21. Buranelli, "Peter Zenger's Editor," 174–181.

may very well have enhanced circulation. We assume that legal restrictions on press freedom, the ever present threat of official reprisals, and occasional exemplary prosecutions by the courts or by legislatures were intimidating; but these may very well have been one of the acceptable risks of doing business in the printing trade. Zenger, for example, does not appear to have been humbled by his brief incarceration from November, 1734, until his release in August, 1735. The *Weekly Journal* continued its vituperative attacks upon the Crosby regime during his Zenger's absence. Zenger emerged from jail a popular hero. When a new regime came to power, he was appointed to the office of public printer for the colony.

More important than government restriction, intimidation, and outright suppression in limiting the press were the sheer physical and technical difficulties of gathering, publishing, and distributing news, the financial risks of printing as a business enterprise, and the professional traditions, attitudes, and practices that governed eighteenth-century journalism. Most of the essential materials of production—newsprint, ink, presses, and type – had to be imported from abroad at considerable expense.[22] No type foundry existed in the American colonies until 1768; the only type available for export out of Britain was secondhand. The first printing press was not manufactured domestically until 1769.[23] Printer's ink was not made in quantity until after the Revolution, although local printers sometimes produced their own at considerable cost and inconvenience. Paper was milled in America, but it was of a cheaper quality than the imported product. Benjamin Franklin, the most successful printer in America, actually derived most of his income at the height of his career from manufacturing and selling ink and newsprint to printers in other colonies.

In addition, in the early days of colonial journalism, local news was not considered important enough to warrant space in a local newspaper. In small communities, everyone knew what happened

---

22. Information regarding the economic aspects of printing trade analysis is provided in more detail in Peter J. Parker's "The Philadelphia Printer: A Study of an 18th Century Businessman," in *Business History Review*, No. XL, (1966), 24–26.

23. Additional descriptions and accounts of the technical aspects of printing in the colonial period can be found in Lawrence C. Wroth's *The Colonial Printer*, (Charlottesville, VA: The University Press of Virginia, 1964), with specific emphasis placed on page 84.

without having to read it in the press. "News" meant foreign news—the latest happenings from abroad—except that the time span separating the event itself and the published report of it was often many weeks or months, so that colonial newspapers were often chronicles of recent history rather than journals of current events. In winter, when bad weather delayed ships or post riders, editors often printed trivia. Successful newspaper printers usually had to keep in touch with regular "correspondents," who forwarded news by letter from the principal towns along the seaboard or even from across the Atlantic.

One of the tendencies of eighteenth-century American journalism was a gradually decrease in interest in foreign news in favor of local and inter-colonial news. As populations grew and social and political affairs became more complex and difficult to understand firsthand, readers began to expect more local reportage, interpretation, and commentary. After extensive analysis of the colonial press, One historian has concluded that, before 1738, only one-fourth of a cross-section of colonial papers published "original"—that is, colonial—news as opposed to foreign news, but thereafter there was a marked increase in local and inter-colonial material and a relative decline in the attention devoted to news from abroad. But as newspapers began striking closer to home, printers faced the increasingly difficult and even risky problem of deciding what local news to include and what to leave out.[24]

Most newspaper publishers were businessmen primarily — printers first and journalists second. What they printed was not nearly as important as keeping the presses going. As a result, newspaper printers were often highly mercurial in their politics. Hugh Gaine, for example, oscillated throughout his career between opposing sides of important public questions.[25] For example, in the early 1750s, on the debate over the founding of King's College in New York, Gaine at first adamantly refused to print the works of

---

24. Studies regarding new methodology and the importance of the colonial press as both a mirror and shaper of a rising "American" consciousness can be found in Richard L. Merritt's "Public Opinion in Colonial America: Content Analyzing the Colonial Press," in *Public Opinion Quarterly*, Vol. XXVII, No. 3 (1963), 356–371. For more on the historically significant elements of the colonial press and life generally, see Richard L. Merritt's *Symbols of American Community, 1735–1775*, (New Haven, CT.: Yale University Press, 1966.)
25. *The Journals of Hugh Gaine,* 214.

the Presbyterian opponents of the Anglican establishment, but later his paper was so filled with anti-Anglican material that he appears to have switched his position.[26] During the Revolution, Gaine began as a printer for the patriot cause; but, when things went badly for the patriots in New York, Gaine went to work for the British when they occupied the city. Gaine was more unpredictable than most, but his attitude was not in conflict with the prevailing ethical standards of the printing profession.[27] Those standards comported well with business necessity.

The newspaper was only an adjunct to the printer's other business activities. The average printer imported and retailed a wide assortment of goods—not only books of all kinds (almanacs, grammars, Bibles, law books, dictionaries, novels, and scientific treatises) but also household remedies, hardware, musical instruments, wax, leather goods, paper, and firearms. His newspaper was his principal means of self-advertisement. A main source of income was job printing—turning out specialty items in lots for private firms, churches, and sundry organizations. For Philadelphia printers, it was the "first order of business."[28]

The newspapers did not, in themselves, make money, but they did keep the printer's name before the public, thus maintaining the flow of orders for specialty work as well as advertising the arrival of the most recent shipment of goods from abroad. That is why delinquent subscribers, sometimes several years in arrears, continued to receive their journals. In 1759, James Parker, the public printer for New York, estimated that at least 25 percent of his subscribers were normally behind on their subscription payments. The printer had to keep his name and his advertising in circulation. But this dependence on subscription tended to dictate the content of what was published. It meant, for one thing, that a printer could not exclude letters or essays with which he disagreed. A "free press" meant an open press. Benjamin Franklin summed up this credo of the trade in his "Apology for Printers":

> Printers are educated in the Belief, that when Men differ in Opinion, both Sides ought equally to have the Advantage of being heard by the Publick; and that when Truth and Error have

---

26. Ibid.
27. Parker, "The Philadelphia Printer: A Study of an 18th Century Businessman," 24–27.
28. Ibid.

> fair Play, the former is always an overmatch for the later: Hence they cheerfully serve all contending Writers that pay them well, without regarding on which side they are of the Question in Dispute. Being thus continually employ'd in serving both Parties, Printers naturally acquire a vast Unconcernedness as to the right or wrong Opinions contained in what they print; regarding it only as the Matter of their daily labour . . . That it is unreasonable to imagine Printers approve of every thing they print, and to censure them on any particular thing accordingly; since in the way of their Business they print such great variety of things opposite and contradictory. It is likewise as unreasonable what some assert, "That Printers ought not to print any Thing but what they approve"; since if all that Business should make such a Resolution, and abide by it, an End would thereby be put to Free Writing, and the World would afterwards have nothing to read but what happen'd to be the Opinion of Printers. That if all Printers were determin'd not to print any thing till they were sure it would offend no body, there would be very little printed.[29]

During the press war over Kings' College, in 1753, Hugh Gaine was assailed for preventing the so-called "triumvirate"—William Livingston, William Smith, Jr., and John Morin Scott—from replying to attacks on *their Independent Reflector* that appeared in Gaine's *New York Mercury.*[30] Gaine was accused, in effect, of restricting the press. However, most printers followed Franklin's philosophy (or business practice) and tried to keep their pages open to opposing viewpoints. This broadened their appeal and sustained interest in the journal's continuous reappearance.

The average printer might avoid publishing controversial material if the effect of continuing to do so would be to terminate

---

29. Background on Smith and Franklin's social life in colonial Pennsylvania may be found in Ralph L. Ketcham's "Benjamin Franklin and William Smith: New Light on an Old Philadelphia Quarrel," in *Pennsylvania Magazine of History and Biography*, No. 88, (1964), 142–163 (quoting in the text the words of Benjamin Franklin, from his "Apology for Printers," in *The Pennsylvania Gazette*, (May 27, 1731)). For additional descriptions of politically shaping movements in colonial Pennsylvania, refer to Ralph L. Ketcham's "Conscience, War, and Politics in Pennsylvania, 1755-1757" in *William and Mary Quarterly*, 3rd Ser., Vol. XX, (1963), 416–439.

30. For additional information on the MacDougall controversy in New York, refer to D. R. Dillon's *The New York Triumvirate: A Study of the Legal and Political Careers of William Livingston, John Morin Scott,* [*and*] *William Smith, Jr.*, (New York: Columbia University Press, 1949), with specific emphasis placed on Chap. 6.

subscriptions. The best illustration of this was, again, the storm raging around the *Independent Reflector*. James Parker published both the *New York Gazette* and the *Reflector*.[31] When twelve subscribers dropped their orders for the *Gazette* after Parker had reprinted material from the early issues of the magazine, he immediately announced a change in policy and thereafter refused to allow the pages of his weekly to be used by the editors of his own monthly. Eventually, he discontinued the *Reflector* altogether. The Parker case is but one example of a general truism about newspaper journalism: newspapers reflected the attitudes of their readership as much as, if not more than, they affected them. The very nature of the colonial printer's enterprise, and the practices of most newspaper publishers in the colonial period, probably had more to do with defining the character of the press than repressive legal doctrines of press freedom and government intimidation.

Given the obstacles to the development of journalism in the colonies—the narrowness of the law, the physical hardships of transporting papers from place to place over long distances, the difficulty of getting news in the first place, the costs of production, the dependence on subscribers, and the limits imposed by business necessity—what is extraordinary is the vitality, the fearlessness, and the polemical character of the colonial press. An examination of the press itself—newspapers and magazines, particularly—shows a general pattern of press freedom existing in reality if not in law. To concentrate on cases of intimidation without reference to the general environment of journalistic energy out of which they emerged is to distort the picture of what the press was really like in colonial America.

Anyone examining the early history of American journalism is bound to be struck by the boldness of expression, the abundance of press controversy, and the frequent defiance of efforts to intimidate. Indeed, in at least one instance—the case of Andrew Bradford and the *American Weekly Mercury* of Philadelphia—a printer was unintimidated by arrest, and his paper apparently became more aggressive after the experience than it had been before.[32] On

---

31. *The Independent Reflector*, ed. Milton M. Klein, (Cambridge, MA: Harvard University Press, 1963), 19.
32. For more on specific facets of colonial journalism, see Anna J. De Armond's *Andrew Bradford, Colonial Journalist.* (Newark, Del.: University of Delaware Press, 1949).

September 18, 1729, the *Mercury* printed No. 31 of the *Busy Body* series, which stressed the dangerous tendency of public officials to perpetuate themselves in power. The essay, plagiarized from *Cato's Letters*, was offensive not so much for its sentiment as for its timing: it appeared just prior to the fall elections. Bradford was held for examination, and his printing office and home were searched for evidence that would reveal the author of the piece. The attorney general was instructed to commence prosecution. But all this seems to have had little effect upon the printer himself. The following week the next installation of *Busy Body* appeared as before, more outspoken than ever. The author explained that he "had not enlarg'd lessened or altered [the essay], for what has happened upon Publishing the other."[33] Bradford was soon released from custody, but his brief scrape with the authorities apparently had the opposite effect from that which was intended; "from this time forward the *Mercury* was bolder than ever."[34]

In the 1730s, Bradford fought a running battle against Andrew Hamilton, the powerful speaker of the Pennsylvania Assembly. On matters of defense policy, the *Mercury* took the side of the governor, who urged more strenuous measures than the pacifist-minded, Quaker-dominated House was willing to accept.[35] Bradford also defended the governor's Chancery Court in 1735, at a time when it was under attack by Hamilton and the legislature. The *Weekly Mercury* defended the executive establishment. In taking on Andrew Hamilton and the Assembly, Bradford was challenging the real political power center in Pennsylvania and, in the aftermath of Zenger, the body most likely to oppress him.

Another illustration of press controversy in Pennsylvania deserves closer analysis.

William Smith (not the same William Smith who was involved with William Livingston and the *Independent Reflector*) first came to Philadelphia from New York in 1753.[36] A native of Scotland and

---

33. Ibid.
34. Ibid.
35. Merritt, "Public Opinion in Colonial America: Content Analyzing the Colonial Press," 356–371.
36. A comprehensive biography of William Smith, provost of the Philadelphia College and co-founder of the *American Magazine and Monthly Chronicle for the British Colonies* may be found in Albert F. Gegenheimer's *Thomas Godfrey: Protégé of William Smith* (Philadelphia: University of Pennsylvania Press, 1943), Part 1: 1–37.

soon to be ordained as an Anglican minister, Smith was interested in promoting higher education. His proposals regarding the Academy and Charitable School in Philadelphia led to his appointment as its first provost when the institution became a college in 1755. However, Smith's ambitions, went beyond educational innovations, and he quickly became the most controversial political and literary figure in the city. His relationship with Benjamin Franklin, Philadelphia's leading citizen, was close at first; Franklin was instrumental in securing Smith's appointment to the College. But their political differences soon drove them into opposing camps, and the breach in their relations lasted for the rest of their lives.

The backdrop for the developing political controversy in Pennsylvania was the French and Indian War, the great contest between France and England for imperial domination in North America. Smith assumed his teaching duties in the Philadelphia Academy in the spring of 1754, about the time when hostilities between the French and the British commenced along the Pennsylvania frontier in the Ohio valley. The English cause did not go well in the early years of the struggle. Washington's surrender at Fort Necessity in July, 1754, followed a year later by General Braddock's disastrous defeat in the battle before Fort Duquesne, gave the French control of the strategic upper Ohio region until November, 1758.[37] During this interval, the fate of Pennsylvania as an English colony was in serous doubt. The French menace, coupled with a breakdown of the traditionally amicable relations between Pennsylvanians and the neighboring Delaware and Shawnee Indians, threatened the very life of the province and seriously challenged the pacifist policies of the dominant Quakers.[38]

The great questions confronting the political leadership of Pennsylvania during this crucial period related directly and immediately to defense. Above all, two measures were required if the colony was to meet its military responsibilities—an adequate supply bill and an effective militia act. However, like so many other issues in colonial politics, these issues were intertwined with the on-going contest between the executive and the legislature for

---

37. For more on the historical control of land in mid-eighteenth century America, see Hutson, J.H., *Pennsylvania Politics: The Movement for Royal Government and Its Consequences*, (Princeton, NJ: Princeton University Press, 1972).
38. Ibid.

control of provincial government. The Assembly was willing to pass the requisite military measures, provided that, in doing so, it did not enhance the powers of the governor of the colony. Historically, executive power increased in time of war because of increases in expenditures and military formations under executive control. The Pennsylvania Assembly was determined to prevent the war from undermining its constitutional position in this way.[39] For example, the Assembly demanded that the proprietor's estates, like all other property, be subject to tax in the general revenue measure it was being called upon to enact. This the governor, Robert Hunter Morris, refused to do, since it contravened the specific instructions he had received at the outset of his administration. The governor and the Assembly remained deadlocked on this question even after Braddock's defeat. Morris would not accede to Assembly demands, but until he did so, the Assembly refused him his militia bill. However, by the fall of 1755, action could no longer be postponed. Indian raids on the frontier in October led to a march on Philadelphia by irate frontiersmen. The Assembly was forced to respond.

The result was a series of compromises between the governor and the Quaker party.[40] A revenue measure was passed, with proprietary estates still exempt from taxation; but an Assembly commission was authorized to superintend the expenditure of funds. A militia act was passed, but in deference to Quaker pacifist principles, the act provided that men could claim exemption from service on the grounds of conscience and company officers could be elected by enlistees. To some extent, Quaker religious principles explain the half-heartedness of the war measures undertaken by the Pennsylvania Assembly in 1755 and 1756, but just as important was Assembly fear that any concessions would mean surrender of

---

39. A detailed account of the colonial Pennsylvania political climate may be found in Dietmar Rothermund's *The Layman's Progress: Religious and Political Experience in Colonial Pennsylvania, 1740–1770*, (Philadelphia: University of Pennsylvania Press, 1961).

40. An examination of the changing political attitudes and behavior of the colonial Pennsylvania Quakers may be found in Richard Bauman's *For the Reputation of Truth: Politics, Religion, and Conflict Among the Pennsylvania Quakers, 1750–1800*, (Baltimore, MD: Johns Hopkins Press, 1971).

constitutional authority to the executive.[41] In the summer of 1756, Robert Hunter Morris was replaced by William Denny, a man of less ability and few political connections. The result was that, despite the war crisis, the power of the Assembly relative to that of the governor was never greater than during the emergency of the middle 1750s.[42]

William Smith moved into the eye of this storm lashing Philadelphia's political life within a year of his taking up permanent residence in the city. He became the voice of the proprietary faction—a loose coalition bent upon overturning Quaker power in the Assembly. As an Anglican clergyman, Smith sided with anti-Quaker religious groups, the Presbyterians in particular. He enthusiastically supported the appointment of an Anglican bishop for the colonies—a major policy objective of the English authorities. In addition, in the war crisis, Smith championed strong measures to deal with the French and Indian threat along the border. Early in 1755, reacting to the French occupation of Fort Duquesne on the upper Ohio River, Smith composed one of his most controversial political essays, *A Brief State of the Province of Pennsylvania.* The pamphlet was published in London but widely circulated in Philadelphia. In it Smith suggested that members of the Assembly should swear an oath declaring allegiance to the King and a willingness to take all necessary measures to defend his interests—in effect, it was a call to Quakers to resign from legislative office. Moreover, Smith urged that the very numerous German residents of the colony be disfranchised, at least temporarily, and that they be barred from public office. As the German Pietist sects were allied with the Quakers, this was another way of striking at Quaker power. *A Brief State* elicited considerable opposition, much of it either written or inspired by Benjamin Franklin to which Smith responded the following year in a second pamphlet called *A Brief View of the*

---

41. For a more in-depth account of the Smith-Moore controversy, see Riddell, William Renwick, "Libel in the Assembly: A Pre-Revolutionary Episode," in *Pennsylvania Magazine of History and Biography*, Vol. LII, No. 2 (1928), 176–192.
42. Additional reference and analysis of the acting governor's decision to favor William Penn and the assembly during the Smith-Moore controversy can be found in Nicholas B. Wainwright's "Governor William Denny in Pennsylvania," in *Pennsylvania Magazine of History and Biography*, Vol. LXXXI, No. 2 (1957), 170–198.

Conduct of Pennsylvania in 1755. Smith "seems to have been constitutionally incapable of resisting an impulse to 'sound off' in public controversy."[43]

The recently enacted militia law calling for the election of officers had led to Franklin's elevation to the command of the Philadelphia militia. Franklin was now at the zenith of his political power. Though not totally in support of the Quakers' halfway defense measures, he was still their most influential spokesman and defender. Gouverneur Morris organized an independent militia company known as the "association," as the counterweight to Franklin's regulars. The rivalry between the regular militia and the "independents," between the Assembly and the governor, and between Franklin and Smith erupted in William Bradford's *Pennsylvania Journal*, already the leading voice of opposition to Assembly measures and the long-time competitor of Franklin's *Pennsylvania Gazette*.[44]

Smith's attacks upon the Quaker-dominated Assembly because of the inadequacy of its defense policy eventually led to a summons to appear before the bar of the House. But Smith refused to be humbled by the encounter and came out with a new pamphlet, *Obediah Honesty*, in which he upheld the freedom of the press. However, Smith's own printer, one James Chattin, *was* intimidated, and he refused to print or sell any more of Smith's essays. Undeterred, and supported throughout by the trustees of Philadelphia College, provost Smith found another instrument for broadcasting his controversial views. William Bradford, grandson of the pioneer American printer, and nephew, adopted son, and apprentice to Andrew Bradford, whose *American Weekly Mercury* had established a tradition of newspaper radicalism in Philadelphia a generation before, became Smith's close ally.

Bradford agreed to publish a periodical that Smith would edit. They called it the *American Magazine and Monthly Chronicle for the British Colonies*. Although it lasted for only a year, it was to become the "most vital and original literary magazine published in

---

43. Ketcham, "Benjamin Franklin and William Smith: New Light on an Old Philadelphia Quarrel," 143.
44. A closer examination of the life of Benjamin Franklin can be found in William S. Hanna's *Benjamin Franklin and Pennsylvania Politics*, (Stanford, CA: Stanford University Press, 1964).

America before the War of the Revolution."[45] The first installment appeared in November, 1757. In it, Smith reprinted a recent English militia law, a scheme for establishing an effective militia in Pennsylvania and an essay that argued that, while militia forces were adequate for general purposes, only hired mercenaries were equipped to deal with marauding Indians. The rest of the magazine was devoted to literary and scientific pieces. The most important, from a political point of view, was an essay by the "Antigallican" that bemoaned, in Spartan spirit, the effects of luxury and ease upon civil society.

On January 6, 1758, William Smith was arrested, cited for contempt, and denied relief on a habeas corpus petition by order of the Assembly. He remained in prison until the adjournment of the house in April and then, in September, was rearrested for a brief period of internment until the Assembly was dissolved.

The ostensible reason for Smith's arrest was his support of one William Moore, a justice of the peace in Chester County. Moore's hostility to the ruling Quaker party was long-standing. As far back as July, 1740, Moore, then an Assemblyman, had antagonized the Quakers by denouncing their refusal to vote for supplies to prepare for possible military operations during an earlier military confrontation with the French known as King George's War. In 1755, with Pennsylvania again facing a military crisis, Moore renewed his urgings that the Assembly enact a strong militia law to deal with Indian raids. On August 25, 1757, Moore was called to appear before the House to answer charges of misconduct in office, but he refused to comply and issued a statement denying that the Assembly had the power to try him as if it were a judicial body. The Assembly and Moore both appealed to the governor, William Denny, each charging the other with malicious behavior. Moore was finally arrested along with Smith, Moore for libeling the House in his petition to the governor and Smith for publishing the petition in his newspaper. The governor was sympathetic to the two men and criticized the Assembly for neglecting urgent matters while engaging "in new heats and disputes, at a time when public danger

———

45. Schlesinger, Arthur M., *Preclude to Independence: The Newspaper War on Great Britain, 1764–1776.* (New York: Alfred A. Knopf, 1958).

surrounds us on every side."[46] The governor dismissed all charges against Moore in August, 1758.

Meanwhile, Smith continued to bait the Assembly from his place of confinement. The February, 1758, issue of the *American Magazine* contained statements by Moore and most of the relevant public documents in the case, including lengthy communications between the governor and the Assembly. Even more significant, however, was the first appearance at this time of the "Watchman" essays. They were published in William Bradford's *Journal*, but there is little doubt that Smith was the author of this series. In defense of Moore, the "Watchman" [i.e., Smith] argued that even the House of Commons itself did not have the power to act in a judicial capacity against an official charged, as Moore had been, with extortion. In addition, the essay quoted generous portions from *Cato's Letters* on press liberty.

At least two of the "Watchman" letters appeared in the *Pennsylvania Journal* while Smith was still confined. Letter III was republished in April, the month of his release, in the *American Magazine*. Here, Smith commented upon the "uncommon endeavors used, for a number of years past, to overawe the Press, and to vilify and intimidate the advocate for *impartial Enquiry*."[47] The third "Watchman" also contained a letter, supposedly written by a Quaker, that declared that the Friends should not have aspired to rule if they were unprepared to employ the instruments of power. It concluded with the charge that the troubles of Pennsylvania were caused by individuals who had their own selfish schemes to pursue.[48]

"Watchman" VI appeared in the *American Magazine* in June. It began on a sharp note of alarm: "There never was a time when activity, diligence, and attention to public affairs, were more necessary than for some years past in this province; and yet no time, perhaps, when less were to be found."[49] In general, the essay was a philosophical discourse analyzing the failings of people in

---

46. Wainwright, "Governor William Denny in Pennsylvania," 170–198.
47. Gegenheimer, *Thomas Godfrey: Protégé of William Smith,* 1–37.
48. For additional useful material regarding individual printers, newspapers, and magazines, see L.N. Richardson's *A History of Early Magazines, 1741–1789,* (New York: Thomas Nelson and Sons, 1931).
49. Merritt, "Public Opinion in Colonial America: Content Analyzing the Colonial Press," 356–371.

power. However, there was no mistaking its intent or the immediacy of its application. It charged those to whom power had been given with selfishness and neglect of the public good.

In July, Smith reprinted the seventh installment from the "Watchman" series, this time a statement on how the cunning and stratagems of "weak and wicked rulers" seek "to suppress all inquiries into their conduct." Smith's description of the techniques of repression had a striking resemblance to his own experiences as a victim of the legislature's animus. His readers did not have to be alerted to the connection. Of men in power, Smith wrote:

> They will always look on the friends of truth, as their own particular enemies. If you examine their conduct, they will be angry, because they know, you must blame. If you blame, they will punish cruelly, because they know, the censure of the just, and are certain that if they cannot put a stop to all enquiries by acts of severity, they themselves soon come to condign punishment. Whence, every word will be termed "*seditious*," every truth "*libelous.*" To tell, what you know, will be call'd "false"; to speak what you think, "*villainous*." When matters come to this pass, Genius will be depressed, Freedom of speech and writing banished, Honesty tongue-tied, and then commences all the political process of *seizing*, *examining*, *imprisoning*, *burning*, and what not.[50]

Smith described how the ancient Athenians spent public funds for festivals and merriment while Philip of Macedon approached their city in strength. "Nothing was more true, than that they were running into destruction; and yet nothing more dangerous than to tell them so."[51] Lest the ancient analogy, however heavily drawn, escape his readers, Smith applied it to present circumstances with breathtaking force and bluntness:

> At the commencement of those murders and outrages [by the Delawares and Shawnees] under which this unhappy country now bleeds, in a certain province we all know [Pennsylvania], tho' like the *Athenians*, they had no law absolutely converting their public revenues to rioting and excess, yet they [the people of Pennsylvania] had placed all confidence and authority in men, whose avowed principles forbid their converting it to that which

---

50. Gegenheimer, *Thomas Godfrey: Protégé of William Smith,* 1–37.
51. Ibid.

> is its real use. . . repelling violence and protecting the innocent from blood and slaughter. Nothing was more certain than that the continuing power in such hands [the presently constituted Assembly], tended to increase the public calamity, and to let in total destruction and distress upon the community. And yet nothing was more dangerous than to say so. [52]

These were defiant words for a man recently imprisoned for criticizing the legislature.

In August, the "Watchman's" eighth letter, a direct attack upon members of the legislative assembly, appeared in the *Pennsylvania Journal* and reprinted in the *American Magazine* soon afterward. Popular rulers needed to be watched more than traditional tyrants, Smith argued, for by linking their names and their interests together with the people they manage to mask their own sinister designs. The "Watchman" warned that "no people ought to entertain such an exalted opinion of the abilities or integrity of their rulers, as to approve of every thing they do without ever suspecting they are capable of error or deceit." He advised his fellow countrymen to pursue wiser policies than those heretofore followed and to get rid of "all those...whose weakness, wickedness, or malice render[s] them unfit for the sacred trust consigned to them."[53]

August, 1758, saw the last appearance of the "Watchman" in the *American Magazine.* Smith was returned to jail in September. In December, he sailed for England, not as an exile or political refugee bust as a petitioner demanding vindication from the only power capable of granting it—the Privy Council itself. In England, Smith was celebrated by the Anglican hierarchy for his activities in Pennsylvania. His strong support for the imperial cause naturally earned him great favor. The Privy Council cleared Smith of all charges. The law officers of the Crown recommended that Moore's address to Governor Denny, which Smith had published, was indeed libelous, but that only the Assembly so libeled could act upon it. Consequently, Smith's arrest by a subsequent assembly was unlawful.

Vindicated, Smith returned to Philadelphia early in 1759. His career as an educator, minister, and essayist was far from over. He opposed the Stamp Act in 1765 and the oppressive measures of the

---

52. Ibid.
53. Ibid.

mid 1770's that led to the break with England. He remained a loyalist, however, and despite the unpopularity of such sentiments in the winter of 1775–1776, he remained unafraid to publish his views. His *Plain Truth* pamphlet answered Thomas Paine's argument for independence in *Common Sense*. Its appearance at the height of the Revolutionary crisis, along with articles by Smith and other advocates of reconciliation with Great Britain, is another example of the Philadelphia press keeping pace with the ongoing public debate over the great issue of colonial independence.

During the stormy period of the French and Indian War, Smith's *American Magazine* and Bradford's *Pennsylvania Journal* together illustrate a side of American journalism in the colonial era that deserves more appreciation. The actions of the Pennsylvania Assembly against Moore and Smith represent a leading example of how legislatures rather than courts had become the agencies for press suppression in the period after Zenger, with "breach of privilege" replacing seditious libel as the major offense charged. Smith's numerous encounters with the Pennsylvania Assembly—like Moore's—failed to silence him. During his imprisonment, he composed the "Watchman" essays for the *Pennsylvania Journal*, and upon his release he reprinted them in the new *American Magazine*. He remained unintimidated by the Assembly, despite the fact that his position was contrary to that of the leading oligarchs of Philadelphia—the Quakers and their supporters—and directly affronted perhaps the most powerful legislative body in all America.[54] To be sure, Smith left for England as a direct result of his incarceration, and the effect of his departure was to terminate the life of his monthly journal. Still, by that time the worst of the military crisis had passed. In November, 1758, the French abandoned Fort Duquesne, and the threat to the life of the colony was ended. But in the months that mattered, Smith wrote and published material offensive to the Assembly. His position was not vindicated by an early change in public attitude, for the Quakers remained the dominating force in Pennsylvania politics until the Revolution. But his activities as a writer and publisher vindicated the reputation of the editors, writers, and printers of the period as

---

54. Bauman, *For the Reputation of Truth: Politics, Religion, and Conflict Among the Pennsylvania Quakers,* passim.

fierce defenders of the liberty of the press despite the numerous legal impediments which they had to confront.

A close examination of political controversies in other colonies would show a similar pattern, so that we need to revise our understanding of the press during the late colonial period. New York maintained a spirited, politically oriented press after the Zenger trial. In the early 1750s, one of the most colorful and animated debates occurred over the founding of King's College, later Columbia. The controversy centered around the *Independent Reflector*, and several minor spin-off publications such as the *Occasional Reverberator* and *John Englishman*. Hugh Gaine's *New York Mercury* was the *Reflector's* chief antagonist. But unlike William Smith's *American Magazine and Monthly Chronicle* in Philadelphia, the *Independent Reflector* did not challenge the provincial Assembly head on, but the explosion it ignited shows that the press in New York provided a more than adequate forum for the discussion of highly sensitive and divisive public questions. And when the power of the Assembly did come into play, vigorous critical debate was even more in evidence. James Parker was called to account in 1759 when Parker published a broadside challenging the wisdom of New York's recently enacted stamp duty on legal documents and newspapers.[55] Probably because it failed to produce sufficient revenue, the tax was dropped. Still, the importance of the episode is not be measured but the effect or lack of effect Parker's statement had but by the fact that he spoke out at all. A printer intimidated by fear of reprisal would hardly have questioned the good sense of the legislature in imposing a highly controversial tax. Still another example, also from New York, points out the futility of legislative attacks upon the press. In the famous McDougall case of 1769–1771, it is clear that the effort to silence McDougall for criticizing the New York Assembly was counterproductive, in that his incarceration was broadcast to the other colonies. The New York Assembly's action in voting supplies for British troops stimulated a major press war. The "Dougliad" essays, defending the Assembly and attacking McDougall, appeared in Hugh Gaine's *New York Gazette and Weekly Magazine* in the spring of 1770, but anti-Dougliad rejoinders were printed in the *New York Journal* and

---

55. McAnear, Beverly, "James Parker Versus New York Province," in *New York History* XXII, (1941), 321–330.

the *New York Gazette* or *Weekly Post-Boy*. Just as William Smith of Philadelphia had done at the height of the French War, McDougall contributed to the controversy from his prison cell. In short, legislative repression, like the license laws and court trials of an earlier era, seem to have had little effect on curbing press freedom.

Recent studies indicate just how important the press was in shaping American consciousness, not only during, but even long before the Revolutionary crisis itself. One student of the press in the pre-Revolutionary period has shown that a sense of an American identity preceded the institutional formations that followed quickly upon the break with England. Symbols of American community were evident in the press in the generation before the great political upheaval of the mid-century.[56] Not pale and anemic, but vigorous, controversial, and fearless, American journalism reinforced an emerging American consciousness and brilliantly reflected the vitality of American political life. Thus despite the existence of the draconian law of seditious libel, "there was almost certainly a much wider degree of freedom of expression in colonial and early national America" than we have been led to believe.[57] The law, after all, responds to social reality as much as it shapes reality. It was the tension between seditious libel and legislative privilege, on the one hand, and the fact of a vigorous press, on the other, that ultimately brought the law into line with the substantial press freedom that prevailed in colonial America during turbulent times.

---

56. See Merritt, *Symbols of the American Community*.
57. For further criticism of Levy's interpretation of freedom of the press, see Smith, James M., "A Review of Levy's 'Legacy of Suppression,'" in *William and Mary Quarterly*, 3d Ser., Vol. XX, (1963), 156–159.

Episode 4

Politics in Late Colonial America

> Unspeakably calamitous have been the consequences of Party Division. It has occasioned Deluges of Blood, and subverted Kingdoms. It always introduces a Decay of publick Spirit, with the Extinction of every noble and generous Sentiment.[1]
>
> *The Independent Reflector*, 1753

In some ways, colonial politics prefigured American political experience in the years to come. Colonial public life was rich in controversy, political institutions were surprisingly open, and participation in government at some levels was widespread. To be sure, there are marked differences between the political attitudes and campaign practices, and the values and goals of public life then and now, and these need to be noted. But politics nourished the roots of colonial public life even as the health of the political system today is our surest safeguard that constitutional government will continue.

One of the great debates in American history has focused upon the extent to which colonial America was a political democracy. Historians are divided on this question into at least three camps. Some have said that it was not democratic, while others have claimed that it was, while still others have challenged the whole question itself, asserting that the issue was foreign to the concerns of the colonial American. The literature on this debate is extensive, and there is no need to review it again. Accordingly, it might be useful to focus upon some of the relatively undisputed claims in the controversy and apply them to a reconstruction of the most important features of colonial political life in general.

---

* Source: Chapter 6 ("The Character of Politics") in George Dargo, *Roots of the Republic: A New Perspective on Early American Constitutionalism* (New York: Praeger, 1974.)

1. William Livingston, "Of Party Divisions," in *The Independent Reflector*, Milton Klein, ed. (Boston, MA: Harvard University Press, 1963), 146.

The right to vote was extensive among adult white males in the colonial era. Chilton Williamson, whose history of the suffrage is a modern treatment, estimates that between fifty and seventy-five per cent of the free, adult white males over twenty-one could vote in colonial America.[2] Both in local and in colony wide elections, qualifications to vote for town selectmen, for "select" vestries, and for deputies to the provincial assemblies were either easily satisfied or ignored altogether. Normally, qualification to vote was based on the possession of real property, but because of the wide availability of land, this was not a serious impediment to the establishment of a fairly broad electorate.[3] In Virginia, possession of real property either as a freehold or as a lease for life or lives was the prerequisite for the voting franchise, but townsmen could also vote if they owned a dwelling and a piece of a town lot.[4] However, slaves or other forms of movable or personal property, regardless of value, did not suffice. Elsewhere, the distinction between real and personal property was not recognized as important. In Massachusetts, a person's property had to be worth £40 sterling[5]; in Connecticut, £40 in current money.[6] Landed property was not required in either province.[7]

More important as a barrier to voting than property restrictions were the physical encumbrances connected with voting procedures. Usually, the poll was taken at the county seat, which meant that some voters living in very large counties had to travel many miles at considerable personal sacrifice to exercise the franchise. Time off from work meant several days or more lost at the harvest or in the planting season. Overnight stays in highway inns while en route

---

2. For a study on early American colonial democracy, see Chilton Williamson, *American Suffrage: From Property to Democracy, 1760–1860* (Princeton, NJ: Princeton University Press, 1960), 20–39.
3. Ibid., 22–23.
4. Ibid., 30.
5. Ibid., 13, 32.
6. Ibid., 13, 27. For more examples of the historical trends emphasizing roles of factions on colonial politics, see Oscar Zeichner's *Connecticut's Years of Controversy, 1750–1776* (Chapel Hill, NC: University of North Carolina Press, 1949).
7. Williamson, *American Suffrage*, 17, 32. For more information on "political factions in colonial society" and a penetrating survey of the recent work and an analysis of its import and thrust of early American history, see Jack P. Greene's "Changing Interpretations of Early American Politics," in *The Reinterpretation of Early American History: Essays in Honor of John E. Pomfret*, R.A. Billington, ed. (San Marino, CA: Huntington Institute, 1966), 151–84.

were costly. Even voting in town elections could prove burdensome. Some New England towns encompassed a number of scattered and separate villages, only one of which was designated as the polling place, and voters might have to travel a considerable distance in order to vote.

Because of the physical hardships that attended voting in some localities, there was a natural tendency for candidates to encourage their known supporters to go to the polls by offering to pay at least some of the costs of food, drink, and, if necessary, lodging along the way. In most colonies, however, statutes prohibited candidates from "treating" voters in these ways prior to the election once the governor had issued a writ of election. In Virginia, such electioneering practices were strictly limited by law, and no candidate could give money, food, entertainment, gifts, contracts, or promises of favor without running the risk of disqualifying himself from office. *The Concessions and Agreements of West New Jersey* provided that "no person or persons who shall give bestow or promise directly or indirectly to the said parties electing any meat drinke money or moneys worth for procurement of their choice and consent shall be capeable of being elected a member of the said Assembly."[8] Nevertheless, these laws were often evaded, and "treating" was widely practiced. Supporters performed the customary catering services, thus relieving the candidate of direct legal liability. Given the difficulties, burdens, and costs of traveling to the polls, voters came to expect some type of recompense, but once the proscriptions of law set in, the "treat" was confined to food and drink offered at or near the poll at the time of voting. Meals, lodging, travel costs, and other expenses for voters residing at a distance became their own responsibility.

Besides the inconvenience, cost, and lost labor time that voting often entailed, the voter also opened himself to various forms of physical and moral intimidation when he went to the polls. Sup-

---

8. Julian P. Boyd, "Concessions and Agreements of West New Jersey," in *Fundamental Laws and Constitutions of New Jersey, 1664–1964* (Princeton, NJ: Princeton University Press, 1964), 95, (referencing the original text of the *Concessions and Agreements*, Ch. XXXIII (1677). Additional information concerning the study of suffrage, voting practices, and legislative apportionment in New Jersey can be found in Richard P. McCormick's *The History of Voting in New Jersey: A Study in the Development of Election Machinery, 1664–1911* (New Brunswick, NJ: Rutgers University Press, 1953), Chaps. 1–2.

porters of one candidate might deliberately attempt to impede voters known to favor another. There are cases of blocked roads, of bridges torn down, and of ferry boats wrecked to prevent opposing voters from reaching the county seat. If all else failed, an outright brawl might be set off at the voting place. Pennsylvania elections were known for their turbulence, and voters were sometimes warned to come armed to the polls. In 1738, in Philadelphia, rival factions fought openly to "control the stairs" leading to the poll in the central market.[9] The "trial of the stairs" was an accepted feature of Philadelphia voting practice.[10] The Philadelphia election riot of 1742 occurred because of special anxieties and tensions, but disorders of this kind were not uncommon in port towns because of the presence of voteless sailors, who often had a stake in the outcome of a local election.

The difficulties of voting—not the qualifications that established voter eligibility—help to explain why some elections were poorly attended. Voters were normally apathetic. Unless the election was hotly contested or the issues were of particular interest, voters preferred to stay home. But voting was not a right or a privilege; it was a civic duty, like militia service. The law not only entitled freeholders to vote; in some colonies, freeholders were penalized if they did not. Virginia imposed a fine of 200 pounds of tobacco if a voter failed to go to the polls.[11] In seventeenth-century Plymouth, freemen were fined for not attending town meetings or for not voting for the town's deputies to the General Court—two reasons why freemanship was not always enthusiastically sought after in that colony.[12] In Massachusetts,

---

9. Sister Joan de Lourdes Leonard, C.S.J., "Elections in Colonial Pennsylvania," *William and Mary Quarterly,* 3d Ser., Vol. 11 (1954): 394. For more information on elections in Pennsylvania, refer to Norman S. Cohen's "The Philadelphia Election Riot of 1742," *Pennsylvania Magazine of History and Biography*, No. 92 (1968): 306–319.
10. Ibid.
11. B.K. Brown and R.E. Brown, *Virginia, 1705–1786: Democracy or Aristocracy?* (East Lansing, MI: Michigan State University Press, 1964), Chaps. 6–7.
12. George D. Landon, Jr., "The Franchise and Political Democracy in Plymouth," *William and Mary Quarterly,* 3rd Ser., Vol. 20 (1963): 520–21 (analyzing democracy in the Plymouth colony, cross-referenced with attendance data from local meetings held).

towns that dodged the responsibility (and the cost) of sending at least one deputy to the legislature were subject to a stiff penalty.[13]

The county sheriff was the principal officer charged with conducting the election procedure. He voted only in cases of a tie and was expected to conduct the proceedings impartially. Yet, officials rarely maintained a neutral position. A sheriff could determine the outcome of contested elections in some provinces by neglecting to notify voters in areas where sentiment was opposed to his own, by moving the poll to another location at the last minute, by excluding qualified and admitting unqualified voters, by closing the poll after those favored had voted, by filing incorrect returns, and, finally, by intimidation. A voter who supported candidates whom the sheriff opposed could be called with bothersome regularity to jury duty, a civic responsibility even more onerous than voting itself.

The voting process itself tells us much about colonial political attitudes and behavior. The voters assembled *en bloc* on the common or before the county courthouse, and when the vote was called they divided according to their choice. The sheriff could decide by visual estimate—"upon the view"—whether there was a unanimous vote, or else which group was larger and, therefore, which candidate was chosen if there were more than one.[14] If many candidates were running or if an election was vigorously contested, a "poll" of the voters might be required. Each voter would then be called by name to step forward and either declare the vote aloud, or submit a written ballot with the voter's own name affixed thereto, or make his selection in a more secret manner.[15] Pennsylvania tried to establish a kind of secret ballot; each voter dropped a bean into a divided container; sometimes different-colored beans were used for different candidates.[16] However, in most colonies, voting was open. To announce one's vote aloud and without fear was a mark of civic pride.

These practices seem unsophisticated and replete with faults and weaknesses to us, and yet colonial Americans probably considered them about as fair, valid, important, and liberal as we do

---

13. For more information on the study of democracy in early colonial Massachusetts see Robert E. Brown's "Democracy in Colonial Massachusetts," *New England Quarterly*, No. 25 (1952): 291–313.
14. J.R. Pole, "Suffrage and Representation in Massachusetts: A Statistical Note," *William and Mary Quarterly*, 3rd Ser., Vol. 14 (1957): 560–592.
15. Ibid.
16. Leonard, "Elections in Colonial Pennsylvania," 392.

ours. To us, any kind of property test for voting is a deprivation of a basic human right; it seems to favor the haves and discriminate unjustly against the have-nots. However, people in the eighteenth century may not have viewed it in just that way. The property restriction was a device—originally a liberal reform—preventing local persons of wealth, power, and influence from controlling the outcome of elections. Given that most voting was oral and that a voter's choice was public knowledge, it was necessary to insulate the voter as much as possible from social pressure. A tenant was not very likely to risk his lease by voting against the known inclinations of the landlord; nor would an apprentice or bound servant vote against the master or a debtor against a creditor. The theory was that tenants and servants, like women, slaves, and children, did not have "a will of their own." Only a person with a minimum of property was sufficiently self-possessed to exercise a free choice. Even though, in reality, tenants often voted with surprising independence, it was widely believed that, in the absence of a property qualification, the rich and powerful would be able to march to the polls at the head of a parade of dependents prepared to vote at their dictation.

Consequently, property qualifications were thought to minimize outside pressure and equalize power among the electorate, just as property qualifications for office were originally designed to reduce the officeholder's incentive to use an official position for personal gain. Historians have tended, by implication, to applaud the fact that the property qualification was not important because it was frequently ignored, the result being to enlarge the size of the voting population.[17] But it is possible that elections in which voter qualifications were not examined may have been less "liberal" than those in which they were. "Fagot voting" and "colonizing" were the terms used to describe customs whereby temporary deeds of property were given to unqualified voters so that they could satisfy eligibility requirements and then vote the way of their benefactors.[18] Such blatant efforts to manipulate elections led to the establishment of residency qualifications and hikes in the minimum amount of property needed to vote. For example, Virginia first defined the size of the minimum freehold necessary to vote in the

---

17. Williamson, *American Suffrage*, 49.
18. Ibid., 50–51.

1786 reform law—one hundred acres of unimproved land of twenty-five acres with a house and plantation—to offset the recently discovered tendency of the rich to lease small parcels of land in return for support at the polls.[19]

The property qualification was also justified on the basis of the "stake in society" theory. Since taxes on real property were the principal source of government revenue, and as English law and tradition dictated that taxes were the "free gift" of consenting freeholders, it followed that taxpayers alone were entitled to vote for officials charged with raising and disbursing public funds. On the basis of such logic, plural voting made good sense.[20] If a freeholder owned land in more than one county or election district, as a taxpayer, he ought to have been able to vote as many times as he was subject to tax. In fact, it was considered an abuse of a voter's privilege if a sheriff in one county called for an election on the same day as that in another county, since this could well deprive freeholders with sufficient land in each of their right to vote twice. Above all, property qualification for voting tended to limit the electorate to persons sharing those traits of character that property ownership reinforced—independence, stability, reliability, honesty, and integrity.[21] Such qualifications made farming virtues into political virtues.[22]

The whole question of secret voting as opposed to public voting also needs some rethinking. To colonial Americans, it was by no means obvious that secret voting was superior to oral voting. There were (and are) certain hidden costs. Secret ballots were by no means immune to manipulation. If the results of a secret ballot were challenged, a new vote was required. In colonial times, this was a considerable hardship. Voters had already been inconvenienced once and were unlikely to undertake the tedious, time-consuming, and costly journey to the poll a second time. A secret ballot would require the validation of all voter qualifications prior to the election, an additional burden to an already encumbered system. Americans knew about secret voting—it was provided for

---

19. For a more descriptive study of colonial Virginia, see Charles E. Sydnor, *Gentlemen Freeholders: Political Practices in Washington's Virginia*, 2d. ed., (New York: Van Rees Press, 1965).
20. Williamson, *American Suffrage*, 5–8, 12–15.
21. Ibid., 19.
22. Ibid., 20.

in the *Concessions & Agreements of West New Jersey* and it was required by law in Pennsylvania and the Carolinas—but there was no significant agitation for it during the colonial era except in New York.[23] On the other hand, an oral vote was less subject to dispute. Each voter's choices were listed next to his name. It was a simple task to recheck the result by going through the poll. If an unqualified voter was on the list, that vote could be crossed off without affecting the validity of the entire canvass.

If colonial voting habits appear quaint to us, their campaign techniques are remarkably less so. Discounting the obvious differences occasioned by modern communications media and transportation technology, the attitudes and practices of colonial nominees running for office parallel our own in a number of interesting and even striking ways. While it was not considered good form to trumpet one's personal assets as a candidate, those who did not were often repudiated at the polls. The accepted conventions of politics required that candidates "standing for election" demurely await the judgment of the candidate's character by fellow citizens. But reality dictated that a serious politician actively solicit votes and advertise his candidacy by appearing at the polling place on election day. Personal contact was the most effective way of winning support. People voted as much on the basis of personal evaluation as on issues. A candidate who was widely known, who managed to visit voters throughout the election district, who shook hands, knew the family, and remembered the names of the children was likely to be more successful than the self-effacing candidate for office who stayed at home. Many politicians lamented the necessity of having to appeal to the people, but they performed the required rituals or risked voter rejection.

In addition to personal contact, candidates for elective office used the public prints extensively. Pamphlets, broadsides, reprints of the *Assembly Journal,* and letters to the editors of newspapers were the accepted and frequently employed techniques for broadcasting the successes of one candidate as opposed to the failings of another. Whispering campaigns, rumor-mongering, and slander were not considered to be in good form, but they were also not

---

23. For a study of early democracy in colonial New York, refer to Milton M. Klein's "Democracy and Politics in Colonial New York," *New York History,* No. 40 (1959): 221–246.

uncommon. In addition, voters were persuaded—at a price—either to vote in support of a particular candidate or to withhold support from an opponent by not voting.

These practices were best known in the most politicized of the colonies. For example, prior to 1755, elections in New York were controlled by "bosses" who rounded up voters by direct or indirect bribes and conducted extensive "paper wars" in the press—all of which was financed through well-stocked campaign treasure chests.[24] In Pennsylvania, the dominant Quakers, more a political than a religious group by the 1750s, used the annual Quaker meeting as a caucus for choosing nominees for the Assembly. "Tickets" were put together and printed, and there is even some evidence of ethnic balancing to attract immigrant votes.

Patronage of one sort or another was also used to collect votes. A member of the Boston delegation to the Massachusetts House of Representatives instructed James Otis, Jr., on how he should conduct his first campaign for election by recounting his own experience:

> I can also tell you, by way of example, some of the steps I take: two or three weeks before an election comes on, I send to the cooper and get all my casks put in order. I say nothing about the number of hoops. I send to the mason and have some job done to the hearths or the chimneys. I have the carpenter to make some repairs in the roof or the wood house. I often go down to the ship yards about eleven o'clock, when they break off to take their drink, and enter into conversation with them. They all vote for me.[25]

All these techniques—campaign literature, trips around the circuit, buying up votes, carefully distributing patronage in the right places—were expensive. In most instances, the candidate had to have either resources of his own or the support of wealthy patrons.

By the end of the colonial period, a surprisingly modern political system had developed in a number of colonies. Rhode Island, the most independent-minded and autonomous province, was also among the most politicized. "Proxy" voting—a system whereby the

---

24. Nicholas Varga, "Election Procedures and Practices in Colonial New York," *New York History,* No. 41 (1960): 249–277.

25. William Tudor, *The Life of James Otis, of Massachusetts: Containing also Notices of some Contemporary Character & Events* (Boston, MA: Wells and Lilly, 1823), 92.

voters submitted printed ballots in their respective towns, which were then forwarded to Newport for tabulation in the General Court—required a high degree of political organization.[26] Each of the two rival factions that dominated Rhode Island politics in the generation before the Revolution caucused to decide on nominees, printed proxy "tickets," organized newspaper campaigns, and sent speakers and "runners" around the province to drum up and hunt for voter support.[27] "*Rhode Islandism*" came to be used throughout the colonies as a derogatory term describing practices that were thought to demean public life but were increasingly discoverable in places other than Rhode Island itself.[28]

The sum of the parts of colonial electoral practices from campaign to election may not add up to democracy. The historians who have criticized the "colonial democracy" school are certainly right in asserting that deference and the need for consensus explain more about early American political culture than its putative democratic character.[29] Still, the degree of public participation, or the effects that such participation had upon colonial public life, should not be underestimated. It was an "age still pre-democratic in its conscious thought, although not in many of its practices and institutions."[30] Those who were white, male, propertied, free, and Protestant who could and did vote in colonial elections were deferential to their "betters" and expected the "natural leaders" of the social order to

---

26. David S. Lovejoy, *Rhode Island Politics and the American Revolution, 1760–1776* (Providence, RI: Brown University Press, 1958), 127–154 (focusing more on general procedural standards and less on voting in colonial Rhode Island).
27. Ibid.
28. Ibid.
29. Roy N. Lokken, "The Concept of Democracy in Colonial Political Thought," *William and Mary Quarterly*, 3rd Ser., Vol. 16, No. 4 (1959): 576–78. This text provides a leading example of literature critical of the "democratic" explanation of colonial politics, showing that the concept of democracy was rooted in classical thought and had a very circumscribed meaning in the colonial period. Additional information on consensus data and its effects can be found in Michael Zuckerman's "The Social Context of Democracy in Massachusetts," *William and Mary Quarterly*, 3rd Ser., Vol. 25 (1968): 524–544 (arguing that on a local level, consensus rather democratic majoritarianism was the purpose of extending the franchise as widely as possible).
30. Williamson, *American Suffrage*, 42.

control the administration of government.[31] But they also had a lively sense that their vote counted—as it surely did in an electorate of limited size where elections often turned on a handful of votes in a canvass of a few hundred—that their needs and desires deserved recognition, and that candidates who failed to defer to the people ought not be returned.

A clear example of the relationship between the voter and their representatives is the Land Bank controversy in Massachusetts in 1740–1741.[32] One of the major economic problems facing colonial America was the chronic shortage of an adequate circulating medium of exchange. Many colonies suffered from almost continuous trade deficits, which meant that specie coming into the country was siphoned off to make up for trade imbalances.[33] Monetary tightness tended to deflate prices and depress business. In order to counteract these effects, colonial legislatures tried various inflationary experiments to increase circulation, raise prices and discourage imports from abroad. The obvious and favorite technique was to print paper. But the British government and English merchants frowned upon paper money for the very same reasons that Americans applauded it: dear money in America meant greater business opportunities and profits for English merchants and manufacturers selling goods to the American market.

In 1730, the English Board of Trade decided to enforce its restrictive monetary policy to Massachusetts whose growing commercial economy was perceived as an economic threat to English merchants and traders. Newspaper issues were to be limited and outstanding notes retired in order to return the province to a specie-based currency within ten years. The new directive had explosive potential. During the 1730s, Governor Jonathan Belcher disregarded Board of Trade instructions and continued to allow paper issues, but toward the end of the decade Belcher began to comply

---

31. J.R. Pole, "Historians and the Problem of Early American Democracy," *American Historical Review*, Vol. LXVII (1962): 626–646 (arguing that colonial society was "deferential" rather than "democratic").
32. For information on the Land Bank controversy in Massachusetts, see George A. Billias, *The Massachusetts Land Bankers of 1740,* University of Maine Studies, *Second Series*, No. 74 (Orno, Maine: University Press, 1959).
33. Theodore Thayer, "The Land Bank System in the American Colonies," *Journal of Economic History*, Vol. XIII, No. 2 (1953): 146–148 (discussing the wide use of land bank measures in other colonies besides Massachusetts).

with royal policy.[34] Large segments of provincial opinion looked upon the governor's growing commitment to financial retrenchment as fraught with disaster. By 1740, a political deadlock between the governor and the cheap money forces in the Massachusetts House of Representatives brought the provincial government to near paralysis.[35] The financial problems had become a burning public issue.

At this point, one John Colman revived a scheme that had been in circulation in Massachusetts for nearly a century and had already been used, with some success, in other colonies.[36] Colman suggested the establishment of a private credit bank based on land mortgages. His proposed "land bank" would issue circulating notes redeemable in twenty years and payable in commodities or company bills.[37] It was a simple device by which land—Massachusetts' major natural resource—would be used as a basis for a needed medium of exchange. The Land Bank and Manufactory Scheme promised to solve the problem of insufficient currency, low prices, excessive imports, and a lagging economy.

Colman's Land Bank quickly became the central political issue in Massachusetts.[38] Some Boston commercial interests tried to set up a silver bank as a conservative alternative to the Land Bank, but the idea had little support.[39] The Land Bank was popular with a broad cross-section of the electorate, and in the spring election of 1740, a lower house dominated by Land Bankers was returned that proceeded to protect the Bank from executive interference.[40] In September, 1740, the Bank issued its first paper notes.[41] Belcher and the Massachusetts Council attempted to outlaw the Bank by

---

34. Schutz, John A. "Succession Politics in Massachusetts, 1730–1741," *William and Mary Quarterly*, 3rd Ser., Vol. 15 (1958) 508–520. For a helpful introduction to issues that arose in colonial financing structures, see E. James Ferguson, "Currency Finance: An Interpretation of Monetary Practices," *William and Mary Quarterly*, 3rd Ser., Vol. 10 (1953): 175–78. This text provides a helpful introduction to issues that arose in colonial financing structures.
35. Billias, *The Massachusetts Land Bankers of 1740*, 32–42.
36. Ibid., 5–6.
37. Ibid., 4.
38. Ibid., 4–6.
39. Ibid., 10.
40. Ibid., 41.
41. Ibid., 12–15.

executive proclamation, but this served only to polarize political alignments even more.[42]

In May, 1741, Land Bankers again won in the provincial elections.[43] The "Land Bank House" proceeded to take reprisals against the council which had sided with Belcher in his attempt to destroy the Bank.[44] Sixteen councilors were purged, but the governor responded by dissolving the new Assembly. Soon afterward, and partly as a result of a petition filed by Massachusetts merchants, Parliament quashed the Bank by applying the Bubble Act of 1720, which proscribed speculative enterprises.[45] In addition, William Shirley was appointed to replace Belcher as provincial governor.[46] In the ensuing months, Shirley managed to work out a series of compromise measures by which the Bank was liquidated with a minimum of hardship and inconvenience to its subscribers.

The political fall-out resulting from the Land Bank explosion was considerable. John Adams once remarked that the turmoil in Massachusetts over the Land Bank exceeded that which followed the Stamp Act a generation later.[47] But what is of special interest here is how the controversy illustrates the relationship between public policy and voter behavior. There was an increase in the number of representatives sent to the General Court [the Massachusetts legislature] from towns usually too apathetic or parsimonious to send their full quota of deputies. For example, the number of deputies to the House of Representatives sent by towns in Worcester county doubled between 1739 and 1741.[48] Land Bank supporters throughout the province gained dramatic voter support with striking results. Seventy percent of the deputies from conservative districts failed to be re-elected in 1741, the year when elections to the General Court were a virtual referendum on the Land Bank scheme.[49] In contrast, districts whose deputies generally supported

42. Ibid.
43. Ibid., 33–35.
44. Thayer, "The Land Bank System in the American Colonies," 150.
45. Ibid., 148–49. The book does not use the phrase "Bubble act."
46. Billias, *The Massachusetts Land Bankers of 1740*, 38–42.
47. Ibid., 16.
48. Ibid., 33.
49. Robert Zemsky, *Merchants, Farmers, and River Gods: An Essay of 18th Century American Politics* (Boston, MA: Gambit, 1971), Chaps. 5–6, (where the author incorporates an argument against debtor-creditor split in the Land Bank Controversy).

the Land Bank, were more likely to be returned to office.[50] George A. Billias, a student of the Land Bank controversy, concluded that the issue "roused the colonists from their apathy and spurred them into political action. The rising tide of votes mustered by the land bankers threatened to engulf the royal governor and to upset the established pattern of government."[51]

The elections to the House of Representatives in 1740 and 1741, when the Land Bank agitation was at its height, clearly demonstrated that, in Massachusetts, the political system was capable of responding to a vital public question. Uncontested elections and elections involving insignificant public issues brought few voters to the polls. But when elections mattered, the electorate acted. Such was the case in the money crisis of Massachusetts in the 1740s, but a similar condition could be found in most of the other provinces. Issues of genuine importance generated meaningful divisions and gave a "surprisingly democratic, even modern cast" to politics.[52] Public-policy questions of sufficient moment significantly affected voter behavior. The electorate was an important variable in government. Colonial political life may not have been democratic, but it did stimulate a political process characterized by frequent elections, competition for office, development of issues, and exposure of official conduct to public scrutiny. Government was not just a matter of administration by "the better sort." Through political activity, the notion of responsible government, responsive to an enlarged and critical public, was gaining ground.

If colonial political life was based on an unusually broad and active electorate, it found its expression in those constituted bodies that actually governed. On the provincial level, the most important of these was the colonial assembly, the focal point of colonial political activity and the central concern of political ideologues. The assemblies represented the voice of the people in the government itself, guarding popular rights and properties and preventing

---

50. Ibid.

51. Billias, *The Massachusetts Land Bankers of 1740*, 42.

52. For a comparison of the origins and divergent concepts of the representative function, see J.R. Pole's "Magistracy, Community, and the Social Order: The Responsibilities of Representation," in *The Seventeenth Century: The Sources of Legislative Power* (Charlottesville, Virginia: The University Press of Virginia, 1969), 50–69.

the executive from overstepping constitutional authority. The assemblies were looked upon as the mediating force between the "rulers" and the "ruled." But representatives were also quasi magistrates. Once elected they were, as a part of the government, rulers worthy of respect and deference. The only check upon abuse of authority was the electoral process itself. In the power to vote, the people retained some ability to pass upon the performance of their deputies. Thus, colonial constitutional ideology consisted of a series of checks—that of the legislature upon the executive and that of the people upon their delegates. Colonial political and social thought was essentially adversarial: the few checked the one, and the many checked the few.

Here again the reality of colonial politics differed from prevailing notions of what political life should be about. If theory posited a politics of popular deference to the wisdom of society's natural leaders, the practice of representative politics was much more assertive, interest-oriented, and independent. As Bernard Bailyn has shown, the tradition of requiring deputies to represent the expressed wishes of the community in the legislature—or pay the price of subsequent repudiation by the voters—goes back to the medieval notion of attorneyship: the legislator was a spokesman for the people who had deputized the legislator to plead their cause before the King. A delegate was not a free agent sent to legislate according to his conscience.[53] At a time when the role of the English parlimentarian was moving closer to the latter, more modern definition of the representative function, the Americans were in the process of resurrecting the older view of the delegate as advocate.[54] During the crisis of the Revolution, these opposite interpretations of the legislator's role were to achieve a clear-cut definition: *virtual representation* (the English view) versus *actual representation* (the American view).[55] However, it is clear that the ideologues of the Revolution merely conceptualized the role of the people's deputy as it had come to be known through the collective experience of most of the mainland provinces.

---

53. Bernard Bailyn, *The Ideological Origins of the American Revolution* (Cambridge, MA: Harvard University Press, 1967), 162–164 (mid-eighteenth century view of the representative functions of democracy).
54. Ibid., 164–167.
55. Ibid., 167–171.

Colonial legislative representation was characterized by residency requirements—a deputy normally had to live, or at least own property, in the district he represented; by "binding instructions"—a deputy was told what course of policy he was to pursue, at first only with regard to local issues, then on public questions of intercolonial concern; by accountability—a deputy's performance in the legislature was measured by the extent of his adherence to his instructions.[56] As stated in Chapter 35 of the *West New Jersey Concessions and Agreements*:

> That the said Proprietors and Freeholders at their choice of persons to serve them in the Generall and Free Assemblys of the Province give their Respective Deputies or Trustees their instructions at large to represent their grievances or for the improvement of the Province and that the persons chosen doe by indentures under hand and seale Covenant and oblidge themselves to act nothing in that capacity but what shall tend to the fitt service and behoofe of those that send and employ them and that in case of failer of trust or breach of Covenant that they be questioned upon complaint made in that or the next Assembly by any of their respective Electors.[57]

To be sure, these elements of the representative function were not universal. The residency requirements obtained in only nine of the mainland colonies; the practice of instructing deputies seems to have been articulated earliest in New England and was less well established in the Middle and Southern Colonies. Yet, even in Virginia, where politics was more staid, where traditional behavioral norms survived longest, and where the politics of deference was more deep-rooted because of the relative stability and homogeneity of the ruling gentry—even in Virginia, a growing effort to

---

56. Gordon S. Wood, *The Creation of the American Republic, 1776–1787* (Chapel Hill, NC: North Carolina University Press, 1969), 173–196. This text traces the shift of American thinking, clarifying collective thought regarding the period of the Revolution lasting until the ratification of the Constitution.
57. Boyd, "Concessions and Agreements of West New Jersey," 96, (referencing the original text of the *Concessions and Agreements*, Ch. XXXV (1677), For more on the study of suffrage reform in New Jersey see J.R. Pole's "Suffrage Reform and the American Revolution in New Jersey," *New Jersey Historical Society Proceedings*, No. LXXIV (1956): 172–94.

bind the delegate to the wishes of his constituents was discernible.[58] The question was debated in the House of Burgesses in 1754.[59] As Landon Carter, a leader of the Virginia gentry, defined it, the issue was "whether a representative was obliged to follow the directions of his constituents against his own reason and conscience or to be governed by his conscience."[60] However, for the most part, Virginians continued to reject the practice of instructing delegates at least until the Revolution. "Instruction was hardly compatible with deference."[61]

In another important way, colonial representative assemblies reflected the activism and assertiveness of American politics. In comparison with the English Parliament, the lower houses of assembly were fairly well apportioned according to population. Until the end of the colonial period, the Board of Trade made no serious effort to restrict their size. As a result, new towns in New England and new counties elsewhere continued to gain representation in the assemblies to the extent desired without much difficulty. Studies of Massachusetts, New York, New Jersey, Pennsylvania, and Virginia show that legislatures were fairly well apportioned.[62] Indeed, direct representation of specific property interests—as opposed to numerical and regional representation— appears to have emerged only later and as a consequence of conservative fears for the rights of property excited by the passions of the Revolution.

The very character of the colonial assembly (its *representativeness*) and the nature of the colonial legislator's function (to be an *advocate* for his constituency) explains why, in most colonies, political activity concentrated on the legislature. Legislators were close to the people. Assemblies contained elements from the different sections of each province. Where regional, economic, ethnic, or religious differences were sharp—as they were in New York, Pennsylvania, and Massachusetts—these differences were reflected in the political struggles for membership in, and control of, the provincial legislatures. Where, on the other hand, a colony,

---

58. Sydnor, *Gentlemen Freeholders: Political Practices in Washington' Virginia,* 94–111.
59. Lucille Griffith, *The Virginia House of Burgesses, 1750–1774,* rev. ed. (Birmingham, AL: University of Alabama Press, 1968), 22–28.
60. Ibid., 65–74.
61. Ibid., 64–65.
62. Bailyn, *The Ideological Origins of the American Revolution,* 162–165.

however large, had an undifferentiated economy and a relatively homogenous population—as in Virginia—political activity in the legislature was less likely to be unhinged by permanent factions separated by difference on fundamental issues. There, personal rivalries and transitory squabbles—surface divisions—tended to be the rule. But most assemblies in the generation before the Revolution, were not as tranquil as the Virginia House of Burgesses. Society in most of the mainland provinces in the late colonial period was increasingly fractured by class polarization, religious feuds, ethnic suspicions, and economic competition among rival interests. Social diversification was reflected in political life. Political factionalism was becoming the most salient feature of American politics.

The emphasis upon factional as opposed to class antagonisms is one of the trademarks of recent colonial historiography. Richard Buel, Jr. refers to the "seething factionalism of provincial politics."[63] Bernard Bailyn writes of "chaotic factionalism," which he explains as follows:

> There was bitter, persistent strife within the provincial governments almost everywhere. There was strife, first of all, between branches of government—between the executives on the one hand and the legislatures on the other—strife so rampant as to be more noteworthy by its absence than its presence and so intense as to lead on occasions to a total paralysis of the government. But it was not only a matter of conflict between branches of government. There was, besides this, a milling factionalism that transcended institutional boundaries and at times reduced the politics of certain colonies to an almost unchartable chaos of competing groups.[64]

---

63. Richard Buel, Jr., "Democracy and the American Revolution: A Frame of Reference," *William and Mary Quarterly*, 3rd Ser., Vol. 21 (1964): 167. Here, the author places emphasis on the importance of the representative assembly as a kind or arbiter between rulers that ruled; explaining that votes had little opportunity to initiate policy and only enough power to keep their elected representatives in check.
64. Bernard Bailyn, *Origins of American Politics* (New York: Vintage Books, 1967), 63–64. Bailyn establishes the ideological context in which colonial politics can be understood, but also details the political situation in the provinces in the pre-Revolutionary period.

In short, colonial Americans were—to use a phrase that Patricia Bonomi has applied to New York, but which has even more general utility—a "factious people."[65]

Evidence of this factiousness is to be found in the growing body of detailed political studies of individual colonies. Reviewing this literature in a very comprehensive essay, Jack P. Greene established a working "typology of political forms" that put the discrete experiences of the separate provinces into a comparative perspective.[66] Greene described four descriptive categories or models: (1) *chaotic factionalism*—a political condition noted by shifting and evanescent alliances among competing groups; (2) *stable* factionalism—on-going rivalry among more permanently divided elements; (3) *domination by a single, unified* group—interludes of relative calm brought about by the emergence of a ruling elite that effectively curbed factional forces; and (4) *faction-free, with a maximum dispersal of political opportunity within the dominant group*—a variation of category three wherein competition was kept within the confines of a large, open, and relatively homogeneous oligarchy rooted in a stable and well-integrated social substructure.[67] According to Greene, individual colonies did not adhere to only one of these models but often shifted from one to another. For example, before the abrogation of its charter in 1684, the pattern of politics in Massachusetts is best described by model three; from 1634 until the Land Bank controversy and the ascendency of William Shirley in 1741, by model one; from 1741 until 1760, factionalism in Massachusetts again was held in check; and, from 1760 until the Revolution, the pre-existing, single-group dominance gave way to the stable factionalism of model two. What is significant in Greene's analysis, in addition to its originality and broad focus, is the substitution of faction for class as the major analytical device for comprehending colonial politics. According to this scheme, the presence (or, for that matter, the absence) of faction became the central feature of the colonial political experience.

The causes of faction in colonial America were many. In addition to the regional, economic, and ethnic divisions, faction resulted

---

65. For more on the notion of a "factious people," refer to Patricia U. Bonomi's *A Factious People: Politics and Society in Colonial America* (New York: Columbia University Press, 1971).
66. Greene, "Changing Interpretations of Early American Politics," 151–184.
67. Ibid.

when political weakness at the executive level stimulated a struggle for power in the assembly among society's elite, itself a shifting group of competing claimants for social and political pre-eminence. The assemblies not only seized prerogatives traditionally assigned to the executive, but they also granted favors in the distribution of land, awarded contracts for the construction of internal improvements, allotted privileges and monopolies, and regulated economic activity and trade. As new communities, the needs were great. In satisfying those needs, the assemblies had to expand the scope of governmental functions beyond traditional limits, thereby increasing legislative competence and the stakes of politics.

Political factionalism was widespread in colonial America. Historiographical efforts to explain its causes have deepened our understanding of the structure of colonial politics, the forces that propelled it, and the way politicians worked. However, political activity was not accepted as part of the normative processes of government in the well ordered state. Rather it was the sign of division and disaffection, a sign of a lapse in government itself. Politics was not, as in modern political culture, an integral part of constitutional government; it was its antithesis. The idea that government was a prize to be fought for by contentious groups was opposed to the purposes for which government was established. Government was the embodiment as well as the servant of society. Its chief end was the promotion of the common good or commonwealth. As the Reverend John Wise put it in his searching essay, *Vindication of the Government of New England Churches,* in 1717:

> A Civil State is a Compound Moral Person whose Will (united by those covenants before passed) is the Will of all; to the end it may Use, and Apply the strength and riches of Private Persons towards Maintaining the Common Peace, Security, and Well-being of all. Which may be conceived as tho' the whole State was now become but one Man.[68]

Representation was desirable precisely because it improved the chances that government would encompass and comprehend the interests, and thus the good, of all. This dominant ideology did not allow for the participation of particular groups, or "parties," in

---

68. John Wise, *Vindication of the Government of New England Churches* (Boston, MA: Congregational Board of Publication, 1860), 40.

government itself. For particularism was opposed to the general good. To introduce particularity, whether in the form of faction or of special interest, was to inject into the very councils of the state those noxious poisons that would open the body politic to the infection of private tyranny. As William Livingston put it in his essay on parties in the *Independent Reflector* (1753):

> Unspeakably calamitous have been the Consequences of Party Division. It has occasioned Deluges of Blood, and subverted Kingdoms. It always introduces a Decay of publick Spirit, with the Extinction of every noble and generous Sentiment. The very Names of Things are perverted. On Fury and Violence it bestows the Appellation of Magnanimity and Opposition, and stiles Resentment and Rancour, Heroic Ardor, and Patriot-Warmth. Nor is it ever at a Loss for Pretences to bubble the Mob out of their Wits, and give its wildest Ravings a plausible Colour.[69]

Party and faction were a blight. Outside the government, they fomented discord; inside, corruption and tyranny. The well ordered polity was free of "party spirit."[70]

However, despite this prevailing antiparty ideology, colonial politics was riven with passionate political controversy. In almost every colony, "factions" were the most visible feature of the political landscape.[71] They badgered well-meaning governors on almost every issue of substance. Those public matters requiring legislative consideration and concurrence, such as tax policy, appropriations, fee schedules, salaries, the establishment of courts of justice, and the regulation of the militia, usually elicited vigorous public debate. Factions representing different groups and opposing points of view were strongest in legislative halls and assemblies. Governors decried the "baneful effects of the spirit of party," but they, in their turn, had to join one of the existing groups or else organize a "governor's party" to counteract this pernicious influence.[72]

---

69. Livingston, "Of Party Divisions," 140–148.
70. Ibid. For a discussion of the growing trends that reject eighteenth-century political judgments, claiming that factions betokened lack of political development, refer to Patricia U. Bonomi's *A Factious People: Politics and Society in Colonial America* (New York: Columbia University Press, 1971).
71. Ibid.
72. Ibid.

This peculiar discrepancy between an antiparty, antifaction ideology and a well-developed, rapidly maturing, and highly volatile political life could not last indefinitely. Political activity was inevitable, given the nature of colonial institutions, the fairly wide exercise of the franchise, the comparative openness of American society to political ambition, and the ever increasing size of the representative assemblies—that natural breeding ground for political controversy and division.

As a result, the conventional wisdom was becoming less and less relevant to the realities of eighteenth-century political life. The first fissures in the wall of ideological orthodoxy were at least visible near the end of colonial times. Wherever faction enlivened politics, people were forced to confront the discrepancy between a prevailing anti-party ideology and the on-going existence and utility of party and faction in daily political life. Indeed, it was in those very provinces where factionalism was most pervasive that the illogic of the conventional wisdom concerning politics was first perceived.

Not surprisingly, one of the earliest manifestations of a new concept of oppositional politics appeared in the *New York Weekly Journal* at a time when its illustrious printer, John Peter Zenger, was in jail awaiting trial. A lead article on March 17, 1734, began with a firm acknowledgment of the conventional wisdom:

> Factions and Parties in a State, or any other Society, are no Doubt very pernicious. . . . He must therefore have very little public Spirit, or even Humanity, who . . . fully either kindles or foments such cruel Disorders in his Country.[73]

Clearly, the speaker—probably the editor, James Alexander—agreed that political faction was evil, and that society ought to be rid of it. However, the remaining portions of the essay are more enigmatic; essentially, they modify the initial theme:

> But however inconsistent with Goodness and Virtue, it is to take a Pleasure in the Divisions of Ones Country, or to be active in the Promoting of them we ought not to extend this so far as some do, who upon such Occurences give Themselves Airs of being

---

73. Editorial, *New York Weekly Journal* March 17, 1734, 1.

> intirely distinterested, and disclaim all Attachment to any of the contending Parties in a State.[74]

Party may be bad, but it is not the worst of evils. To feign disinterest while pursuing party purposes is to aggravate the bad effects of political division:

> It may therefore be of some Use to enquire, how far an honest Man in a Time of public Dissentions ought to embark in them, and take part in the Debates relating to them, so as to discover his Opinions and Inclinations for one Party or Principle more than another.[75]

Better to own up to one's particular position than to dissemble. What was there to hide? After all, each conceives his own cause to be good, not evil:

> If we are engaged in a good Cause, and I fancy no Man willingly espouses what he thinks a bad one, what should make us either ashamed or afraid of owning our Affection for it?[76]

Moreover, not only is it better to declare one's position openly; it may be unrealistic to suppose that a disinterested position is possible:

> . . . it is impossible for a Man who converses at all in the Wourld, to conceal his Sentiments about any Maner of Importence which happens to be agitated in it. And therefore none should aim at a Qualification which cannot be attained without impairing their Virtue.[77]

The *Weekly Journal* did not state that "party spirit" was good, only that "public spirit" may not be possible and that it is better to air the diversity of views than to attempt to disguise them behind

74. Ibid.
75. Ibid.
76. Ibid., 2.
77. Ibid.

masks of pretended virtue.[78] Man has the right "freely to examine and debate all matters either in Philosophy or Religion."[79]

Two other examples are illustrative of this new trend of thought. Both are products of the cacophonous 1750s. One is an outgrowth of the fight in New York over the establishment of King's College as an Anglican school; the other, the result of William Smith's paper war against the Quakers in Pennsylvania.[80] In his essay on parties in the *Independent Reflector,* William Livingston managed to stake out new ground after reiterating the standard conventions of his time. In its concluding portion, Livingston went on to argue that harmony in government *was not* a sign that all was well in the well-ordered state:[81]

> It must after all be allowed, that a long and uninterrupted Calm in a Government divided into separate Branches, for a Check on each other, is often presumptive, that all Things do not go well. Such is the restless and aspiring Nature of the human Mind, that a Man intrusted with Power, seldom contents himself with his due Proportion. For this Reason, an unremitted Harmony between several Persons created as a Counterpoize to each other, is suspicious. Their Union may be the Consequence of their keeping within their proper Limits, and it may be the Effect of an iniquitous Coalition.[82]

From here, Livingston proceeds to draw out the implications of this logic. If a false tranquility in government may camouflage hidden motives and sinister designs, then healthy conflict and vigorous dissent in society at large may better preserve the liberty of the subject:

---

78. Ibid.
79. Ibid., 2–3.
80. Milton M. Klein, "Democracy and Politics in Colonial New York," *New York History,* No. XL (1959), 221–246.
81. Livingston, "Of Party Divisions," 146; Buel, Jr., "Democracy and the American Revolution: A Frame of Reference," 169. In reference to voting themes and political favoritism in early New York colonial politics, see the descriptive and informative work of Stanley N. Katz, *Newcastle's New York: Anglo-American Politics, 1732–1753* (Cambridge, MA: Harvard University Press, 1968).
82. Ibid., 146–147. For more information, see Lokken, "The Concept of Democracy in Colonial Political Thought," 568–580.

> To infer, therefore, that the Liberties of the People are safe and unindanger'd, because there are no political Contests, is illogical and fallacious. Such a Tranquility may be the Result of a Confederacy in Guilt, and an Agreement between the Rulers to advance their private Interest, at the Expence of the People. But this can never be our Case. Agreeable to the generous Spirit of our Constitution, we have a Right to examine into the Conduct and Proceedings of our Superiors; and upon discovering them in a Combination of Roguery, if we cannot set them together by the Ears, we can form a Party against their united Strength: And such a Party, I hope we may never want the Spirit to form. To conclude, shou'd a future Governor give into Measures subversive of our Liberties, I hope he will meet with proper Opposition and Controul.[83]

Thus, the evil spirit of party might capture men in government as well as men outside of it. The separation of the branches of government was not an ironclad warranty against such an occurrence. Consequently, the formation of a party outside the government to counteract factious elements within was justified. The Fathers of the Republic would later compose, in Richard Hofstadter's efficient phrase, a "Constitution against parties;" the principal device they would employ to render party useless was to be the Separation of Powers, the fundamental structural foundation of the Constitution of the United States.[84] Only afterward would it be realized that separated powers were not sufficient, and that party was a vital extra-constitutional check upon the abuse of power by government. William Livingston's prophetic essay, written in 1753, anticipated this realization by at least half a century.

Another essay by Smith, "On the good and ill Effects of civil DISSENTION," published in the very first edition of the *American Magazine and Monthly Chronicle* (1757–1758), justified in advance the oppositional stance that that periodical would assume during its brief career. It also mirrored the growing awareness of the existence of party and faction and the need to legitimize the

---

83. Ibid.

84. This theme may be found in more detail in the discussion of American party evolution in Richard Hofstader's *The Idea of a Party System: The Rise of Legitimate Opposition in the United States, 1780–1840* (Berkeley, CA: University of California Press, 1969).

reality of political conflict. As the "Planter" argued in a bold formulation of the new theory:

> . . . political evil, internal discords, and civil commotions, which threaten the dissolution of a state, are frequently no more than the efforts of the constitution to expel certain noxious principles, and the proper effect of them is to establish the public weal in a more vigorous, regular and permanent state. . . . [H]appy is the state which is informed by it in the requisite degree. Its operation is salutary; and the consideration of this has often lighted up the hopes of the patriot.[85]

It is a brilliant statement. Faction is no longer the source of social decay but a sign of health—it is society purging itself of "noxious principles." Smith was suggesting that political dissent may not be merely an acceptable evil but a "salutary" and even necessary good if the public interest is to be made "vigorous, regular and permanent."

To be sure, political dissension had evil effects if pushed to extremes. Developing the medical metaphor, a favorite literary conceit of the period, Smith explained just why party could exist only to the "requisite degree:"

> . . . *Dissensions* in a state . . . are productive sometimes of good, sometimes of evil effects. They resemble a fever in the human body, the general intention of which is salutary; namely, by the increased action of the solids and fluids upon each other to expel the morbific matter, which has disordered the constitution, and to restore the animal machine to its wonted health and vigor. Yet such may be the violence of the conflict, as intirely to destroy the function of some principal organs; or, carried to a still greater height, to bring on a dissolution of the whole fabric.[86]

Smith did not completely abandoned the old ideology. Dissent, like fever, had bad as well as good effects. Nevertheless, Smith departed from the conventional wisdom in significant ways. He has recognized that political dissent and division would exist every-

---

85. William Smith, "To the Proprietor & Co., The Planter, No. 1," in *American Magazine and Monthly Chronicle for the British Colonies*, Vol. 1, William Bradford, ed. (Philadelphia, PA: The Society of Gentlemen, 1757), 33–38.
86. Ibid.

where. It was part of the design of God, Nature, and the Universe—indeed, dissension was as necessary to liberty as fever was to health, and as evil was to virtue:

> . . . collisions are more or less the fate of every State; that they discover the defects and weak sides of a government to those who had delayed repairing and fortifying them, for no other reason than that they had not before the same opportunity, of knowing them; that they give a clearer insight into the constitution, make people examine and understand their rights and liberties, and thereby teach them where to stand upon their guard against attacks from abroad, as well as the no less dangerous reforms of pretended patriots at home.[87]

The modalities of colonial political life were tied to the past. Politics was viewed in traditional terms: it was the conflict between the government and the governed. In the context of the Anglo-American world, this was perceived as a fundamental struggle between the royal prerogative and its colonial agents and surrogates, on the one side, and representative assemblies, on the other. The political conflicts that resulted from this polarization were not viewed as normative but as extraordinary conditions occasioned by disequilibrium among the branches of government. In the well-balanced state, politics was not only unnecessary, it was undesirable. At the time of the Revolution, many believed that, once the colonial governors were stripped of their arbitrary powers, the basis for further political conflict would dissolve and the long-sought unanimity of interest and opinion so fundamental to the commonwealth idea would finally be achieved. But the highly factious politics to be found in most colonies, some more than others, gave the lie to these traditional notions. Nor would political conflict diminish with the coming crisis of the Revolution; it would, in fact, intensify. And as it intensified, the anti-party ideology of the earlier period would become increasingly irrelevant to the emergent reality—now visible to all—of continuing and deepening party conflict.

The colonial political process consisted of many components: interest-group representation, deference toward popular opinion, the development of vote-getting procedures, and ideological

87. Ibid.

movement toward new concepts of oppositional politics. Political institutions—parties and factions, in particular—began to have a life of their own. Like modern political parties, the interest of party and faction began, in some places, to transcend the particular issues, personalities and interests that had given them birth. Recent emphasis on the pervasive the "politics of deference" in the late colonial period—a welcome reaction to the excessive claims of the "colonial democracy" school of historical thought—has partially obscured the vigor and the surprisingly mature state of development that colonial politics had reached. Long before the War of Independence, Americans had achieved political competence; the "public accepted the reality and pertinence of political conflict."[88] Not only did America *have* a political culture; increasingly, America *was* a political culture—discrete in its separate provincial parts but sharing common experiences; above all, sharp, often fierce, political battles resolved by political procedures of astonishing modernity.

88. Bailyn, *Origins of American Politics,* 63–64.

Nineteenth Century Episodes

Episode 5

Law in the New Republic

> The legitimate powers of government extend to such acts only as are injurious to others. But it does me no injury for my neighbor to say there are twenty gods, or no god. It neither picks my pocket nor breaks my leg.
>
> Thomas Jefferson, 1781

In the half century after the Revolution, America transformed itself from a British colony into an independent nation. From an economic appendage of the British mercantile system, America became a developing commercial power in its own right. This national achievement was impressive. Between 1776 and 1820 America fought two major wars, the war that achieved independence and the war that preserved it. American diplomats negotiated the Paris peace settlement in 1783, which capitalized on America's military successes in the Revolutionary War, and the Treaty of Ghent in 1815, which minimized American military losses in the War of 1812. In the turbulent years that followed the French Revolution and the rise of Napoleon Bonaparte, from 1789 to 1815, America maintained its neutrality for over twenty years. Thereafter, it asserted itself as an independent force in the Western Hemisphere. With the drafting of the Constitution and its subsequent ratification in 1787, the nation forged a new relationship among the several states and between the states and the central government. The United States government, a fledgling federal entity, developed viable domestic policies, a two-party system, and an enduring set of political institutions that were the foundation for permanent governmental stability.

During this time, the social and economic fabric of America passed through a rapid sequence of changes. When the shooting

---

* Source: Chapters 1–4, (1–47) in George Dargo, *Law in the New Republic: Private Law and the Public Estate* (New York: Alfred A. Knopf, 1983) (Borzoi Books in Law and American Society).

started on Lexington Green in the spring of 1775, the American colonies were isolated agricultural settlements clinging to the littoral edge of the vast North American continent. Communication was rudimentary, and inter-colonial transportation was dependent on coastal travel by sea. The vast majority of the American people were engaged in agricultural work. There was no national or "continental" economy, but rather a series of fragmented economic zones dependent on the English connection. Such credits in international exchange which the colonists did manage to earn resulted from the production of basic raw materials for export to European markets. Only four cities— Philadelphia, New York, Boston, and Charleston—had populations in excess of 10,000, and the populations were widely scattered by hundreds of miles. On the eve of the Revolution, total population was just over 2 million.

By 1820 the nation had grown enormously. Total population was approaching 10 million. Territorial acquisitions from the Treaty of Paris, the Louisiana Purchase, and various treaties and land cessions from Spain put the southern border of the United States on the Gulf of Mexico and its farthest northwestern reaches on the Pacific. Westward migration was well under way, and the land area east of the Mississippi River was settled, populated, and by 1822, divided into twenty-two separate states and two organized territories. Roads and canals had breached the major geographic land barriers and shortened distances. The first textile factories were already in operation, and steamboats plied the inland rivers. American banks serviced the commercial needs of farmers and townspeople alike while cities, growing rapidly, were beginning to encounter the social problems of modern urban life—crime, fire, and contagion. In short, by 1820 America had attained not only political independence, but considerable economic self-sufficiency and social development.

The conventional wisdom about America's early growth and development holds that the American Revolution, the separation from Great Britain, and the establishment of the federal system of government set loose a spirit of enterprise that was boundless in its ambition, awesome in its energy, and continental in its reach. That spirit was born out of the American passion for freedom, once it was released from the political and legal constraints of English mercantilism. However, in the 1940s and early 1950s, a small band of revisionist historians challenged this view. Sponsored by the Committee on Research in Economic History, and partly funded by the Social Science Research Council, these historians produced a body of work that had a profound impact on American historical writing. The revisionists focused their research on the role of governmental support in American economic development.[1]

The influence of the New Deal on the revisionist historians was clear. The 1930s had witnessed an unprecedented expansion of government intervention in the economy. The "regulatory state" had become a fact of American life. The New Deal transformed the American economic system into a mixed economy in which governmental management moderated the extreme fluctuations of the business cycle. These changes had not come about easily, and the political scars they had caused were still fresh in the 1940s when the work of the revisionist historians appeared.

The revisionists, although not ideological in a formal sense, were clearly sympathetic to the basic goals and methods of the Roosevelt administration. The results of their work, "a multi-pronged attack on the question of the influence of . . . government on the economy of the United States,"[2] was a series of impressive state studies that showed that government, particularly at the state and local levels, had played a crucial role in American economic growth from the very beginning.[3] As one sympathetic writer put it in the introduction to a book on Pennsylvania history: "On the basis of the evidence here presented it seems reasonable to conclude that governmental participation was as great, perhaps greater, in Pennsylvania in 1830 as in 1930, if one takes into account the scale and range of economic development."[4] Without conscious design, but with considerable effect, these post-New Deal historians

---

1. Oscar Handlin and Mary F. Handlin, *Commonwealth: A Study of the Role of Government in the American Economy: Massachusetts, 1774–1861* (rev. ed., Cambridge, MA: Harvard University Press, 1969), ix.
2. Ibid.
3. In addition to the Handlins' *Commonwealth*, these studies included Louis Hartz, *Economic Policy and Democratic Thought: Pennsylvania, 1776–1860* (Cambridge, MA: Harvard University Press, 1948); Milton S. Heath, *Constructive Liberalism: The Role of the State in Economic Development in Georgia to 1860* (Cambridge, MA: Harvard Univeristy Press, 1954); and Carter Goodrich, *Government Promotion of American Canals and Railroads* (New York, NY: Columbia University Press, 1960).
4. Benjamin F. Wright, "Foreward" in Hartz, *Economic Policy and Democratic Thought*, ix.

established the legitimacy of the New Deal program by demonstrating its source in the American past.

That it was legitimizing in no way diminished the value of the revisionist contribution to historical knowledge. Awareness of the important supportive role of state and local government in the formative era of America's commercial and industrial growth continues to be a vital corrective to simplistic formulations about "laissez faire," "private initiative," and the "genius of American private enterprise"—clichés that reinforce the mythology of American history—a harmless mythology in itself were it not for its abuse by those with a particular economic and political philosophy.

Some of the more extreme conclusions of the revisionist historians can be challenged. While acknowledging that government enterprise, public subsidies, land distribution policies, state construction of roads and canals, and tax, monetary, and tariff policies contributed substantially to the dramatic growth of the antebellum economy, we can point to the role of American law in sanctioning private decisions, private determinations of value, private standards of liability, and private agreements in American economic development. To that extent it undercuts the stress placed by the revisionists on the role of public law and public authority.

Are these real divergences of interpretation or merely matters of emphasis and focus? The revisionists analyzed the most visible examples of public policy, principally legislation and regulation. Their orientation was economic. Their research design, as they put it, "focused upon the role of government in the economy as the central subject of . . . investigation." Given such an orientation, it is not surprising that they found that "out of the Revolutionary era emerged a vigorous conception of the state."[5]

In contrast, if we draw upon the material of legal history, which focuses upon common law rather than statutes, courts rather than legislatures, and litigation rather than politics, we can pose new questions and see different perspectives. While there can be little doubt that government played a critical role in American economic development, the changes that were taking place in American law indicate that there was a decided movement in this period away

---

5. Handlin and Handlin, *Commonwealth*, preface to the first edition (1947).

from objective, external, and public values toward subjective standards and private decision making. The character of these deep changes in law and the legal system necessarily diminished the "public estate." Despite the acknowledged importance of public authority in fostering development and change, the legal system increasingly emphasized the private resolution of conflict. If the highest social imperative of the eighteenth century had been the pursuit of "public virtue"—a willingness of the individual to sacrifice private interest for the good of all—then the decline of the public estate in the nineteenth century represented a basic transformation in not only American culture, but also in the American republican experiment itself.[6]

The period did not simply see the establishment of a new relationship between government and society as suggested by the revisionists. Rather, it saw the emergence of that special reverence for the values, standards, goals, and claims of what has come to be called the "private sector." In that sense, the post-Revolutionary period anticipated future historical development to a surprising extent. It was a period in which the conflict between what is public and what is private first appeared, creating one of the most enduring tensions in American life.

We know that the Revolution ushered in a period of extraordinary legal activity, which required the participation of a whole new generation of lawyers. At the outset, they were not the best known, the most experienced, or even the ablest lawyers, since many of these sided with the Loyalists and eventually left the country.[7] Nevertheless, the Revolution was very much a "lawyers' revolution." Patriot lawyers played important roles at the state and continental levels of government. The attitudes, values, and institutional changes that emerged in the aftermath of the Revolu-

---

6. For a discussion of the concept of public virtue in the eighteenth century, see Gordon S. Wood, *The Creation of the American Republic, 1776–1787* (Chapel Hill, NC: University of North Carolina Press, 1969), 65–67.

7. A recent study of the American Loyalists concludes that while a majority of lawyers were Whig (i.e., Patriots), most of the leaders of the bar, the "giants of the law," remained loyal to the Crown. See Wallace Brown, *The King's Friends: The Composition and Motives of the American Loyalist Claimants* (Providence, RI: Brown University Press, 1965), 265. For a discussion of the impact of the Revolution upon the legal profession in one state see Gerard W. Gawalt, *The Promise of Power: The Emergence of the Legal Profession in Massachusetts, 1760–1840* (Westport, CT: Greenwood Press, 1979).

tion, and which continue to animate American public life to this day, were rooted in the legal traditions, common to this unique generation of legal professionals. But if the Revolution was a "lawyers' revolution," and if it did cause significant legal change in America, the changes were uneven affecting only some legal institutions and some areas of American law but not others.

One way of capturing that differentiation is to distinguish between public law and private law. The words "public" and "private" are generally used as opposites. "Private" means belonging to or concerning an individual person, company, or interest. "Public" pertains to the people as a whole—to the nation, state, or community at large. A law is private if it is in the interest of the individual, as distinguished from being for the benefit of the public. Public laws affect the community and all persons within the law's jurisdiction while private law is law that is enforced by individual actions on the basis of established legal doctrines securing private rights. Public law embraces those areas of law that spell out the powers and limitations of government (constitutional and administrative law), those wrongs that the state will prosecute and punish (criminal law), and the methods, processes, and procedures of the legal system itself (procedural law). Lawmaking by the agreement of private parties (contract law), laws that define injuries and wrongs of one party against another in the absence of contractual obligation (tort law), the body of law that establishes the rights, powers, and privileges as well as the duties, obligations, and responsibilities of those owning property (property law), and a host of other subjects (such as the law of agency, landlord and tenant; master and servant, family law; and commercial law) comprise the body of private law.[8]

The American Revolution had a deep, abiding, and immediate impact on American public law. In terms of private law, however, its effects were less dramatic and direct. Thus, while changes in American law and in the American legal system in the fifty years

---

8. Statues of general application are public laws, but private bills—those passed at the petition of individuals—are not. While statutes that have systematized large areas of commercial law, such as the modern Uniform Commercial Code, are part of public law, the body of substantive law thus codified and the continuing interpretation and construction of the UCC is the result of the litigation of private parties and is, to that extent, still part of private law.

following the Revolution were profound, those changes cannot be traced directly to the Revolution itself. What is striking is the strong continuity of private law in the revolutionary era. Private law was one of those social systems that resisted deep change.[9] To be sure, the law's evolution in the half-century following 1776 was very much the product of social forces that the Revolution had released. But the relationship between law and society is complex, and without more evidence, we cannot conclude that the American Revolution and the changing American legal system were directly connected in a relationship of cause and effect.

This uneven distribution of the reform impulse, as between public and private law, tells us something about the character of the Revolution itself and the rather narrow way Americans who supported the Revolution defined the liberties for which they fought. Their overwhelming desire was to contain and control political power and to protect private, local rights from governmental interference. The revolutionary generation wanted to circumscribe authority and to define precisely the legitimate functions of government. Consequently, constitutionalism stood at the very center of revolutionary agitation, and constitutional change was the most salient manifestation of the Revolution's effect on American law.[10] Viewing the Revolution retrospectively, the main legal event of the period was the gathering of the Philadelphia Convention of 1787 and the ratification conflict that followed. But for Americans living at the time, the federal structure and the powers of the central government, although important, were questions of far less significance than the constitutional foundations of those governments closest to the people—namely, the states.

On May 10, 1776, almost two months before the Second Continental Congress declared that the North American colonies

---

9. As one noted legal historian has concluded with reference to New England: "The War of Independence had virtually no effect upon the system of private law administered in New England." Richard B. Morris, "Legalism *versus* Revolutionary Doctrine in New England," *The New England Quarterly* 4 (1931): 195–215. For more on the subject, refer to Stanley N. Katz, "Republicanism and the Law of Inheritance in the American Revolutionary Era," *Michigan Law Review* 76 (1977): 1–29, which examines the modest impact of the Revolution on inheritance law.

10. Wood, Gordon S. *The Creation of the American Republic, 1776–1787,* Chaps. 4, 5, and 6.

(except for Quebec) were independent from Great Britain, the Congress resolved:

> that it be recommended to the respective assemblies and conventions of the United Colonies, where no governments sufficient to the exigencies of their affairs have been hitherto established, to adopt such government as shall, in the opinion of the representatives of the people, best conduce to the happiness and safety of their constituents in particular and America in general.[11]

From 1776 until nearly the end of the War of Independence, most of the states went through an intensive process of constitution-making. Some states even experienced a series of constitutional "revisions" in the course of just a few years as they experimented with various forms of government and different processes of constitutional adoption.[12]

So central was this preoccupation with constitution-making that it at times interfered with the war effort. For example, in 1777, the New York delegation to the Continental Congress, then meeting in Philadelphia, complained that:

> tho' the Enemy is daily expected an astonishing Langour prevails, and the embodying a competent Force to oppose the meditated Invasion, seems to be a distant Object. The Seat of this Disease is not an Indifference to the Cause. . . . The unhappy Dispute about [the] Constitution is the fatal Rock on which [Pennsylvanians] have split . . . which threatens them with Destruction. We ardently wish that in our own State the utmost Caution may be used to avoid a like Calamity. Every wise Man here wishes that the Establishment of new Forms of Government had been deferred.[13]

---

11. Worthington C. Ford. Ed., *Journals of the Continental Congress, 1774–1789* (4 Vols., Washington, DC, 1904–1937), 342.
12. Willi Paul Adams, *The First American Constitutions: Republican Ideology and the Making of the State Constitutions in the Revolutionary Era* (Chapel Hill, NC: University of North Carolina Press, 1980); Elisha P. Douglass, *Rebels and Democrats: The Struggle for Equal Political Rights and Majority Rule during the American Revolution* (Chicago, IL: Elephant Paperbacks, 1965).
13. "Phillip Livingston, James Duane, and William Duer to Abraham Ten Broeck, (April 29, 1777)," in *Letters of Members of the Continental Congress*, E.C.

Robert Morris, chief financial officer of the Confederation, reported to General Horatio Gates that the entire Maryland delegation had gone home in order to participate in the formation of a state Constitution. "This seems to be the present business of all America, except the Army," he lamented.[14] As a Virginia delegate concluded regretfully: "Constitutions employ every pen."[15]

But if some members of the Continental Congress understandably saw things from the perspective of the military emergency, many other Americans viewed the constitution-making process much less casually. For them, this was what the Revolution was all about. If the results of independence were to be nothing more than the substitution of one form of oppressive government for another, then the effort was not worth making. Climactic moments in history are infrequent, but this was clearly one of them, and the moment had to be seized. An article in a Philadelphia newspaper printed on July 1, 1776, one day before independence was declared and three days before the Declaration of Independence was adopted, put it best:

> The affair now in view is the most important that ever was before America. In my opinion it is the most important that has been transacted in any nation for some centuries past. If our civil Government is well constructed, and well managed, America bids fair to be the most glorious state that has ever been on earth. We should now at the beginning *lay the foundation right*. . . . The plan of American Government, should, as much as possible, be formed to suit all the varieties of circumstances that people may be in. . . . For we may expect a variety of circumstances in a course of time, and we should be prepared for every condition.[16]

How to "lay the foundation right" was, however, a source of bitter dispute and continuing conflict. The issues were many, some procedural and others substantive. On the procedural side, a much debated question was whether state legislatures or the people, acting directly through special constitutional conventions, should draft constitutional instruments. The latter was a novel idea, and,

---

Burnett, ed. (Washington, DC: Carnegie Institution of Washington, 1921–1936), vol. 2, 344.

14. Morris to Gates, (October 27, 1776), Ibid., 135.

15. F.L. Lee to Landon Carter, (November 9, 1776), Ibid., 149.

16. Pennsylvania Packet (July 1, 1776) (emphasis added); Wood, *The Creation of the American Republic*, 127–132, et passim.

like most truly revolutionary ideas, it was not immediately accepted. The Town Meeting of Concord, Massachusetts, stated the problem with penetrating clarity:

> [If] the same body that forms a Constitution have of consequence a power to alter it [then there is no security for liberty] because a Constitution alterable by the Supreme Legislature is no security at all to the subject against any encroachment of the governing part on any, or on all of their rights and privileges.[17]

If the legislature had the power to draft and adopt a constitution then there would be no true difference between an ordinary statute and fundamental law. The constitution had to be kept safe from legislative tampering and interference. The most effective way to achieve such a goal was to call into being a special body whose sole purpose was the adoption of a constitution. Once adopted, the body would dissolve forever. A constitutional convention fit that purpose, for it was not a continuing body, but a special institution organized for a special purpose.[18]

Substantive issues such as the structure of government, the powers of the different branches of government, and the relations between local and central authority were the most vexing. There was deep division between "radicals" who wanted to give maximum authority to the people and "conservatives" who preferred to limit popular sovereignty as much as possible.[19] Included on the radical agenda for constitutional change were the following: (1) the reduction of the role and power of "governors" to that of mere

---

17. Massachusetts (State) Archives, Vol. 156, 167; Robert J. Taylor, ed., *Massachusetts Colony to Commonwealth: Documents on the Formation of its Constitution, 1775–1780* (New York: W.W. Norton & Co., 1972), 45–46.
18. While a minority of the states used the convention device either as part of the drafting process or as part of ratification, the federal Constitution of 1787 was both proposed and ratified by the convention method. Thus, the process of federal constitution-making was truly innovative, even radical, in its time. Contemporary critics—and liberal historians—focused more upon the conservative substance of the Constitution than the manner of its adoption. See Richard Hofstadter, *The Progressive Historians: Turner, Beard, Parrington* (New York: Knopf, 1968), Chaps. 5–6; Charles A. Beard, *An Economic Interpretation of the Constitution of the United States* (New York: The MacMillan Company, 1913); and Wood, *The Creation of the American Republic,* Chap. 12.
19. Adams, *The First American Constitutions,* Chaps. 6–13; Douglass, *Rebels and Democrats,* passim.

"executives;" (2) a provision for legislative impeachment for "executive maladministration;" (3) frequent elections of representatives to the state legislatures; (4) the substitution of residency for property tests in setting voting requirements; (5) separation of the powers of the three functional branches of government to reduce executive influence; and (6) unicameralism in the legislative branch. The most extreme example of radical constitutionalism was the Pennsylvania Constitution of 1776, which completely eliminated a single chief executive, established a unicameral legislature, and set up a procedure for periodic revision of the state's constitution.[20]

On the other hand, conservatives wanted: (1) to maintain property qualifications for voting and for office holding; (2) bicameral legislatures so that each branch would serve as a check on the other; and (3) an increase of the power of the executive to counteract the excesses of runaway popular legislatures. While radicals wanted the executives to be chosen by and responsible to the legislatures, conservatives preferred to have the executives elected on their own so that they would have an independent power base that would enable them to withstand legislative "encroachment."[21] Above all, conservatives advocated judicial review of legislative action by an independent judiciary.

The constitutional convention idea, while innovative and even revolutionary in concept, was also part of the conservative program. Putting the constitution-making process into the hands of the people was one way of keeping it from the legislatures. Conservatives playing on fears of "legislative tyranny" emphasized the distinction between "ordinary law" and "fundamental law." They supported this distinction by giving the people the power to declare the fundamental law in the form of a written constitution and by giving the courts the function of preserving the distinction through the exercise of the power of judicial review.

The first suggestion that courts should exercise some power of review over legislative enactments came from the conservative camp. New York established a Council of Revision, consisting of the highest executive and judicial officers of the state, whose job it

---

20. Ibid., Chap. 14.
21. Wood, *The Creation of the American Republic*, Chap. 2.

was to review the acts of the legislature.[22] The New York Constitution of 1777—in which the constitutional powers of the governor were unusually broad—was a victory for constitutional conservatism. As such, it served as a model for the framers of the federal constitution in the design of the office of the presidency.[23] The creation at the national level of a powerful chief executive chosen by a special electoral college, rather than by Congress or the state legislatures directly, can be fairly interpreted as a conservative triumph.

On some constitutional issues there was little disagreement between radicals and conservatives. All agreed that a written constitution was preferable to England's unwritten constitution. Americans believed that fixed principles of government were among the immutable "laws of nature."[24] The task of political theorists was to discover those fixed principles while the task of political activists was to implement those principles in the day to day work of governance. The strength of the English constitution lay in its fluidity and its responsiveness to political change, while the strength of American constitutionalism was the detachment of day-to-day politics from those timeless truths about government that needed to be preserved for all time.

In the development of an "American jurisprudence" responsive to the special circumstances of American life, legislative bodies and courts of law had to mold both statutory law and case law to the standard of a written constitution. American law in this formative period of its modern growth was rooted in two very different sources. The first was a positivist tradition, going back to the colonial period, which stood for the proposition that law was primarily an instrument to be used to meet societal demands and exigent circumstances. The second source was a natural-law tradition embodied in the written constitutionalism of the revolu-

---

22. Francis Newton Thorpe, ed., *Federal and State Constitutions*, Vol 5 (Washington, DC: Government Printing Office, 1909); E. Wilder Spaulding, *New York in the Critical Period, 1783–1789* (New York, NY: Columbia University Press, 1932, 1963), Chap. 5.

23. Compare *New York Constitution,* 1771: Arts. XVII and XVIII; with *U.S. Constitution,* 1777: Art. II.

24. George Dargo, "Parties and the Transformation of the Constitutional Idea in Revolutionary Pennsylvania," in *Party and Political Opposition in Revolutionary America,* P.U. Bonomi, ed. (Tarrytown, NY: Sleepy Hallow Press, 1980), 110.

tionary period itself, which held that there were certain fundamental principles or laws of nature which antedated the legal regime and to which statutes and judicial decisions had to conform. Constitutions were enacted to codify these antecedent natural laws and natural-rights principles, and lawmakers and judges were bound within this constitutional framework.[25]

These ideas were codified in constitutional provisions that defined the constitution as law. The Massachusetts Constitution of 1780 put it this way:

> This form of government shall be enrolled on parchment, and deposited in the Secretary's office, *and be a part of the laws of the land;* and printed copies thereof shall be prefixed to the book containing the laws of this Commonwealth, in all future editions of the said laws.[26]

The notion of written charters having the force and effect of law was not new to Americans. Ever since early colonial times, "charters," "compacts," "orders," "liberties," and "agreements" had been recognized as having legal force.[27] But if these were not new ideas, the Revolution gave them special force and powerful articulation. The use of written constitutions as law was, and remains, a uniquely American contribution to the development of modern government. In contrast, the French drafted a series of written constitutions during the French Revolution, but these were little more than frames of government, constitutional blueprints, and statements of political purpose—not enforceable legal tools. In America, constitutions had legal authority to which all other law had to conform. As declared by the Massachusetts Constitution of 1780:

> [F]ull power and authority are hereby given and granted to the said General Court, from time to time, to make, ordain, and establish, all manner of wholesome and reasonable orders, laws, statutes, and ordinances, directions and instructions, either with

---

25. Wood, *The Creation of the American Republic*, 291–305.
26. *Massachusetts Constitution*, 1780: Chap. VI, Art. XI (emphasis added).
27. George Dargo, *Roots of the Republic: A New Perspective on Early American Constitutionalism* (New York: Praeger, 1974), Chap. 3.

> penalties or without; *so as the same be not repugnant or contrary to this Constitution.*[28]

Provisions of this kind were significant for two reasons. First, and most important, they made constitutional guarantees of personal liberty enforceable in the courts. In many states these were called "bills of rights."[29] Second, they laid the basis for judicial review. While some would argue that "nonrepugnancy" clauses—such as the Massachusetts provision cited above—were not a justification for court review of legislative enactments, particularly in the absence of specific constitutional authorization, it was surely inevitable that high appellate courts would use the written constitution to monitor the decisions of lower courts within their jurisdictions. Thus, while the broad reach of John Marshall's decision in *Marbury* v. *Madison*,[30] outraged many, who labeled it "judicial usurpation," some sort of special constitutional role was bound to be played by the courts in a system with a written constitution defined as law.[31]

In the end, the idea of a written constitution appealed to radicals and conservatives alike, in different ways. Radicals liked it because it made legally enforceable such individual rights as religious freedom, security from unlawful arrest, and the right of peaceable assembly and petition. Conservatives favored the idea because it secured the right to property and was a potential basis for exercising the power of judicial review, a power that state as well as federal courts began to exercise with increasing frequency in the decades following the Revolution. Contemporaries perceived the Pennsylvania constitution of 1776, with its unicameral legislature and its plural executive, as the most "radical" of the state constitutions. The New York constitution of 1777, on the other hand, was thought to be a model of "conservatism" because of the great power of the governor's office and the establishment of a special body, the Council of Revision, to review acts of the legislative branch. In

---

28. *Massachusetts Constitution,* 1780: Chap. I, Art, IV (emphasis added).
29. See e.g., *Virginia Declaration of Rights* (1776.)
30. 5 U.S. (1 Cranch) 137 (1803).
31. For a discussion of judicial review and the intent of the framers, see Raoul Berger, *Congress* v. *The Supreme Court* (Cambridge, MA: Harvard University Press, 1969), Chap. 7.

fact, almost every state constitution contained some elements of both the "radical" and the "conservative" program. But this should not be surprising since state constitutions were usually adopted after political conflict and debate usually resulting in compromise and accommodation.

The United States Constitution, drafted and ratified by Federalists[32] (who were seen as "rich and well-born") and opposed by Antifederalists (who had a reputation for radicalism) contained within it some aspects of the radical program. These radical elements (representation by population in the House of Representatives, congressional control over military budgets, the power to impeach, the machinery for amendment, specific enumeration of legislative powers, the reservation of powers to the states, and, eventually, the adoption of a federal Bill of Rights) showed the impact of radical thought at the federal level. But conservatives could also claim victories—a bicameral Congress, a powerful chief executive, an independent federal judiciary, the equality of the House and Senate, and a prohibition on state legislative impairment of private contractual obligations.

However, in the federal Constitution there was also one overriding concept on which both radicals and Conservatives could agree, each for their own separate reasons. This was the Supremacy Clause in Article VI, which can be thought of as the single most important provision of the original Constitution of the United States as drafted at the Philadelphia Convention in the summer of 1787:

> This Constitution, and the laws of the United States which shall be made in pursuance thereof, and all treaties made, or which shall be made, under the authority of the United States, shall be the *supreme law of the land* And the Judges in every State shall be bound thereby, *anything in the Constitution or laws of any State to the contrary notwithstanding.*[33]

---

32. The term "federalist" was used in the 1780s to denote strong nationalistic proclivities while the term "antifederalist" referred to that political persuasion which would preserve the sovereignty of the states. These terms should not be confused with the Federalist Party and the Jeffersonian opposition which grew out of the policies of the Washington administration in the early 1790s.
33. *U.S. Constitution*, 1787: Art. VI (emphasis added).

The Supremacy Clause was principally designed to give effect to nationalists like John Jay, Alexander Hamilton, Gouverneur Morris, and George Washington. The Clause bound the states into an organic nation under one supreme law that would be applied by national (or "federal") courts. But in the context of the whole constitutional movement, state as well as federal, the Supremacy Clause had independent and additional significance. It is the element that most distinguished the Constitution of the United States from the Articles of Confederation that was finally ratified in 1781. In giving the Constitution the force of law, the framers created an instrument of government comparable to state constitutions. The Constitution was no mere "league of friendship"[34] among the several states, but a true government of great potentiality. In that respect, the Constitution's opponents, who feared the enhanced power of the central government, were right to clamor for limitations on the national authority—a clamor that led to the adoption of the federal Bill of Rights.[35] The Supremacy Clause made the guarantees codified in the Bill of Rights legally enforceable limitations, first on Congress and, much later, on government at every level.

For all of its economy of statement, therefore, the United States Constitution was extraordinary in its scope. It bound the states as well as the national government into a union of law, and it made the government of the United States truly a "government of laws and not of men." The innovations in constitutional government at the state and national levels represented the deepest, most enduring, and most important contribution the revolutionary generation made not only to America but to the political development of many new countries in the two centuries since 1776. The American colonial experience had taught that the exercise of public power, when unrestrained, was dangerous. Americans were more comfortable with private decision-making, and regarded the enhancement of private power as a necessary check on potential governmental abuse. This predilection resulted in the *privatization* of American law.[36]

---

34. See Worthington, *Journals of the Continental Congress,* 342.
35. Alpheus T. Mason, *The States Rights Debate: Antifederalism and the Constitution* (Englewood Cliffs, NJ: Prentice Hall, 1964), 1–7.
36. The concept of privatization is receiving much current attention both in legal and general literature. See John R. LeClaire, "Public Wealth, Privatization, and the

Privatization presupposes that all individuals are equal before the law, that the law is neutral, and that the good of all is best promoted by shifting power from public bodies to private, preferably individual, actors. However, in reality all individuals are not equal in relation to law, and collective action by individuals with common interests is inevitable. Privatization makes some sense in a perfectly individualized and atomized society, but in a society in which competing interests and pluralistic groupings jockey for power, privatization tends to create novel forms of unchecked authority.

Americans perceived the threat to liberty as largely a problem of public power, and the revolutionary generation had fashioned legal remedies to deal with that problem. But no similar sensitivity to the challenge of private power existed at the time of the Revolution. *Privatization* did extend the reach of human freedom in some respects, but in other respects it had the effect of desensitizing Americans to the dangers posed by a class system based on sharp inequalities of wealth and power. Such inequalities were already much in evidence by the end of the colonial period. For example, *privatization* manifested itself in liberalized procedures for personal manumission. Slave codes in most colonies made emancipation exceedingly difficult even for masters who wished to manumit their slaves by either *inter vivos* gift or by testamentary bequest. But after the Revolution, some slave codes were eased and increasing numbers of blacks achieved freedom through private acts of manumission.[37] Still, both in the North as well as the South, the law of slavery and freedom remained an area of primary concern to public law.

In the century following the Revolution, the problem of power and its control shifted from the public to the private sector. Social, commercial, and (eventually) industrial exploitation would replace political and legal oppression as the major challenge to personal freedom. Caught in the tension between positive law and natural law, between economic power and constitutional values, state legislatures required high appellate courts to give reasoned expla-

---

Constitution: The Alaska Example," *Boston University Law Review* 61 (1981): 969–1006; T. Ohashi and T. Roth, eds., *Privatization: Theory and Practice* (Vancouver, BC: Frasier Institute, 1980); Albert O. Hirschman, *Private Interest and Public Action* (Princeton, NJ: Princeton University Press, 1981).

37. Arthur Zilversmit, *The First Emancipation: The Abolition of Slavery in the North* (Chicago, IL: University of Chicago Press, 1967), 18, 122–124, 155–190.

nations of the logic that led to particular results in individual cases as these competing values and pressures came into conflict.

State legislatures also provided for the appointment of official court reporters to publish high court decisions for the guidance of lower courts and legal practitioners.[38] A body of case law emerged out of these reports and with it, the doctrine of "binding precedent."[39] The emergence of this body of decided cases meant that American courts were in the process of developing a distinctively American common law. In the 1820s, 1830s, and 1840s, treatise writers systematized this body of American law in a remarkable series of books that finally ended the dependence of the American legal profession on English legal learning.[40] In addition, state and federal courts assumed the power of judicial review whereby appellate courts heard challenges to statutes, executive orders, and lower court rulings and decided these cases according to the standard of the written constitution both at the state and the federal level.[41] Judicial review was a uniquely American institution. Under this power courts of law resolved basic social conflicts within a framework of law.

Although the Revolution ushered in a period of growth and change in public law, particularly in the field of constitutional law, there is no doubt that the greatest growing point in the legal system was in the field of private law. Here, policy judgments of the courts had substantial effects upon the values, groups, and interests that competed for legal recognition. These policy judgments often had one-sided effects. Law played a critical role in distributing resources, in allocating costs and benefits in the process of economic

---

38. See *Laws of the Commonwealth of Massachusetts* 3 (1804), 227. See also Lawrence M. Friedman, *A History of American Law* (New York, NY: Simon & Schuster, 1973), 282–285.
39. Harold J. Berman and William R. Greiner, "The Historical Development of the Doctrine of Precedent," in *The Nature and Functions of Law* (Brooklyn, NY: The Foundation Press, Inc., 1966), 491–494.
40. Leading examples of the early nineteenth-century treatises are James Kent, *Commentaries on American Law*, 4 vols. (1826–1830); Joseph Story, *Commentaries on Equity Jurisprudence* (1835); Theodore Sedgwick, *Treatise on the Measure of Damages* (1847). For a discussion of the treatise-writing tradition, see Roscoe Pound, *The Formative Era of American Law* (Boston, MA: Little, Brown and Company, 1938), Chap. 4.
41. William E. Nelson, "Changing Conception of Judicial Review: The Evolution of Constitutional Theory in the States, 1790–1860," *University of Pennsylvania Law Review* 120 (1972): 1166–1185.

development, and in encouraging the organization of certain economic groupings, such as corporations, while discouraging others, such as the early trade unions. The courts acted as mediating bodies among conflicting political forces and changing value systems. If the overall thrust of legal policy in the period favored venture capital over established wealth, corporations over labor unions, milldam owners over simple farmers, this was because of an emerging ideological consensus that preferred growth to stability, action to inaction, risk to certainty, and individual initiative, choice, and decision over community custom, old values, and social consensus.[42]

* * *

The law of eminent domain, still in its infancy in the immediate post-revolutionary period, already reflected many of the forces pushing and pulling American law in new directions. Although few of the state Constitutions adopted in the revolutionary era contained just compensation provisions, the principle was widely recognized that private property could not be appropriated for public use unless the owner was compensated for the taking.[43] The Fifth Amendment to the Constitution put it most succinctly: "nor shall private property be taken for public use without just compensation."[44] The words are simple and straightforward. Even in states with no expressed constitutional provision for just compensation, courts adopted the federal constitutional provision or applied compensation law as an equitable remedy or by reason of natural justice. "Eminent domain" became the absolute right to private property. Indeed, the "devolution" of the eminent domain power to "private takers" eroded absolutist conceptions of private property to such an extent that eminent domain law can be said to have prepared the way for the regulatory state.[45]

---

42. James Willard Hurst, *Law and the Conditions of Freedom in the Nineteenth-Century United States* (Madison, WI: University of Wisconsin Press, 1964), passim.
43. Morton J. Horwitz, *The Transformation of American Law: 1780–1860* (Cambridge, MA: Harvard University Press, 1977), 63–66.
44. *U.S. Constitution*, Amend. V.
45. See Harry N. Scheiber, "Property Law, Expropriation, and Resource Allocation by Government, 1789–1910," *Journal of Economic History* 33 (1973): 323.

The difficult questions of eminent domain law were not subject to automatic resolution by reference to fundamental constitutional sources, or to simple principles of compensation. Did milldam owners who raised water levels in a river or stream in order to operate a waterwheel subject an upstream neighbor to an involuntary taking when the latter's land was flooded? Was such a taking by a private party equally compensable as when the taking was by public authority? Did the construction of a milldam constitute a benefit sufficient to satisfy a "public use" test? What if the person whose land was flooded also benefited from the taking? Was the benefit to be "offset" against the loss, and how was compensation to be paid, in kind or in money, and if in money, what would be the appropriate measure of damages?[46]

These were serious issues not easily resolved and often not settled in ways indicated by constitutional provisions. In Massachusetts, for example, the 1780 constitution declared that "whenever . . . publick exigencies require that the property of any individual should be appropriated to public uses, he shall receive a reasonable compensation therefor."[47] However, in *Commonwealth v. Sessions of Middlesex* (1812), the Massachusetts Supreme Judicial Court decided that when private land was taken for a public road, if the proprietor's benefit from the construction of the road exceeded his damage from the taking, then no compensation was due because there was no loss.[48] Takings such as this, despite judicial sanction, were recognized as confiscatory by at least some offended contemporaries. As the reporter of the Middlesex case noted:

> [T]he justice of the rule is certainly very questionable. The expense of making a highway is a common burden, incurred for the common good of which burden, each citizen, in proportion to his ability, ordinarily sustains his part, and if one accidentally, whether by dwelling or having his lands near the highway, or from any other circumstance, derives more benefit from it than another, this does not seem to afford any sound reason for imposing a heavier tax upon him merely on that account. Indeed, it would be impracticable, in taxation, to apply the rule generally,

---

46. For further discussion of milldam law, see Horwitz, *The Transformation of American Law,* 47–53.
47. "Declaration of Rights" in *Massachusetts Constitution,* 1780: Art. X.
48. *Commonwealth* v. *Sessions of Middlesex*, 9 Mass 388 (1812).

> and assess the expenses of public works upon each citizen in exact proportion to the supposed benefit he may be expected to derive from them. *Where, then, is the equality or justice of applying the rule in a case like that reported in the text?*[49]

In fact, courts sometimes upheld small individual proprietors against powerful interests when it was not at all clear that the "taking" would result in a genuine public benefit. For example, a Massachusetts case held that:

> [W]here private persons or corporations prevail on towns to layout town ways, colorably for the use of the inhabitants, but really for their own benefit, over lands of others who are opposed to the way . . . a jury may discontinue a way thus irregularly obtained; and they ought to do it, whenever they are satisfied that private emolument, and not the interest of the inhabitants, has caused the way to be located.[50]

Accordingly, the emerging ideological commitment to economic growth and development—which the extension of the power of eminent domain power to private actors promoted—created tension with the competing social imperative to prevent the abuse of public power for purely private gain. The devolution of eminent domain from public authority to private actors was a trend that greatly accelerated after the middle of the nineteenth century. But consciousness of the natural rights basis of American constitutionalism was still keenly felt. In short, while the law clearly moved in directions that promoted growth, the law did not simply ratify all of the demands of favored economic interests. Rather, it mediated between conflicting values and competing social goods.

Traditional property rights, such as quiet enjoyment and just compensation, were subjected to other challenges besides the expanded usage of the eminent domain power. Internal improvements and changing technologies necessarily brought values and interests into new areas of conflict. If property owners in the eighteenth century enjoyed settled traditions of just compensation and the right to peaceable possession, the opening of the nineteenth century witnessed a growing number of modifications of these customary rules as builders of roads, canals, bridges, public

---

49. Ibid., 389 (emphasis added).
50. *Commonwealth* v. *Cambridge,* 7 Mass 158 (1810).

buildings, mills, and factories increasingly interfered with other people's property. A classic example of this development occurred in Massachusetts, a just compensation state whose law was transformed in this period into an instrument for the promotion of economic growth.[51] In 1795 the Massachusetts General Court, the state legislature, passed a milldam act that created a procedure for compensating riparian landowners whose lands were flooded when a neighbor constructed a dam in order to work a waterwheel."[52] The statute provided for the payment of yearly damages, the damages to be appraised by a jury. But the effect of the enactment was to force a complainant to lease away part of his land in return for an annual rent for as long as the mill owner wished to flood. Not only was the plaintiff thereby deprived of the use of his own land, but the award of an annuity rather than a lump sum payment meant that plaintiffs could not invest in alternative resources, nor did they receive compensation in years when no flooding occurred for the permanent damage to the value of their land.

An important decision of the Massachusetts Supreme Judicial Court, *Stowell v. Flagg*, established that the award of annual damages as provided for by the 1795 law was to be the exclusive remedy for plaintiffs whose lands were flooded. Such plaintiffs were barred from resorting to more traditional remedies such as self-help, or actions at law or in equity for relief.[53] Under self-help, the property owner whose quiet enjoyment had been disturbed could go onto someone else's land and remove the disturbance because the complainant had justification. Thus, a property owner whose lands were flooded by a neighbor's dam could destroy the dam without incurring liability. In the alternative, the injured party

51. Morton J. Horwitz, "The Emergence of an Instrumental Conception of Law," in *Law in American History*, D. Fleming and B. Bailyn, eds. (Boston, MA: Little, Brown and Company, 1971), 287–326.

52. "An Act for the Support and Regulation of Mills (Feb. 27, 1796)," in *Massachussetts Act and Resolves* (1794–1796), 443.

53. Horwitz, "The Emergence of an Instrumental Conception of Law." *Self-help* is the taking of an action by an aggrieved party to remedy a wrong without use of the legal process. A *suit at law* is a civil action undertaken in accordance with established rules of civil procedure, seeking damages as the remedy. *Injunctive relief* is an equitable remedy granted by a court at the instance of a party plaintiff against a party defendant, forbidding the latter from doing an act that will cause irreparable injury to the complaining party.

could file a lawsuit for damages in trespass or nuisance, if equity for an appropriate injunction to be fashioned by the court. If the complaining party did file a suit on a theory of trespass, the claim to damages would not be limited to the actual value of the loss because the law would seek to deter as well as to compensate. Similarly, in a nuisance action, the damages awarded might be higher than the loss.

A North Carolina decision summarized the reasons why damages for nuisance ought not to be either light or merely compensatory; the same reasoning would also apply to punitive damages available in trespass:

> [I]f the keeping up of the nuisance will afford more profit to the wrongdoer than the small damages assessed by a jury, he will keep it up forever; and thus one individual will be enabled to take from another his property against his consent, and detain it from him as long as he pleases. The damages ought not to be for what the incommoded property is worth, but competent to the purpose in view; that is, a demolition of the erection that occasions the nuisance. Sometimes the profits of such erections as merchant mills for instance, are of much greater value in one year, than the fee simple of the annoyed property. In such cases the object of the law cannot be obtained but by damages equivalent to the profits gained by the erection, or by damages to such an amount as will render those profits not worth pursuing.[54]

But the Massachusetts Milldam Act, instead of preserving the *plaintiff's prospective remedy* for preventing damage (e.g., through injunctive relief), authorized *prospective takings* by the mill owner. This represented a major departure from the practice followed in a number of states where statutes required prior authorization for each dam before it was constructed.[55] Even more significant, the Milldam Act of 1795, in conjunction with the Supreme Judicial Court's decision in *Stowell* v. *Flagg*, signified a fundamental incursion into traditional notions about the right to private property. This departure from customary understandings did not escape the concern of contemporaries. One critic of *Stowell* v. *Flagg* ques-

---

54. *Bradley* v. *Amis*, 3 NC 399 (1806).
55. Horwitz, "The Emergence of an Instrumental Conception of Law," 48.

tioned whether such an "unusual and extraordinary provision of the law" could be constitutional:

> I may not seize my neighbor's goods, except by process of law, against his consent, even though I may offer him their full value in return. I may not plough my neighbor's land, even though the thorn and the thistle alone flourish there under the sluggish husbandry of its owner. I may not obscure the light from the ancient cottage window, though poverty and weakness alone may have enjoyed its cheerful influence; nor may I poison the water or air that has, for years, given health and comfort to my neighbor, though the trade I may follow would enrich my coffers, and accommodate the neighborhood. But the ordinary rules of right and wrong, as to the enjoyment of private property, seem not to apply to estates which border upon any of the beautiful and healthy streams which enliven our scenery. They may be sacrificed to the speculating spirit of the manufacturer.[56]

The fundamental right to property guaranteed by the state and federal constitutions was the right not to have property taken, even for public use, without consent. Unconsented taxation, after all, was the triggering cause of the American Revolution. However, in this case, the legal innovation represented by the Massachusetts Milldam Act, as interpreted by the Massachusetts high court, authorized a taking for private use that deprived owners of property without ordinary legal process. As the writer cited above put it: through the mill act and *Stowell v. Flagg* the law authorized "the occupation and enjoyment of another's estate forever; which . . . is altogether unlike any other assumption of private property usually contemplated by our constitution."

* * *

One of the most important developments in private law in the nineteenth century was the emergence of negligence as a limitation on liability for injuries to persons and property.[57] The eighteenth century was a period when plaintiffs were compensated under a

---

56. Joseph K. Angell, "The Law of Water Privileges," *American Jurist* 2 (1989): 25.
57. *Negligence* is the failure to do some act that a reasonable or prudent person would do, or the doing of an act that a reasonable or prudent person would not do, under similar circumstances.

system of what we would call "strict liability."[58] Under strict liability, defendants were liable in damages for having caused loss or injury even if they were not at fault or negligent for having failed to observe reasonable precautions. People acted at their risk, and if their action caused loss, then aggrieved plaintiffs would be compensated. However, in the early nineteenth century, the regime of strict liability began to break down. Social values were in transition. Action was now to be encouraged, not penalized, and devices were needed to shield risk takers from liability. The burden was put on the injured party to establish that the defendant had acted carelessly or with negligence. If the plaintiff failed to carry that burden, then the law deemed the loss to have been accidental and it "must lie where it falls"—that is, on the injured plaintiff. In a negligence regime, plaintiffs became "self-insurers."[59]

In the age of strict liability, negligence had generally meant neglect of a duty imposed by office, contract, or status.[60] If a town failed to keep up a bridge or road, and if someone was injured as a result, the liability was not determined on the basis of carelessness, but for nonperformance of the duty imposed by law to maintain the facility. For example, if a prisoner escaped from a jailhouse, the sheriff was usually found to have "neglected" his official duty of safekeeping even if he had not acted carelessly in the performance of his office. However, the negligence standard that emerged by the middle of the nineteenth century would come to mean something else—not neglect but fault, misfeasance, or failure to observe a "standard of care;" a failure on the part of the defendant that the plaintiff had to prove in order to recover.

The shift from strict liability to negligence first occurred in cases where there were joint actors and where each party to the dispute had exposed the other to some risk or danger. Where there was such mutuality of risk or danger, the law would determine which party would bear responsibility for the injury or loss that resulted from the encounter. It did so by inquiring whose negli-

---

58. In *strict liability* the plaintiff does not have to show that the defendant was at fault or was negligent, but only that the defendant did the act which caused the injury.
59. *Self-insurance* means simply that the injured party must bear any loss suffered; the law will not distribute the loss through "social cost spreading" or some other system of relief.
60. Horwitz, *Transformation of American Law*, 85–87.

gence was causative—in other words, which of the parties was at fault. The earliest cases that raised these questions were collision cases involving ships moving in harbors, or travelers and stage-coaches on roadways.

Increasingly, the law confined the strict liability doctrine to those cases where the plaintiff had not exposed the defendant to a "reciprocity of risk." It is for this reason that the New York case of *Clark* v. *Foot* represents such a radical, even astonishing, departure from the old regime of strict liability.[61] Clark and Foot were neighbors. Foot set fire to some of his fallow land and the fire spread, causing damage to Clark's property. Clark sued Foot and lost because he failed to prove that Foot, or his servant, had been careless or negligent. Interestingly, it is not a collision case with two joint actors, but a land case where only the defendant was active while the plaintiff was passive. There was no question of causation. The plaintiff was disturbed in the quiet enjoyment of his property. But for the defendant's action, there would have been no loss. Yet, the plaintiff failed to recover. Moreover, the loss was caused by a spreading fire. Fire damage had always been and continued to be the classic instance for the application of the rule of strict liability. Use of fire was lawful, but one used it at one's peril because fire was inherently dangerous. In both English and American law, any damage caused by fire was compensable regardless of fault. Therefore, the New York court's decision in *Clark* v. *Foot* ran counter to an ancient rule of common law.

The emergence of the negligence doctrine in the nineteenth century and the narrowing of strict liability corresponds to the privatization model observable in other areas of the developing law. Both in strict liability and in negligence, a duty owed to the world was imposed by law. But in the strict liability regime, the duty was highly generalized, external, and objective. Action was risky, for damage was compensable regardless of fault. But in a regime governed by the negligence standard the duty was confined, specified, and determined according to some standard of conduct to which the individual actor-defendant was expected to conform. Whether or not he had acted non-negligently was a subjective

---

61. *Clark* v. *Foote*, 8 Johns 421 (NY 1811); Gary T. Schwartz, "Tort Law and the Economy in Nineteenth Century America: A Reinterpretation," *Yale Law Journal* 90 (1981): 1717–1775.

judgment made relative to each person and to the circumstances of each case. To be sure, the law might impose a general "standard of care" as defined by reasonable or prudent persons, but the parameters of that standard were not determined by the law or by the community, but by the customary conduct of actors in the same situation or occupation as the defendant. In fact, in some cases, the standard of conduct was created by the defendant's own past record of conduct. Not action per se, but deviation from an acceptable standard of action—defined either by the defendant or by actors similarly situated—gave rise to liability. In this sense, the standards of liability were privatized and narrowed.

Clark v. Foot foreshadowed the new theory of negligence that was later defined by the phrase: "there is no liability without fault." It is one of the first in what was to become a steady and growing volume of cases in which plaintiffs would lose because they failed to prove the defendant's negligence to the satisfaction of courts and juries. In this sense, the case is a turning point in American law. The erosion of traditional property values coincided with the emergence of negligence law, which was soon to become an important limitation on liability. *Clark v. Foot* in New York and *Stowell v. Flagg* in Massachusetts were classic instances of how old legal ideas in the most ancient field of the common law—the law of real property—were going through revolutionary changes under the impact of forces that the courts had only begun to perceive.

* * *

Related transformations were also affecting the law of contracts. Under the chief justiceship of John Marshall, the Supreme Court of the United States made the Contract Clause of the U.S. Constitution a major force behind legal privatization. That clause prohibited any state from enacting a "law impairing the obligation of contracts."[62] By including that provision in the original constitution, the framers hoped to curb the more radical state legislatures from enacting debtor relief laws and other measures that outraged creditors in the economic depression of the 1780s.[63] However, the

---

62. *U.S. Constitution,* Art. I, Sec. 10.
63. Benjamin F. Wright, *Consensus and Continuity, 1776–1787* (New York: W.W. Norton & Company, 1958), 53.

early decisions interpreting the Contract Clause were applied not to contracts between private parties but to state land grants to developers and charter grants to public corporations. The Supreme Court said that such grants were really contracts between the state and the grantee, and that legislation which altered the terms of a grant, or repealed it altogether, would adversely affect those property interests that might have vested under such a grant.[64] Legislation of this kind, therefore, was invalid under the Contract Clause of the federal constitution because of the consequent "impairment" of contractual obligations that the state had undertaken. While states later would protect their freedom of action by reserving authority to alter prospectively a legislative or charter grant, the effect of these early Supreme Court decisions was to liken the state to an ordinary private party.

Thus, for the Supreme Court under John Marshall, the Contract Clause became a device for limiting state action—not merely when such action might interfere with private contractual relationships, but also when the state itself was one of the contracting parties. Under such an interpretation of its meaning, the clause became an instrument for reducing the state to the status of a private party in order to prevent it from altering the terms of its grants and charters to private interests. While later cases would cut back on Marshall's broad interpretation, the privatization model remained deeply embedded in constitutional law.[65] Privatization limited the exercise of state authority unless that exercise could be rationalized on the basis of the state's inherent police powers, or of some other doctrine of public utility or need.[66]

---

64. See, for example, *Fletcher* v. *Peck,* 10 US (6 Cranch) 87 (1810); *Dartmouth College* v. *Woodward,* 17 US (4 Wheat) 518 (1819).
65. See, for example, *Ogden* v. *Saunders,* 25 US (12 Wheat) 213 (1827), and *Charles River Bridge* v. *Warren Bridge et al.*, 36 US (11 Pet) 420 (1837).
66. Not until 1948 did the privatization model in contract law get turned on its head. In that year, the U.S. Supreme Court outlawed racially restrictive covenants in the sale of real property. In *Shelley* v. *Kraemer*, 334 US 1 (1948), private decision makers were barred from performing acts that the Constitution prohibited the states from performing if such acts required state support of subvention, however indirect. In the early contract clause cases, state legislatures had had to shape their conduct as if they were private parties, but under the doctrine of "state action" as expanded in *Shelley* v. *Kraemer*, private parties were subjected to the requirements imposed on states and their instrumentalities.

In the early nineteenth century, contractual freedom was "privatized" in still other ways. The modern theory of contract law is that private individuals are lawmakers who, through the instrument of a bargained-for private agreement, create a legal regime that will govern their future conduct, as if that behavior had been conditioned by statute, regulation, or court order. Behind this "contract theory" stands the psychology of free will and the political philosophy of self-government; mature human beings in a free society are capable of ordering their affairs in ways they best understand.

This had not always been the case. In the eighteenth century, the law stood as a pervasive "omnipresence in the sky," particularly in the contract area. Parties could enter into a contract, or "covenant," only if the terms of their bargain did not violate group values, rules of social conduct, or community norms. The law of contracts was undeveloped, its rules were traditional, and its design fitted the mold of a stable, pre-modern society where relationships were face to face, obligations were undertaken and discharged according to well-established customs, and deviations from the norm were controlled by carefully defined rules and procedures.[67]

A contract action brought by a Massachusetts physician a decade before the Revolution illustrates the old law. The doctor's bill was for drugs, travel costs, and medical attention, but there was no written contract defining the terms of remuneration. Nevertheless, the court decided that these costs "had as fixed a Price as Goods sold by a Shopkeeper. . . . The jury did, according as the Law was laid down to them, and struck off about £7 from the Account, lowering the Charges, probably, to what they thought '*reasonable*.'" The doctor's charges, in other words, were fixed by local custom as established by jurors drawn from the local community who were familiar with local customs.[68]

While many traditional elements of the old law of contracts persisted well into the nineteenth century, by 1820 the law showed signs of rapid change in the direction of modern contract theory. The deepest change was the shift away from community values toward individual intent as the test for an enforceable agreement.

---

67. William E. Nelson, *Americanization of the Common Law: The Impact of Legal Change on Massachusetts Society, 1760–1830* (Cambridge, MA: Harvard University Press, 1975), 54–62.

68. *Pynchon v. Brewster*, Quincy 224 (Mass 1766). See Horwitz, *Transformation of American Law*, 165.

The purpose of the developing rules of contract law was to carry out the will of the parties even when their agreements reflected judgments of value or mandated behavior or performance that ran contrary to accepted custom. For example, courts increasingly allowed the amount of "consideration" to be determined by the parties.[69] Even nominal amounts would be permitted if the parties so intended. This was in opposition to eighteenth century usage, where courts would not enforce contracts where the items exchanged had not been of roughly equivalent value.[70]

Powerful historical forces generated these changes in contract law. The new commercial economy was creating novel products, distant markets, and fluid price structures, as well as a whole range of complex commercial relationships among buyers and sellers, employers and workers, producers and consumers. Shifting patterns of trade, the growth of commodity and "futures" markets, and greater impersonality in the relations between contracting parties all forced substantial changes in the rules that governed agreements. In addition, behind the demanding requirements of the new commerce and industry lurked the ideology of private decision-making, an ideology rooted as much in political and social attitudes as in hard economic fact. On every level, post-revolutionary legal thought emphasized the lawmaking role of the private individual while simultaneously criticizing the superintending power of the state. The private contract was, in essence, a private statute; the law of contracts facilitated "private ordering" of markets and resources. In a word, the private contract represented self-government in private law, just as republicanism promoted the representative principle in public law.[71]

The triumph of what has been called "the will theory of contracts" carried the republican impulse to the smallest unit in society—two individuals, who in concert formed a micro-legislature and made law. Modern contract law theory brought Americans closer to a regime of direct democracy. However, in practice "liberty of contract" was based upon the illusion that

---

69. *Consideration* is the benefit that accrues to the promisor or the loss incurred by the promisee in a bargained-for agreement.
70. Horwitz, *Transformation of American Law,* Chap. 6.
71. Morton J. Horwitz, "The Historical Foundations of Modern Contract Law," *Harvard Law Review* 87 (1974): 917–956.

parties entered into agreements on the basis of genuine negotiating equality. In fact, the myth of "liberty of contract" eventually became part of an ideological justification for social and economic exploitation. The theory of contracts was sound, but its implementation in a world where wealth and power were not equally distributed inevitably brought distortions in results not unlike the distortions seen in the legislative process, which occurred when powerful interests, or lobbies, corrupted political institutions in the name of representative democracy.

The decline of the eighteenth century's so-called "substantive theory of contracts" meant that the law concerned itself only with the formalities of contract formation. Neither the relative bargaining positions of the parties nor the substance of what they agreed to was any longer a central issue. This opened the door to widespread abuse by the powerful over the weak, the informed against the ignorant, and too often, the rich against the poor. The emergence of modern contract theory in the nineteenth century was the clearest expression of the tendency of American law to ratify underlying social relationships. Of all the branches of the legal system, the law of contracts became the least responsive to the demands of social justice and economic equality.

* * *

The rise of the will theory of contracts also contributed to the development of the modern American business corporation. The public corporation is an ancient legal institution with the oldest example being the municipality incorporated by the sovereign—in England by the King-in-Parliament, and after independence, by the state legislatures in America. Still another form of public corporation was the joint stock company. Many of the original American colonies, such as Plymouth colony, Massachusetts Bay colony and early Virginia were established and settled in this way. Joint stock companies pooled the financial resources of participating adventurers in order to promote England's expansion overseas. While these public corporate entities were largely self governing in day-to-day operations, the power of the government to alter their corporate charters and to reach the personal assets of individual shareholders was unlimited.[72]

But the law of corporations went through significant transformations in the period after the American Revolution. Chief among these was the concept of limited liability—individual assets would no longer be available to cover the debts of a corporation unless the member shareholders had so agreed. The intentions of the parties governed this critical aspect of corporate life—a significant departure from earlier practice where the obligations of the members were determined by their status as corporate shareholders rather then by the contractual relationship between each shareholder and the corporation. This transformation in the law of corporations is an example of Sir Henry Maine's famous generalization concerning the evolution of modern law in "progressive societies," which he characterized as "a movement from status to contract."[73] The law now prevented forced assessments against shareholders by the corporation, by corporate creditors, or by public authorities. The corporation thereby became a private, voluntary association of a most unusual kind.[74]

In place of the public purposes that public corporations asserted as the primary justification for their special legal status, the new private corporations of the nineteenth century utilized new theories of political economy. These theories held that indirect public benefit was best achieved through the pursuit of private gain. Adam Smith, the great Scottish philosopher and founder of modern political economy, supplied the ideological basis for this proposition. In his *Wealth of Nations*, first published in 1776, the year of American independence, Smith advanced the novel notion that the public good was best promoted not by disinterested individual "virtue," but through harnessing the passion for private gain.

> [E]very individual necessarily labours to render the annual revenue of the society as great as he can. He generally, indeed neither

---

72. Joseph S. Davis, *Essays in the Earlier History of American Corporations* (New York, NY: Russell & Russell, 1965), vol. 2, Chaps. 1–5.
73. Sir Henry Maine, *Ancient Law*, rev. ed. (London: John Murray Publishers, 1930), 18.
74. See Horwitz, *Transformation of American Law,* 111–114; and Nelson, *Americanization of Common Law,* 133–136.

> intends to promote the public interest, nor knows how much he is promoting it. By preferring the support of domestic to that of foreign industry, he intends only his own security; and by directing that industry in such a manner as its produce may be of the greatest value, he intends only his own gain, and he is in this, as in many other cases, led by an *invisible hand* to promote an end which was not part of his intention. By pursuing his own interest he frequently promotes that of the society more effectually than when he really intends to promote it.[75]

Smith's metaphor of the *invisible hand* had a profound impact on America, where entrepreneurs increasingly asserted the principle of the free market and competition over special privilege.

The major legal victory that new private corporations won in America during the period following the Revolution was the establishment, as a principle of constitutional jurisprudence, that corporations had legal standing and were entitled to the same legal protections and constitutional guarantees as individuals. In the *Dartmouth College* case,[76] Chief Justice Marshall held that the New Hampshire state legislature, in amending the corporate charter granted to the original trustees of Dartmouth College, had violated the contract clause by impairing the contractual obligation of the state to the trustees. Marshall's holding that a corporate charter was simply a contract had been suggested by earlier decisions,[77] but never enunciated as a doctrine of constitutional law. With more force than reasoned justification, Marshall simply stated that a "charter is a contract," thereby radically altering the status of corporations in American law.

Commercial corporations, in particular, benefited from this landmark Supreme Court decision. The *Dartmouth College* case transformed the Contract Clause—designed by the framers of the Constitution to protect individual property rights—into an instrument for the benefit of the business corporation, which were already becoming the most dynamic form of private aggrandizement of wealth and power in America. Associate Justice Joseph

---

75. Adam Smith, *The Wealth of Nations* 6th ed. (London: Methuen, 1950), vol. 1, 421 (emphasis added).
76. *Dartmouth College* v. *Woodward*, 17 US (4 Wheat) 518 (1819).
77. *Fletcher* v. *Peck*, 10 US (6 Cranch) 87 (1810); *New Jersey* v. *Wilson*, 11 US (7 Cranch) 164 (1812); *Terrett* v. *Taylor*, 13 US (9 Cranch) 43 (1815).

Story's concurring opinion in the *Dartmouth College* case further contributed to this trend by dividing corporate entities into private corporations and public corporations. According to Story, a corporate charter granted by the state to achieve a public purpose, whether to build a road, dig a canal, or establish a bank, was nonetheless private if the corporate stock was privately owned.[78]

But private corporations held onto their quasi-public character when it was convenient to do so. For example, when an established corporation wanted to block new competitors, or when a turnpike company wished to exercise eminent domain power in order to secure a right-of-way, it was useful to claim that the corporation was an arm of public authority, that it was established for a public purpose, and that it was entitled to special protections. While such claims came under mounting criticism by opponents of special privilege, such attacks did not reach a climax until the 1830s and 1840s. However, by then corporate law had been sufficiently privatized to make the corporation, whether new or old, virtually impervious to political challenge. The *Dartmouth College* case had made that certain. Chancellor James Kent, the author of the single most influential treatise on American law in the nineteenth century, commented that *Dartmouth College* "did more than any other single act, proceeding from the authority of the United States, to throw an impregnable barrier around all rights and franchises derived from the grant of government; and to give solidity and inviolability to the literary, charitable, religious and commercial institutions of our country."[79] For Kent, *Dartmouth College* was a great decision, but Ichabod Bartlett, attorney for the state of New Hampshire in the *Dartmouth College* litigation, concluded that "the government must control these institutions [the corporations] or they shall control the government!"[80]

---

78. Francis N. Stites, *Private Interest and Public Gain: The Dartmouth College Case, 1819* (Amherst, MA: University of Massachusetts Press, 1972), Chaps. 7 and 9.
79. Kent, *Commentaries on American Law,* 418.
80. Quoted in Charles G. Haines, *The Role of the Supreme Court in American Government and Politics, 1789–1835* (New York, NY: Russell & Russell, 1960), 416.

* * *

The growth of the private corporation notwithstanding, the notion persisted that some organizations were of such profound public concern that they should remain within the control of public law. Early labor unions fell into this category. In the eyes of the law, labor unions were "criminal conspiracies." Indeed, at the time when the corporate form as a legal entity was breaking away from public control, American courts established the doctrine that labor associations were conspiracies in restraint of trade—a doctrine of labor law that remained virtually unbroken until 1842.[81]

In the late eighteenth century, journeymen cordwainers (shoemakers) in eastern cities organized for the purpose of establishing minimum rates of pay. They attempted to set up what would later be called the "closed shop"—closed, that is to non-associating workers. When master craftsmen tried to hire "nonunion" journeymen, the cordwainers struck. In retaliation, the masters organized their own associations and proceeded to initiate prosecutions against the organized journeymen for criminal conspiracy. This was the beginning of what would be a major trend in American labor history—use of the courts and of the legal process by employers to curb union activity. In the case of the cordwainers, the heavy hand of the criminal law was used successfully to destroy voluntary associative activity by working people.[82]

The issues that came to a head in the *Cordwainer* cases were central questions of American law. Despite the fact that this was a period when the English common law was under attack in America, the common law of criminal conspiracy—the most shadowy and oppressive part of the entire body of English criminal law—was applied to labor unions and put into effect in many American jurisdictions.[83] In the *Cordwainer* cases, the courts held that labor combinations were illegal conspiracies if the *purpose* of the combination, such as to raise wages, or the *means* employed, such as calling a work stoppage, were illegal. Unions that coerced

81. *Commonwealth* v. *Hunt*, 45 Mass (4 Metc) 111 (1842).
82. John R. Commons, et al., *History of Labour in the United States* (New York: A.M. Kelley, 1966), vol. 1, Chap. 5.
83. The issue reinforced political divisions between the Jeffersonians, who in principle opposed the wholesale application of English legal rules to America, and the Federalists, who generally were in favor of the "reception" of English law.

nonunion journeymen or threatened master craftsmen with strikes, or other actions "in restraint of trade" that were prejudicial to the public, easily satisfied either the "illegal purpose" test or the "illegal means" test. For all practical purposes, any activity undertaken by a journeymen's union was bound to result in criminal indictment and conviction under these legal doctrines.

The problem of jury bias also surfaced in these cases. In an 1806 case, of the twelve members of the jury that convicted members of the Federal Society of Journeymen Cordwainers, nine were merchants and three were master craftsmen—hardly a balanced panel to decide whether journeymen could organize.[84] However, what is most interesting from a broad historical perspective is the comparison between the posture of the law toward early trade unionists and its posture toward the process of business incorporation. While private incorporators, in furthering their own economic interests, could limit their civil liability under the new law of incorporation, journeymen craftsmen invited criminal sanctions by associating together in pursuit of their common economic interests. Moreover, the law imposed no liability, criminal or civil, on associations by master craftsmen. Thus, the law permitted employers to organize to fight their employees, but it prohibited employees from organizing in their own self-interest to fight their employers.

Indeed, while the right to associate freely was generally recognized in almost every important sphere of life, noneconomic as well as economic, associations of wage earners were singled out for special attention and control. As defense counsel in the Philadelphia *Cordwainer* case argued:

> Shall all others, except only the industrious mechanics be allowed to meet and plot; merchants to determine their prices current, or settle the markets, politicians to electioneer, sportsmen for horse-racing and games, ladies and gentlemen for balls, parties and [banquets]; and yet these poor men be indicted for combining against starvation?[85]

Political, religious, and social associations of all kinds were perfectly legal. Political parties and religious sects, once the targets

84. Commons, *History of Labour,* 147.
85. Ibid., 141.

of criminal prosecution, were now legitimate. Even some economic associations—private incorporating investors and unions of master craftsmen—were acceptable. But working people who sold their labor for wages still felt the sting and punishment of public law despite constitutional provisions protecting the "right in a peaceable manner to assemble together for the common good."[86] Clearly, powerful class bias was at work. This is particularly evident in view of the jury selection process, which, as exemplified by the Philadelphia *Cordwainer* case, was heavily weighted in favor of the master craftsmen. Thus, at the same time that the law was in the process of releasing the business corporation from political control, by transforming it from a public law to a private law entity, the *Cordwainer* decisions made early trade unions vulnerable to criminal prosecution.

On the surface, because of the continued application of the criminal law to the cordwainer unions, these cases appear to be truly exceptional to the general trend of privatization. But on a deeper level, the anomaly can be reconciled. In the limited-liability private corporation cases, as in the *Cordwainer* cases, the courts put much emphasis on the issue of coercion. In the developing law governing the new private corporation, neither the corporation itself nor its creditors could assess the personal assets of shareholders beyond what shareholders had assented to by contract. Similarly, under the *Cordwainer* decisions, journeymen could not force union membership on recalcitrant craftsmen. For example in the New York *Cordwainer* case, the union had secured the discharge from employment of a member who had not paid his dues. This was coercion, and for this reason the court found that the methods used by the cordwainers were illegal. The underlying ideology was the same. Just as monopoly and special privilege placed unwanted restraints on capital resources, the economic restraints imposed by labor unions disrupted the workings of Adam Smith's "invisible hand." In both instances, the stress was on individualism, voluntary association, and non-coercion—the same themes animating other zones of law in the post-revolutionary period.

The *Cordwainer* cases illustrate the ways in which the transition from public law to private law was arrested in the labor

---

86. *Pennsylvania Constitution*, 1790: Art. IX, Sec. 20.

market, where society preferred to retain firm control because of deep fears about working-class power. These fears have persisted. The special posture of the law toward employer-employee relations has had a continuing history in America. Long after the collapse of the labor conspiracy doctrine, antitrust legislation, fashioned to curb the excesses of industrial combinations in the late nineteenth century, was turned against industrial unions. The failure of the journeymen cordwainers in the prosecutions brought against them in the early nineteenth century must have convinced many working people that the legal constitutional system was a system built for the wealthy and the powerful, not for the indigent and the politically weak.

* * *

Why did the deep changes in American law, outlined above, occur in the period after the American Revolution? What social forces generated these changes in direction away from public law values toward private law? In short, why was the public estate diminished in so many areas by the advance of the private law? Clearly, one answer is that the legal profession's special orientation to American society had much to do with this legal transformation. The recruitment, education, and socialization of lawyers into the legal profession, and the emergence of that profession as a powerful and independent force in American life, supplied the basic underpinnings for substantive legal change.

In the period after the American Revolution there was an increase in the number of lawyers—not merely in absolute terms but in numbers relative to population growth itself. One social historian has estimated that from 1783 to 1820 the number of lawyers grew four times faster than the general population, which itself was expanding at a rapid rate because of natural increase and immigration.[87] The figures in Table I give some indication of that increase.

---

87. David Hackett Fischer, "The Legal System," (NEH Seminar Paper, Brandeis University, Waltham, MA, 1979), 10–41 (by permission).

TABLE I

Number of Lawyers in Three Selected States, 1740–1820

	Number of Lawyers	**Lawyers per 10,000 population**
		Massachusetts (including Maine)
1740	15	10
1775	71	24
1780	34	11
1785	92	24
1790	112	24
1800	200	35
1810	492	70
1820	710	87
		Connecticut
1790	129	54
1800	169	67
1820	248	90
		South Carolina
1771	24	19
1820	200	40

Source: David H. Fischer, "The Legal System;" Gerard W. Gawalt, The Promise of Power: the Emergence of the Legal System in Massachusetts, 1760–1840 (Westport, Conn., 1979), 14.

The statistics for Massachusetts are particularly arresting because they show that while there was a net decrease in the number of lawyers as a result of the emigration of Loyalists during and immediately after the American Revolution, the rapid growth of the legal profession that had taken place in Massachusetts in the late colonial period had resumed by the mid-1780s.

How were these new lawyers trained? What were the larger implications of that training to the growth and shape of American law? Legal education in the early years of American history was quite different from what it became in the nineteenth and twentieth centuries. In the colonial period most lawyers who were trained in America rather than at the English Inns of Court[88] worked as

88. The Inns of Court in London, "little more than living and eating clubs" by the eighteenth century, were near the central common-law courts. Students read law

apprentices in the law offices of established attorneys. Each practitioner defined the tasks and the education of his apprentice-clerks differently, and the amount of time served varied greatly. Law clerks usually spent most of their working hours copying forms, drafting pleadings and briefs, and doing whatever office chores were required. The oral instruction the novice received was entirely within the control of his teacher, and most of the time the practitioner was too busy to give much attention to his clerk. The chief benefit the student received was the experience of working in a law office, ready access to the published books or manuscript folios in the office library, and personal contact with lawyers, clients, and the legal process.

For such privileges, students or their families paid handsome fees—as in the case of one famous general who paid tuition so that his nephew, a future Supreme Court justice, could study law:

> Phila. March 22, 1782. I promise to pay James Wilson Esq. or order on demand one hundred guineas, his fee for receiving my nephew Bushrod Washington as a student of law in his office.
>
> G. Washington.[89]

Bushrod Washington's teacher, James Wilson, went on to become an associate justice of the United States Supreme Court as did Bushrod Washington himself sometime later. Wilson was also one of the great legal and political thinkers of his day. But Wilson was not, apparently, a great law teacher. Another contemporary reported that:

> [A]s an instructor he was almost useless to those who were under his direction. He would never engage with them in professional discussion; to a direct question he gave the shortest possible answer and a general request for information was always refused.[90]

The reminiscences of early American lawyers reflecting on their days as law office clerks are replete with such complaints about the neglect, boredom, and tedium of the life of a law student.

---

and observed trials while living at the Inns. See Friedman, *A History of American Law*, 84.

89. Quoted in Charles Warren, *A History of the American Bar* (Boston, MA: Little, Brown and Company, 1911), 166.

90. Quoted in ibid., 167.

William Livingston of New York, for example, who in 1745 was a student of James Alexander, John Peter Zenger's famous attorney, wrote to a New York newspaper complaining about his teacher:

> [I]f [lawyers] deserve the imputation of injustice and dishonesty, it is in no instance more visible and notorious, then in their conduct towards their apprentices.[91]

Livingston called his teacher's conduct "scandalous, horrid, base, and infamous to the last degree."

The great Justice Joseph Story also suffered as a student. Left alone by his law teacher to fathom the depths of *Coke on Littleton*, a standard English law book, Story later reported: "[I] took it up, and after trying it day after day with very little success, I sat myself down and wept bitterly. My tears dropped upon the book, and stained its pages."[92]

Some students were more fortunate. John Quincy Adams was lucky enough to have Theophilus Parsons, later chief justice of the Massachusetts Supreme Judicial Court, as his teacher:

> Nov. 27, 1787. It is of great advantage to us to have Mr. Parsons in the office. He is in himself a law library, and proficient in every useful branch of service; but his chief excellency is, that no student can be more fond of proposing questions than he is of solving them. He is never at a loss, and always gives a full and ample account, not only of the subject proposed, but of all matters which have any intimate connection with it. I am persuaded that the advantage of having such an instructor is very great, and I hope I shall not misimprove [sic] it as some of his pupils have done.[93]

The first American law schools were outgrowths of this law office apprenticeship system. Practitioners who were better at teaching than they were in representing clients or winning cases began to attract a student following. Their offices expanded as the numbers of their students grew. Table II (page 151) lists the private law schools founded in this period that are based on this expanded

---

91. Quoted in ibid.
92. Quoted in Albert J. Harno, *Legal Education in the United States* (San Francisco, CA: Bancroft-Whitney Co., 1953), 20.
93. Quoted in Warren, *A History of the American Bar,* 169.

apprenticeship model. Some lasted well into the nineteenth century. The most famous of these was the Litchfield Law School established by Tapping Reeve in 1784 in Litchfield, Connecticut. In the half-century of its existence, Litchfield produced over one thousand graduates.[94] Students came from all over the country to attend the law lectures given there. The Litchfield Law School was not only one of the earliest law schools in the country; it was also the first law school of national reputation. Many of its graduates became famous lawyers and judges. Three among them, Levi Woodbury of New Hampshire, Henry Baldwin of Pennsylvania, and Ward Hunt of New York, were appointed associate justices of the United States Supreme Court. Two other Litchfield graduates, John C. Calhoun of South Carolina and Aaron Burr of New York, later achieved political stature (and in Burr's case, subsequent disgrace) as Vice Presidents of the United States. Still others became prominent in business, journalism, and education.

Teaching at Litchfield was by the lecture method. Extant student notebooks and teacher memoranda reveal the subject matter covered in these lectures, most of which were given by Judge Reeve and his close associate, Judge James Gould. Litchfield law teachers concentrated on the major fields of private law and gave scant notice to the main areas of public law. For example, in one Litchfield course twenty-six pages of lecture notes were devoted to "municipal law" (the law of local government) and eighty-seven pages were devoted to "public wrongs or required sixty pages, "contracts" required ninety-seven pages, "bailments" required one hundred and twenty-nine pages, "bills of exchange and promissory notes" required seventy-three criminal' But the lectures on "private wrongs or torts" pages, and "mercantile law" required one hundred

94. Samuel H. Fisher, "Litchfield Law School, 1774–1833: Biographical Catalogue of Students," *Yale Library Law Publications* 11 (1946).

TABLE II

Private Law Schools Before 1835, by State

Name of Law School	Location	Date Founded (if known)	Date Closed (if known)
Virginia			
Wythe's Law School	Williamsburg	1779	
	1791		
Wythe's Law School	Richmond	1791	c. 1806
Taylor's Law School	Needham	1821	
St. George Tucker's Law School	Winchester	1824	
	1830		
Lomax's Law School	Fredericksburg	1830	—
Connecticut			
Litchfield Law School	Litchfield	1784	1833
Staple's Law School	New Haven	1800	1824
Gilbert's Law School	Hebron	1810	1816
Swift's Law School	Windham	—	—
New York			
Van Schaak's Law School	Kinderhook	1786	1828
New York Law Institute	—	1826	—
Kentucky			
Transylvania Law School	Lexington	1799	1861
Tennessee			
Powell's Law School	Blountville	c.1800	—
Haywood's Law School	Nashville	1807	-
Vermont			
Turner's Law School	Fairfield	1806	1812
Massachusetts			
Howe's Law School	Northampton	1823	1829
Metcalf's Law School	Dedham	1828	c.1829
Pennsylvania			
Dickinson's Law Academy	Philadelphia	1821	—
Maryland			
Dorsey's Law School	Baltimore	—	1823

Adapted from Fischer, "The Legal System," 10–44. See also Alfred Z. Reed, Training for the Public Profession of the Law (New York, 1921), app. B.

sixty-seven pages.[95] Clearly, courses on private law subjects received extensive treatment at Litchfield whereas attention to public law was minimal.

However, in contrast with Litchfield's narrow and technical definition of the elements of legal training was the broader conceptual approach taken by David Hoffman of Maryland. Hoffman published his *Course of Legal Study* in 1817 in preparing for the law lectureship at the new University of Maryland. His book on legal education is an extraordinary contrast with the training available at Litchfield. In it Hoffman, himself a leading member of the Maryland bar, made an attempt to open the mind of the student to a larger universe of learning peopled by ancients as well as moderns; philosophers, theologians, historians, and statesmen as well as lawyers and jurists.

Five of the thirteen "titles" of Hoffman's book were devoted to public law subjects: The Elementary and Constitutional Principles of the Municipal Law of England, of the United States, and of the Roman or Civil Law (Title II); The Law of Crimes and Punishments (Title VII); The Law of Nations (Title VIII); The Constitution and Laws of the United States (Title XI); and The Constitution and Laws of the Several States of the Union (Title XIII). Three further titles were: Moral and Political Philosophy (Title I); the Civil or Roman Law (Title X); and Political Economy (Title XIII). The remaining five titles, less than half of the total, dealt with subjects that generally would fall within the private or commercial law sphere: The Law of Real Rights and Real Remedies (Title III); The Law of Personal Rights and Personal Remedies (Title IV); the Lex Mercatoria or Merchant's Law (Title VI); and Maritime and Admiralty Law (Title IX).

Hoffman captured the spirit of his work in the introduction to his book:

---

95. Samuel H. Fisher, "The Litchfield Law School," Connecticut Tercentenary Commission, *Committee on Historical Publications*, 6–8; reprinted in Henry L. Shepherd, *Litchfield: Portrait of a Beautiful Town* (Litchfield, CT, 1969), 40–62; Ronald L. Coleman, "Learning the Law at Litchfield," *Connecticut Bar Journal* 34 (1960): 270–276; Samuel H. Fisher, *The Litchfield Law School, 1775–1833*, Tercentenary pamphlet XXI (1933); Charles C. Goetsch, *The Litchfield Law School: A Modern View* (Hartford, CT: University of Connecticut Law School Press, 1981); Burton S. Hill, "Litchfield, First American Law School," *Michigan Alumnus Quarterly Review* 56 (1950).

> He who aspires to a thorough acquaintance with legal science, should cultivate the most enlarged ideas of its transcendent dignity, its vital importance, its boundless extent, and infinite variety. As it relates to the conduct of man, it is a moral science of great sublimity; as its object is individual and national happiness, it is, of all others, the most important; as it respects the moral actions of men, and of nations, it is infinitely varied; and as it concerns all his rights and obligations, either derived from, or due to his God, his neighbour, his country, or himself, it must necessarily be a science of vast extent.[96]

In short, David Hoffman conceived of the law as a "liberal" profession. Its study and practice would broaden the mind and uplift the spirit.[97]

Hoffman's *Course of Legal Study* influenced curriculum development at Harvard Law School, founded in 1817, and at the University of Virginia Law School, founded in 1826. At Columbia, law lectures were given by James Kent in 1794 and 1795 and then again in the mid-1820s. Kent published his lectures in his great four-volume treatise, *Commentaries on American Law*. Like Hoffman's *Course of Legal Study*, the *Commentaries on American Law* contained more public law content than anything offered at Litchfield. The entire first volume of the work, one-fourth of the whole, was devoted to the law of nations, American constitutional law, and the sources of municipal law in the several states. While *Commentaries on American Law* lacked the broad philosophical and historical orientation of Hoffman's book, it did contain numerous references to ancient law and to European civil law. James Kent, who served as Chancellor of New York—the highest legal position in the state—was widely read and thoroughly educated, and his influential book, which went through numerous editions in the nineteenth century, was the product of his own liberal education.

Nevertheless, despite its narrow technicalism, or perhaps because of it, Litchfield was unquestionably the most influential national law school in America prior to the emergence of law schools with academic affiliations, such as Harvard, Columbia and

---

96. David. Hoffman, *A Course of Legal Study* (2nd ed., Baltimore, MD: Joseph Neal, 1836), 23.
97. Perry Miller, ed., *The Legal Mind in America: From Independence to the Civil War* (Garden City, NY: Doubleday, 1962), 84.

the University of Virginia. In the period of its professional dominance, Litchfield emphasized the practitioner's arts rather than legal theory. This meant that leading lawyers from every state spent the formative years of their professional development in an intellectual environment in which technical competence in the fields of private law was valued more highly than proficiency in public law. The training that great numbers of lawyers received, in law offices and in apprentice schools modeled after Litchfield, stressed mastery of those skills most highly prized by private litigants. The teaching, although intensive and sometimes masterful, lacked a broad philosophical or humanistic basis.

Thus, legal training and general education remained separate and distinct. The divorce between professional training and general education is best exemplified by the institutional detachment of schools, such as Litchfield, from the leading colleges of the day. Indeed, even when academic law schools replaced private academies and became the focal point of legal education, they were run and taught by practitioners. Like medical schools and other vocational satellites of early universities, academic law schools were not organically connected to the liberal arts colleges and universities of which they were a part. This detachment remained a dominant characteristic of American legal education, although in the twentieth century this has been mitigated by the emergence of a regular law professoriat with full-time teaching and academic commitments

But the practitioners and former practitioners who taught at Litchfield, at other private law schools, and at the early academic centers of legal education had virtually no opportunity to develop a wider vision of the role of law in the achievement of broad social purposes. Preoccupation with mastery of the technical arts of legal practice meant that the strictures that David Hoffman had enumerated in his introduction to *A Course of Legal Study* had little meaning for a large proportion of the first several generations of post-revolutionary American lawyers. As Hoffman wrote in the preface to the second edition of his book: "The prejudices of early education adhere . . . with wonderful tenacity."[98] Those prejudices helped to determine not only the values that the legal profession

98. Hoffman, *A Course of Legal Study,* ix.

continued to consider of preeminent importance, but the substance of the law they practiced and of the legal system they shaped.

The spirit of the law taught in institutions such as Litchfield was pervasive because of the enormous influence of lawyers in American society. Lawyers not only occupied key positions in government, but were achieving increasing importance in the emerging corporate bureaucracies. To be sure, there were divisions within the profession between frontier lawyers and the urban bar, between untrained "pettifoggers" and the products of law schools, between those who represented the poor and the "middling" classes and those associated with the rich and the well-born. Such divisions explain much about anti-lawyer sentiment and the battles fought over professional standards, bar admission procedures, and methods of judicial selection.[99] But historical attention to divisions within the legal profession has slighted the great importance of the profession as a brotherhood with common interests sharing a single universe of discourse.

No one understood this better than Alexis De Tocqueville. After an extensive journey through the United States in the early 1830s, which he undertook in order to examine American prisons, De Tocqueville wrote what has become the classic study of American democracy. The young French aristocrat viewed the legal profession as a separate rank within American society. According to De Tocqueville, lawyers "naturally constitute a *body*; not by any previous understanding, or by an agreement that directs them to a common end; but the analogy of their studies and the uniformity of their methods connect their minds as a common interest might unite their endeavors."[100]

In the absence of a native aristocracy, and in a nation where "the people" were sovereign, lawyers occupied a mediating position between the democratic majority and the governing elite. Committed to the preservation of the legal order, which they controlled, the legal profession provided a natural counterpoise to the radical inclinations of the popular will. One result of this restraint

---

99. Maxwell Bloomfield, *American Lawyers in a Changing Society, 1776–1876* (Cambridge, MA: Harvard University Press, 1976), Chaps. 2 and 5; Alfred Z. Reed, *Training for the Public Profession of the Law* (New York, NY: Arno Press, Inc., 1921), pt. 2, passim.

100. Alexis De Tocqueville, *Democracy in America*, Phillips Bradley, ed. (2 Vols., New York, 1944), vol. 1, 283.

was the absence of innovation in private law, compared to the radical transformation in public law, which the American Revolution had brought about. As De Tocqueville put it:

> The Americans, who have made so many innovations in their political laws, have introduced very sparing alterations in their civil laws, and that with great difficulty, although many of these laws are repugnant to their social Condition. The reason for this is that in matters of civil law the majority are obliged to defer to the authority of the legal profession, and the American lawyers are disinclined to innovate when they are left to their own choice.[101]

De Tocqueville likened the lawyers to the "hierophants of Egypt," keepers of "an occult science," who by profession rather than by birth harbored aristocratic pretensions. The profession "secretly opposed [its] aristocratic propensities to the nation's democratic instincts, their superstitious attachment to what is old to [the people's] love of novelty, their narrow views to its immense designs and their habitual procrastination to its ardent impatience."[102]

The power of the legal profession as a cohesive force in American life was strengthened by the joinder of the bench and the bar. Lay advocacy disappeared in most states after the revolution. In addition, the colonial practice of elevating laypersons as well as lawyers to the highest courts in some of the colonies came to an end in most states.[103] These developments meant that the bar became thoroughly professionalized and the bench would be drawn from its ranks. Accordingly, judges and lawyers would emanate from the same pool of training and experience. Furthermore, the courts wrested control over bar admission requirements from county bar associations, thereby increasing the fusion of bench and bar and weakening the independence of lawyers from the courts.[104]

The growth of judicial independence reinforced these tendencies. The Constitution recognized the principle of an independent judiciary when it provided that federal judges would have perma-

---

101. Ibid., 290.
102. Ibid., 289.
103. Friedman, *A History of American Law*, 109–110.
104. Ibid., 276; Reed, *Training for the Public Profession of the Law,* Pt. 2.

nent tenure in office and could be removed only for extraordinary causes. Once appointed by the president, federal judges could not be removed except by impeachment, a device rarely used. Most of the original states adopted some form of judicial appointment either by the governor or by the legislature or some combination of the two.[105] The elective principle only became popular in the mid-19th century, but even then, judicial offices were usually not contested in the same way as other elective positions. The state judiciaries became non-political—at least with respect to recruitment to the bench. Thus, both the federal and the state judiciaries, in different ways, became independent of day-to-day politics. This independence was a source of great influence. "The courts of justice are the visible organs by which the legal profession is enabled to control the democracy," De Tocqueville observed.[106] Clearly the legal profession, the judges together with the lawyers, had become a force with unmatched social leverage and influence.

The extraordinary power of the legal profession in American life was the result not only of the peculiar legal, constitutional, and political framework of American society, but also of the fusion of the bench and the bar into a cohesive force. Of equal importance was the enormous deference the American people gave to legal professionals and the degree to which the American public absorbed the ideas and habits of the legal profession. The very language of the lawyers became what De Tocqueville called the "vulgar tongue" of public life. Several forces combined to make it so. Because lawyers played such a prominent role in politics and occupied a disproportionate number of public offices, political issues of great consequence were often distilled into erudite legal questions, and political positions were defined as doctrines or propositions of law. Thus, the greatest public issue of the nineteenth century, racial slavery, the issue over which the nation was to break apart in 1861, was addressed not in moral terms or in terms of social cost, but primarily as a series of technical problems of constitutional law—such as whether African Americans could be citizens, or whether or not Congress had the power to exclude

105. Glenn R. Winters, "Selection of Judges—An Historical Introduction," *Texas Law Review* 44 (1966): 1081–1087.
106. De Tocqueville, *Democracy in America,* 289.

slavery in the territories, a place occupied by very few masters and slaves by the outbreak of the Civil War.

Alexis De Tocqueville attributed this penetration of the social fabric by the legal mentality to the jury system. "The jury," he wrote, "is preeminently a political institution."[107] The civil jury especially "cannot fail to exercise a powerful influence upon the national character."[108] De Tocqueville had a very positive view of the jury system and its effects. He found that jury service was as widespread as the franchise and about as frequently exercised. This exposure to the judicial process imparted a sense of equity, social responsibility, and participation in self-government to the citizen. De Tocqueville also thought that jury service was a highly educative experience teaching both a rudimentary knowledge of the law and its application to actual cases. Jury service transmitted to the citizenry the spirit of the judges, whose influence upon the jury panel was almost unlimited. Their influence, in fact, extended:

> [F]ar beyond the limits of the courts; in the recreations of private life, as well as in the turmoil of public business, in public, and in the legislative assemblies, the American judge is constantly surrounded by men who are accustomed to regard his intelligence as superior to their own; and after having exercised his power in the decision of causes, he continues to influence the habits of thought, and even the characters, of those who acted with him in his official capacity.[109]

The justification for a jury in a system of constitutional democracy has always been that it represents a check upon the power of the judges through citizen participation in the execution of the laws.[110] But De Tocqueville showed that the contact between judge and jury worked both ways. The deference of the typical jury to the judge's instructions on the law, and the judge's abiding influence on the mind of the jurors even after the trial had ended, exposed a fundamental truth. De Tocqueville put it best:

---

107. Ibid., 294.
108. Ibid., 295.
109. Ibid., 297.
110. By 1820, a clear functional differentiation between the role of the judge and the jury had come about. The jury was the finder of *fact* and the judge was the definer of *law*. See Friedman, *A History of American Law*, 137.

> The jury, then which seems to restrict the rights of the judiciary, does in reality Consolidate its power; and in no Country are the judges so powerful as where the people share their privileges, it is especially by means of the jury in civil causes that the American magistrates imbue even the lower classes of society with the spirit of their profession.[111]

Thus, the shift in emphasis from public law to private law in the period after the Revolution was a result not only of the pivotal role of the legal profession in public life, but also of the power the legal profession exercised over the American mind.

---

111. De Tocqueville, *Democracy in America,* 297.

Episode 6

Louisiana's First Civil Law Digest

> However our present interests may restrain us within our own limits, it is impossible not to look forward to distant times, when our rapid multiplication will expand itself beyond those limits, and cover the whole northern, if not the southern continent, with a people speaking the same language, governed in similar forms, and by similar laws; nor can we contemplate with satisfaction either blot or mixture on that surface.
>
> Thomas Jefferson, 1801

We can think of historical memory—the ordering of past events—as falling into three categories. The first includes those events that were famous in their own time as well as in the present. The Louisiana Purchase itself is such an event: momentous in 1803 and certainly well known today. The second category of historical events—again using an example from Louisiana—would be the controversy between Thomas Jefferson and Edward Livingston over the New Orleans Batture—well known in its day, but obscure today except to people with very particular historical interests. And then there is the example of the Digest (or Code) of 1808. Famous today as the cornerstone of the Louisiana's mixed legal system, the Digest was not highly noticed outside of Louisiana at the time of its adoption. Nationally, it was hardly noticed at all.

In 1811, speaking in opposition to the admission of Louisiana into the Union in one of the most memorable speeches ever made in the early Congress, Josiah Quincy of Boston argued that the Constitution did not permit the admission of a state on the other side of the Mississippi, a state peopled by a foreign nation, speaking a foreign tongue, and following strange laws and customs. "It was not for these men that our fathers fought." As Quincy declared: "It was not for them this Constitution was adopted. You have no

---

* Source: George Dargo, *The Digest of 1808: Historical Perspectives* originally published in *Tulane European and Civil Law Forum* Vol. 24, 2009, 1–30.

authority to throw the rights and liberties, and property of this people, into a "hotch-pot" with the wild men of the Missouri, nor with the mixed, though more respectable race of Anglo-Hispano-Gallo Americans, who bask on the sands, in the mouth of the Mississippi. I make no objection to these from their want of moral qualities or political right. The inhabitants of New Orleans are, I suppose, like those of all other countries, some good, some bad, some indifferent. . . . But," he concluded, "I oppose this bill from no animosity to the people of New Orleans, but from the deep conviction that it contains a principle incompatible with the liberties and safety of my country. . . . The bill, if it passes, is a death-blow to the Constitution."[1] Josiah Quincy had mined every source for his Constitutional arguments against Louisiana's admission, but notably absent is any reference to the 1808 Digest whose enactment, had it come to his attention, surely would have figured large in his lengthy discourse on the floor of the House.

This is not to say that Digest of 1808 was totally ignored. In one instance, the notice came indirectly in an article that can be called the "barbarous yoke" encyclical. This was a piece that apparently first appeared in a Paris newspaper and then picked up and reprinted by *La Lanterne Magique*, a highly politicized fly-by-night journal that had a brief half-life in New Orleans in 1808. Entitled "French Views With Respect to Louisiana" the complete text is as follows:

> "The Province of Louisiana, though separated for the present, from the GREAT EMPIRE, by a certain concurrence of events, continues to evince the highest veneration for all our political institutions. To avoid the barbarous yoke of a Gothick system of jurisprudence called the common law of England, the principles of the civil law have been expressly and exclusively adopted as the basis of a new code which is shortly to be promulgated in that Province. M. Louis Moreau Lislet, a French jurisconsult, has the honour of digesting this code; which in fact is a paraphrase of the Napoleon code.
>
> We regret to miss, in this digest, that admirable combination of principles, and perspicuity and elegance of style, which distin-

---

1. Josiah Quincy, Speech Against the Admission of New States, Debates, 11th Cong., 3rd Sess., 524–42 (January 14, 1811), reprinted in *The Annals of America* vol. 4 (Cambridge, Ma.: Hilliard and Brown, 1968) 283, 538, 542.

guish this grand work of the most eminent geniuses of our nation. We presume that Mr. Moreau thought it necessary to disguise the glorious plagiary, lest he might excite the national jealousies of his new fellow citizens. And he has disguised it effectually. So flattering a compliment to his native country, however, deserves our highest commendation, particularly as his labours will tend to preserve in that colony, for some time longer, the practice of those laws which it is our interest TO FIND THERE."[2]

A number of Federalist newspapers, most notably *The Repertory* of Boston but others around the country as well, reprinted the "barbarous yoke" piece in order to bolster the Federalist argument that the purchase of Louisiana had been a dangerous and improvident mistake and that Louisianians were preparing for the day when they would return—or be returned—to France. And this was just a few short years after some New England Federalists, including Boston's Josiah Quincy, had seriously advocated something called the Northern Confederacy, a scheme that contemplated northern state secession from the Union in part because of the Louisiana Purchase.[3]

The *Connecticut Herald*, another Federalist newspaper, provides a further example of the notice taken of the Digest's enactment. The *Herald* reprinted in full the speech of John Hughes, the representative to the Orleans territorial legislature from Ouachita Parish, given in March, 1809. In his address to the legislature—the same body that had enacted the Digest the previous year—Hughes fulminated against the early admission of Louisiana then under debate. But he also took note of the recently adopted civil digest this way:

> The imperfect knowledge which the tribunals and their officers had of the Spanish laws which remained in force on the taking possession of this country, was made the pretence for the introduction of a new code; and that code is not the ancient law of the territory, of which it purports to be a digest, but almost verbatim

---

2. *The Repertory* (Boston), March 24, 1809.
3. Kevin M. Gannon, "Escaping 'Mr. Jefferson's Plan of Destruction'": New England Federalists and the Idea of a Northern Confederacy, 1803–1804," *Journal of the Early Republic*, Vol. 21, No. 3, (2001), 413–443.

> *the new system of France—the Napoleon Code.*"[4]

As the editors of the *Herald* concluded in an editorial footnote to the reprint of Hughes' speech: "It is a lamentable fact that the civil law now in force in this territory is not a digest of the ancient laws of Louisiana, but of the present imperial law of France."[5] Both documents—the "barbarous yoke" piece and the Hughes address—provide evidence that the Louisiana civil digest was perceived by contemporaries as having been largely patterned after the French *Code Civil.*

* * *

Distance and remoteness shrouded Louisiana in mystery in the early years of the 19th century. Added to that were the numerous barriers to travel and the impossibility of easy communication between New Orleans and the population centers of the United States far to the east. There is no better description of this than that of Henry Adams in his *History of the Jefferson and Madison Administrations.* On the division of the west from the east, this is what Adams had to say in one of the opening paragraphs of Adams' great work:

> The entire population, both free and slave, west of the mountains, reached not yet half a million; but already they were partly disposed to think themselves, and the old thirteen States were not altogether unwilling to consider them, the germ of an independent empire, which was to find its outlet, not through the Alleghenies to the seaboard, but by the Mississippi River to the Gulf. Nowhere did eastern settlements touch the western. At least one hundred miles of mountainous country held the two regions everywhere apart.[6]

---

4. *Connecticut Herald,* May 16, 1809, 2 (original ital.).
5. Ibid.
6. Henry Adams, *The United States in 1800* (Ithaca, NY: Cornell Paperbacks, 1955; 1974), 112–113. Adams continued: "Nearly every foreign traveler who visited the United States during these early years, carried away an impression sober if not sad. A thousand miles of desolate and dreary forest, broken here and there by settlements; along the seacoast a few flourishing towns devoted to commerce; no arts, a provincial literature, a cancerous disease of negro slavery,

To these elemental geographic conditions must be added the strategic vulnerability of that city in the era following the Purchase —a problem not fully resolved until the Battle of New Orleans in early 1815.[7] Located on the "Island of Orleans", the city of New Orleans was surrounded on nearly every side by water, and, as such, was exposed to naval or amphibious attack from Spain, or France, or Britain. New Orleans was part of the Gulf Coast and the western anchor of a developing chain of river outlets which connected southwestern settlers in the interior with Caribbean and Atlantic trade.[8] Indeed, Americans in the Mississippi Territory (which encompassed what later became the states of Mississippi as well as Alabama) would have gladly exchanged all of Louisiana for Florida in order to guarantee access to the gulf via the Pearly, the Tombigbee, or the Alabama river.[9] As one resident of the region reported to the President: "[I]t will be best for us to have no more Territory beyond the Mississippi than what is necessary to secure the Navigation; now to *ascertain*, *extend*, *establish*, and *maintain*

and differences of political theory fortified within geographical lines,—what could be hoped for such a country except to repeat the story of violence and brutality which the world already knew by heart, until repetition for thousands of years and wearied and sickened mankind? Ages must probably pass before the interior could be thoroughly settled; even Jefferson, usually a sanguine man, talked of a thousand years with acquiescence, and in his first Inaugural Address, at a time when the Mississippi River formed the Western boundary, spoke of the country as having 'room enough for our descendants to the hundredth and thousandth generation.' No prudent person dared to act on the certainty that when settled, one government could comprehend the whole; and when the day of separation should arrive, and American should have her Prussia, Austria, and Italy, as she already had her England, France, and Spain, what else could follow but a return to the old conditions of local jealousies, wars, and corruption which had made a slaughter-house of Europe." For a recent effort to restore Adams to his rightful place in American historiography, and to correct some of the misconceptions that still bedevil interpreters of this pioneer of the historical profession, see Gary Wills, *Henry Adams and the Making of America* (New York: Houghton Mifflin Harcourt, 2005).

7. The Battle of New Orleans not only made Andrew Jackson a national hero, but the victory also demonstrated that New Orleans and all of Lower Louisiana could be held as a secure American possession. It also settled, once and for all, the nagging question of the loyalty of Louisianians to their new sovereign.

8. "New Orleans was a focus of immigration and a center of influence linking the Caribbean with the Mississippi valley" long after the Purchase. See, Richard W. Bailey, "the Foundation of English in the Louisiana Purchase: New Orleans, 1800–1850," *American Speech*, Vol. 78 (Winter 2003), 363–384, 368.

9. On the essential geographic unity of the region, see I.J. Cox, *The West Florida Controversy, 1798–1813: A Study in American Diplomacy* (Baltimore, 1918); 1967), esp. 1–6.

the Frontiers . . . [of] Louisiana, would be *expensive, troublesome, dangerous and consequently impolitic in the highest degree.* But to obtain east and west Florida, *would be the reverse.*"[10] Robert R. Livingston, the minister to France, was specifically instructed by Jefferson and Secretary of State James Madison to acquire New Orleans and Florida.[11] Spain had governed West Florida and Louisiana as a single entity with New Orleans as its capital.[12] New Orleans without Florida made no sense and would be difficult, perhaps even impossible, to hold.

The negotiated purchase of New Orleans and all of Louisiana—without West Florida—came not only as a surprise but as a serious strategic problem.[13] With West Florida still in Spanish hands most important access routes to the city were, technically at least, under Spanish control. Baton Rouge, eighty miles northwest of New Orleans and occupying the last high ground overlooking the Mississippi, was the site of a Spanish fort. This gave to the Spanish the potential to sever communications between the settled part of Lower Louisiana and the rest of the mainland.[14] Spanish naval units patrolled Lake Pontchartrain and could easily fortify Fort Petites Coquilles which guarded the Rigolets, the most important strait connecting the lake and the gulf.[15] Ship Island off the Florida coast was the major staging area for naval operations on the Gulf Coast until the Civil War, but in 1803 Ship Island was in

---

10. Thomas M. Potter to Jefferson, Sept. 17, 1804, in Jefferson Papers, Library of Congress. [original italics].

11. Alexander DeConde, *This Affair of Louisiana* (N.Y., 1976), 110.

12. A.P. Whitaker, *The Mississippi Question, 1795–1803: A Study in Trade, Politics, and Diplomacy* (New York, D. Appleton-Century Co., 1934) ("The geographical unity of Louisiana and West Florida was recognized by their union under the authority of a single governor, with New Orleans as the capital."), 29.

13. West Florida would remain disputed territory until the American settlers revolted in 1810 and declared an independent republic only to be absorbed first into the Orleans Territory and then into the new state of Louisiana as the Florida Parishes.

14. Ibid., 262; Kenneth Drude, "Fort Baton Rouge," *Louisiana Studies*, 7 (1968), 259–269.

15. Wilburt S. Brown, *The Amphibious Campaign for West Florida and Louisiana, 1814–1815: A Critical Review of Strategy and Tactics at New Orleans* (Tuscaloosa, AL: University of Alabama Press, 1969), 65.

the hands of the Spanish.[16] As to the overland routes from the northeast, principally the Natchez Trace and the Pearl River route, these also had to traverse Spanish West Florida.

Clearly, the Spanish presence all around New Orleans could be troublesome. And while Spanish military power was feeble on a global scale especially after the Franco-Spanish defeat at the Battle of Trafalgar in 1805, Spain was strong enough to assert its interest in and around the island of Orleans. Spain was still a respectable naval power.[17] The Spanish fresh water navy was not inconsiderable. In 1800, it was "essentially a river fleet [whose] chief value lay in [its] ability to cooperate in the defense of the posts on the Mississippi."[18] In short, "West Florida was necessary for the defense of New Orleans."[19] When in the summer and early fall of 1806 a Spanish-American military conflict seemed imminent, the United States' position in all of Lower Louisiana appeared to be in danger of complete collapse.

Secretary of the Treasury, Albert Gallatin, the longest serving treasury secretary in the nation's history and Jefferson's principal cabinet advisor on matters having to do with Louisiana, considered West Florida even more vital than New Orleans itself.[20] With his European background—born and educated in Switzerland, a native French speaker, multi-lingual, and knowledgeable about international affairs—Albert Gallatin was the figure that Jefferson turned to in the days immediately preceding and following the Purchase for advice on how his administration should act. As early as September 1803, three months prior to the formal delivery and

---

16. One military historian has considered the Rigolets to be "the most strategic spot in Louisiana." Richard P. Weinert, "The Neglected Key to the Gulf Coast," *Journal of Mississippi History*, 31 (1969), 269–301.
17. Whitaker, *Mississippi Question*, 262.
18. Ibid., 35; ("It was out of the question for such meager and widely scattered [military] forces to defend the province [all of Louisiana] against invasion, and indeed they were not expected to do so. Though they could not maintain Spanish sovereignty, they could at least assert it, and they could preserve order among the king's subjects. For the latter purpose they were fully adequate. . . .[A]s a police force for a colony of 45,000 inhabitants . . . they were rather impressive.") 35–36.
19. Cox, *West Florida Controversy*, ("West Florida rendered New Orleans susceptible to attack by . . . a foreign enemy, and its own weakness was a constant temptation to seize it."), 546.
20. See, Gallatin to Madison, Feb. 7, 1803, in *Letters and Other Writings of James Madison*, 4 vols., (Philadelphia: J. B. Lippincott, 1865), II, 179–180.

transfer of Louisiana scheduled for December 20th, Gallatin wrote to the president: "Permit me to suggest the propriety of having everything in readiness to take possession of New Orleans."[21] Gallatin detailed what military forces were available for deployment should there be doubt as to "whether the prefect and Spanish officers shall be willing to give it up or not." Only recently, Spain had retroceded all of Louisiana west of the Mississippi to France with the understanding that France would not cede the territory to any third party such as the United States. But Spain did not relinquish its claim to the Floridas. Therefore, there was grave doubt as to what the disposition of the Spanish authorities would be when France handed over all of Louisiana to the Americans. "Although I do not share in the alarm of our ministers," Gallatin wrote at the time to the President, "I think it wise to be as perfectly prepared as if it had a real ground . . . and to prepare the way with the inhabitants [of New Orleans] so as to meet no opposition from them." He then continued: "If it shall be found necessary to take possession of New Orleans against the will of the possessors, there can be no doubt of the propriety of occupying at the same time that part of West Florida which we claim. But if New Orleans and West Louisiana shall be yielded without difficulty, the policy of occupying the rest of what we claim against the will of the Spanish officers is a subject which deserves serious consideration."[22]

In a subsequent letter written soon afterwards, Gallatin went into greater detail about the military situation in the southwest as the date for the Louisiana transfer approached:

> [If] the Executive shall think it necessary to call any militia or volunteers in that part of the country [the southwest], it may be confidently relied on that within a fortnight after the reception of the orders by the Executives of Tennessee and Kentucky fifteen hundred horsemen, all of them volunteers and well selected, shall be at Nashville, and then proceed immediately to Natchez, which they may reach within twenty days afterwards at most.
>
> About one-third of that number might meet at Nashville a few days earlier, and march across the wilderness within a fortnight,

---

21. Gallatin to Jefferson, 5th September, 1803, in Henry Adams (ed.), *The Writings of Albert Gallatin* 3 vols., (Philadelphia: J. B. Lippincott, 1879), Vol. I, 152–153.
22. Ibid., 153.

> the rest to follow in divisions of two or three hundreds . . . from the more distant parts; which will also be more convenient on account of forage for the horses. (. . .) All agree that as to the number of men, considering that all the crops are in, the season the most favorable in point of health of the whole year, and the general zeal of the country, five thousand men could be raised at once without any difficulty, and that the only struggle will be for having permission to go.[23]

Others besides Gallatin were concerned about the problem. General James Wilkinson, the supreme commander of American military forces in the west—such as they were—who was stationed in New Orleans, warned the Secretary of War that "Every Hour evinces more and more the necessity of a strong garrison here. . . . [O]ur puny force has become a subject of ridicule, and the old women begin to exclaim '*quel triste Governement* [sic].'"[24] Wilkinson feared "for the preservation of our immense Acquisitions in this quarter." He understood the urgency of the need for additional military support to shore up the tenuous American position in that remote corner of the continent.

As it happened, the transfer of all of Louisiana—minus the disputed territory of West Florida—went off without a hitch. But Jefferson remained convinced that military defenses needed substantial reinforcement if Louisiana was to remain in American hands. Gallatin continued to advocate for a military build-up in and around the city. "Observe also that the approaches by Lake Pontchartrain must be defended, as well as those by the Mississippi," he wrote to Jefferson late in 1806.[25] Some months later he advised that "with a moderate force, properly distributed on water and in the forts, which command the navigation, it is the most easily defended place, of equal importance, in the United States."[26]

---

23. Gallatin to Jefferson, October 28, 1803, Ibid., 163.
24. Wlkinson to Henry Dearborn, Jan. 11, 1804, in Clarence E. Carter (ed.), *The Territorial Papers of the United States* (26 vols., Washington, United States Government Printing Office, 1934–1962), vol. IX, 159.
25. Gallatin to Jefferson, Nov. 16, 1806, in Gallatin Papers, supra note 21, vol. I, 317.
26. Gallatin to Jefferson, July 25, 1807, Ibid., 344. ("New Orleans, like Savannah and Norfolk, cannot be defended by its population alone. Its defenses in support of gunboats in the river and in the lake, should be strong forts at Plaquemine and St. John. A garrison and forts in the city do not appear to be of any use. If an enemy

The isolation of New Orleans was one of the most vexing problems facing Jefferson after 1803. In the remainder of his first term in office and throughout his troubled second term, he returned again and again to this issue of strategic vulnerability and the need to take remedial measures there.

Coupled to the on-going problem of exterior exposure was the hair-trigger volatility of the local populations whose reaction to the recent change in sovereignty was still not fully known or understood. Thomas Jefferson came to believe that nothing less than radical demographic change would shore up Louisiana's defenses and solidify America's hold of its grand new possession. To effect such change, Jefferson proposed that Congress adopt a militia scheme that would transplant thousands of Americans to the new territories west of the Mississippi to strengthen the defenses of New Orleans. Albert Gallatin was sympathetic to the idea, and Jefferson consulted with him about it with some frequency. But the plan was first proposed by others. As early as the summer of 1803—following the Purchase but preceding the transfer—none other than Thomas Paine suggested sending "thousands and tens of thousands in England and Ireland and also in Scotland" to settle Louisiana. Paine even suggested that the very name—"Louisiana"—be stricken and that all vestiges of French culture and influence could be permanently erased.[27] Ephraim Kirby of Connecticut, the compiler of the very first set of state law reports in America and one of Jefferson's early judicial appointments to the Mississippi Territory, observed in 1804 that "a strong American settlement . . . will offer an excellent Barrier against the approach of a foreign enemy at the southwestern point of our territories. Upon any emergency succor might be thrown into New Orleans with more ease from this place (i.e., the Mississippi Territory) than any

---

lands on terra firma, he will take the town and garrison, and we must retake it from the upper country.")

27. M.D. Conway, ed., *The Writings of Thomas Paine*, 4 vols., (New York: G. P. Putnam's Sons, 1894–1896), III 430–436. The final designation of Lower Louisiana as the Territory of Orleans fulfilled Paine's recommendation. The change in nomenclature did not go unnoticed for it was commented upon in the Louisiana Remonstrance (1804). "Remonstrance of the People of Louisiana Against the Political system Adopted by Congress for Them" (Dec. 31, 1804), in *American State Papers*, Class X, Misc., I: 396–399, communicated to the House, Dec. 3, 1804, to the Senate, Dec. 31, 1804, Annals of Congress, 8th cong., 2nd Sess., 727–728.

other."[28] Throughout his first and second terms Jefferson continued to advocate for the deployment of a strong militia force in the region. The proposal, though never enacted by Congress during his presidency, fitted nicely with Jefferson's general philosophy of relying on militia rather than a standing army while achieving the budgetary retrenchment with a modest federal military establishment which Gallatin strongly favored.

The idea had ripened by 1806. The Administration prepared a bill providing allotments of 160 acres in fee-simple estate to white males between the ages of eighteen and thirty-five who agreed to reside in the territory for no less than seven years, during which time they would render two years of active service to the regular army. Recruiters would receive grants of 640 acres for every hundred men they brought into the program. The federal government would bear the costs of transportation and settlement.[29] Introduced into Congress for the first time by Senator Thomas Worthington of Ohio in March 1806, it was described and summarized by Senator William Plumer of New Hampshire:

> The President observed to me that he considered this bill as one of the most important now pending in Congress. That no part of the U.S. was so much exposed as Louisiana—That it was absolutely necessary to provide means for its defense—That near half of its present inhabitants were such that they could not be depended on in case of an invasion. [And] that it would be impolitic and expensive to raise a standing army.[30]

Jefferson himself described the militia plan to John Dickinson of Pennsylvania in January 1807:

---

28. Kirby to Jefferson, April 20, 1804, in the Ephraim Kirby Papers, Duke University.

29. A Bill for the Settlement of a Part of the Territory of Orleans; Sketches of parts of a bill for encouraging settlers in territory of Orleans; and, Notes on the Bill for the defense of Orleans—all of which appear in manuscript as well as in Jefferson's published writings. See, P.L. Ford, ed., *The Writings of Thomas Jefferson*, 10 vols., (New York: G. P. Putnam's Sons, 1892–1899),VIII, 425–427; also, E.S. Brown, "Jefferson's Plan for a Military Colony in Orleans Territory," *Mississippi Valley Historical Review*, vol. VIII (1922), 373–376.

30. E.S. Brown (ed.), *William Plumer's Memorandum of Proceedings in the United States Senate, 1803–1807* (NewYork: Macmillan Co., 1923), 474.

> I proposed to the members of Congress . . . the enlisting [of] 30,000 volunteers, Americans by birth, to be carried at public expense, and settled immediately on a bounty of 160 [acres] of land each on the West side of the Mississippi; on the condition of giving two years of military service, if that country should be attacked within 7 years. The defense of the country would thus be placed on the spot, and the additional number would entitle the territory to become a state, would make the majority American, and make it an American instead of a French state. This would not sweeten the pill to the French; but in making that acquisition we had some view to our own good as well as theirs, and I believe the greatest good of both will be promoted by whatever will amalgamate us together.[31]

But there were other reasons for the militia scheme—Jefferson's Settlement Project—besides security. In fact, Jefferson wanted to completely transform the cultural and legal character of his vast acquisitions, or, as he wrote to Gallatin, "to draw their laws and organization to the mold of ours by degrees as they find practicable without exciting too much discontent."[32] The evidence for this is indisputable. In his very first year as president, with Louisiana already in his sights, Jefferson told James Monroe (the future minister plenipotentiary to France) that "however our present interests may restrain us within our own limits, it is impossible not to look forward to distant times, when our rapid multiplication will expand itself beyond those limits, and cover the whole northern, if not the southern continent, with a people speaking the same language, governed in similar forms, and by similar laws; nor can we contemplate with satisfaction either blot or mixture on that surface."[33] As he later would put it (somewhat more colorfully) when comparing the two legal traditions then in competition for recognition in Louisiana: "For however I admit the superiority of the civil over the common law code, as a system of perfect justice, yet an incorporation of the two would be like Nebuchadnezzar's

---

31. Jefferson to Dickinson, Jan. 13, 1807, in Jefferson, *Writings* (Ford ed.), supra note 29, vol. IX, 8.
32. Jefferson to Gallatin, Nov. 9, 1803, Gallatin Papers, New York Historical Society.
33. Jefferson to Monroe, Nov. 24, 1801, quoted in De Conde, *This Affair of Louisiana*, 110.

image of metal and clay, a thing without cohesion of parts."[34] Or, as he would write to Gallatin, "If by giving 100 miles square of that country we can secure the rest and at the same time create an American majority before Orleans becomes a state, it will be the best bargain every made."[35]

The perception that the Louisianians were unfit for self-government under the American system was widespread in Washington. Gallatin believed that they "seem[ed] to be but one degree above the French West Indians, than whom a more ignorant and depraved race of civilized men did not exist. Give them slaves and let them speak French (for they cannot write it) and they would be satisfied," he said. One United States senator believed "those people are absolutely incapable of governing themselves" while another simply feared that "they are not yet bound to us by any ties."[36] Thomas Paine was unrestrained in his contempt for native Louisianians whom he thought unworthy of rights or powers of self governance until, as he put it, "as you become initiated into the principles and practice of the representative system of government, of which you have yet had no experience, you will participate more, and finally be partakers of the whole."[37]

Jefferson's plan to plant an American majority in the future state of Louisiana never succeeded. The militia scheme came toward the end of his second term, and by then Jefferson had become a lame duck president. In addition, even though Jefferson's political party still dominated the nation and the Congress, events across the Atlantic assumed ever-increasing importance; they eventually succeeded in undermining Jefferson's political power and personal influence. The so-called peace of Amiens collapsed in

---

34. Jefferson to John Tyler, June 17, 1812, in A.A. Lipscomb and A.E. Bergh, ed., *The Writings of Thomas Jefferson*, ed., 20 Vols. (Washington, D.C.: Thomas Jefferson Memorial Association of the United States, 1904–1905), XIII, 166.

35. Jefferson to Gallatin, Jan. 31, 1807, Ibid., XI, 145. "Congress . . . sought to secure the region further by flooding the Louisianas with 'loyal' American settlers who presumably already understood the benefits of the American Union." John Craig Hammond, "'They Are Very Much Interested in Obtaining an Unlimited Slavery': Rethinking the Expansion of Slavery in the Louisiana Purchase Territories, 1803–1805" *Journal of the Early Republic*, Vol. 23, No 3, (2003), 353–380, quote at 365.

36. Quotes collected in ibid., 363–364.

37. Thomas Paine, To the French Inhabitants of Louisiana, (1804), supra, note 27.

1803, and by 1807 the Wars of Napoleon were back in full force.[38] In addition, through the use of naval force and an economic blockade Jefferson had succeeded in bringing a naval dispute with the Tripolitan States in the Mediterranean to a successful conclusion during his First Term, so that he came to the mistaken belief that a similar approach could be applied when the rights of neutrals were threatened on the high seas. As a result, and at Jefferson's direction, Congress put into place the policy known as the Embargo Act which soon developed into a draconian system for stopping American trans-Atlantic shipping altogether. This resulted in widespread commercial depression. New England and much of the eastern seaboard were in abject revolt while Jefferson's popularity went into freefall. His attempts to enforce the Embargo with the use of military force made him the target of increasing political attack.[39] Moreover, other issues diverted Jefferson's attention and depleted his political resources thereby blocking the completion of the settlement project for Louisiana: The Burr Conspiracy and its fallout in 1806–1807, the litigation over the New Orleans Batture after 1807, the ending of the slave trade after January 1, 1808, the volatile status of West Florida, and the growing conflict with Great Britain over impressments and the rights of neutrals were the most salient. In such a climate, an ambitious plan like the militia scheme had no chance of succeeding in Congress. Nevertheless, again and again, Jefferson returned to this idea of transforming Louisiana.

The settlement project was Thomas Jefferson's boldest attempt to institute Anglo-American law in Louisiana. When it failed, Jefferson had no choice but to recognize that the laws in force would remain in force. Recognized principles of international law, well known at the time, supported such a policy. As summarized by a leading American treatise published years later but reflecting the

---

38. The Spanish had also tried, without much success, to "superimpose their culture and institutions." Jerah, Johnson, "Colonial New Orleans: A Fragment of the Eighteenth-Century French Ethos", in A.R. Hirsch and J. Logsdon (eds.), *Creole New Orleans: Race and Americanization* (Baton Rouge: Louisiana State University Press, 1992), 12–57.

39. Leonard W. Levy, *Jefferson and Civil Liberties: The Darker Side* (Cambridge, Mass., 1963), esp. chaps. 5, 6.; also, Dumas Malone, *Jefferson the President: Second Term, 1805–1809* (Boston: Little, Brown & Co., 1974), chaps.16, 31, 32, et passim.

state of the law in 1800: "The change of sovereignty does not obliterate the subject-matters of property or obligations. . . . Accordingly, it is held that the municipal private code remains in force . . . in the absence of new laws displacing them."[40] Or, as Blackstone had written back in the middle of the 18th century, "[i]n conquered or ceded countries, that have already laws of their own, the king may indeed alter and change those laws; but, till he does actually change them, the ancient laws of the country remain [in force]."[41] Louisiana had been ceded by France to the United States by treaty which provided that "the inhabitants of the ceded territory shall be incorporated in the Union of States, and admitted as soon as possible, according to the principles of the Federal constitution, to the enjoyment of all of the rights, advantages, and immunities, of citizens of the United States."[42] The inhabitants of Lower Louisiana were well aware of the terms of the treaty of cession. But the Louisiana Government Act of 1804 vested all legislative power in a governor and council of thirteen notables appointed by the President of the United States with "power to alter, modify, or repeal the laws which may be in force."[43] All legislative enactments were subject to Congressional oversight. The Act of 1804 had a sunset clause providing for its termination in 1805, but it contained no guarantee of self-government or admission to the union thereafter. Nevertheless, Louisianians perceived the Louisiana Government Act of 1804 as a violation of the treaty of cession even though, in other respects, the act was fully in conformity with customary practice—a territorial government in the first stage of a three-stage process of territorial development.

As soon as the terms of the first Louisiana Government Act became known, a political protest was mounted in New Orleans. Within weeks of the passage of this first organic law, the mayor of

---

40. Henry Wheaton, G.G. Wilson, ed., *Elements of International Law* (Oxford: The Clarendon Press, 1866; 1936), 365 n(4).
41. William Blackstone, *Commentaries on the Laws of England*, 4 vols., (Dublin: Printed for John Exshaw…, 1771); I, 107.
42. F.N. Thorpe, comp, *The Federal and State Constitutions, Colonial Charters and Other Organic Laws of the . . . United States of America*, 7 vols., (Washington, D.C.: Government Printing Office, 1909) Vol. III, 1364–1371.
43. An Act erecting Louisiana into two territories" (8th Cong., 1st Sess.), Ibid., 1364–1371.

New Orleans called for a formal *demarche* to Congress.[44] The ensuing agitation focused upon the apparent violation of the cession agreement.[45] Foremost among the complaints listed in what became known as the Louisiana Remonstrance was the failure of Congress to provide for immediate statehood—"the immediate establishment of the said territory into a free state." This was a primary concern of the three memorialists who traveled to the District of Columbia bearing the Remonstrance in the fall of 1804.

The Remonstrance was a remarkable expression of an instinct for self-government which was thoroughly unexpected in Washington. In forceful and colorful language, it expressed the deepest longings of native Louisianians:

> Persuaded that a free people [i.e., Americans] would acquire territory only to extend the blessings of freedom, that an enlightened nation would never destroy those principles on which its Government was founded, and that their Representatives would disdain to become the instruments of oppression, we calculated with certainty that their first act of sovereignty would be a communication of all the blessing they enjoyed, and were the less anxious to know on what particular terms we were received. [W]e passed under your jurisdiction with a joy bordering on enthusiasm, submitted to the inconveniences of an intermediate dominion without a murmur, and saw the last tie that attached us to our mother country severed with less regret. . . . But we cannot conceal, we ought not to dissemble, that the first project presented for the Government of this country [Louisiana] tended to lessen the enthusiasm which . . . had been universal, and to fix our attention on present evils, while it rendered us less sanguine as to the future.

Recounting the revolutionary history of the Americans and the principles that guided the American Revolution and the Constitution, the Remonstrance continued:

> Are truths, then, so well founded, so universally acknowledged, inapplicable only to us? Do political axioms on the Atlan-

---

44. Etienne, Bore, New Orleans City Council Records, Vol. I, No. 1, 94.
45. For a close study of the legislative history of the Louisiana Government Act of 1804, see James E. Scanlon, "A Sudden Conceit: Jefferson and the Louisiana Government Bill of 1804," *Louisiana History*, Vol. 9 (1968), 139–162.

> tic become problems when transferred to the shores of the Mississippi? or are the unfortunate inhabitants of these regions the only people who are excluded from those equal rights acknowledged in your declaration of independence, repeated in the different State constitutions, and ratified by that of which we claim to be a member? Where, we ask respectfully, where is the circumstance that is to exclude us from a participation in these rights? Is it because we have not heretofore enjoyed them?
>
> This, on the contrary, would seem a reason to hasten the communication, to indemnify us by a futurity of freedom, for the years we have been deprived of it, and enable us, experimentally, to compare the blessings of a free Government with the evils of another kind of dominion. . . .We may then again become the victims of false information, of hasty remark, or prejudiced opinion; we may then again be told that we are incapable of managing our own concerns, that the period of emancipation is not yet arrived, and that when, in the school of slavery, we have learned how to be free, our rights shall be restored. . . . If there is force in our reclamations, on the great question of fundamental rights; if we are entitled to legislate for ourselves as a member of the Union, and to establish the forms on which that legislation shall be conducted, by framing a constitution suited to our own exigencies, then no further observations need to be made on other parts of the law, for the right of local legislation implies that of making the alterations we might deem expedient. . . . [46]

But of utmost importance to the Louisiana memorialists was their emphasis upon the restriction placed by the Act of 1804 upon further importations of slaves into the territory:

> There is one subject, however, extremely interesting to us, in which great care has been taken to prevent any interference even by the Governor and council, selected by the President himself. The African trade is absolutely prohibited, and severe penalties imposed on traffic free to all the Atlantic States who choose to engage in it, and as far as relates to procuring the subjects of it from other States, permitted even in the Territory of the Mississippi. It is not our intention to enter into

---

46. Remonstrance of the People of Louisiana, supra note 27; published in New Orleans in French as *Memoire presente au Congres des Etas-Unis d'Amerique par les habitants de la Louisiane* (New Orleans, J.B.L.S. Fontaine, 1804); in English as *Memorial Presented by the Inhabitants of Louisiana to the Congress of the United States* (Washington, D.C., Samuel Smith (publisher), 1804).

> arguments that have become familiar to every reasoner on this question. We only ask the right of deciding it for ourselves, and of being placed in this respect on an equal footing with other States. To the necessity of employing African laborers, which arises from climate, and the species of cultivation pursued in warm latitudes, is added a reason in this country peculiar to itself. The banks raised to restrain the waters of the Mississippi can only be kept in repair by those whose natural constitution and habits of labor enable them to resist the combined effects of a deleterious moisture, and a degree of heat intolerable to whites; this labor is great, it requires many hands, and it is all important to the very existence of our country. If, therefore, this traffic is justifiable any where, it is surely in this province, where, unless it is permitted, cultivation must cease, the improvements of a century be destroyed, and the great river resume its empire over our ruined fields and demolished habitations.[47]

When their mission appeared to have failed, the Louisiana memorialists published several advocacy documents which illustrate just how completely Louisianians understood the terms of the cession and the degree of self-government to which it entitled them and that the American government had failed to provide.[48] Most notable was the speed, focus, and discipline of the Louisiana protestors. Their agitation for immediate change would continue unabated. Louisianians continued to insist upon their political and legal rights with a determination that was as single-minded as it must have been surprising. As noted in an unpublished letter by Joseph Dubreuil de Villars, a Louisiana planter, the Americans had totally misconstrued the political intentions of the Louisianians, and the ideological posture of its people. Dubreuil wrote to a personal correspondent, "It is not unknown here, after reading over Northern public papers, that the ceded territory has been described to

---

47. Ibid., 399; For a thorough analysis of the importance of this provision of the Louisiana Government Act of 1804 and the objections to it by the Louisiana Remonstrators, see John Craig Hammond, "'They Are Very Much Interested in Obtaining an Unlimited Slavery': Rethinking the Expansion of Slavery in the Louisiana Purchase Territories, 1803–1805" *Journal of the Early Republic*, Vol. 23, No 3, (2003), 353–380.
48. *Reflections on the Cause of the Louisianians Respectfully Submitted by their Agents* (Washington: n.p., 1805); *Analysis of the Third Article of the Treaty of Cession of Louisiana* (n.p.: n.p., n.d.).

Congress as some sort of Tower of Babel, suffering from the confusion of tongues, and the Louisianians as men stupefied by despotism or ignorance, and therefore unable to elevate themselves, for a long time to the heights of a free constitution."[49] But this was far from the case, for as Dubreuil then observed in referring to the three deputies bearing the Remonstrance to Washington in the winter of 1804:

> [T]he Deputies [were] specially instructed to send copies of this memoir to all the legislative bodies of individual States, and to all the printing houses and journalists who have the best reputation and who are most widely known. By this means we would be sure to have as many advocates and supporters with Congress as there may be worthy citizens all over the United States. This last step . . . is perfectly well planned. In absolute governments, the oppression of an individual is really a special evil about which nobody worries, because from the very nature of things, everyman is left alone and is obliged to fight things out for himself, but under Democratic Constitutions the oppression of one individual is necessarily a general evil, because all rights and liberties included therein are in a real and imminent danger, the minute the public authority dares to violate a single one of the rights of even the most obscure of their citizens.[50]

The letter by Dubreuil de Villars is an extraordinary document. It is yet another testament to the political sophistication of the people of Louisiana who fully understood the gulf separating perception and reality in the Louisiana mind and heart at the dawn of its history as an American possession. The Louisiana Government Act passed a year later was, in part, a response to the agitation caused by the Act of 1804. The provision of the Act of 1804 barring slavery from Lower Louisiana was dropped in the revision of 1805; sixth article of the Northwest Ordinance, which prohibited slavery, was specifically omitted from the new Louisiana organic law.[51] This second stage of territorial governance provided for an

---

49. J. Dubreuil, Letter of June 2, 1804, Joseph Dubreuil de Villars Papers, Special collections, Perkins Library, Duke University.
50. Ibid.
51. Sec. 5. And be it further enacted, That the second paragraph of the said ordinance, which regulates the descent and distribution of estates; and also the sixth article of compact which is annexed to and makes part of said ordinance, are

independent elected legislative assembly that, along with the governor's council, constituted the legislative branch.[52] The rapidity with which Orleans went through these stages of territorial governance—first outlined in the Northwest Ordinance of 1787—showed the efficacy of political protest. Statehood would come in 1812, less than a decade after the Purchase. The expedited treatment that Louisiana received in the period was a product of the political energy that the Louisianians themselves were able to bring to bear.

* * *

In the first decade of the 19th century Louisianians had been "booted from one corner to another on the field of world politics"[53] by shifts in political sovereignty—from France to Spain, then back to France, and then to the United States—all in the short space of a single generation. While considerable uncertainty still lingered as to how permanent Louisiana's newest political arrangement would prove to be, by 1808 it was clear that the Americans were serious about staying. The Burr Conspiracy had shown that New Orleans was not nearly as volatile as once thought while, by 1808, Spanish imperial contraction had demonstrated that its power in the Mississippi Region—despite the dire warnings of such self-serving alarmists as General James Wilkinson—was nothing more than an elaborate *trompe d'oeil.*[54] As to West Florida—the object of America's original and most ardent desire—its final acquisition by force was only two years away, and no one expected Spain to have

---

hereby declared not to extend to but are excluded from all operation within the said territory of Orleans. Act Further Providing for the Government of the Territory of Orleans (1805), Thorpe, *Federal and State Constitutions*, supra note 43, at 1372; Hammond, "Rethinking the Expansion of Slavery", supra note 47, at 374.

52. An Act further providing for the government of the territory of Orleans (8th Cong., 2nd Sess.), in Thorpe (comp.), *Federal & State Constitutions*, supra note 32, at 1371–1373; see also, Jack E. Eblen, *The First and Second United States Empires: governors and Territorial Government, 1784–1912* (Pittsburgh: University of Pittsburgh Press,1968).

53. Whitaker, *Mississippi Question*, supra note 13, at 243.

54. Spain's attitude toward the defense of Louisiana was once characterized up by Manual de Godoy, Spain's foreign minister, this way: "*No es posible poner puertas al campo*" {"You can't lock up an open field."]; Whitaker, *Mississippi Question*, supra note 13, 180; "Even the military was surprisingly unSpanish." Johnson, "Colonial New Orleans," supra note 38, 47.

much to say in the matter.[55] Finally, the territorial government under William Claiborne's management acted with increasing competence and assurance. In short, "political hegemony" was quickly becoming less the great issue that it had been at first.

But "cultural hegemony" was another matter altogether. As explained by the historian, Jackson Lears, "[C]ultural hegemony can . . . reconcile the apparent contradiction between the power wielded by dominant groups and the relative cultural autonomy of subordinate groups . . . Ruling groups do not maintain their hegemony merely by giving their domination an aura of moral authority through the creation and perpetuation of legitimating symbols; they must also seek to win the consent of subordinate groups to the existing social order." [56] Or, as explained by a literary theorist, "[H]egemony is not only the political process by which a particular group constitutes itself as 'the one' or 'the majority' in relation to which 'minorities' are defined and know themselves to be 'other,' but it is equally the process by which positions of otherness may ally and constitute a new majority, a 'counter-hegemony.'"[57]

The concept of "cultural hegemony" has great force when applied to conditions in Lower Louisiana in this period. While the number of new American settlers continued to increase, French was still the dominant language, and the vast majority of people were French speakers. In fact, a significant "Frenchification" was ongoing at the time of the transfer which continued thereafter. "In New Orleans in 1800, one quarter of the white population was Spanish, but the Spanish, too, lived as Frenchmen and, as with the Germans, the French language was the general means of social

---

55. By 1804, there was nary a single fortified Spanish post in the entire Mississippi Valley. The garrisons that did exist numbered very few Spanish troops. See Whitaker, *Mississippi Question*, supra note 13, 263 (". . . the two Floridas together could muster less than two thousand Spanish regulars; . . . Kentucky alone had 30,000 men enrolled in its militia.")

56. T.J. Jackson Lears, "The Concept of Cultural Hegemony: Problems and Possibilities," *The American Historical Review*, Vol. 90, No. 3, (Jun., 1985), 567–593, quotes at 568, 569.

57. See, Lisa Lowe, "Heterogeneity, Hybridity, Multiplicity: Marking Asian American Differences," in *Literary Theory: An Anthology*, 2nd ed., J. Rivkin & M. Ryan, eds., (Oxford: Blackwell Publishers, 2003), 1031–1050, quote at 1036.

discourse."[58] Many, including such prominent individuals as William Claiborne and Edward Livingston, both of whom having been widowed, married French Creole women—twice in Livingston's case. Moreover, a surge of French-speaking refugees from the island of Saint Domingue reinforced the process of Frenchification following the outbreak of the Haitian Revolution in 1791.[59] Thousands of refugees sought asylum in New Orleans. From 1791 to 1812, about 15,000 Saint Dominguais settled in Lower Louisiana with most staying in the capital city.[60] Many came directly from Saint Domingue or via Cuba and Jamaica thus swelling the Francophile population of the Territory of Orleans in the first decade of the 19th century.[61]

"New Orleans . . . was ultimately the destination for the largest number of refugees from the Haitian Revolution."[62] According to Daniel Clark, the American consul in the city at the time of the transfer in 1803, New Orleans numbered 8,056.[63] By 1810, the Dominguais had more than doubled the size of the city to over 17,000.[64] Overall, the number of blacks (free people of color and black slaves) exceeded the number of white inhabitants. But French remained the dominant vernacular in a sea of languages and cultures. "United by their Creole language and culture and by their common misfortune, these newcomers from the islands permitted New Orleans to preserve for a few more years its colonial charac-

---

58. Vernon Valentine Palmer, "Two Worlds in One: The Genesis of Louisiana's Mixed Legal system, 1803–1812," in V.V. Palmer , ed., *Louisiana: Microcosm of a Mixed Jurisdiction* (Durham: North Carolina Academic Press, 1999), 23–39, quote at 29.
59. For a useful overview of the Haitian Revolution, see Laurent Dubois, "The Haitian Revolution and the Sale of Louisiana, *The Southern Quarterly*, Vol. 44, Issue 3, 18–41; idem., *Avengers of the New World: The Story of the Haitian Revolution* (Cambridge, Mass.: Belknap Press, Harvard University, 2004).
60. R.L. Paquette, "Revolutionary Saint Domingue in the Making of Territorial Louisiana," in D.B. Gaspar & D. P. Geggus, *A Turbulent Time: The French Revolution and the Greater Caribbean* (Bloomington, Ind.: Indiana University Press, 1997), 204–225, at 214.
61. Paul Lachance, "An Empire Gone Awry," *Humanities* (2002), Vol.23, Issue 6, 17–20.
62. Ned Sublette, *The World That Made New Orleans: From Spanish Silver to Congo Square* (Chicago: Lawrence Hill Books, 2008), 250.
63. See, Whitaker, *Mississippi Question*, supra note 13, at 277, n31 (3,948 whites, 1,335 free blacks, 2,773 black slaves).
64. Ibid., 242, 250–251.

ter, its exotic charm, and a life-style similar to that of an island just offshore from the continent, even as thousands of Americans were arriving from the eastern states."[65] This meant that ". . . Creole political ascendancy, or at least group preservation, seemed assured. . . . "[66] Even in the 1820s, New Orleans was still perceived as a nearly ungovernable *melange* of peoples. As Benjamin Latrobe, the pioneering engineer and architect, would observe, "[O]n arrival in New Orleans in the morning, a sound more strange than any that is heard anywhere else in the world astonishes [a stranger]. It is a more incessant, loud, rapid, and various gabble of tongues of all tones than was ever heard at Babel."[67]

Accordingly, while political hegemony was becoming "closed", cultural hegemony was still "open"—an area for interaction, accommodation, negotiation, and compromise.[68] Cultural commitments were not fixed but highly fluid, open-ended, and still undefined. In Louisiana, despite the growing political power of the Americans, the possibility for the creation of a "counter-hegemony" left a "third space" for the emergence of competing cultural expressions. While political hegemony may get closed off by a dominant over a sub-dominant group—as in the ultimate case of political sovereignty—the sub-dominant (or "subaltern") group can still assert itself not only through participation in the very institutions of political dominance upon which the architecture of sovereignty itself is built but also by continuing to assert a separate

---

65. G. Debien & Rene Le Gardeur, "The Saint-Domingue Refugees in Louisiana, 1792–1804", in C.A. Brasseaux and G.R. Conrad (eds.), *The Road to Louisiana: The Saint-Domingue Refugees, 1792–1809* (Lafayette, La. : Center for Louisiana Studies, University of Southwestern Louisiana, 1992), 113–243, quote at 114–115.
66. Thomas Fiehrer, "From La Tortue to La Louisiane: An Unfathomed Legacy," in Ibid., 1–30, quote at 25.
67. Benjamin Henry B. Latrobe, January 12, 1819, quoted in Jon Kukla, *A Wilderness So Immense: The Louisiana Purchase and the Destiny of America* (New York: Knopf, Inc., 2003), 333. "Linguistic abundance" was the dominant feature of cultural life in New Orleans well into the 1820s and '30s. See, Bailey, "Foundation of English in the Louisiana Purchase," supra note 9, 363–384, at 366.
68. "[O]ne might imagine hegemonic cultures placed anywhere on a continuum from 'closed' to 'open.' In the 'closed' version, subordinate groups lack the language necessary even to conceive concerted resistance; in the 'open' version, the capability for resistance flourishes and may lead to the creation of counter-hegemonic alternatives. (. . .) [T]he line between dominant and subordinate cultures is a permeable membrane, not an impenetrable barrier." Lears, "Concept of Cultural Hegemony," supra note 57, at 573, 574.

cultural identity. Moreover, the subaltern group has the potential, if not to reverse then at least to arrest the pace and extent of cultural transformation. And if there are many such subaltern groups, these can coalesce and form a united cultural identity thereby finding a place within an emerging "hybrid" culture. In this way, the subjugated group (or groups) effectively resist total domination. Through this process, they are able to achieve recognition, respect, even permanent identification as part of a new cultural milieu.

Consequently, the historical concept of "cultural hegemony" leads inevitably to the idea of "*hybridity*"—a cognitive field most closely associated with modern post-colonial thought. *Hybridity* has been defined as "a fruitful metaphor in the idea of cross-fertilization between . . . constitutive elements. . . .[t]he interleaving of practices [to] produce new forms even as older forms continue to exist"[69]—"a positive, resistive force to cultural hegemony."[70] The term is most often associated with contemporary writers—most notably Homi K. Bhabha and Anjali Prabhu—who have created a distinctive cultural discourse from a modern post-colonial perspective:

> What is theoretically innovative, and politically crucial, is the need to focus on those moments or processes that are produced in the articulation of cultural differences. These 'in-between' spaces provide the terrain for elaborating strategies of self-hood— singular or communal—that initiate new signs of identity, and innovative sites of collaboration, and contestation, in the act of defining the idea of society itself. . . . The social articulation of difference, from the minority perspective, is a complex, on-going negotiation that seeks to authorize cultural hybridities that emerge in moments of historical transformation.[71]

---

69. Ashcroft, Bill, Gareth, & Tiffin (eds.), *The Post-Colonial Reader* (London: Routledge, 1995), 184.
70. Anjali Prabhu, *Hybridity: Limits, Transormations, Prospects* (Albany: State University Press of New York, 2007), 7; e.g., ". . . ways in which different cultures encountering one another in contingent historical circumstances transform themselves and each other into new and unforeseeable entities. Such a concern is central to other theories that abound in postcolonial studies as expressed in terms such *as creolization, metissage, hybridity*, and even *diaspora*."Prabhu, "Interrogating Hybridity: Subaltern Agency and Totality in Postcolonial Theory," *Diacritics* (2005), 76–92, quote at 76.
71. Homi K. Bhabha, *The Location of Culture* (New York: Routledge, 1994; 2006), 2, 3.

Or, as Homi Bhabha explains:

> [F]or me the importance of hybridity is not to be able to trace two original moments from which the third emerges, rather hybridity to me is the 'third space' which enables other positions to emerge. This third space displaces the histories that constitute it, and sets up new structures of authority, new political initiatives, which are inadequately understood through received wisdom. . . . The process of cultural hybridity gives rise to something different, something new and unrecognizable, a new area of negotiation of meaning and representation."[72]

There is no need to engage here in the complex discourse of post-colonialism in order to apply it to early Louisiana. While this may appear to be anachronistic—post-colonialism being largely a phenomenon of the second half of the 20th century—it should be recalled that the first truly modern anti-colonial revolution was that which took place on the island of Saint Domingue: the great black revolt led by Toussaint L'Overture (1791–1803).[73] The refugees from that revolt went to other islands and borderlands of the Caribbean, including New Orleans and Lower Louisiana. The "broad and deep influence of revolutionary Saint Domingue" cannot be overemphasized.[74] Saint Domingue in the 18th century was the richest colony in the Caribbean. It had strong economic, social and cultural ties to the Louisiana settlement throughout the late 18th century, and the diaspora of Saint Dominguais following its revolt from colonial French control was very large. The "common wind" of revolutionary ideas emanating from republican France after the Revolution "was stirring people of all colors and statuses in the greater Caribbean" and that certainly included territorial Louisiana.[75] "The radical French ideals of liberty,

---

72. "The Third Space: Interview with Homi Bhabha" in J. Rutherford (ed.), *Identity: Community, Culture, Difference* (London: Laurence & Wishart, 1990), 207–221, quote at 211.
73. C.L.R. James, *The Black Jacobins: Toussaint L'Ouverture and the San Domingo Revolution* (2nd rev. ed; New York: Vintage, 1989); Carolyn Flick, *The Making of Haiti: The Saint Domingue Revolution from Below* (Knoxville: University of Tennessee Press, 1990).
74. Robert L. Paquette, "Revolutionary Saint Domingue," in *Turbulent Time*, supra note 61, at 205.
75. Ibid., quote at 216.

equality, and fraternity spread quickly to and through Louisiana and by means of books, newspapers, correspondence [as well as by] sailors, merchants and refugees."[76]

Accordingly, there is a direct link between this first anti-colonial revolt and the events that transpired in the first decade of Louisiana's history as a U.S. possession. Using the metaphor of the Nigerian novelist, Chinua Achebe, whose great novel, *Things Fall Apart*, described how the interaction between colonizer and colonized caused a disintegration of indigenous culture in his native Nigeria, we can assert that in Louisiana, things did not "fall apart." The Civil Digest of 1808 was one of a number of acts of self-governance that Louisianians achieved in the territorial period of their history. Not only the Digest, but the Practice Act and the Crimes Act of 1805, and even the Black Code of 1806, evidence an extraordinary ability to identify specific legal needs and to act upon them. Other acts of social cohesion such as the organization of a rudimentary public school system as well the organization of one of the very first urban police force in the South, the New Orleans "City Guard," attest to the same instinct for governance.[77] Even the "free people of color"—separate and apart from the dominating white planter, merchant and professional classes—attempted to reconstitute their own militia guard;[78] they petitioned the courts in legal disputes; and, they mobilized politically for collective action.[79]

Overall, the story of Louisiana in this period is a dramatic tale of energetic self-government manifested by examples drawn from "civil administration, the law, education, religion and the military institutions and institution-making defined the boundaries of incorporation and exclusion, creating the networks through which people expressed their goals and grievances."[80] The potential for fragmentation, discord, and cultural conflict was great even without

---

76. Kimberly S. Hanger, "Conflicting Loyalties: The French Revolution and Free People of Color in Spanish New Orleans," in *A Turbulent Time*, supra note 61, 178–203, at 194.
77. Peter J. Kastor, "Young Men and Strngers: Institutions, Collaborations, and Conflicts in territorial Louisiana," *Journal of the West*, Vol. 43, No. 3 (2004), 13–22.
78. See, "Address From the Free People of Color" to Gov. Claiborne on Jan. 17, 1804, cited in K.S. Hanger, "Conflicting Loyalties," in *A Turbulent Time*, supra note 61, at 192.
79. Thomas N. Ingersoll, "Free Blacks in a Slave Society: New Orleans, 1718–1812, *William & Mary Quarterly*, 3rd Ser., Vol. 48, No. 2 (1991), 173–200.
80. Kastor, "Young Men and Strangers", supra note 78, at 13.

the Anglo-American influence coming from outside. But instead of breaking apart, all of the indigenous groups—mostly the French,[81] but also the German, the Spanish, the Irish, the Caribbean, the Creole, and the African—all coalesced around this shared tradition of customary civil law. These groups identified with the old law and were able to see past particular differences. The "ancient laws of Louisiana" (whatever they were) became the signature of an emergent "hybrid" culture. And Louisiana's geographic position helped to produce a climate for cultural compromise by isolating its new American governors from central command and control in Washington. Such isolation required local American leaders to interact and to compromise across cultural lines in order to achieve social stability. That is why the failure of the militia scheme was so important. It meant that the cultural isolation of the Americans would continue just long enough for codification to proceed while taking advantage of a unique historical moment—a moment that might not be repeated.

The Louisiana experience is the great exemplar of the role of *convergence* and *contingency* in human history. As explained by the deconstructionist philosopher, David Wood, *convergence* refers to the fact that "events don't just happen, they don't just come from nowhere. They [are] made possible by convergences . . . by various factors coming together and making the emergence of something new possible,"[82] while *contingency* refers to the "vagaries of [the] unpredictable . . . in [human history]."[83] Not *causation* but *convergence* and *contingency*. These are the historical forces that helped to shape Louisiana's mixed legal system. There was no inevitability about this. The timing had to be just right. Another few years and the demographics would have been sufficiently altered to make it more difficult to implant the civil law with any kind of permanence. Private civil law triumphed at a critical juncture of European

---

81. Even the "French" were split into sub-groups: the "foreign French" who emigrated from France, the French speakers native to Louisiana, and the refugees (black and white) from Saint Domingue. See, Paul F. Lachance, "The Foreign French", in *Creole New Orleans*, supra note 38, 101–130.
82. "Thinking Against the Grain," An interview with David Wood, May 29, 2008 (Vanderbilt University Philosophy Department), 4, [at http://www.vanderbilt.edu/AnS/philosophy/faculty/wood-interview.html].
83. R.L. Schuyler, "Contingency in History", in *Political Science Quarterly*, Vol. LXXIV (Sept. 1959), No. 3, 321–333, at 333. (ital added).

—largely French—socio-cultural hegemony in Louisiana. Within fifty years this strength on the ground would largely disappear, having passed into the hands of the Americans. As Professor Vernon Palmer has concluded:

> It is a reasonable conjecture that had the founding period of the legal system been delayed perhaps even twenty years the entire story might have been scripted differently, so rapid was the parallel process of Americanization which in effect raced with Creole efforts to entrench civil law in Louisiana law and constitution. The story of this race against time is the story of the founding of common law and civil law in Louisiana.[84]

Contrary to the suppositions of astute observers such as Thomas Paine, Albert Gallatin, Thomas Jefferson and many others, Louisianians knew what they wanted, and they knew how to get it. Timing was all. The political stars had to be properly aligned, and the energy for effective and concerted action had to be present. With the central administration distracted, weakened, distant and unable to do much about it, Louisianians enacted the Digest (or code) of 1808 when the occasion was right. But the future was still filled with uncertainty. As the "barbarous yoke" encyclical republished by the *Lanterne Magique* would declare, a return to France was contemplated by those who still hoped "to preserve in that country, for some time longer, the practice of those laws it is our interest TO FIND THERE."[85]

* * *

The late Richard Hofstadter, the great Columbia University historian, used to say that—much like novelists and dramatists—historians tended to emphasize conflict because it made a far better

---

84. Palmer, "Two Worlds in One," supra note 59, at 27–28. Kastor, "Young Men and Strangers," supra note 78, at 14. ("It was during the territorial period, when local residents suddenly found themselves part of another country and federal officials expressed deep concerns about the fate of the union, that the struggle to create, control, and direct institutions was so profound. Time and again, members of a diverse population turned to these issues in an effort to reshape Louisiana, to define its social character and its relationship to the United States. And all of these people were committed to doing so on their own particular terms.")
85. Supra, note 2.

story than consensus. "Literature . . . traffics in conflict"[86] and, thought Hofstadter, so do writers of history. In the 1960s, Hofstadter became a target for intense historical criticism, but his critics did not always appreciate that Hofstadter was applying to historiography the same sort of critical sensibility that people like Alfred Kazin and Lionel Trilling, two of Hofstadter's closest friends, had deployed in the field of letters and literary criticism.[87]

The issue of conflict in history has been raised with respect to Louisiana during the territorial and early statehood period – did it exist or not? Some have suggested that it did not—at least not to an extent that made any real difference. However, there are historians (this one included) who have continued to use words such as "clash" and "conflict" in describing relations between rival groups and competing cultural traditions in the territorial period and early statehood period of Louisiana's rich history.[88] Writing from Paris in the early 1820s, Bernard Marigny, descendant of a distinguished line of French Creoles dating back to one of the founders of the city of New Orleans, provides further evidence for this view of turbulence in the history of early Louisiana:

> Called upon twelve years ago to take part in public affairs, I have supported and defended with all my ability and strength the rights and interests of the inhabitants of Louisiana of the same origin as myself. I found myself in the opposing party, and I have never left it. If this system [of opposition] had not been carefully and constantly carried on by Messrs. Blanque, Thierry, and myself, the seat of government would long since have been transferred from New Orleans to Baton Rouge, and the civil laws, by which we are [now] governed, annulled and replaced by the famous Common Law of England, a veritable *grimoire*, which, like the languages of Aesop, one can make another say

---

86. Richard Posner, *Law and Literature* (Cambridge: Harvard University Press, Rev. & Enlarged Ed., 1998), 22.
87. David. S. Brown, *Richard Hofstadter: An Intellectual Biography* (Chicago, IL.: University of Chicago Press, 2006).
88. E.g., Joseph G. Tregle, Jr., "Creoles and Americans," in *Creole New Orleans*, supra note 38, 131–185; George. Dargo, *Jefferson's Louisiana: Politics and the Clash of Legal Traditions* (Cambridge: Harvard University Press, 1975).

> whatever one wishes, to the great detriment of the unfortunate litigant.[89]

Observations such as that provided by the Marigny memoire, support the validity of the "conflict" interpretation. Recent historians have challenged the "conflict approach," however. These scholars have suggested that while there were, indeed, ethnic and political differences and tensions in Lower Louisiana, such groups were not necessarily battling for political or even cultural control. In fact, in some places and on some issues they worked together on the basis of common interest.[90] Despite their differences in language, personal background, and political affiliation, American immigrants forged marital, commercial, and social alliances with French Creoles. Issues of land acquisition and the availability of slaves provided the material basis for such alliances. The French had the land and the Americans had access to slaves thereby providing a nexus for cooperation and compromise particularly in rural Louisiana. This was particularly true in the parishes away from the capital in New Orleans where political, ethnic, linguistic and cultural conflict tended to be more intense.[91] Thus, these historians conclude, there was consensus as well as conflict in territorial Louisiana.

The central concept of *hybridity* provides a way to resolve this historiographical debate between conflict and consensus. *Hybridity* allows room for conflict but also—in the words of Homi Bhabha,

---

89. Memoire of Bertnard Marigny addressed to his fellow citizens of New Orleans (Paris, 1822), trans. Olivia Blanchard, in Howard-Tilton Memorial Library, Tulane University. John Blanque was a member of the Orleans territorial legislature in the year of the Digest. Thierry was the editor of the *Louisiana Courier* (French and English).

90. Warren M. Billings & Mark F. Fernandez (eds.), *Essays in the New Louisiana Legal History* (Baton Rouge, LA: Louisiana State University Press, 2001), esp. 1–22; see also, Richard Holcombe Kilbourne, Jr., *A History of the Louisiana Civil Code: The Formative Years, 1803–1839*, Baton Rouge, LA: Louisiana State University Press, 1987, esp. chaps. 1, 2.; also, Robert L. Paquette, "Revolutionary Saint Domingue," supra note 61, at 215.

91. "While migrants depended on French Louisianian residents for access to land, French Louisianians, in turn, relied on newcomer Anglo-Americans for slaves.... Thus, a bargain was struck between the two ethnic groups of aspiring planters." Sarah Russell, "Ethnicity, Commerce, and Community on Lower Louisiana's Plantation Frontier, 1803–1828," *Louisiana History* (1999), Vol. 40, 389–405, quotes at 401, 402.

for "collaboration and contestation in the act of defining the idea of society itself—the social articulation of difference, [in] . . . a complex, of on-going negotiation that seeks to authorize cultural *hybridities* that emerge in moments of historical transformation."[92] Louisiana's mixed legal system is the legacy of such "a moment of historical transformation." *Hybridity* produced a rich interaction—call it conflict, contestation, or negotiation—from within the mix of languages, cultures and legal traditions that the Americans found in their first true colony.

Thomas Jefferson once thought Lower Louisiana a territory totally different and distinct. As he put it philosophically at the very start of the American occupation: "[I]n a whole composed of parts, no one part must carve for itself."[93] But Louisiana refused to be a "part of the whole." It resisted with *energy* and *agency* in a sufficiency of time to transform its legal and its cultural heritage into something genuinely new and decidedly different—a difference that continues to this day. A landmark in American as well as in Louisiana history, the Digest (or Code) of 1808 was by no means inevitable or predetermined. Its enactment was *contingent* upon an alignment and *convergence* of historical forces, a record of events and personalities that could not have been predicted with certainty. In time, Louisiana would be transformed by the inevitable changes which participation in the American federal union would require. But for the moment, Louisianians were able to resist successfully the forces of cultural as well as political and legal hegemony which possession by the United States portended. Thus, the Civil Digest of 1808 was not only a foundational legal document but a constitutive cultural moment in historical time—an effort by the people of Louisiana to preserve language, culture, and historical memory as well as law. Viewed in this way and through such a lens, the Civil Digest can best be perceived and understood.

---

92. See supra, note 72.
93. Jefferson to Claiborne, Dec. 2, 1804, in *Territorial Papers*, supra note 24, at IX, 342.

Edward Livingston and the New Orleans Batture

> Hence the shores of the Mississippi present every where bends or points, of which, the bends, or curves, being exposed to the more immediate and direct action of the current, are constantly excavated or abraded, which the points, under the influence of the countercurrent generally increase in extent by the alluvial accretions formed around them. These alluvial deposits, which are often of great extent and value, are called battures.
>
> Gustavus Schmidt, 1841

On May 23, 1807, the Superior Court of the territory of Orleans rendered a unanimous decision in the case of *John Gravier* v. *The Mayor, Aldermen, and Inhabitants of the City of New Orleans*. The court hoped that its judgment for the plaintiff would extinguish a smoldering and potentially explosive public question—a hope not soon realized. With the aftereffects of the Burr storm and the Wilkinson "terror" still lingering, a new and inflammatory public debate commenced in the highly volatile political atmosphere of Orleans. The controversy enmeshed the people and their government on every level but, even more significantly, it dramatized the importance of legal questions in public life. The problem was that of the New Orleans Batture.

The Batture in front of the city was best described by a great Louisiana legal scholar a generation later this way:

> New Orleans is situated on an alluvial plain, evidently formed, like the surrounding country for a great distance, by the transporting and creating power of the Mississippi in the course of

---

* Source: Chapter 4 ("Edward Livingston and the New Orleans Batture") in George Dargo, *Jefferson's Louisiana: Politics and the Clash of Legal Traditions* (Clark, NJ: Lawbook Exchange, 2009 (Rev. Ed.); originally published by Harvard University Press, 1975.

> centuries. This plain, which constituted a portion of the Delta of the Mississippi, contains a soil of incomparable fertility, through which the current of the majestic river winds its way with resistless impetuosity, sweeping along in large, graceful and singularly regular curves, which mould its channel, and make the shores, which limit and restrain its waters, conform to their meanderings. Hence the shores of the Mississippi present every where bends or points, of which, the bends, or curves, being exposed to the more immediate and direct action of the current, are constantly excavated or abraded, which the points, under the influence of the countercurrent generally increase in extent by the alluvial accretions formed around them. These alluvial deposits, which are often of great extent and value, are called battures.[1]

The Batture St. Mary was part of a land parcel granted to the Jesuit Order in 1726 by the French Crown. In 1763, the Society of Jesus was suppressed in France and its lands in Louisiana were sold. The grounds in question were divided into separate lots. The lot nearest the city was sold to one Jean Pradel, who passed it on to an Andre Renard. The widow of Renard married Bertrand Gravier in 1785, and upon her death the entire estate was left to him. In 1788 Bertrand Gravier established a suburb on the part of the estate that fronted the Mississippi River, sections of which were sold during the 1790s. Bertrand Gravier died intestate in 1797 and the remainder of his property went to a brother, Jean Gravier, whose title to the property was later contested by the other heirs of Bertrand.[2]

The "batture," or alluvial ground which the Mississippi deposited on the suburban lots fronting the river, remained unimproved prior to 1800. The inhabitants of New Orleans used batture soil and sand to fill in streets, to construct sidewalks, and to maintain the

---

1. Gustavus Schmidt, "The Batture Question," in *Louisiana Law Journal* (1841), 87–88. The "batture" (now called "*batcher*") is the sand and silt which lies between the river at its low water point and the levee.
2. The best analysis of the Batture controversy is still William B. Hatcher, *Edward Livingston: Jeffersonian Republican and Jacksonian Democrat* (University City, Louisiana: Louisiana State University Press, 1940), chap. 8. The basic documentary material can be found in U.S. Congress, *American State Papers: Documents, Legislative and Executive of the Congress of the United States* (18 vols., Washington, D.C., 1832–1861), *Public Lands*, II, 1–84. See also Francis P. Burns, "The Graviers and the Faubourg Ste. Marie," *Louisiana Historical Quarterly*, 22 (1939), 385–427.

levee. The batture itself, through long established custom, was used as a place for anchorage and wharfage.

Traditionally, as the batture widened, riparian owners moved the levee further toward the water's edge at the high-water mark. By this process of gradual enclosure they were able to increase the size of their holdings. However, when Jean Gravier attempted this in 1804, he elicited an outcry from the local inhabitants. The ensuing confrontation between Gravier and the city of New Orleans raised the question of title.[3] Gravier sued the city in Superior Court in an effort to establish his claim, once and for all, but the court postponed a judicial resolution of the problem for more than a year.[4] The difficulty regarding Gravier's title arose from the peculiar fact that his plantation no longer fronted the river but was separated from the Batture by the suburban lots which had been sold by Bertrand Gravier in the 1790s. No one ever challenged the proprietary rights of ordinary riparians to alluvial accretions. The question was whether or not private title to an alluvion formed by a navigable waterway and adjoining a municipal suburb could be enjoyed by an individual whose lands were not adjacent to the river.[5] This, in turn, rested upon disputed points of fact: was a batture already in existence at the time of the original sale of the Jesuit lots in 1763, and did the batture, in the absence of a specification in the deeds of sale, comprise a portion of the properties of those who, by succession or sale, had acquired title to those lots? The court, basing its decision upon the Spanish laws then in force in the territory, decided that an alluvion *had* formed by the time Bertrand Gravier sold his suburban lots, but that since the Batture was not

---

3. The city responded to Gravier's efforts to enclose the Batture as early as February 1804 (City Council Records, vol. 1, bk. 2, 42, 63 in New Orleans Public Library).

4 Judge Prevost delayed the trial of the case until a full complement of three was present on the court (ibid. [Dec. 21, 1805], 158). During the delay, Prevost permitted the use of Batture soil only for the upkeep of the levee (ibid. [Jan. 4, 1806), 162; [May 3, 1806], bk. 3, 51–52). This caused considerable annoyance. William Spriggs, George Matthews, and Joshua Lewis were the three judges of the Superior Court at the time the case was decided.

5. There was no question as to the title of the other battures along the river, such as that of Bernard Marigny. For example, see ibid. [Dec. 24, 1806], 145, where the city contemplated the acquisition of the battures of Villere and Lachaise, apparently anticipating little difficulty.

included in the instruments conveying title, the heir of Bertrand, that is Jean Gravier, remained the rightful owner of the property.

* * *

For Edward Livingston the Batture represented an enormous opportunity to reverse the direction of his declining fortunes. He had come to New Orleans soon after the cession of all of Louisiana to the United States, in order to find some way of liquidating a debt of $44,000 which he owed the federal government. Livingston looked upon Louisiana as a place of voluntary exile where he could reestablish his reputation at the bar while amassing sufficient funds to enable him to settle his accounts, return to his New York home, and retire in comfort. Edward wrote his sister, Margaret B. Livingston, less than two months after his arrival in New Orleans that he was "engaged in business that will ultimately prove extremely profitable and I am so much pleased with the country that I shall make it my place of abode at least until my labors enable me to re-establish my affairs which, if I am suffered to pursue them without interruption, I hope will be in three or four years at the farthest."[6] He wished merely to be left alone. He hoped the government would not distract him "by pursuing their demands" in New Orleans.[7] Livingston was convinced that Gravier's title to the Batture was good, and that the property had tremendous commercial potential.[8] Gravier engaged Livingston as counsel in his suit against the city. Then, after the court decided in Gravier's favor, Livingston acquired one-third of Gravier's interest, then estimated to be worth $200,000 which was, of course, an enormous sum of money in those days.[9] As time went on the value of the Batture steadily appreciated, but even in 1807 a one-third interest was more

---

6. Edward to Margaret B. Livingston, March 30, 1804, Simon Gratz Papers, Historical Society of Pennsylvania.
7. Livingston to [?] May 13, 1804, ibid.
8. Court action was commenced by Livingston in behalf of Gravier in October 1805 (City Council Records [Dec. 7, 1805], vol. I, bk. 2, 152; Hatcher, *Edward Livingston*, 145).
9. Claiborne to Jefferson, May 20, 1807, *Territorial Papers of the United States*, ed. Clarence E. Carter (26 vols., Washington, D.C.: Government Printing Office, 1934–1962), IX, 736. There is no certainty about what Livingston actually paid for the property. Livingston said that it cost him $80,000, but the inhabitants of New Orleans believed that he received the property in lieu of fee. See Hatcher, *Edward Livingston*, 144–145.

than enough to relieve Livingston of his financial obligations. The batture was a good investment if title could be sustained.

Livingston began a series of works and improvements which, he explained, would benefit the public, but popular indignation was aroused by what seemed to be his impudent interference in the customary use of the ground. To Livingston's surprise, his workers were driven from the batture on repeated occasions during the spring and summer of 1807. By September of that year public sentiment in New Orleans was inflamed. A crisis had been reached, and William Claiborne, the governor of the territory, was once again placed in the awkward position of having to decide between two valid but conflicting claims. He could defy neither the court nor the people without precipitating a breakdown of public order. Claiborne succeeded in quieting the crowd which assembled on the batture on September 15th by assuring them that the President of the United States would settle the matter equitably. The problem, he informed the people, would be transmitted to the general government in Washington. He agreed to authorize John Baptiste MaCarty, a local notable, to collect affidavits attesting to the public's historic right to the batture and to convey them to the capital.[10]

Meanwhile, the city of New Orleans initiated the legal maneuver of transferring its alleged title to the batture to the U.S. government. Claiborne notified Jefferson that he believed the "United States are the legal claimants of the land in question,"[11] but it was not until December 1807 that the city officially requested the governor to intercede in its behalf and to notify the Administration of its desire that the public right to the batture be defended by the federal government.[12] However, as early as November Jefferson had decided to review the matter. The President consulted separately with Attorney General Caesar Rodney, Treasury Secretary

---

10. City Council Records (Sept. 23, 1807), vol. 11, bk. 1, 37. Laminated copies in French and English of these affadavits are in the Louisiana Miscellany, Library of Congress (LC).
11. Claiborne to Jefferson, May 20, 1807, *Territorial Papers*, ed. Carter, IX, 736.
12. The first resolution to this effect was passed on Sept. 16, 1807 (City Council Records, vol. II, bk. 1, 35). The official request was made on Dec. 5, 1807 (ibid., 82). Documents were forwarded to Washington by action taken on Dec. 12, 1807 (ibid., 84–85). Claiborne and the city had conferred on the desirability of transferring the city's claim to the United States as early as May 25, 1807. As a result of this decision Livingston was confronted by a coalition of municipal, territorial, and national authorities.

Albert Gallatin, Jefferson's closest advisor on Louisiana affairs, and then with his entire cabinet. He then instructed the Secretary of State, James Madison (the Department of State was directly responsible for U.S. territories) to order the U.S. marshal in New Orleans to occupy the batture in conformity with an act of Congress of March 3, 1807, which empowered the government to evict squatters from public lands. On January 25, 1808, the order was executed. The marshal, Le Breton D'Orgenois, evicted Livingston and his workmen. Subsequently, the city passed a resolution calling for the destruction of works already commenced by Livingston and the restitution of the batture to its traditional usages.[13] Governor Claiborne himself received the official thanks of the municipality for his intercession with the U.S. government on this important question.[14]

Jefferson acted hastily in his batture policy. Madison issued the instructions to the U.S. marshal on November 30, two weeks prior to the city council's decision, and a full month before any official request could have been received from New Orleans.[15] Three considerations explain the swiftness with which the Administration acted. First, on the basis of the fragmentary material available to the Cabinet at the time, the court decision appeared to be a miscarriage of justice, but the only legal argument Jefferson had was a brief by Pierre Derbigny, the attorney for the city in the original suit. In a note to Gallatin on November 4th the President wrote: "As it will be necessary to decide how this question of the batture is to be settled, we must of course take the trouble of understanding it. I therefore send you a very able opinion of Derbigny's to be returned when read to Mr. Rodney. Happening to have an Encyclopedia which he quotes, I have turned to it and find it able and satisfactory. Mr. Rodney is in possession of the opinion of the court assigning their reasons."[16]

---

13. (Jan. 27, 1808), ibid., 124. Claiborne refused to authorize destruction of Livingston's works (Feb. 6, 1808, ibid., 141–142). The city also feared precipitous action (Feb. 13, 1808), ibid., 143, and it did not authorize the use of Batture silt for filler. The city passed ordinances prohibiting further construction on the levee (*Louisiana Gazette*, Feb. 19, 1808).

14. City Council Records (Feb. 6, 1808), vol. II, bk. 1, 139.

15. Madison's letter to the U.S. marshal is cited in *Livingston* v. *D'Orgenoy*, 7 Cranch (U.S.) 577 (1813), at 578.

16. Jefferson to Gallatin, Gallatin Papers, New York Historical Society.

Derbigny's brief, Rodney's opinion, and a copy of the French *Encyclopedia*—plus the court's brief opinion—this was the sum of the reference material at Jefferson's disposal when he summoned the Cabinet meeting of November 27th, at which time the decision to evict Livingston was taken. Early in December, Livingston sent Gallatin documents and proofs in support of his title in order to answer the city's argument.[17] But by that time, policy had already been decided, and orders were en route to the marshal. Jefferson would discover to his regret that the legal issues involved were not as simple as he first thought—indeed, that the Batture could be a legal quagmire as well as a sandy shoal.

The second reason for haste was Jefferson's antipathy to Livingston. William Hatcher, in his biography of Edward Livingston, lists four sources of this hostility: Livingston's lackluster support for Jefferson in his fight for the presidency in 1801, the financial scandal in New York in which Livingston was involved, the reports the President had been receiving from Governor Claiborne detailing Livingston's political activities, and Livingston's alleged association with Burr and his interference with Wilkinson during the latter's "reign of terror" in New Orleans a year earlier.[18] For these reasons Jefferson did not hesitate to take a position which he knew would damage a man he had cause to dislike. Personal animosity between the two deepened as the batture litigation continued. It abated only on the very eve of Jefferson's death many years later.

The third reason for Jefferson's swift action in the developing dispute was the political opportunity it presented to the Administration. Political considerations dominated Jefferson's policy on the batture. His first moves were to freeze the situation, evict Livingston, and halt further construction, confident that a final arbiter in the dispute would decide favorably for the government. The New Orleans public was not uniformly against Livingston, but there is little doubt that a presidential decision in Livingston's favor would have alienated most of the local inhabitants.[19]

---

17. Livingston to Gallatin, Dec. 2, 1807, ibid.
18. Hatcher, *Edward Livingston*, 150–151.
19. The *Orleans Gazette*, itself pro-Livingston, admitted that the French favored the public's right to the batture. One "B" scored a telling point in a fabricated debate when, referring to the Mississippi River as "our good old father," he said "that the batture is a

Jefferson presumed that Congress would either leave the matter with the federal land commissioners in the territory or, as he suggested in a note to Gallatin, appoint a special board of higher standing "at least for the batture, which is of too much value and too much involved in prejudices there to be safely trusted to the present Commissioners."[20] By "prejudice," Jefferson meant politics. He wrote this note in March 1808, but he was fully aware of the explosiveness of the issue when he acted back in November. The attitude of the land commissioners was not clear, but Jefferson suspected they were vulnerable to Livingston's allegedly profound and beguiling influence.[21] Consequently, Jefferson favored a special commission appointed solely for the purpose of deciding the Batture question "to whom the evidence and arguments in writing shall be sent, without any necessity of their going there."[22] But Gallatin did not like the idea of a special commission. He preferred to have the United States' claim transferred to the New Orleans municipality by an act of Congress, thus allowing the city to continue litigation in the courts.[23] However, U.S. title would first have to be firmly established.

Jefferson acted on the batture with the expectation that he would be sustained by the subsequent decision of either an impar-

---

part of his inheritance, and consequently that his legitimate issue ought to enjoy his succession, without giving any part of it to the adopted children, who have but lately come into the family" (Oct. 1, 1807). Elizabeth Trist, who often reflected American attitudes on local public questions, described the demonstrations in mid-September as "Mob Government." E. Trist to Jefferson, Oct. 27, 1807, Nicholas P. Trist Papers, Southern Historical Collection, University of North Carolina.

20. March 2, 1808, Gallatin Papers, New York Historical Society.

21. Jefferson was not sure of the position of James Brown, then the most influential of the land agents in Orleans. For one thing, the Browns had been named by Wilkinson as having been soft on Burrism. On the batture question itself, Brown had been one of the attorneys for Gravier in the original law suit against the city (U.S. Cong., *American State Papers: Public Lands*, II, 16). Claiborne would later write that Brown did indeed support Livingston. See Claiborne to Jefferson, Sept. 1, 1808, *Official Letter Books of W. C. C. Claiborne, 1801–1816*, ed. Dunbar Rowland, 6 vols., (Jackson, Miss.: State Dept. of Archives & History, 1917), IV, 202. The presence of James Brown on the projected board of land commissioners rendered it suspect in Jefferson's view. That Brown may, in fact, have been sympathetic with the government's claim is suggested by a letter he wrote to Philip Grymes (Nov. 25, 1808, James Brown Papers, LC), Brown's successor as U.S. attorney.

22. Jefferson to Gallatin, Dec. 24, 1807, Jefferson Papers, LC.

23. Gallatin to Jefferson, March 2, 1808, ibid.; Daniel Clark to the Mayor and Alderman of New Orleans, Dec. 16/24, 1807, American Documents, New Orleans Public Library.

tial tribunal or Congress. The order to the U.S. marshal to remove Livingston, an act designed to quiet the excitement until a final decision could be made, was the only decisive action ever taken by the federal government in the matter. Hastily conceived with thin evidentiary support, Jefferson's batture policy would subsequently have to stand or fall on its insubstantial merits.

* * *

The Batture controversy generated almost as much heat in the Orleans territory as the Burr conspiracy. Several local newspapers devoted much attention to it. The *Orleans Gazette,* the leading English language newspaper, was sympathetic to Livingston even though the editor opened its pages to advocates for the city. The paper defended the decision of the Superior Court, condemned MaCarty's mission to Washington, linked the Gravier-Livingston Batture with the battures of other riverfront proprietors in the hope that this would enlist their powerful support behind the cause, and strenuously condemned the city for transferring its claim to the U.S. government.[24]

The *Louisiana Courier*, the leading French newspaper, defended the municipality. In fact, the first appearance of the *Courier* in mid-October 1807 was occasioned by the absence of an adequate vehicle for presenting the public's position on the issue. The *Courier*'s ardent and continuous advocacy of the public right to the batture during the ensuing months was the result of the editor J.B.S. Thierry's conviction that he was the solitary defender of the community against the "usurpers" of its property.[25] Indeed, the

---

24. *Orleans Gazette*, Sept. 21, 1807; see also ibid., Sept. 24, Oct. 1, Nov. 16, 1807; Dec. 2, 1808; Sept. 8, 1809.

25. *Courier*, Oct. 14/30 (supplement), Nov. 4 (supplement), 1807. Thierry's penchant for lone advocacy was again revealed in the Batture fight. Thierry staked out his own position on the legal issues and then defended it as one besieged, even refusing to reconcile his forensic posture with any of the other supporters of the public's claim, such as Pierre Derbigny. The result was a rift which the friends of Livingston were quick to exploit. Thierry also fought bitterly with one H. P. Nugent, another ardent champion of the public's cause. See H. P. Nugent, *A Letter to his Excellency Wm. C. C. Claiborne, Govr of the Territ. of Orleans and a Letter to James Brown—A Defence of the Honorable John Rowan and Daniel Clark, Members of Congress Against the Slanders of the Tergiversant Redacteur of the Courier* (New Orleans: Printed for the author, 1808).

appointment of Thierry to the office of public printer in November 1808 was due, in part, to the position he had taken on the batture question.[26]

In addition to the 'warm newspaper discussion,"[27] a pamphlet war was fought over the disputed alluvial grounds of the Mississippi. Great bodies of law were marshaled by each side. Leading legal luminaries took part, some from as far away as Philadelphia, and their briefs were exchanged in volleys of argument and counterargument. Livingston was his own best advocate, but he also solicited the help of Peter S. DuPonceau, then one of the leading lawyers in America. The scholarship of Pierre Derbigny and Louis Moreau Lislet (one of the two principal draftsmen of the 1808 *Digest of the Laws in Force*), and the argumentative skill of editor Thierry were arrayed on the other side.

Pierre Derbigny published the first pamphlet in the summer of 1807. Derbigny opened his argument with general remarks concerning the great utility of the batture in the life and commerce of New Orleans and its importance both to the inhabitants of the city and to the people of the United States. He then proceeded to raise the pivotal point which would serve as the connecting link between the batture problem and larger legal questions:

> The peculiar situation of this territory, newly acquired to the United States, governed by the civil law, so different from that which rules the rest of the Union, so lately transferred from a government which manifests the sovereign authority more frequently by ostensible acts than by writings, must surely, it should seem be powerful motives to induce the General Government to bestow on the examination of this cause, all the attention and consideration it deserves! Will not the general government reflect that Louisiana, by the very nature of the Provisional government which rules it, is deprived of a part of the advantages enjoyed by the other citizens of the Union, in their judiciary contests, and that the fate of their fortunes, and their lives is definitively submitted to one sole tribunal, composed of three judges, who decide at once in the first instance, and in the last resort, in a

---

26. Just as important, of course, was Thierry's position on the Burr Conspiracy a year before. The Burr and Batture issues earned Thierry Claiborne's support for the post of public printer.
27. Claiborne to Madison, Oct. 17, 1807, *Letter Books*, IV, 135.

country whose languages, manners, usages, and even sometimes whose laws are little familiar to them; and that the acknowledged integrity and information of those three judges are not always a solid security for the irrefragability of their judgment? [28]

Peter Stephen DuPonceau, in a very persuasive brief, would later reply that the civil law itself—that is, those very same elements of the civil law to which Derbigny would refer—supported the contentions of Gravier and Livingston and that the decision in favor of private right was not in violation of the accepted customs, usages, and laws of the country but rather derived from them. Nevertheless, Derbigny's point was critical. Public opinion, unfamiliar with the legal sources, unimpressed by scholarly citations, unpersuaded by the logic of learned counsel, and unprepared to understand lengthy and difficult legal treatises, would remain convinced that the decision, rendered by judges trained at common law, was a corruption of justice resulting from the adulteration of the community's customary practices by an alien legal system.[29] The questions raised by the batture stimulated a social awareness of the importance of legal issues in general and a hostility to American common law in particular.[30] Consequently, the batture controversy was popularly perceived as a conflict between two diverse legal traditions.

Derbigny's second point was also important. He argued that the original sale of the Jesuit lots occurred while Louisiana was still under French dominion and governed by French law. Therefore, he

---

28. Case laid before counsel for their opinion on the claims to the Batture, situated in front of the suburb St. Mary, August 21, 1807, reprinted in U.S. Cong., American State Papers: Public Lands, II, 28–33, quote at 29.

29. This belief was reflected in the newspaper debate. For example, on October 1, 1807, the *Orleans Gazette* printed a piece that was critical of the Superior Court's decision on the batture. It was charged with ignorance of local laws and usages: "A fair trial of the cause could not be expected from three judges speaking a different language . . . and bred under different laws, usages and religion."

30. The batture question quickened the hostility toward judges, judge-made law, and lawyers and thereby cultivated the needed sentiment to sustain the repudiation of the common law. The *Courier* voiced these feelings in an article on the batture on Nov. 4, 1807: "It is certain that a general and well founded belief prevails in New Orleans that a conspiracy of lawyers is formed to rob the city of its property; and that the judges are of a conspiracy, their judgment in the cause of the batture gives strong reason to suspect. . . . Such dextrous lawyers can with ease, Twist law and judges as they please."

wrote, "the French laws must . . . direct our judgments as to the effect of those sales, and the extent of the right which they could transfer to Pradel and other purchasers of the Jesuits' property."[31] The question of property in a batture formed adjacent to those lots existing at the time of the original sale, he argued, should also be decided by French law. After reviewing the history of the batture from the time of the Jesuit proprietorship, Derbigny explained that alluvions or accretions along navigable rivers belonged to the sovereign, according to the civil law of France. To support this contention he cited the French legal commentators Pothier and Denizart and the Encyclopedist Larasle. He attempted to demonstrate that the Batture St. Mary was the kind of alluvion whose possession was governed by the edicts of successive French monarchs. Its existence at the time of the sale of the Jesuit property, the existence, also, of a royal road separating the river and the batture from private lots, the subsequent acts of Spanish governors in controlling public access to the batture, and the acquiescence of the Graviers to these regulations all supported Derbigny's major contention. Thus the burden of the rebuttal would have to be directed toward the main point that French municipal law clearly provided for battures and that, in the absence of written evidence of a grant to private owners, the Batture St. Mary continued to be the possession of the sovereign power, which had now become the United States government.

Derbigny's brief was the most efficacious. In particular, his contention that French law would have to be the rule of decision—a contention which the Superior Court did not accept—and that French law favored the sovereign was the theoretical foundation underlying Jefferson's action in dispossessing Livingston. Subsequently, other writers abandoned Derbigny on specific points, but until the end of the dispute, and despite cogent refutations, Jefferson himself adhered to this first published brief with a doggedness and tenacity at which Edward Livingston himself marveled.

Livingston was the first to rebut Derbigny. His *Examination of the Title of the United States to the land called the Batture* was published on December 10, 1807.[32] On the questions of fact

31. Case laid before counsel, U.S. Cong., American State Papers: Public Lands, II, 29.
32. Reprinted in ibid., 33–41.

Livingston argued that the lots of the old Jesuit plantation extended to the river itself and were not bounded by a public high road on the levee, that the Graviers never abandoned their claim to the batture, and that, since the sale of the Jesuit lands occurred after the cession of Louisiana to Spain on November 3, 1762,[33] the Spanish Crown could not acquire rights to those properties by virtue of French law.

On questions of law, Livingston challenged the accuracy of Derbigny's contentions. He argued that the custom of Paris, in conformity with both Roman and Spanish law, bestowed upon owners of riparian estates all soil accretions made by changes in the courses of rivers.[34] In any case, Livingston wrote, Spanish, not French, law was the rule of decision in the batture case, and Spanish law held that although the public retained prescribed usages in riverbank alluvions, the alluvions themselves belonged to the riverfront proprietors.[35] He emphatically denied that customary usage of the batture established public ownership. According to the civil law, he wrote, the public had a perfect right to the use of the banks of navigable streams, but private title remained unimpaired. Livingston admitted that it was unlawful for riparian owners to erect structures that would impede access to the grounds and that it was within the power of the authorities to order the demolition of such structures. Legal title, however, would not be affected by any such decrees.

The lines of argument between Livingston and Derbigny were clearly drawn. They differed on whether the river or the levee bounded the lots of the front proprietors, on which body of law governed title to the batture, and on the meaning of acts undertaken by the local government prior to 1803.

Louis Moreau Lislet, Louisiana's leading civil law authority, supported Derbigny. As one of the attorneys for the city in the original Gravier suit, Moreau Lislet was familiar with both the facts and the law of the case. However, in one important respect he broke through the forensic mold set by the original court decision, Derbigny's attack upon it, and Livingston's defense. Later on, both

---

33. This was the date of the secret transfer of Louisiana prior to the formal peace settlement of 1763.
34. U.S. Cong., American State Papers: Public Lands, II, 40.
35. Note F, ibid., 44.

Thierry and Julien Poydras would make it the keystone of their position in the aftermath of Peter Stephen DuPonceau's definitive demolition of Derbigny's position. Moreau Lislet wrote: "The city's claim was maintained in a law of the *Partidas* which expressly declares that sand-banks or sandy tracts (*arenales*) on the borders of rivers, in the front of towns, make part of the commons of those towns (*Partida* 3, Title 28, Law 9)."[36] This citation of Spanish *Partidas* was important. It represented a wise tactical switch from French law to Spanish law as the basis of argument. Moreau Lislet wrote that "whether the Batture belonged to the king, as we have proved, or were the property of B. Gravier, as was pretended, it must have changed proprietor at the time B. Gravier established a suburb on the front of his plantation." For a suburb was a part of the city, and by the law governing cities, as defined by the *Partidas*, the sandy banks bordering rivers were part of the commons. In the future, defenders of the public's claim would no longer rest their case upon the law of alluvions but on the fact that the batture constituted part of the port of New Orleans, and hence could not be owned privately.

Moreau Lislet's analysis of the Superior Court's decision was significant in one other way. He noted that the court was composed of judges trained in common law. "Whatever be the integrity of the judges who rendered this judgment," he wrote, "still must we deplore the situation to which they have reduced New-Orleans, possibly through an imperfect acquaintance with our usages and laws, which made it difficult for them to apprehend the arguments of the Counsel for the city."[37] Defenders of the decision tried to disprove this charge by showing that the Gravier case rested on a foundation built of Roman, Spanish, and French legal materials. Nevertheless, the allegation survived the disproof s. Moreau Lislet and others fed the suspicion that the batture decision represented another triumph of foreign over local justice.

The pamphlet war over the batture continued unabated for the next few years. Peter Stephen DuPonceau contributed a lengthy and

---

36. Examen de la Sentence Rendue Dans La Cause entre Jean Gravier et la Ville de la Nouvelle-Orleans (New Orleans: Jean Renard, 1807), 21 (author's translation).
37. Ibid., 23. Others also attacked the judges for siding with Livingston. For example, Nugent, *Letter to Claiborne*, 14, *et passim.*

well-argued brief in the summer of 1808.[38] He riveted his attention upon Derbigny's basic argument: that French law favored the sovereign's title. So thoroughgoing was Peter Stephen DuPonceau's refutation that no writer, with the exception of Jefferson himself, ever again founded his case for the public's right upon this point. As a result, J.B.S. Thierry, in answer to Peter Stephen DuPonceau, discarded Derbigny completely and developed a new approach.[39] Thierry argued that the batture was not an alluvion at all, but the bed of a river which could never belong to a private proprietor. He defended Jefferson's expulsion of Livingston as an exercise of sovereign power over rivers and harbors. Later on, when Julien Poydras presented the case for the public to Congress, he too would use this argument.

Subsequently, all of the major contributors to the public debate over the legal questions at issue in the Batture controversy submitted rejoinders to their respective critics. Derbigny sent the still-uncompleted manuscript of his own *Refutation* of Peter Stephen DuPonceau to Jefferson in order to reassure the President that his batture policy was well-founded in law,[40] but Derbigny's new pamphlet added very little to what he had already published.[41] Peter Stephen DuPonceau came out with his second work on the subject early in 1809. He ridiculed his opponents, pointed to the divisions within their ranks, scolded Jefferson for not having reinstated Livingston, and admonished the government for hiring Thierry as its new advocate.[42] Otherwise there was little in Peter Stephen DuPonceau's second published work that he had not already set

---

38. Opinion on the Case of the Alluvion Land, or Batture, Near New Orleans, reprinted in U.S. Cong., American State Papers: Public Lands, II, 45–54.
39. Examen des Droits des Etats Unis et des Pretentions de M. Eduourd Livingston sur la Batture en Face du Faubourg Ste. Marie (New Orleans: De l'imprimerie de Thierry, 1808).
40. Derbigny to Jefferson, Nov. 14, 1808, Jefferson Papers, LC.
41. Refutation Du Memoire en forme de consultation Redige par M. Peter Stephen DuPonceau au sujet des pretentions des Etats Unis sur Ia Batture du fauxbourg Ste. Marie (New Orleans: De l'imprimerie du telegraphe, 1808).
42. "A Review of the Cause of the New Orleans Batture, and of the discussions that have taken place respecting it; containing answers to the late publications of Messrs. Thierry and Derbigny on that subject," (Philadelphia, 1809), reprinted in *American Law Journal*, 4 (1812), 517–562.

forth in his first. Nor did Thierry add to the debate in his reply to Peter Stephen DuPonceau.[43]

The newspaper debates and the pamphlet war revealed the depth of public interest in the batture question. The city council ordered 500 copies of one of Thierry's briefs for distribution. Claiborne reported that public interest in the legal debate was lively and that some of the briefs were "exhibited on the 'Exchange, and read for the instruction of the bye standers."[44] The fact situation was complex, and the legal arguments became increasingly prolix. The simplicities to which they were reduced by publicists like Thierry, and later by Poydras, distorted accurate perception. For example, Thierry wrote that "the judges of the Superior Court were not sufficiently versed in the study of the Roman law to render, in such an important matter, a judgment founded upon the principles of that sacred code,"[45] despite Peter Stephen DuPonceau's attempt to demonstrate that both Spanish and French law provided ample support for the court's decision.

Peter Stephen DuPonceau's first brief was undoubtedly the most persuasive, and yet there was a dimension to the city's position not susceptible to scholarly refutation. The whole notion that a question of such trancending importance as that of the Batture St. Mary could be settled by parties in court was an alien one. Louisianians could not understand a legal proceeding which equated public interest and private right. Learned treatises alone would never convince them that their rights had been adequately safeguarded in an ordinary law court, especially one in which the judges were newcomers to their region. Moreover, the frontier between law and politics had been crossed when Jefferson expelled Livingston from his property, and legal scholarship availed little against the consequent array of power, interest, and reputation. It was on this level that the batture question had to be decided. Edward Livingston was already aware of this by the spring of 1808.

---

43. J. B. S. Thierry, *Reply to Mr. Duponceau . . .* (New Orleans: s.n., 1809).
44. Claiborne to Jefferson, Sept. 17, 1808, *Letter Books*, IV, 218.
45. Examen des Droits. . . , 33.

* * *

Although Livingston was surprised by Jefferson's course of action in the Batture case, he hoped that difficulties could be resolved by mail. He forwarded documents and proofs to Albert Gallatin in the early part of December 1807 and even offered his share of the batture in return for a financial settlement with the government.[46] The Administration's reply came in the form of the *posse comitatus* led by the U.S. marshal who drove Livingston's workers from the batture on January 25, 1808. Three days later Livingston wrote to his brother in New York that "a most extraordinary event [has] again suspended my hopes for independence."[47] Livingston recalled how he had gained possession of the property the previous May, and that he had commenced improvements at a personal cost of $12,000. Now he expected his investment would be swept away by the violence of the river. "What makes it more extraordinary," he wrote, "is that my property and Mr. Delabigarre['s][48] are singled out while there are hundreds of alluvians in the territory depending on the same title and a long quantity adjoining mine held under the identical title by which we held that [remain] untouched." He was shocked at the government's reaction to what he considered his own conciliatory approach. He wrote, "I am so astonished at the . . . despotic nature of the [Administration's] attack that I have yet formed no plan. I can scarcely believe myself in a country that boasts of having a constitution."

Livingston realized that a negotiation by mail was now out of the question and that he would have to go to Washington. Professional commitments delayed his journey until mid-April 1808. Meanwhile, Claiborne alerted Madison to Livingston's impending trip and warned that his purposes were "several subjects private and political: Among the former the case of the Batture will be introduced; among the latter, the acts of General Wilkinson during the winter of 1806, and of Governor Claiborne generally are to be

46. Livingston to Gallatin, Dec. 2, 1807, Gallatin Papers, New York Historical Society.
47. Edward Livingston to Robert R. Livingston, Jan. 28, 1808, Robert R. Livingston Papers, New York Historical Society.
48. Peter Delabigarre was the actual purchaser of two-thirds of the Batture from Jean Gravier, which the heirs of Delabigarre and Livingston then divided after Delabigarre's death. Delabigarre paid the court costs in the litigation of the case between October 1805 and May 1807. See Hatcher, *Edward Livingston*, 144–145.

much complained of."[49] The governor was trying to deflate criticism by anticipating it.

Livingston arrived in Washington on May 5, and Gallatin immediately scribbled a note to his chief, "what should I do with E. Livingston . . . "[50] to which Jefferson replied, "if you can possibly have him arrested here for his public debt, the opportunity ought not to be lost."[51] But that was for Gallatin to decide. As for Jefferson, he was leaving town altogether. Livingston wasted no time in contacting the elusive President. He wrote to him from his hotel in Georgetown the very evening of his arrival, hoping for "a short audience."[52] Jefferson's icy response was composed the next day. He referred Livingston—"whatever be the subject of [his] application," pretending not to know it—to the appropriate department head.[53]

Livingston was indefatigable. He composed a long letter to Madison on the same day, May 6th, and recounted the circumstances which brought him to Washington. Livingston could not understand the "peculiar Displeasure of the Executive." He reminded the Secretary that he had not appealed to the public "in a case which [he] could easily have shown regarded every individual in the community."[54] However, he chose not to spare Madison some evidence of his displeasure, commenting on his "ill fortune in arriving after a voyage of some thousand miles at a moment when the President's affairs would not permit him to give half an hour's audience." Livingston was convinced that within that time he could have persuaded Jefferson as to the justice of his petition. Nevertheless, in spite of the President's absence, Livingston was willing to have the Attorney General examine his documents and issue a counter-order to the U.S. marshal restoring his property to him. If, on the other hand, the government was still adamant in its position, Livingston would be glad to place the matter before a competent tribunal. He closed his letter to Madison with an offer to supply an attorney trained in the civil law to aid Rodney in his deliberations.

---

49. Claiborne to Madison, April 18, 1808, Madison Papers, LC.
50. Gallatin to Jefferson May 5, 1808, Jefferson Papers, LC.
51. Jefferson to Gallatin, May 6, 1808, ibid.
52. U.S. Cong., American State Papers: Public Lands, II, 25.
53. Jefferson to Livingston, May 6, 1808, Jefferson Papers, LC.
54. Livingston to Madison, May 6, 1808, in U.S. Cong., *American State Papers: Public Lands*, II, 65.

By the brevity of their notes to Livingston and their pretense at unfamiliarity with Livingston's business, both Madison and Jefferson feigned disinterest. In fact, they were nervously preoccupied with Livingston's appeal. Letters exchanged later in the month between these two principal officers of the United States government betrayed their true feelings.

After examining papers and documents which Livingston presented, Madison wrote to the President that he had "not had time to do more than skim over his pivotal argument."[55] His examination must indeed have been perfunctory, for the analysis which followed was opaque and confusing. Madison wrote:

> I observe he labors more to establish the identity of the French with the Roman and Spanish law, than to show that the proceeding on which his title depends, was under the Spanish, not the French law. At the time this took place France retained the possession, after having executed a Treaty of alienation. If France had a right to do what was done, it would seem, that the French not the Spanish law, would be the rule in that as in all other transactions during the interval of non-delivery of the ceded country: If the proceeding was not of right, the title derived from it must be a nullity also; unless made good by some subsequent sanction under the Spanish authority. To consider France as the Trustee of Spain, would make the Spanish code her guide, and vitiate all proceedings under the French code. To consider France as the sovereign de facto, not de jure, would make the French law, equally the law de facto, tho' not de jure, and exclude the Spanish law as the criterion in the case. Unless therefore the French law of alluvian, be in reality the same with that of Spain, the title of Mr. E. will depend on the course of things relating to it, after the possessory transfer to Spain. These are very hasty ideas, and would not be hazarded without a knowledge that if incorrect they will be superceded by your better view of the subject.[56]

Jefferson's reply was somewhat clearer:

> Your observations on [Livingston's] allegations that Gravier's grant must be under the Spanish law, because after the cession of

---

55. Madison to Jefferson, May 11, 1808, Jefferson Papers, LC.
56. Ibid.

> the province by France to Spain, tho' before delivery of possession are conclusive, to which must be added that Louis XIV having established the Coutumes de Paris as the Law of Louisiana, this was not changed by the mere act of transfer; on the contrary the Laws of France continued and continues to be the law of the land except where specially altered by some subsequent edict of Spain or act of Congress. He has not in the least shaken the doctrine that the bed of the river, and all the atterrissements or banks which arise on it by the depositions of the river are the property of the king by a peculiarity in the law of France, so that nothing quoted from those of Spain or the Roman law is of authority on that point.[57]

Madison's uncertainty on so fundamental a matter as the law in force in Louisiana is an indication of the untidiness of the government's legal position at what was, by May 1808, a very late moment in the unfolding drama. Madison's confusion on a vital part of the government's case reveals how ill-conceived that position was when policy was determined. Jefferson's grasp of some of the fundamentals was better, or at least clearer, but his avid search for weaknesses in Livingston's opinion revealed deep vexation.

The decision to remove Livingston from the batture had been made in the Cabinet on November 27, 1807. The grounds for his removal were the Act of Congress of March 3, 1807, authorizing the eviction of squatters from public lands; this, together with the opinion of Pierre Derbigny, constituted the legal basis for Jefferson's action.[58] He little suspected that his policy would later be vigorously contested. It was not until after Peter Stephen DuPonceau's opinion was published in July 1808 that it proved necessary for the government to find additional grounds to sustain the action undertaken the previous November. Thierry's *Examen* partly answered this need. Meanwhile, from November 1807 until July 1808, the government felt assured that Derbigny's case, built upon

---

57. Jefferson to Madison, May 19, 1808, ibid.

58. U.S. Cong., *Statutes at Large*, comp. Richard Peters, vol. II (Boston: Little and Brown, 1845), 445–446; Jefferson later wrote, "on the 27th of November, 1807, I asked the attendance of the heads of Departments to whom the papers received had been previously communicated for their consideration. . . . We took of the whole case such views as the state of our information at that time presented" (U.S. Cong., *American State Papers: Public Lands*, II, 65).

his particular interpretation of the French laws of alluvion, would hold up in any future litigation. From the exchange of letters between Jefferson and Madison in May 1808, it is clear that the President, at least, felt that his policy in regard to the Batture was legally sound.

Livingston waited for Jefferson and Madison to respond to his personal petition. They tried to divert him by saying that the batture question had been referred to Congress and was out of their hands, but he was not satisfied.[59] On the eve of his departure for Philadelphia and from there to return to New Orleans, Livingston wrote again to Madison, this time allowing his mounting irritation to show through his transparent self-restraint. "It having been deemed inconsistent with official duty to examine my proof or listen to my argument, I must at present content myself with having done everything that a sense of justice and the extreme of moderation could require," he wrote, intimating that they had not seen the last of him.[60]

Livingston's patience was at an end. He wanted to know if the President seriously intended to submit the entire business to Congress who, in turn, would determine whether or not the President had been invested "with the power of reviewing the decision of a court, of opposing the execution of its decrees, and depriving a citizen of his property without even the form of trial or affording him the means of defence." Livingston warned Madison that unless some satisfactory arrangement was worked out between them, he would charge Jefferson before the bar of public opinion with having committed serious violations of law. He had refrained from such action until then, he wrote, to avoid a confrontation between the executive and judicial branches of the government—a conflict that would unsettle the public mind. He had hoped for a chance to demonstrate amicably and in good faith the error which had misled the Administration, but his appeal had failed. Madison was obdurate.[61]

---

59. Jefferson to Madison, May 19, 1808, Jefferson Papers, LC; Madison to Livingston, May 20,1808, in U.S. Cong., *American State Papers: Public Lands*, II, 26. Livingston had gone to New York. He returned to Washington, however, and managed to see both the Attorney General and the President, but they remained unmoved.

60. Livingston to Madison, July 13, 1808, ibid.

61. Madison to Livingston (undated memorandum in answer to Livingston's letter of July 13), ibid., 26.

From Philadelphia, Livingston remained in communication with Administration officials. Jefferson informed him, through Madison, that the Attorney General concurred in the government's position. Livingston desired to examine Caesar Rodney's opinion in order to demonstrate its weaknesses. He still hoped for a settlement short of a full congressional and public debate. Despite his warnings to Madison and his confidence in the soundness of his position, Livingston realized his disadvantage in any open battle with the President. He sent Rodney a note requesting Rodney's written legal opinion on the batture. In his reply the Attorney General explained that the original was not in Madison's office but had been sent over to Congress with all of the other relevant materials. Not having a copy for Livingston to see, he merely noted that it coincided with Derbigny's opinion in the case.[62] Livingston was astounded at Rodney's blissful admission to having based his opinion upon Derbigny's brief when it directly contradicted the decree of the Superior Court of the Orleans territory. He queried the Attorney General as to which was more deserving of credence, "the solemn deliberate decision of three judges, . . . sworn to do justice between the parties, or the ex parte statement of a lawyer feed to maintain a contrary opinion?"[63] But Rodney was unshaken. In a short note penned a few days later, the Attorney General promised Livingston that he would write to him when the latter was back in New Orleans. He mentioned Moreau Lislet and John Gurley as having concurred in Derbigny's opinion—another anemic defense of his position.

Livingston's appeal to Rodney had failed; the Administration was immovable; the visit to Washington accomplished nothing. In spite of this, Livingston remained hopeful. He planned to return in the fall of the year to renew his petition,[64] but by October he had changed his mind. Professional obligations and living expenses forced him to remain in New Orleans. There was little he could do.[65] Frustrated in his efforts to secure his property and redeem his

---

62. Rodney to Livingston, July 17, 1808, ibid., 26.
63. Livingston to Rodney, July 20, 1808, ibid., 27.
64. Edward Livingston to Margaret B. Livingston, July 26, 1808, C. J. Ingersoll Papers, Historical Society of Pennsylvania.
65. During the fall months, Livingston made use of the legal Opinions sent to him by William Rawle, Edward Tilghman, William Lewis, and Jared Ingersoll —all leading

name through a direct appeal to the government, Livingston decided to lay his case before the nation.

* * *

In his *Address to the People of the United States*, Edward Livingston arraigned Thomas Jefferson for what he called his oppressive, unconstitutional, arbitrary, and illegal policy in regard to the New Orleans batture. "Private injuries," he wrote, "when offered in violation of Constitutional principles, become proper objects of public attention. . . . The selection of a remote scene for the exercise of arbitrary power, and of an unfriended or unpopular individual for its object, render the case more dangerous. . . ."[66] Livingston was attempting to utilize his unpopularity to his own advantage. For a year he had experienced the consequences of political isolation and the insufficiency of logic, truth, and justice—as he understood them—to restore him to his fortune. Now he was throwing himself upon the people in a last effort to win public support.

In the course of his long review of the events following the decree of the Superior Court of May 23, 1807, Livingston reflected upon the reasons for the injustice he had suffered. He knew that the malice of his enemies was active against him. He considered Governor Claiborne "the most malevolent among them."[67] The governor had staked his reputation on the cause of the batture, and he had convinced the people of New Orleans that his influence with the President would counteract the decision of the Superior Court. He, Livingston, was alert to this, but he still:

---

members of the Philadelphia bar. Their short briefs, along with Peter Stephen DuPonceau's were posted on the exchange coffee house and read and discussed at length by the public, as was Thierry's *Reply to Duponceau.* Accretions of silt on the Batture for the year 1808 were very considerable (Claiborne to Jefferson, Sept. 17, Oct. 24, Nov. 17; 1 *Letter Books*, IV, 218, 232–233, 252–253). The city of New Orleans undertook expensive surveys of these accretions because while "imperceptible" accretions favored private rights to alluvions, measurable increases bolstered public title.

66. Address to the People of the United States on the measures pursued by the Executive with respect to the Batture at New Orleans (New Orleans, 1808), reprinted in U.S. Cong., American State Papers: Public Lands, II, 7–13, quote at 7.

67. Ibid., 9.

> found it difficult to believe that the First Magistrate of a great people would quit the care of a nation to participate in the petty disputes of a corporate town; or, to secure the popularity of a favorite, that he would have set at defiance the very forms of law, braved the authority of the courts, and broken through the most important barriers of that constitution he had sworn to defend. If he had only effected my ruin, I should not have been surprised; for I am no longer in a situation to serve him; but that the suffrage of a party in an inconsiderable town should be purchased at this prodigal expense of principle, I own astonished me.[68]

Here Livingston was hitting one of the touchstones of affairs in the territory. The ominous clouds of defection in Lower Louisiana, the proximity of the hostile Spanish, and the remoteness of New Orleans had indeed transformed a local dispute into an urgent national issue. Instances of personal injustice carried little weight in such great affairs of state. This was no "petty dispute of a corporate town"; the "suffrage of a party in an inconsiderable [place]" was not insignificant. Livingston was beginning to realize that the politics of the batture controversy warranted even more attention than the legal merits of the batture case.

Livingston planned to distribute copies of his *Address* to Congress. He asked his brother Robert to help win over the members of both houses.[69] Peter Stephen DuPonceau and Livingston's other brother, John Livingston, advised that he suppress the work, but Livingston disagreed. For one thing, the *Address* had already appeared in all of the local newspapers. Secondly, he did not see the value of further self-effacement. "I tried moderation and silence longer than I ought," he wrote to his brother Robert in January, "and I found that they produced nothing but insolence and an accumulation of injuries."[70] Livingston contemplated the effect upon Jefferson of a renewed personal petition but concluded that "his tyranny will have increased with my submission." Yet, while Jefferson was but six weeks away from retirement, Livingston did not lose sight of the possibilities which the incoming Administration offered. He suggested that his brother might intercede with

---

68. Ibid.
69. Edward Livingston to Robert R. Livingston, Oct. 24, 1808, Robert R. Livingston Papers, New York Historical Society.
70. Edward Livingston to Robert R. Livingston, Jan. 22, 1809, ibid.

President-elect Madison. He himself would not ask for favors. "If he [Madison] should persist in the measures of his predecessor," he speculated, "I will not be the only sufferer, but I hope better things from his character."

Livingston demonstrated in his *Address* a growing awareness that the root of his batture troubles lay deeper than mere questions of law or fact. But it was J. B. S. Thierry, editor of the *Louisiana Courier*, who first perceived the full political dimensions of the batture controversy. The Aaron Burr conspiracy was a live issue in the Orleans territory. And while the embers of those fires were still glowing, the batture controversy had burst out into the open.[71] On both questions Livingston was vulnerable, and editor Thierry was quick to punish him for it. Entries in the *Courier* in April and May of 1808 sought to damage Livingston by linking him with well-known Burrites, thereby connecting *Burrism* with *Batturism*. Thierry viewed Livingston's batture misfortune as another defeat for the "swarm of locusts from the United States."[72] Thierry attributed Louisiana's political troubles to a fundamental fact: the existence in the territory of "the ambitious members of [Aaron

---

71. For a full discussion of the impact of the famous Burr Conspiracy on the politics of New Orleans, see George Dargo, *Jefferson's Louisiana: Politics and the Clash of Legal Traditions* (Cambridge: Harvard Press, 1975; rev. ed., Clark, N.J.: Lawbook Exchange, 2009), chap. 3.

72. The piece in the *Courier* was a reprint from a letter to the editor of the Philadelphia *Aurora,* March 3, 1808:

> The expulsion of Edward Livingston and his associate speculators, from the *Batture*, on behalf of the United States, has produced the liveliest emotion of joy and satisfaction at New-Orleans, and throughout the whole country; for a swarm of those locusts from the United States had taken such daring strides, and held themselves up as objects of menace to the Government, and superior to the laws, that for a time, the Government was considered as too imbecile either to assert its own authority or to protect its own laws.
>
> This affair of the Batture, has however restored confidence to the honest and faithful citizen; and has spread dismay and confusion among 'the choice spirits.' *Livingston, Clark, Watkins and Co.* have found that their efforts to excite commotion, and their rides through all the districts to asperse the Government, and stir up sedition, have at length turned out to their confusion, and to the honor of the General Government. The Legislature have in consequence of this salutary decision of the executive, transmitted their thanks to the President by an express.
>
> *Courier*, April 25, 1808

Burr's] broken faction." Thierry praised Claiborne's devoted service in behalf of the public interest in the matter of the batture.[73]

In his response to Livingston's December *Address*, Thierry commented upon a number of its allegations and again endeavored to connect the batture affair to the other public issues agitating the territory.[74] In the December 12th issue of the *Courier*, Thierry again alluded to the Aaron Burr conspiracy of 1806 and tried to entangle Livingston with all the others who had unluckily been caught up in those events. Thierry likened Livingston's declamations against invasions of individual liberty to the cries of those against whom General Wilkinson had acted in suppressing the

---

73. Thierry wrote:

> In spite of all the intrigues of the honorable Daniel Clark, the governor is still in place, and, if Louisiana has been affected with some misfortunes, it is meantime evident that we ought to attribute them to Burr, and to the ambitious members of his broken faction, who still remain amongst us. No one, at present questions the paternal interest which governor Claiborne feels for all our citizens. He has not recourse to all those petty tricks which lead to popularity; he has not on all solemn occasions a band of fawning favorites to offer up vows for his health, and to prepare sets of toasts which, being afterwards exhibited in the gazettes, strike the world with astonishment; but he is sincerely attached to whatever interests the country; he is entirely devoted to the prosperity of its citizens, and it is to his earnest solicitations that we shall owe the reinvestiture of the corporation in the possession of the Batture, on the ground of that prescription, which may be considered as immemorial, without the citizens having to dread the injurious consequences which some have wished to deduce there from against the right of proprietors bordering on the river to the accessions made to their lands by the alluvions.
>
> No one is ignorant at this day of all the means which the governor has incessantly employed to obtain the reestablishment of the public in this interesting property; but we do not yet know what our honorable delegate has done on this subject. I believe that all the world, as well as myself would be charmed, should he [Clark] design to set forth that which he has done in Congress in this important business.
>
> *Courier*, May 16, 1808

A letter to the editor by one "A.P." in the *Courier* of August 8, 1808, said that Clark's public position was to support the city in the Batture affair, but that privately "he was a strong advocate for Mr. Livingston."

74. One H. P. Nugent also connected Burrism and Batturism. In 1811 Nugent wrote, "It has been asserted at the seat of government, that some of our judges were concerned in the Burrite plot, and hence, it is natural to suspect that the project of robbing the banks having been defeated, the Burrites have changed their battery, and have determined to rob the corporation of their lands, by the assistance of their accomplices on the bench" (*H. P. Nugent's Reply to the Calumnies of the Honorable F. X. Martin, One of the Judges of the Superior Court of the Territory of Or leans* [Natchez: Printed for the author, 1811], 35).

supporters of the infamous Burr.[75] A week later Thierry again defended Claiborne as a champion of Louisianians and attributed Livingston's "implacable hatred" of the governor to his failure to gain appointment as a director of the Louisiana Bank."[76] Thierry attributed Claiborne's popularity not to his batture policy, as Livingston alleged, but to "his firm and wise conduct whilst he was almost involved in the elements of the Burrite faction." This established Claiborne's right to the affection of the inhabitants and the confidence of the Administration. "Such a popularity could not receive any increase from the affair of the batture," argued Thierry. The governor was merely doing his duty. But whether it was duty or popularity that directed Claiborne's policy, he had acted properly both during the Burr conspiracy and in the Batture controversy. Thierry was applauding the governor's performance.[77]

* * *

At the urging of his brother Robert, Livingston made another trip to the northeast in the spring of 1809.[78] Peter Stephen DuPonceau was very active on his behalf at this time. Robert Livingston suggested that a final settlement with the government could be reached if Edward indicated a readiness to accept a cancellation of his claim to the batture.[79] Robert believed that Congress would be

---

75. This is how Thierry put it:

> Always faithful! to his system of destruction, Mr. Livingston does not fear to call on his head all the suspicion of his complicity with Burr, by explaining himself thus: 'Where the destruction of personal liberty is permitted with impunity, the invasion of private property must be a venial crime. . . .' It is very simple that he should speak of the destruction of individual liberty, when there was no alternative left between the momentary destruction of the liberty of some incendiaries and the destruction of public liberty, as is natural enough for him to cry out that private liberty is violated when there is in fact nothing more but that obstacle in his usurping the public property.
>
> *Courier*, Dec. 12, 1808

76. *Courier*, Dec. 21, 1808.
77. Thierry's December editorials were later reprinted as an appendix in his *Reply to Duponceau.* The appendix was called "Refutation of Mr. Livingston's Pamphlet Entitled An Address to the People of the United States."
78. Robert R. Livingston to Edward Livingston, Jan. 19, 1809, Robert R. Livingston Papers, New York Historical Society.
79. Robert R. Livingston to Edward Livingston, April 19, 1809, ibid.

glad to "find some way out of the scrape" and was hopeful that the Madison Administration would not be difficult about it.

The optimism which Robert conveyed to Livingston was contagious. Apparently the mood in Washington in 1809 was not unfavorable. Livingston reported that he believed a satisfactory arrangement was possible. "I am well received by the President and my old Congressional friends," Edward wrote to his brother some time after arriving on his second trip to the capital. "[My] misfortunes have arisen from some prejudices excited against me in Mr. Jefferson's mind of which I can neither discover the substance nor the certain author — as they do not seem to have affected me with my former friends!"[80] He felt sufficiently confident to pursue his claim even more immoderately than he had the previous year. Livingston composed a letter that he distributed among a number of the members of Congress in which he restated his position, recounted his trials and sacrifices, and requested legislative aid. He asked for Congressional interference "as a matter of the highest public duty, which in my present position, I am content to solicit as a private favor."[81]

In the spring of 1809, Livingston did have some cause for optimism. In June resolutions were introduced in the House of Representatives by Daniel Sheffey of Virginia calling for a temporary restoration of Livingston's rights to the batture and the appointment of a presidential commission consisting of three referees to decide the question. In an alternative proposal, the President would be empowered to reach a compromise settlement pending a hearing in the federal courts. Livingston was prepared to accept either of these suggestions. Sheffey's resolutions were put before the House repeatedly in 1809, but no action was ever taken.[82]

By January 1810, the buoyancy of the previous spring had evaporated. Livingston lamented the absence of leadership and men

80. Edward Livingston to Robert R. Livingston, May27, 1809, ibid.

81. Circular letter of Edward Livingston to members of Congress, June 23, 1809, Miscellaneous Papers, New York Historical Society.

82. Livingston's activities continued to alienate him from the city government. Early in 1809 he helped the saloon-keepers to oppose a municipal tax on taverns. The mayor and the council were thoroughly outraged. Livingston's motive, it seemed to the authorities, was to exhaust the city's resources in needless litigation so that it would be unable to oppose his other "spoilations of public properties" ([Jan. 28, 1809], City Council Records, vol. II, bk. 2, 14–16).

of talent in the Congress.[83] Debate was desultory. His own cause had been relegated to the discussion of private claims which took place every Friday. He had little hope that Congress would act in his favor. "Should I be disappointed at this session," he wrote sadly, "I must abandon it forever—a life of solicitation is of all others the most insupportable." One month later the situation was unchanged. Congressional debate continued, but interest flagged. Arguments long since refuted were refurbished and advanced anew. Livingston wrote to his brother that "the wretches have caught some tag ends of ten times refuted arguments in the case and after repeating them gravely say that the title of the United States is so clear that they cannot reconcile it to their consciences to subordinate it to a trial."[84] He contemplated a return to New Orleans and a sale of his lands at one-quarter their value in order to free himself of debt.

The Batture debate in Congress in the spring of 1810 centered on the proposal introduced by George Poindexter, the delegate from the Mississippi territory.[85] It provided that a suit be brought by Livingston in the U.S. District Court in New Orleans against the United States; that the nearest federal circuit court consider an appeal according to the law and the forms of law then in force in Orleans; and that the Supreme Court of the United States review the decision of the circuit on a writ of error.[86] In opposition to this

---

83. Edward Livingston to Robert R. Livingston, Jan. 25, 1810, Robert R. Livingston Papers, New York Historical Society. Apparently, Livingston had stayed in Washington and New York without returning to New Orleans.

84. Edward Livingston to Robert R. Livingston, Feb. 14, 1810, ibid.

85. U.S. Cong., *Debates and Proceedings*, 11th Cong., 1st and 2nd.sess. (March 1/5/14, 1810), 1469, 1485–86, 1539–58. For earlier debates on the Batture, see ibid., (June 17/20/26, Dec. 7/11/15/18, 1809; Feb. 2/7/28, 1810) 323, 349, 418–419, 701, 707, 739, 744, 1373, 1379, 1468. The debates for this period are not fully reported in the *Debates and Proceedings*. However, from the available evidence it appears that many members feared that a decision on the Batture would serve as a precedent for a disposition of the Yazoo land claim dispute then pending.

86. The bill was later amended to provide for a special commission to be set up to look into the matter and for a compromise to be worked out between the federal government and Livingston. Agreement was reached in the Senate, but final action was postponed indefinitely on April 21. See *Debates and Proceedings*, 11th Cong., 2nd sess., 1607 (March 21, 1810), 1618 (March 23, 1810), 1694–1699 (March 30, 1810), 1700 (March 31, 1810), 1704–1705 (April 2, 1810), 1858 (April 16, 1810), 1879–1880 (April 17, 1810), 1886 (April 18, 1810), 1935 (April 21, 1810).

proposal Julien Poydras, the territorial delegate from Orleans, lectured Congress on the subject of the Batture.

Poydras had written and spoken on the question before. His past arguments in defense of the public's right to the Batture were based upon Thierry's *Examen*. Poydras himself was a planter, not a lawyer, and he added little to the prodigious heap of law that had already been unearthed. His published work on the Batture, however, was notable for its rhetorical flourishes. His writings were studded with those hyperbolic epithets so characteristic of the style of Livingston's opponents. The "usurpers" of the batture, Poydras had written, were "artful adversaries" and "griping attornies" supporting "illegal claims." They "packed juries" and made "poor clients" suffer through "the cunning of chicane."[87] He called the Batture decision an "atrocity" unparalled in human history,[88] and an impossibility had the judges been familiar with the local language, customs and laws of Orleans.[89]

Poydras's views sharpened public suspicion in the Orleans territory that the Superior Court's Batture decision in favor of Gravier and Livingston was a gross miscarriage of justice, a suspicion that was the one constant factor amidst the variables of legal argumentation in the protracted controversy,[90] all of which had quickened the opposition of the settled population to the introduction of American common law. This hostility to judicial proceedings in general—"judicial piracy" as Poydras called it—animated Poydras's last speech on the Batture. Opening with an eloquent restatement of "the sacred right of the public to the property of the port of the suburb St. Mary," Poydras quickly went to the heart of the question:

---

87. Further Observations in Support of the Right of the Public to the Batture of New Orleans or Port of St. Mary (Washington, D.C.: A.& G. Way, 1809), 14.
88. Speech of Julien Poydras, Esq., the delegate from the territory of Orleans, in support of the right of the public to the batture in front of the suburb St. Mary, Friday, Feb. 2, 1810 (Washington, D.C., 1810), 28.
89. A Defence of the Right of the Public to the Batture of New Orleans (Washington, D.C., 1809), 19; Speech (of Feb. 2), 27.
90. That the Batture decision was only one manifestation of the oppressions of the legal profession was reflected repeatedly in contemporary publications. See for example, *H. P. Nugent's Reply to the Calumnies*, 59, *et passim*.

> The honorable delegate from the Mississippi Territory [Poindexter], has told us in a very soft and persuasive tone, that he had a resolution to offer to the consideration of this honorable house very conciliatory indeed, and which he hoped would prove satisfactory to all parties, being calculated to insure an impartial and fair investigation of the titles of the invaders of the port of the suburb St. Mary. How has he fulfilled this promise, so engagingly announced in his soft sounding preamble? By a resolution, sir, objectionable in every point of view; the artful production of the combined exertions of practitioners profoundly skilled in all the tricks and windings of deceitful chicane. It is a masterpiece of duplicity. Its style is natural and flowing, like the limpid water of a gentle stream. Its language fascinating as a magic charm. "*Impartial trial . . . investigation of title, etc.*" Who can oppose himself to propositions seemingly so just? I, sir, do, and will be joined by everyone who knows that the language of a pleader is always calculated to conceal his real intent. It is the artificial blaze which dazzles the eye of the understanding. It is the melodious but bewitching voice of syrens. It is the smooth but perfidious current which dashes the unwary voyager against the rocks of Scylla or plunges him into the whirlpool of Charybdis. It is the golden sheath which conceals the dagger ready to stab you.[91]

For Poydras what must have been particularly exasperating was the absurdity of equating private and public right to the property. Such an equation was built into the adversary procedure of a common law court. The civilian in Poydras rebelled against what he conceived to be the inherent inequity of having a question such as the Batture decided in ordinary courts of law.[92] In view of the

---

91. U.S. Cong., Debates and Proceedings, 11th Cong., 1st and 2nd sess., (March 14, 1810) 1551. Poydras's speech was published in pamphlet form. See Speech of Julien Poydras, Esq., the delegate from the territory of Orleans, in support of the right of the public to the batture in front of the suburb St. Mary, Wednesday, March 14, 1810 (Washington, D.C., 1810).

92. The distinction between public law and private law is embedded deep in the civil law tradition. Thus, in his chapter on "Legal Categories," John Henry Merryman writes: "It was a kind of negative implication of [the] private law ideology that an entirely different attitude was appropriate in public law matters. There the role of government was not limited to the protection of private rights; on the contrary, the driving consideration was the effectuation of the public interest by state action. . . . In private legal relations the parties were equals and the state the referee. In public legal relations the state was a party, and as representative of the public interest (and successor to the prince), it was a party superior to the private individual" *The Civil Law Tradition: An Introduction to the Legal*

decision of the territorial court in *Gravier v. New Orleans,* Poydras was profoundly distrustful of American law courts in general, but the Poindexter proposal was all the more outrageous because it would have moved the forum for a final disposition of the Batture problem to the courts of the United States, thereby subverting his territory's right to have "every suit originating within its jurisdiction decided according to the local laws and in the ordinary way of judicial proceedings." Working from within this cast of mind, Poydras could not quite see how a public question such as the Batture could be resolved in an ordinary law court by a private civil suit in disregard and defiance of important public interests.

Poydras's stated fears were specific. He dismissed the "impartial trial" gambit as "mere pleading." Only in New Orleans, were there "people sufficiently acquainted with the civil law, and with the facts and circumstances of the case able to give a just and legal verdict." Elsewhere ignorance would prevail. Jurors would be vulnerable to "artful adversaries" interested only in misleading them.[93] Poydras did not concede that a good argument actually had been made by learned authorities for private ownership of the Batture. He spoke in behalf of the special nature of the case and of the peculiarities of the law governing it. The ambiguity of the whole question, the fact that the laws were subject to interpretation and the facts to dispute, was unacknowledged. Any other opinion represented ignorance of local "law, customs and manners." Thus Julien Poydras interpreted the batture decision in favor of Livingston as a thinly disguised effort to overturn the civil law itself. Despite the fact that the rule of decision had been Spanish law, Poydras insisted upon depicting the issue as a conflict between common law and civil law: "A spurious monster, the mongrel offspring of injustice and chicane, has been introduced into my country by our usurpers, who endeavor to pawn it on us as the lovely child of truth and justice; but we have with horror rejected this hideous imp, this illegitimate monster. Its foster parents are now attempting to have him regenerated, and legitimated, and for

---

Systems of Western Europe and Latin America [Stanford, Stanford University Press, 1969], 101, and chap. 14, *et passim*). On these points, see also Max Rheinstein, "Common Law and Civil Law: A Comparison," *Pennsylvania Bar Association Quarterly* 12 (1940), 7–19, esp. 13–15.

93. *Speech* (March 14, 1810), 7–8. Apparently, Poydras did not realize that federal circuit courts, when hearing cases on appeal, sat without juries.

this purpose they pursue means which are new, circuitous and dark; but I ardently hope their schemes may once more prove abortive."[94] What was this "monster," this "imp," this "mongrel offspring of chicane" if not the common law? Poydras could not say so outright, for he was speaking before an American Congress, many of whose members were common lawyers. And yet it is certain that this was his meaning. The batture had become, for him, a symbolic issue—a test to see whether Congress was willing to recognize some kind of cultural distinction in the territory of Orleans.[95]

* * *

Meanwhile, having failed to stir Congress into action, Livingston turned to the courts for relief. In the spring of 1810 he brought an action of trespass against Le Breton D'Orgenois, the U.S. marshal, in the U.S. district court in New Orleans and against former President Thomas Jefferson in the federal circuit court at Richmond. Livingston was determined to have a trial of his cause one way or another.[96]

To defend himself in court Jefferson requested the legal aid of some of the leading members of the Virginia bar.[97] He was advised to seek a full hearing of the case so that U.S. title to the batture would be established beyond question.[98] But Jefferson preferred a dismissal of the case on any technical point of pleading that would spare him a judgment of the merits.[99] He was no longer confident that the removal of Livingston and his workmen from the batture back in 1807 had been legal. He now believed that the federal statute authorizing the eviction of squatters from public lands did

---

94. Ibid., 9–10.

95. The mayor of New Orleans conveyed to Poydras the thanks of the city government "for the firmness, the talent and the zeal" with which he had defended the cause of the Batture in Congress (Message of Oct. 25, 1810, New Orleans Papers, New York Historical Society).

96. Edward Livingston to Robert R. Livingston, April 25, 1810, Robert R. Livingston Papers, New York Historical Society; *Livingston* v. *D'Orgenoy,* 1 Martin (O.S.) 87 (1810), and 7 Cranch (U.S.) 577 (1813); *Livingston* v. *Jefferson,* 15 Federal Cases (8411) 660 (Va. Cir. 1811).

97. Jefferson to William Wirt and George Hay, May 19, 1810, Jefferson Papers, LC.

98. George Hay to Jefferson, July 15/20, 1810, ibid.

99. Jefferson to Wirt and Hay, May 15, 1810, ibid.

not cover him.[100] And with respect to local law, that "we are all ignorant, except so far as instructed by the counsel of that place [i.e., Derbigny] who have written on the case," but in view of the published arguments of Livingston and Peter Stephen DuPonceau he realized that Derbigny's brief was not the last word.[101]

During the summer of 1810, Jefferson explored the whole question of the Batture and prepared what he hoped would be the definitive treatise on the subject as an aid to counsel.[102] He understood that the case against him rested on Spanish municipal law, and so he requested Claiborne to mail him Louis Moreau Lislet's "compilation of the laws of Orleans" [i.e., the Digest of 1808] plus "the book of Spanish laws called the Recopilacion de Indias and the Partita [sic] of the laws of Castille. . . . I suppose they would be very important!"[103] But Jefferson recognized that French civil law still provided the best color of legality to the position he had taken on the batture. Consequently, the brief he composed, and later published, was an elaborate argument purporting to prove that the law of France was the law in force in Orleans.[104]

Because of his lingering uncertainty over the legal questions at issue, Jefferson did everything possible to guarantee a favorable disposition of his case in any way that he could. This went beyond erudite legal treatise-writing and included the deployment of the now former president's considerable influence in the new Madison Administration to tilt the courts in his favor. Two crucial vacancies on the federal bench could affect the outcome of the litigation.[105] The declining health of Judge Cyrus Griffin of the Virginia district would soon open a seat on the federal circuit court where the case would be tried. Jefferson considered Griffin a "wretched . . . fool" and "a cypher," probably because he was a Federalist. Even worse, Griffen was likely to be heavily influenced by John Marshall whom

---

100. Jefferson to Gallatin, Sept. 27, 1810, in *The Writings of Thomas Jefferson*, ed. Paul L. Ford (10 vols., New York: G. P. Putnams, 1892–1899), IX, 283n.

101. Jefferson to Claiborne, June 11, 1810, Jefferson Papers, LC.

102. Jefferson to Wirt, June 18, 1810, *ibid.*

103. Jefferson to Claiborne, Oct. 16, 1810, *ibid.*

104. See below, n. 118.

105. The text account of Jefferson's efforts to influence Madison's judicial appointments at this time is based upon Albert J. Beveridge, *The Life of John Marshall*, 4 vols., (Boston: Houghton Mifflin, 1919), IV, 100–116; and Hatcher, *Edward Livingston*, 156–165, supplemented by other materials as noted.

Jefferson despised and feared. Virginia was part of the Chief Justice's federal circuit, and the ex-president was convinced that Marshall's "twistifications of the law in the case of Marbury, in that of Burr, & the late Yazoo case show how dexterously he can reconcile the law to his personal biases: and nobody seems to doubt that he is ready prepared to decide that Livingston's right to the batture is unquestionable, and that I am bound to pay for it with my private fortune."[106] Jefferson urged Madison to appoint Governor John Tyler of Virginia to the District Court. He thought Tyler would have the "character of firmness enough to preserve his independence on the same bench with Marshall.[107] In pushing Tyler's candidacy Jefferson was not above reminding Madison that in 1807, as a member of the Cabinet, Madison had been one of Jefferson's "associates in the proceedings" against Livingston and therefore liable to summons as a material witness in the case—a source of possible embarrassment to the new president.[108]

The other key vacancy occurred in September 1810, when Justice William Cushing died, leaving the Supreme Court evenly divided between three Republicans and three Federalists and opening up to Madison the first opportunity to create a Democratic-Republican majority on the high court. Jefferson was worried because of the possibility of an appeal from the Virginia circuit, should the Batture decision go against him there.[109] He recom-

---

106. Jefferson to Madison, May 25, 1810, in Jefferson, *Writings*, ed. Ford, IX, 276.
107. Ibid., 275.
108. Jefferson sent his brief on the Batture to all of the former members of his Cabinet ostensibly for the purpose of getting their advice, but with the thinly veiled threat that they were deeply involved and were possible targets of future litigation. As he explained to Caesar Rodney, "Believing my late associates in the executive would feel an interest in the justification of a conduct in which all concurred and also in the issue of it, I have thought it a duty to consult them as to the grounds to be taken, and to take none against their advice" (*The Writings of Thomas Jefferson*, ed. A. A. Lipscomb and A. E. Bergh [Memorial Ed. 20 vols., Washington, D.C., 1904–1905], XII, 424).
109. The urgency of Jefferson's interest in the Supreme Court appointment was best revealed in his Sept. 27 letter to Gallatin: "What the issue of the case ought to be, no unbiased man can doubt. What it will be, no one can tell. The judge's [Marshall's] inveteracy is profound, and his mind of that gloomy malignity which will never let him forego the opportunity of satiating it on a victim. His decisions, his instructions to a jury, his allowances and disallowances and garblings of evidence, must all be subjects of appeal. I consider that as my only chance of saving my fortune from entire wreck. And to whom is my appeal? From the judge in Burr's case to himself and his associate judges in the case of *Marbury* v. *Madison*. Not exactly, however. I observe old Cushing

mended Levi Lincoln, his former Attorney General, but Lincoln declined because of failing eyesight; he then recommended Gideon Granger, the Postmaster General since 1801.[110] Jefferson was determined to get a friend on the Supreme Court one way or another. Madison's fourth choice to fill Cushing's seat (Granger was unacceptable, Alexander Wolcott of Connecticut was rejected by the Senate, and John Quincy Adams, the ambassador to Russia, declined) was Joseph Story, a Massachusetts Republican whom everyone, except Jefferson, trusted.[111]

Meanwhile Jefferson turned to Congress for additional support. With the Cushing replacement pending and Griffin's demise distressingly protracted, Jefferson requested William Branch Giles, a leading Senate Republican, and John Wayles Eppes, his nephew and son-in-law (Eppes married Jefferson's daughter Mary, a first cousin), a staunch Administration supporter in the House, to stifle congressional action on the batture question despite Livingston's repeated petitions.[112] Jefferson was fearful that any legislative undertaking even partially favorable to Livingston would prejudice his position in a court proceeding.

Jefferson sent Giles and Eppes copies of the brief he had laboriously prepared over the summer, cautioning them to show it only to trusted intimates such as Julien Poydras of the Orleans territory. "I have thought that I might rely on your justice as well as your friendship to attend to this case," he wrote, "so far as to prevent his [Livingston's] obtaining there [in Congress] any vote injurious to a fair trial."[113] But Jefferson was not interested in a "fair trial" as that phrase was (and is) commonly understood. He had already agreed with his counsel to try for a dismissal on technicalities while at the same time he remained busily engaged in his concerted effort to manipulate the personnel on the courts about to try the case or likely to hear it on appeal. No doubt Jefferson had persuaded himself that the bench was inveterately opposed to him. He assured Giles and Eppes that "were this case before an impartial court it would never give me a moment's concern. . . . [But] the deep-

---

is dead. At length, then, we have a chance of getting a Republican majority in the Supreme judiciary" (Jefferson, *Writings*, ed. Ford, IX, 284n.)

110. Jefferson to Madison, Oct. 15, 1810, ibid., 282–283.

111. Beveridge, *Marshall*, IV, 110.

112. Jefferson to Eppes and Giles, Nov. 12, 1810, Jefferson Papers, LC.

113. Ibid.

seated enmity of one judge [Marshall] and utter nullity of the other [Griffin] . . . lessens the confidence which the justice of my cause would other wise give me." But it was one thing for Jefferson to believe that all he wanted was a fair trial—quite another to try to win the sympathy of others by passing himself off as an innocent victim of an oppressive bench. One month later, Griffin died. Madison appointed John Tyler to the Virginia district court, thus consummating Jefferson's disingenuous bench tampering.

Tyler understood Jefferson's role in getting him onto the federal bench and, more importantly, what was expected of him. Jefferson had spelled it out in May 1810, when the possibility of replacing Griffin first arose. Referring to the Virginia district, to Marshall's "base prostitution of law to party passions," to Griffin's "imbecility," and to the need for a judge to extend the protection of law to all citizens, he admonished Tyler: "I believe you will do it, and where you cannot induce your colleague to do what is right, you will be firm enough to hinder him from doing what is wrong, and by opposing sense to sophistry, leave juries free to follow their own judgment."[114]

Jefferson was not to be disappointed. On December 5, 1811, the federal Circuit Court for the Virginia district rendered a decision in *Livingston* v. *Jefferson*. The court found that an action for a trespass committed on lands within the United States but outside the jurisdiction of the Virginia district was beyond its power to adjudicate. Refusing to overturn an ancient rule of English common law, the court said that a trespass was local in nature and had to be tried where the land in question lay. The proper venue for an action of trespass involving the Batture, therefore, was a court of competent jurisdiction in the Orleans territory, not one in Henrico County, Virginia.

Both Tyler and Marshall concurred on the venue question, but Tyler congratulated Jefferson's attorneys for their "Herculean strength of forensic ability which . . . sheds luster over the bar of Virginia," while accusing John Wickham, Livingston's advocate, of trying to make "the worse appear the better cause" and using "high-sounding words . . . [to] fill up a vacuum in . . . argument."[115] Marshall, on the other hand, implied that a decision on the merits

---

114. Jefferson to Tyler, May 26, 1810, Jefferson, *Writings*, ed. Ford, IX, 276n.
115. 15 Fed. Cases (8411) 660 (Va. Cir. 1811), 661, 663; see also Hatcher, *Edward Livingston*, 162–163.

would have been in favor of Livingston. This was blocked by the defendant's assertion of the technical distinction between transitory actions and local actions which the weight of previous judicial opinion forced Marshall to uphold. However, whatever the reasons for the technicality, said Marshall, "[t]hey are countervailed, and more than countervailed by the opposing consideration, that if the action be disallowed, the injured party may have a clear right without a remedy in a case where a person who had done the wrong [i.e., Jefferson] and who ought to make the compensation, is within the power of the court."[116]

Tyler later informed Jefferson that the Chief Justice was eager to adjourn and remove the case for hearing before the United States Supreme Court. He would have done so, he said, had Tyler—at the time, gallantly resisting the "severe . . . paroxysms" of a bladder condition—not insisted on a decision at the circuit level "letting the parties act as they pleased, by appealing, if they disliked the decision, to which he [Marshall] consented."[117] Tyler's moral debt to Jefferson for his judgeship was thereby paid in full.

Having been unwilling to risk a legal trial on the merits but eager to establish his innocence in the courtroom of public opinion, Jefferson published the lengthy brief he had prepared as an aid to counsel once the legal proceeding was behind him.[118] The work was a clever but unoriginal synthesis of old arguments plus some new ones concocted by Albert Gallatin.[119] The following year, in a

---

116. 1 Brockenbrough [Marshall's circuit opinions] (1811) 208; 15 Fed. Cases (8411), 664; Hatcher, *Edward Livingston*, 163–164.

117. Tyler to Jefferson, May 17, 1812, *Letters and Times of the Tylers*, by Lyon G. Tyler (3 vols., Richmond, 1884–1896), I, 264.

118. The Proceedings of the Government of the United States in maintaining the public right to the beach of the Mississippi, adjacent to New Orleans, against the intrusion of Edward Livingston. Prepared for the use of counsel (New York, 1812); reprinted in U.S. Cong., *American State Papers: Public Lands*, II, 59–83; and in *American Law Journal* 5 (1814), 1–103.

119. See Gallatin's "Memorandum respecting the suit instituted by E. Livingston against T. Jefferson late President and Letters to and from Mr. Jefferson," Gallatin Papers, New York Historical Society (filed among the 1807 papers). Jefferson's position had been thoroughly refuted by Peter Stephen DuPonceau. Even the *American Law Journal*, in an editorial footnote to a reprint of Peter Stephen Du Ponceau's *Review*, commented critically upon Jefferson's return to Derbigny's position and his failure to answer Peter Stephen DuPonceau's arguments. Many years later, however, Jefferson's position was supported by Gustavus Schmidt, a leading Louisiana jurist of the mid-nineteenth century

characterically exhaustive reply, Edward Livingston would marvel at how Jefferson could "persevere in the same pretence of understanding the laws of France better than gentlemen bred to it from their childhood, and who, engaged on the same side of the controversy with himself, have abandoned the ground he has taken."[120] To Livingston's gratification, the eminent James Kent, Chancellor of New York, wrote him that, on the merits, Livingston's case was stronger and that he had been the victim of an "atrocious injustice." Joseph Story would later declare that Jefferson's conduct in the matter of the Batture was regrettable.[121]

Meanwhile, Livingston had reoccupied the batture in November 1810, a year before his suit against Jefferson came to trial. This time he deferred to local custom by permitting the unloading of boats and the filling of watercarts, but he warned that anyone caught digging in or carting off batture soil would be sued.[122] Nevertheless, Livingston's gesture, however conciliatory, was resisted—by Thierry in the *Louisiana Courier* and by the United States attorney, who ordered J. M. Fortier, the new U.S. marshal in New Orleans, to retain possession for the government. Livingston promptly sued Fortier.[123]

Batture litigation continued for another decade. Livingston remained hopeful and energetic throughout, despite personal grief and continued legal harassment. He was partially vindicated by a Supreme Court decision ordering the U.S. District Court in New Orleans to restore him to his property, but the local authorities blocked effective implementation of the court order, and litigation

---

in articles published in the *Louisiana Law Journal* (1841–42). (I am grateful to Mr. John H. Tucker, Jr. of Shreveport for bringing this work to my attention.) For further discussion, see below, chap. 7.

120. An Answer to Mr. Jefferson's Justification of His Conduct in the Case of the New Orleans Batture (Philadelphia, 1813); reprinted in American Law Journal (1814), 113–299. The quote is ibid., 289.

121. Beveridge, *Marshall*, IV, 114–115.

122. Claiborne to Jefferson, Dec. 24, 1810, *Territorial Papers*, ed. Carter, IX, 907.

123. These events were reported to Jefferson by James Mather in a letter of November 30, 1810 (Jefferson Papers, LC). Edward Livingston to Dominick A. Hall (District Court judge); J. M. Fortier to Robert Smith (Secretary of State), both Nov. 30, 1810 (Miscellaneous letters, Dept. of State, National Archives). Fortier was about to resign and had notified Smith of his intentions in August. No replacement had been picked by October, however. With Edward Livingston out and about, the position called for a courageous man, or at least one who was indifferent to law suits.

went on.[124] Not until the 1820s, after a compromise settlement with the city of New Orleans had been reached, did Livingston begin to enjoy the fruits of his numerous trials and arduous labors.

In time, Livingston even regained the sympathy of those who had opposed him during the bitter fight. Bernard Marigny, one of his strongest opponents in the Batture affair, expressed warm admiration for Livingston's "imperturbable constancy" and "personal courage." "Such a man," he thought, "inspires interest and deserves consideration even from those who oppose him."[125] Even the aged Jefferson was eventually reconciled. In 1824, in a letter to James Monroe, he wrote that Livingston "may be assured I have not a spark of unfriendly feeling toward him . . . Mr. Livingston would now be received at Monticello with as hearty a welcome as he would have been in 1800. . . . I bear ill will to no human being."[126]

* * *

The Batture controversy had wide-ranging ramifications. On the political level it led to the isolation of Edward Livingston.[127] Livingston was Claiborne's chief rival for political preferment in the territory. He was a man of two worlds—an American with important links to the central government whose own brother had been a central figure in the negotiations leading to the purchase of Louisiana, and a resident of Louisiana who had married a French refugee from Saint Domingue, learned the local languages, specialized in civil law, and championed most of the interests of the

---

124. *Livingston* v. *D'Orgenoy*, 7 Cranch (U.S.) 577 (1813); Hatcher, *Edward Livingston*, 165–169.

125. "Memoire of Bernard Marigny addressed to his fellow citizens of New Orleans," (from Paris, 1822), trans. Olivia Blanchard, in New Orleans Municipal Papers, Howard-Tilton Memorial Library, Tulane University, 27–28 (in typescript).

126. Jefferson to Monroe, March 27, 1824, Jefferson Papers, LC.

127. In 1811 Livingston failed to win election to the Lousiana constitutional convention. In 1812, his efforts to prevent Claiborne's election as the state's first governor also failed. Favorable federal court judgments with regard to the Batture in 1813 merely inflamed popular sentiment against him. See Edward Livingston to Robert R. Livingston, July 26, Sept. 28, 1811, Simon Gratz Papers, Historical Society of Pennsylvania; and *Edward* to *Robert R. Livingston*, May 12, June 23, 1812, Robert R. Livingston Papers, New York Historical Society.

inhabitants. Livingston was a serious rival for leadership in the territory. However, the batture controversy dissipated Livingston's popularity, and because of it, he remained politically isolated at least for a time. It is significant that Livingston had to reach out to Peter Stephen DuPonceau and other members of the Philadelphia bar for legal support. No important local lawyer would come to his assistance.

There is no one-to-one relationship between the batture fight and the larger conflict of legal traditions in Lower Louisiana. The rivals for control of the batture did not parallel the civil law/common law antagonists which were described in the previous essay on the Louisiana Civil Digest. From the very first, Livingston fought for the civil law. The practice act of 1805, which he authored, his translation of some of the books in the *Corpus Juris Civilis*, and then, in the 1820's, his projects on behalf of legal codification, all attest to long and devoted service to local legal traditions. On the other hand, Thomas Jefferson, the leading proponent of the common law in Lower Louisiana, defended the public right to the Batture. On one issue the President's position coincided with that of the American minority; on the other he allied himself with the Latin majority.

Still, the struggle for the Mississippi alluvion criss-crossed larger legal questions at many points. Edward Livingston was the best-known American attorney in New Orleans. Because of his exploitation of the batture, Louisianians viewed him as the most notorious example of those "vexatious lawyers" which the cession seemed to have produced. The American judges on the territorial superior court had consigned to Livingston public properties of enormous importance and value. The Batture controversy seemed to be the classic instance of how the law could be twisted and local inhabitants thereby deprived of their ancient rights and privileges.

The original decision in *Gravier v. New Orleans* may have been based upon sound civil law principles. Yet Thierry's *Courier* articles and Poydras's speeches in Congress showed that the public would perceive the Superior Court's ruling as a legal calamity brought on by the bench's profound ignorance of the customs of the country. The batture litigation stimulated an awareness, in the popular mind at least, that important public interests could be lost by legal means. Questions of law, therefore, assumed a new gravity and awakened wide concern.

Thus, in its own special way, the controversy over the Batture of the Faubourg St. Marie dramatized the confrontation between diverse legal cultures. The political, social, and legal issues raised in the course of the batture fight impinged with unparalleled immediacy upon larger questions of law and the overall problem of the conflict of legal traditions in Lower Louisiana. At the same time it prepared the ground at the territorial and national levels of government for the adoption of the *Digest of the Laws in Force* on March 31, 1808, a moment when the clamor over the New Orleans batture was at its height.

Episode 8

Steamboats and Tugboats on the Mississippi

> All the boilers bursting simultaneously—machinery, vast fragments of the boilers, huge beams of timber, furniture and human beings in every degree of mutilation, were alike shot up perpendicularly many hundred fathoms in the air.
>
> *Louisiana Chronicle*, 1843

Here is a short description of the Mississippi as it appeared to the River's most astute observer, surely the most famous and probably the most talkative river pilot who ever lived:

> The majestic bluffs that overlook the river, along through this region, charm one with the grace and variety of their forms, and the soft beauty of their adornment . . . And then you have the shining river, winding here and there and yonder, its sweep interrupted at intervals by clusters of wooded islands threaded by silver channels; and you have glimpses of distant villages, asleep upon capes; and of stealthy rafts slipping along in the shade of the forest walls; and of white steamers vanishing around remote points. And it is all as tranquil and reposeful as dreamland, and has nothing this-worldly about it—nothing to hang a fret or a worry upon.[1]

The writer was, of course, Mark Twain. The approach of a Mississippi steamer and the commotion and excitement that it caused in every river town is what first drew boys like the young Samuel Clemens to a life aboard those boats.[2]

---

* Source: "Steamboats, Towboats and Legal Historiography: The Law in Louisiana and the New Nation" by George Dargo from Edward F. Haas (ed.), *Louisiana's Legal Heritage* (Pensacola: The Perdido Bay Press, 1983), 129–141.

1. *Life on the Mississippi* (New York: Heritage Press, 1944), 338.
2. Ibid., 29.

And here is Mark Twain describing one of the great pastimes of river pilots, steamboat racing:

> I think that much of the most enjoyable of all races is a steamboat race . . . two red-hot steamboats raging along, neck-and-neck, straining every nerve, —that is to say, every rivet in the boilers, —quaking and shaking and groaning from stem to stern, spouting white steam from the pipes, pouring black smoke from the chimneys, raining down sparks, parting the river into long breaks of hissing foam—that is sport that makes a body's very liver curl with enjoyment.[3]

A somewhat more obscure source, an account that appeared in a newspaper called the *Louisiana Chronicle*, described in some detail what sometimes happened during such a steamboat race—a boiler explosion that struck a steamboat called the *Clipper* in the year 1843:

> All the boilers bursting simultaneously—machinery, vast fragments of the boilers, huge beams of timber, furniture and human beings in every degree of mutilation, were alike shot up perpendicularly many hundred fathoms in the air. On reaching the greatest height, the various bodies diverged like the jets of a fountain, in all directions—falling to the earth, and upon roofs of houses, in some instances as much as two hundred and fifty yards from the scene of destruction. The hapless victims were scalded, crushed, torn, mangled, and scattered in every possible direction – many into the river, some in the streets, some on the other side of the Bayou, nearly three hundred yards – some torn asunder by coming in contact through the solid walls of houses at a great distance from the boat. . . . [The] 2nd engineer [was] thrown against the fence—one arm torn off and fragments of his carcass scattered over the trees. The watchman . . . was thrown alive, one hundred yards through the solid wall of Baker's Hotel, into a bed. He retained his senses perfectly for some time after, but the poor fellow expired during the evening. The cabin boy was thrown about two hundred yards through the roof of a shed, and was picked up in a mangled condition.[4]

---

3. Ibid., 268–269.
4. L. C. Hunter, *Steamboats on Western Rivers: An Economic and Technological History* (Cambridge: Harvard University Press, 1949), 288.

In recalling the romantic days of the Mississippi steamboat (as well as one of its less romantic moments), we are reminded of the great dependence of the western settlements upon inland water transportation in the early and middle decades of the nineteenth century. This was particularly true in Louisiana, whose trade and commerce were so completely tied to the Mississippi Basin's vast network of rivers, bayous, and canals. Prior to the War of 1812, goods and people often came to New Orleans by flatboat, a journey that was long, arduous, and hazardous. Average time from Pennsylvania in 1810, for example, was about six weeks in fair weather. But the return journey could take as much as four months, sometimes even longer. In fact, the common practice was simply to break up the flatboat, sell the wood, and return to the point of origin on horseback. Interestingly enough, while the steamboat would eventually displace the flatboat, the two forms of river transportation grew side by side for several decades. The steamboat solved the problem of the return voyage for flatboatmen, so that until the mid-1840's the annual number of flatboats arriving in New Orleans actually increased—from about 600 in 1814 to more than 2,500 in 1846.[5]

Clearly, however, this was to be the Age of Steam. In the west it began in the winter of 1811 when a ship appropriately called *The New Orleans*, owned by the Fulton-Livingston group of New York, steamed from Pittsburgh to New Orleans. Thereafter steamboats became "the most important factor in the great industrial [and commercial] development of [the] region. . . ."[6] Indeed, no other section of the country was so dependent upon steam for transport as was the Mississippi Basin. In no other part of the world were so many steamboats built or operated. New Orleans led the way in this expansion. In the year 1820, for example, there were 198 reported arrivals of steam-powered vessels in this city. Not until the mid-1820s did any other western inland port even approach that figure.[7]

But along with the increase in the number of steamboats in use was the growth in the number of steamboat accidents. The hazards of steamboating were unique, dramatic, and even awe inspiring as

---

5. G. R. Taylor, *The Transportation Revolution: 1815–1866* (New York: Rinehart & Co., 1951), 65.
6. Ibid., 63.
7. Hunter, *Steamboats on Western Rivers*, 644 (Appendix, Table 2).

the explosion aboard the *Clipper* in 1843 graphically demonstrated. Steamboat accidents represented the first major example of industrial accidents that affected the general public. While steam-powered machines were already injuring, maiming, and killing early industrial workers, particularly in textile factories, steamboat accidents put the public in direct contact with the dangers of the new technology.

Given the riskiness of life in that era of frontier violence, economic scarcity, and primitive public health it is surprising how agitated the public became over steamboat accidents and their resulting causalities. Perhaps the explanation lies in their communal impact which neither railroad accidents nor factory accidents ever duplicated. Railroad mishaps often occurred somewhere along the right-of-way, and their effects were confined to the passengers, the crew, or the hapless farmers whose flax or grain near the tracks caught fire. Similarly, factory accidents usually happened behind closed doors and were restricted in their social impact to workers and their families. But steamboat explosions occurred most often on the approach or the departure from the river port. As in the case of the *Clipper*, these events were witnessed by entire communities. Their dramatic character can best be compared to airline disasters in our own century and the obsessive concern we have about them even though we all know that statistically we run a much greater risk when we take a cab to the airport than in the flight itself.

Exploding boilers on steamboats were clearly the most startling and novel kind of accident. One half of the number of lives lost on steamboats before the Civil War was caused by these explosions. But fires were equally spectacular and, in terms of property loss if not mortality, equally devastating. However, much like boiler explosions, fires had a certain comforting familiarity about them. But while the threat of fire on sailing vessels or flatboats were always a possibility, fires aboard steamboats occurred with greater frequency because of the proximity of combustible cargoes to flying sparks, smoldering embers, and blazing furnaces. As one writer has put it:

> [The] floors and partitions [of these boats, their] light framing and siding, soft resinous woods, the whole dried out by the sun and wind and impregnated with oil and turpentine from paint,

> made the superstructure . . . little more than an orderly pile of kindling wood.[8]

With cargoes of cotton, hay, straw, oil, spirits, and even gunpowder, and with dry wood for fuel, it is truly amazing that any steamboats completed a voyage on any inland river without mishap. Lifeboats and life preservers were unknown. Tiller ropes made of hemp burned along with everything else on board so that there was no way to steer a blazing boat back to shore. With nothing but wooden buckets for fire control, it is no wonder that fires aboard steamboats often caused considerable loss of life and property.

Snags, collisions, and storms were the other main causes of accidents to steamboats on western waters. Snags were the biggest single cause of accidents, but they were also the least costly. Snags were usually caused by logs or other debris which breached the hull with tremendous force. Collisions occurred because navigational space was limited, rules of the road were rudimentary at best and ships were not yet required to have running lights at night. The sharp bends in the river and the flat bottoms of the boats afforded limited maneuverability. Foundering caused by sudden storms or by running aground on hidden shoals were another familiar source of mishap.

Of these five major causes of steamboat accident—boiler explosions, fires, collisions, snags, and founderings—the last two were thought to be beyond human control, pure accident which even the most careful seamanship could not avoid. On the other hand, fire and collision, on the other hand, were attributable to human error which created at least a presumption of careless neglect. But boiler explosions fell somewhere in between. Their cause or causes were not yet fully understood in the early years of steam navigation. One body of opinion held that boiler explosions were "unavoidable accident," a "peril of the sea" (or the river). Thus in a marine insurance case decided as late as 1845, the Supreme Court of Missouri concluded "that whatever natural philosophers may think of this . . . the elements which combine to create the power of steam, . . . entirely within the reach of accident. . . ."[9] On the other hand, in a similar case decided just a few years

---

8. Ibid., 278.
9. *Citizens Insurance Co.* v. *Glasgow, et al.*, 9 Mo. 243, 246 (1845).

before, the Supreme Court of Ohio held that "a steam engine, properly constructed, is entirely within man's control. . . . The laws of steam are as well understood as the laws which regulate any other power. . . . Of all the great moving powers, [steam] is the most completely manageable. [A]n explosion . . . presupposes negligence."[10]

The Louisiana courts adopted the second theory. In an explosion case decided in 1859 the Louisiana Supreme Court rejected the argument that "an explosive something, probably electricity, is generated in the steam boiler, which no care can prevent." Instead it held that despite the

> unsatisfactory state of science on the subject of the explosion of steam boilers . . . we think it might be safely assumed that where steam boilers and engines are properly constructed, of good materials and proper strength, and are managed with the prudent and reasonable care which the powerful agent employed requires, they will not explode. . . . The long period of prosperity and freedom from explosions which followed the passage of the Act of Congress of 1852, and the comparative security of steamboats constructed and managed under the regulations of the French Government . . . give great weight to this inference.[11]

The movement for statutory regulation of steamboating to which this Louisiana case referred began with the catastrophes of the 1820s. At first the states most immediately affected tried their hand at regulatory schemes. Legislative investigations of accidents, licensing requirements for engineers, and the imposition of penalties and fines for violators evidenced an emerging governmental interest in the subject. None of the legislation proposed was designed to protect steamboat crews however, only the life and property of the public at large, which is not surprising since it was public outrage over steamboat accidents that triggered these regulatory efforts. State regulation had little effect since steamboat traffic was interstate. There was not much that local authorities could do to regulate out-of-state companies.

Thus what little legislation there was in the 1830s caused no change in the general trend of accident statistics. The decline in the

---

10. *Adm'rs. of Perrin* v. *Protection Insurance Co.*, 11 Ohio 148,152–154 (1842).
11. *Poree* v. *Cannon, et al.*, 14 La. Ann. 506–507 (1859).

average age of steamboats destroyed on western rivers continued: from 1811 to 1819 it was 4.2 years, from 1820 to 1829 it was 4.0 years, and from 1830 to 1839 it was 2.65 years.[12] Not until Congress stepped into the regulatory field, first in 1838 and again in 1852, was there significant change. But until the 1850's steamboats continued to blow up, burn, collide, and founder with alarming regularity. As Charles Dickens, one of many European travelers to America in these years, once put it, "Western steamboats usually blow up, one or two a week, during the season."[13] Or as Mark Twain later reported: "between St. Louis and Cairo . . . steamboat wrecks average one to the mile—two hundred wrecks, altogether."[14]

But while statutory solutions were slow in coming the courts were called upon to deal with the steady flow of litigation that the high rate of accidents produced. The question presented in many of these cases turned on the standard of liability to be applied to the steamboat as a carrier of goods or of passengers. The Louisiana Digest of 1808 (also known also as the Civil Code of 1808) established a statutory scheme that often but not always was the starting point of analysis. Article 63 of the Digest provided that

> Carriers and watermen may be liable for the loss or damage of the things entrusted to their care unless they can prove that such loss or damage has been occasioned by accidental or uncontrollable events.[15]

The source for Article 63, as confirmed by the de la Vergne edition of the Digest, was Article 1784 of the Civil Code of Napoleon.[16] The chief difference in the Louisiana version of the provision is that the mandatory language of the Napoleonic formulation ("they *are* liable for the loss or damage") was changed to the permissive language of Article 63 of the Digest ("carriers and watermen *may* be liable"). Interestingly enough, the Revised Civil

---

12. Hunter, *Steamboats on Western Rivers*, 654 (Appendix, Table 13).
13. Charles Dickens, *Pictures From Italy and American Notes for General Circulation* (New York, 1892), 366.
14. *Life on the Mississippi*, 153.
15. La. Civ. Code, Bk. 3, Tit. 8, Art. 63, 384 (1804).
16. See. R. Batiza, "The Louisiana Civil Code of 1808: Its Actual Sources and Present Relevance," 46 *Tul. L. Rev.* 4 (1971).

Code of 1870 returned to the mandatory language of the French Code possibly because the leading cases decided in the aftermath of the adoption of the 1808 Digest pointed in that direction, as we shall see.

The Digest seemed to offer an open invitation to judicial construction that the Louisiana courts did not hesitate to accept. In *Hunt* v. *Morris*, the first important case to construe Article 63, goods placed on board a steamboat in New Orleans for delivery at Natchez were destroyed by fire when, in preparation for the voyage, the vessel went on a short nighttime excursion to secure wood for fuel.[17] The Louisiana Supreme Court applied an ordinary care standard to the defendant's conduct. The Court held that a carrier was not an insurer as at common law but a bailee for hire answerable only for ordinary neglect that it defined as "the omission of that care, which every man of common prudence . . . takes of his own concerns."[18] But the Court also held that loss by fire created a presumption of negligence that put a burden of proof of non-negligence on the defendant. Since masters of steamboats were "in the constant habit of running them by night" the master of this one did not deviate from what later courts would call the "standard of care" of his profession. The Court also noted that the risk of fire was less by night than by day "because its commencement in any part of the boat would be more readily discovered in the dark."[19] In effect, the defendant in this case met the burden of proof of accident by showing that he had acted with due diligence.

However, more important than *Hunt* v. *Morris* in terms of the influence of Louisiana law upon other American jurisdictions was another steamboat vessel case decided about ten years later. In

---

17. 6 Mart. (O. S.) 676 (1819).

18. Id., 680.

19. Id., 684. *Hunt* v. *Morris* remained good law until the early twentieth century. In *Lehman, Stem & Co.* v. *Morgan's La. & Tex. Rail & Steamship Co.*, 38 So. 873 (La. 1905), the Louisiana Supreme Court placed a greater burden on the defendant at least in fire cases. Defendants now had to show, in addition to proof of care, evidence of causation. See C. Guard Davidson, "Liability of Carrier for Destruction of Goods Through Fire Originating on Premises of Shipper," 6 *Tul. L. Rev.* III (1931). While *Hunt* v. *Morris* had established the ordinary care standard, it was not as favorable to defendants as it might appear since it did create the rebuttable presumption of negligence which placed the burden of proving non-negligence on the defendant. See 6 Mart. (O. S.), 682.

Smith v. *Pierce* the captain of a vessel under tow by a steamboat was ordered to come around to starboard.[20] As was the practice, the two boats were lashed together. The towed vessel went aground and was damaged. There was a dispute as to the number of degrees to starboard the steamboat captain had ordered and whether or not the shouted orders were obeyed at all. The defendant steamboat owners alleged negligence on the part of the captain and crew of the towed vessel as a defense. The Louisiana Supreme Court upheld a judgment for the plaintiff and applied to steam towboats the same standard of liability as any other common carrier. Judge George Mathews, one of Louisiana's distinguished early jurists who had also written the opinion in *Hunt* v. *Morris*, reasoned that towboats were common carriers since their "trade is to carry goods for hire."[21] Mathews allowed no "distinction . . . between the towers [sic.] of vessels by means of steamboats and ordinary carriers" even though the master of the steam towboat had no direct control over the rudder of the towed vessel because "the vessels which are towed are almost entirely passive."[22] The master of the steamboat was bound to carry the vessel in tow safely to its destination even if this required placing his own men on board the vessel. Only uncontrollable events would relieve the steamboat master of liability.

The defendants in *Smith* v. *Pierce* attempted to put steamboats within one of the exceptions to strict common carrier liability developed by Chief Justice John Marshall in a Kentucky case where four black slaves drowned while being transported from shore to a steamboat in the steamboat's tender.[23] Marshall said that slaves were not goods but passengers. He reasoned that since slaves were, as he put it, "intelligent beings," the master of the vessel did not have the same control over them as he would over inanimate objects. Marshall applied the lower standard of liability applicable to passengers. But in *Smith* v. *Pierce*, Judge Mathews rejected this reasoning. Instead, the court, following *Hunt* v. *Morris*, said that the accident created a presumption of negligence rebuttable by evidence of ordinary care. Since the defendant had failed to meet that burden, judgment for the plaintiff was upheld.

---

20. 1 La. 349 (1830).
21. Id., 355.
22. Id., 356.
23. *Boyce* v. *Anderson*, 27 U. S. (1 Pet.) 150 (1829).

The rule that steam towboats (or tugboats) would be held to the same standard of liability as ordinary steam carriers in Louisiana was not followed in most other American jurisdictions.[24] But *Smith* v. *Pierce* was cited as authority in order to establish the proposition that steamboats would be held to the strict common law standard of common carrier liability in the ordinary carriage of goods. A leading New York case, *Alexander* v. *Greene*, cited Judge Mathews' opinion in *Smith* v. *Pierce* at some length. In particular the New York Court of Error s noted the importance of Louisiana decisional law in this area:

> Situated as the people of that state are, upon one of the greatest inland thoroughfares of the new world, their example should have great weight in deciding this cause.[25]

While the New York case was a steam towboat case similar on its facts to *Smith* v. *Pierce*, its holding was later used as authority to extend common carrier liability to steamboat carriers rather than to tugboats in that jurisdiction.[26]

Thus, in a curious and roundabout way, Louisiana's application of common carrier liability to steam towboats helped to establish the foundations for the extension of common carrier liability to ordinary steamboat carriers in common law jurisdictions even though Louisiana itself was a state that placed the lighter standard of the civil law upon regular steam carriers of goods.

This narrow area of the law's development illustrates the importance of Louisiana law to the law of the nation in its formative period. In these early steamboat cases the courts were

---

24. See, Joseph K. Angell, *A Treatise on the Law of Carriers* (5th ed. 1877) § 86, 668. The two great nineteenth century authorities on American common law, Chancellor James Kent of New York and Justice Joseph Story, differed on this issue. Kent included tugboats in his list of carriers held to the higher common law standard of strict liability whereas for Story tugboats represented an exception to that rule. Compare 2 J. Kent, *Commentaries on American Law* 599 (3rd ed.) with J. Story, *Commentaries on the Law of Bailments* § 496 (4th ed. 1846). See also *Bussey & Co.* v. *Miss Valley Transp. Co.*, 24 La. Ann. 165–167 (1872); 80 C. J. S. Shipping § 101; 86 C. J. S. Towage § 13; 63 D. J. Towage at 19 (n. 19).
25. *Alexander* v. *Greene*, 7 Hill 533, 550 (1844).
26. See *e.g.*, *Dorr* v. *New Jersey Steam Navig. Co.*, 11 N. Y. 475 (1854). Likewise for Massachusetts see *Sproul* v. *Hemmingway*, 31 Mass. (14 Pick.) 1 (1833) and *Vermont & Mass. Railroad Co.* v. *Fitchburg Railroad Co.*, 96 Mass. (14 Allen) 462, 470 (1867).

pressed into developing a searching analysis of the meaning of negligence. In the early nineteenth century negligence had not yet become a separate cause of action.[27]

Historians have traced the origins of negligence law to cases drawn from such pre-industrial contexts as jailhouse escapes and stagecoach collisions where negligence simply referred to something like "neglect in the performance of a duty or an office."[28] It would seem, therefore, that this explanation requires significant modification and amplification.

But these early industrial accident cases involving steamboats do suggest that negligence law really got going with the dramatic increase in accidents generated by the new energy technology. Louisiana steamboat cases are especially apposite precisely because Louisiana applied a standard of ordinary care rather than strict common carrier liability to steamboats and towboats. The fault principle and industrialization were growing side by side.

This excursion into early steamboat law suggests that such insularity is not only unfortunate but misplaced. Early nineteenth century Louisiana jurists faced the same kinds of commercial and technological realities that confronted their counterparts in common law jurisdictions. The reasoning in *Alexander* v. *Greene* by the New York Court of Errors was not all that different from what must have been in the mind of Judge George Mathews in deciding *Smith* v. *Pierce.* The New York Court of Errors was faced with the obvious commercial fact that in New York, as in Louisiana, "[t]he towing of boats by steam power has become a matter of great and increasing importance to the interests of the whole community." The application of enhanced standards of liability to this new form of transportation would encourage shippers to use it. Clearly, the same impulses worked upon the Louisiana Supreme Court in *Smith* v. *Pierce.* The case was decided as it would have been in any common law state at that period of our history—on the basis of its facts and through the application of law and ordinary legal reasoning. Public policy considerations, while unstated, lurked just beneath the surface, and the Civil Code of Louisiana was not even cited.

---

27. G. Edward White, *Tort Law in America: An Intellectual History* (New York: Oxford University Press, 1980, 2003), 16, and chap1, passim.
28. Morton J. Horwitz, *The Transformation of American Law, 1780–1860* (Cambridge, MA: Harvard University Press, 1977), 85–89.

The law of common carrier liability as applied to the new technological phenomenon of the steamboat was in an unsettled state in the early decades of the steamboat era.[29] But while Louisiana law was different from the common law in the standard that it applied to steamboat carriers, the result in practice was not all that different. By shifting the burden of proof of non-negligence (or due care) onto defendants, the Louisiana rule approached the exacting tests of common carrier liability in the common law. Moreover, with respect to tugboats, the standard of liability proved to be even higher in Louisiana than it was in common law jurisdictions. There the prevailing rule was that tugboats were not common carriers at all but bailees for hire bound only by an ordinary care standard with proof of negligence on the plaintiff. Thus, Louisiana law seems to have been more natural, less counter-intuitive, and more consistent.

These doctrinal developments suggest that the law was shaped by historical forces that transcended the difference in the given rules of law that separated the civil law and the common law worlds. This point is best reinforced with comments drawn from the writings of two of the most eminent scholars which the civil law and the common law have produced in America, Gustavas Schmidt of Louisiana and Oliver Wendell Holmes, Jr., of Massachusetts. First Schmidt:

> Customs, when not contrary to good morals, or opposed . . . to positive legislation, have . . . in all civilized countries, acquired the dignity of laws; but customs vary from age to age, and what may be regarded as reasonable and just at one period, often becomes obsolete at another; this proves the necessity of studying with care the spirit of every epoch, at which a custom has been formed and has received judicial sanction, in order to appreciate its force and effect.[30]

And finally Holmes:

> The life of the law has not been logic: it has been experience. The felt necessities of the time, the prevalent moral and political

---

29. See *Gordon* v. *Little*, 8 Sergo & Rawl. (Pa.) 533 (1822); *Harrington et al.* v. *McShane*, 2 Watts (Pa.) 443 (1934); *supra*, note 26.
30. "History of the Jurisprudence of Louisiana," 1 *La. L. Journ.* 1, 3–4 (1841).

> theories, intuitions of public policy, avowed or unconscious, even the prejudices which judges share with their fellow-men, have had a good deal more to do than the syllogism in determining the rules by which men should be governed. The law embodies the story of a nation's development through many centuries, and it cannot be dealt with as if it contained only the axioms and corollaries of a book of mathematics.[31]

We need to look searchingly into the underlying historical processes and social realities that did as much to shape the law in modern times as the ancient systems of law that are part of the American and the Louisiana legal heritage. We need to be as sensitive to the history that lies beneath the surface of legal doctrine as were the judges who had to decide these early steamboat cases. Above all, we have to be alert to the fact that courts of law in the civil law world as well as in the common law community were faced with novel but shared problems in the nineteenth century, problems caused by a rapidly changing economic, technological, and social environment. More often than not, these problems were approached in much the same fashion in both the common law and civil law worlds.

---

31. *The Common Law* (Boston: Little Brown, 1881) 1.

Episode 9

The Sarah Roberts Case and the Origins of "Separate but Equal"

> Caste and Equality are contradictory. They mutually exclude each other. Where Caste is, there cannot be Equality; where Equality is, there cannot be Caste.
>
> Charles Sumner, 1849

In the early years of the nineteenth century, Boston's African American school children had the right to attend the public schools as were all of the other children in the city.[1] At first, there was no official rule or policy of racial segregation. However, the physical and psychological intimidation to which black youngsters were subjected forced their parents to remove them from the public schools and have them taught privately. This became the Boston pattern in the early years of the nineteenth century: whites went to the public schools while blacks went to one or two exclusively black private schools.[2]

---

* Source: "The Sarah Roberts Case in Historical Perspective," *Massachusetts Legal History*, Vol. 3 (1997), 37–51 by George Dargo.

1. *Sarah C. Roberts v. City of Boston*, 59 Mass. (5 Cush.) 198 (1849). The best overall treatment of the Sarah Roberts Case is Stephen Kendrick and Paul Kendrick's *Sarah's Long Walk: The Free Blacks of Boston and How Their Struggle for Equality Changed America* (Boston, MA: Beacon Press, 2004), which is comprehensive and detailed in an accessible narrative. Useful overview can be found in each of the following sources: S.K. Schultz, *The Cultural Factory: Boston Public Schools, 1789–1860* (New York: Oxford University Press, 1973), Chaps.7–8; G. Gillerman, "Sarah Roberts, Charles Sumner, And The Idea of Equality," *Boston Bar Journal* 31 (1987): 40; Leonard W. Levy and Douglas L. Jones, eds., *Jim Crow in Boston: The Origins of the Separate But Equal Doctrine* (New York: DaCapo Press, 1974); Leonard Levy, *The Law of the Commonwealth and Chief Justice Shaw* (New York: Oxford University Press, 1957), Chap. 7.
2. Morgan Kousser, "The Supremacy of Equal Rights: The Struggle Against Racial Discrimination in Antebellum Massachusetts and the Foundations of the

This was the world that Sarah Roberts, a four-year old black child living with her family of free African Americans, had to confront when her father brought her to school for the very first time in 1846. Turned away from the five white schools that were nearest her home, she was forced to walk with her father, all the way from the North End to Beacon Hill to the all-black elementary school on Belknap (now Joy) Street. At the second neighborhood school, the Otis School, Sarah was actually admitted for a while by a sympathetic principal only to be forcibly removed by a constable on orders from the Boston School Committee in traumatic circumstances that can only be imagined.

The origins of the Sarah Roberts case, *Roberts* v. *City of Boston*, the first legal case about racial discrimination in Massachusetts schools, are in the school founded in 1798 by an African American named Primus ("Prince") Hall. He opened a small school in his own home. Then, in 1806, Hall moved his school to the basement floor of the newly constructed African Meeting House on Belknap (now Joy) Street on the north slope of Beacon Hill. The city soon began to make an annual appropriation of $200 for the support of the Belknap Street School. A few years later, a white merchant, Abiel Smith, left a bequest to the city to maintain the Belknap School exclusively for black children.[3] Subsequently, Boston's Primary School Committee—the sub-committee of the Boston School Committee responsible for the education of four-to-seven year olds—assumed control of the school's day-to-day operations, but the Belknap School was now called the Smith School for its chief benefactor, Abiel Smith.

The Smith School became the established primary school for black children, while other small primary schools failed after just a year or two. In 1835, the city erected a new building for the Smith School adjacent to the African Meeting House. Within two years the school had four teachers and some 300 pupils. (The Smith School was the one which 4-year old Sarah Roberts would have attended had her parents agreed to send her to a

---

Fourteenth Amendment," *Northwestern University Law Review* 80 (1988): 941, 949–950.

3. The majority report of the Grammar School Committee (1849) upholding the policy of racial segregation, used the argument that integration of the races would have violated the express terms of the Smith bequest. See Levy and Jones, *Jim Crow in Boston*, 122–124.

racially segregated school.) Despite its new construction, conditions were not good at the Smith School from the beginning. The city appropriated only a fraction of what an equivalent school for whites would cost to construct. As a result of pressure from parents, improvements were ordered by the Primary School Committee.[4] These renovations were completed in 1849, just three months before the appeal in the *Roberts* case was argued before the Supreme Judicial Court, a fact of some consequence in the decision itself. But by that time a boycott of the Smith School by militant, anti-segregationist parents was already five years old, and boycott supporters would be satisfied with nothing less than complete desegregation of the lower schools.[5]

Besides segregation of the schools, other kinds of racial discrimination were practiced in Massachusetts in the mid-nineteenth century. For example, pupils with the highest marks in each of the public schools were awarded Franklin scholarship medals presented at a special awards dinner at Faneuil Hall at the end of the school year. But in 1829, William Cooper Nell, top scholar at the all-black Smith School, received a copy of Benjamin Franklin's *Autobiography* instead of the usual medal. Nor was Nell invited to the customary dinner at Faneuil Hall. Nell was then only thirteen years old, but, as he later reported, he never forgot the discrimination which he suffered as a youngster. He attributed his activist political career in later life to his early experience at the Smith School. Years later, it was Nell, by then a journalist and author, who would organize the equal school rights committee, the organization principally responsible for the eleven-year boycott of Boston's segregated schools that eventually led, in

---

4. Blacks were divided on the issue of desegregation of the schools. Opponents of desegregation wanted nothing more than equal facilities and black teachers, demands that the School Committee was prepared to meet. See B. Rushing, "Black Schools in White Boston, 1800–1860," in *From Common School to Magnet School: Selected Essays in the History of Boston's Schools*, James W. Fraser, ed. (Boston, MA: Trustees of the Public Library of the City of Boston, 1979), 24.

5. The two high schools, English High School and the Latin School, were not operated on a segregated basis, and a few graduates of the Smith School did enter the Latin School even before desegregation was mandated by the legislature in 1855.

1855, to the enactment of the state law abolishing racial segregation in the public schools of Massachusetts.[6]

The 1840s was a decade of spectacular social agitation in Boston's African American community. In addition to issues such as abolition, the status of free blacks, and the proposal in Congress for a new, more draconian Fugitive Slave Law, African Americans in Boston fought successfully to end the practice by the new railroad companies of segregating railway cars. Blacks also succeeded in ending the legal proscriptions against racial intermarriage.[7] Places of public amusement were opened to people of every race, and the city's practice of listing citizens in the city directory by color was abandoned.[8] But the fight to end racial segregation in the schools—successful in Salem, New Bedford, Nantucket, Worcester, and Lowell—failed in Boston. "Boston's schools provided the state's last legal refuge for the prejudice of color."[9]

Petitions to the Boston school committee to end racial segregation were repeatedly rebuffed. In 1846 the primary school committee, and then in 1849 the grammar school committee, issued reports explaining the reasons behind the policy of "complexionary classification." These reports were

---

6. 1855 Mass. Acts 256. See also R.P. Smith, "William Cooper Nell: Crusading Black Abolitionist," *Journal of Negro History* 55 (1970), 182. Part of the support for the equal school rights bill came from supporters of the much maligned "Know Nothing" [American] party who forged an alliance with antislavery forces and with African American proponents of school integration. Even before desegregation was mandated by statute, the primary schools began to integrate on their own, no doubt because of social pressures that were brought to bear on the school committee.

7. Louis Ruchames, "Jim Crow Railroads in Massachusetts" *American Quarterly* 8 (1965): 61; Louis Ruchames, "Race, Marriage, and Abolition in Massachusetts," *Journal of Negro History* 40 (1955), 250.

8. Charles W. Slack, "Address in Proceedings of the Presentation Committee Honoring William Cooper Nell (December 17, 1855)," reprinted in Levy and Jones, *Jim Crow in Boston*, 278–279.

9. Levy, *The Law of the Commonwealth*, 328. Despite the victories of the 1840s, Blacks continued to be excluded from juries in the Bay State. C.L. Reymond, *Address in Proceedings of the Presentation Committee Honoring William Cooper Nell* (*December 17, 1855*), reprinted in Levy and Jones, *Jim Crow in Boston*, 278. For the historical context in which the fight for equal school rights was waged in Massachusetts, see Leon F. Litwack, *North of Slavery: The Negro in the Free States, 1790–1860* (Chicago, IL: University of Chicago Press, 1961), Chap. 4.

even more significant than Shaw's opinion in the *Roberts* case itself, in that they provided the arguments for future legal and political justifications of what would become the doctrine of "separate but equal."[10]

The arguments are all too familiar. According to these reports, the petitioners behind the effort to end racial segregation in the city's schools represented only a minority of Boston's African American population. The majority report argued that most of those who signed the petitions to abolish the Smith School and end segregation had no school age children and, therefore, they lacked standing to protest. In addition, it was argued that segregation was best for black children and was the only way to keep school attendance high. Moreover, unlike smaller communities, such as Nantucket and Salem, Boston had a large black population and, therefore, racial classification was both justified and necessary for the good of all. Above all, said the reports, the power to classify by race did not differ materially from the power to classify by age, gender, or ability, and since the graded school was considered, at the time, to be a major advance in public education, the majority reports took the position that any concession on the issue of race would undermine school committee power to classify altogether. As to the legal arguments raised by counsel for the petitioners, the majority reports deferred to the courts of law.[11] Peleg Chandler, the city solicitor and an expert on municipal law, rendered an advisory opinion that racial segregation was legal. As long as school facilities and teachers were roughly equivalent in the all-white schools and the all-black schools, there was no violation of constitutional equality.

Petitions and boycotts having proved to be unsuccessful in ending racial classifications in the schools, a third approach was needed and a new strategy decided upon. Benjamin F. Roberts, an activist who attended political meetings at the African Meeting House, brought a legal action on behalf of his daughter, little Sarah Roberts, in Boston's Court of Common Pleas. Roberts had petitioned the local district superintendent as well as

---

10. The Majority Reports and the Minority Reports are reprinted in Levy and Jones, *Jim Crow in Boston*, 1–163.

11. On the central question of constitutional equality, the school committee deferred to the courts, while the courts deferred to the school committee.

the Primary School Committee for permission to register Sarah at the public school nearest her home on Andover Street, but his petition was rejected. Each time Roberts tried to enter Sarah at her neighborhood school, she was turned away. The Boston School Committee as a whole informed Roberts that he could enter Sarah in the Smith Grammar School, but this he refused to do.

Roberts was no ordinary citizen of the city of Boston. He came from a long line of activist free blacks. His grandfather had fought in the American Revolution and later was an outspoken critic of segregation in the church. Sarah was named after Benjamin's mother who, as a child, had had to endure discrimination first hand. Roberts was a printer by profession with an office on Cornhill Street. In fact, Roberts was one of the first African American printers in America. He was the publisher of two black newspapers—the *Anti-Slavery Herald* (1838) and the *Self Elevator* (1853) both of which were short-lived.[12] William Lloyd Garrison's *The Liberator*, the principal organ of the American Anti-Slavery Society, served as a local community newspaper for Boston's African American population, and Garrison's readers were loyal subscribers. Consequently, Benjamin Roberts's efforts to establish a competing journal never succeeded. Instead, Roberts earned his living by publishing books, pamphlets, broadsides, and occasional pieces for various private organizations and local abolitionist groups.

Sarah Roberts's two attorneys were also not ordinary. Her principal attorney, Robert Morris, was then a young lawyer just starting out and only the second African American, after Mason B. Allen, ever admitted to the practice of law in Massachusetts. Morris was involved in a number of causes, not only the movement for school integration, but also the agitation to end segregated railroad cars and to rescind the state law prohibiting interracial marriages. Morris was also active in the underground railroad and, during the Civil War period, he would work for the equal treatment of black soldiers in the Union Army.

Morris initiated the *Roberts* litigation against the Primary School Committee in October, 1848, but it was Charles Sumner,

---

12. Roderick T. Baltimore and Robert F. Williams, "The State Constitutional Roots of the 'Separate But Equal' Doctrine: Roberts *v.* City of Boston," *Rutgers Law Journal* 17 (1986), 537–538, n8.

Roberts' other attorney, who handled the appeal. Sumner was quickly becoming a national figure. He had been unsuccessful as a candidate for the Boston School Committee when he ran as an advocate of primary school reform, but within a few short years he would be elected to the United States Senate, where he served as anti-slavery's chief spokesman in the nation's capital. Sumner's prominence, his oral argument to the Supreme Judicial Court in the *Roberts* case, and the wide circulation that his legal brief received when it was published by Benjamin Roberts in pamphlet form, meant that, for good or for ill, the case would not soon be forgotten.

The suit brought by Robert Morris and Charles Sumner was based upon an 1845 statute that provided for monetary damages if any pupil was excluded from a public school.[13] Sarah Roberts had been excluded from the public schools that were closest to her home in the West End, this despite the Boston School Committee's general rule that "scholars [were] to go to schools nearest their residences."[14] Instead of attending the nearest neighborhood school, some 900 feet from where she lived, Sarah would have been forced to walk nearly half a mile and climb up the side of Beacon Hill from Andover Street to Belknap Street. Sarah's exclusion from her neighborhood school was the basis for the lawsuit.

The Court of Common Pleas found for the city and upheld the decision of the majority of the Primary School Committee which required Sarah attendance at the Smith School. The case was then appealed to the Supreme Judicial Court. The parties agreed to a lengthy statement of facts thus squarely presenting the Court with the fundamental legal and constitutional issues at stake in the case. This was the court of Lemuel Shaw, one of the great state judges of the nineteenth century and probably the most

---

13. 1845 Mass. Acts 214. The purpose of the statute is not clear. It may have been to discourage arbitrary actions by school officials, or perhaps, to create a voucher system. A student wrongfully excluded from a public school could then pay for private tuition. The statute did not provide for injunctive or any other kind of equitable relief.

14. "Statement of Facts," in *Sarah C. Roberts* v. *City of Boston*, 59 Mass. (5 Cush.) 198, 199 (1849); Charles E. Walker, Jr., "Fighting for Freedom and Equity: Blacks and the Law in Early Massachusetts," *Supreme Judicial Court Historical Society Journal* 1 (1995), 82, 88.

influential chief justice in the long history of Massachusetts' highest court. Of Lemuel Shaw it was said that he had "the absolute power of a [mountain] crag vitalized by the human spirit."[15] In the words of Leonard Levy, "No other state judge . . . had so great an influence on the course of American law."[16]

In its decision in *Roberts* the court was unanimous.[17] That unanimity, the great prestige of the court itself, and the fact that the opinion was written by Lemuel Shaw in what Benjamin Cardozo would later call "the grand style"[18] all help to explain the enormous influence and the lasting effects the case would have in our constitutional jurisprudence for more than a century at both the state and federal levels. In his opinion for the court, Shaw developed his legal analysis by deferring to the power and authority of the School Committee:

> It will be considered, that this is a question of power, or of the legal authority of the committee entrusted by the city with this department of public instruction; because, if they have the legal authority, the expediency of exercising it in any particular way is exclusively within them.[19]

For Lemuel Shaw, the case of Sarah Roberts was not about equal rights but what we today would call administrative power. Shaw had no quarrel with the principle of equality. For Shaw, the equality provisions of the Massachusetts Declaration of Rights were, as he put it, "perfectly sound."[20] But what those rights consisted of, how they were to be applied, and under what

---

15. Quoted in Levy and Jones, *Jim Crow in Boston*, xxiii.
16. Ibid.
17. The one member of the Court who might have dissented, Robert Fletcher, did not participate in the decision. As a lawyer, Fletcher had prepared an advisory opinion for the Salem School Committee arguing that segregation of the Salem schools on the basis of race was unconstitutional. Fletcher's public identification with the anti-segregationist position may have caused him to recuse himself from the *Roberts* case possible as a result of pressure from his Chief. See Baltimore and Williams, "The State Constitutional Roots," 544; Levy and Jones, *Jim Crow in Boston*, xiv.
18. Benjamin N. Cardozo, "Law and Literature," *Yale Review* 14 (1925): 699–718, reprinted in *Selected Writings of Benjamin N. Cardozo*, rev. ed., Margaret E. Hall, ed. (Albany, NY: Matthew Bender, 1980), 338, 448.
19. *Sarah C. Roberts v. City of Boston*, 59 Mass. (5 Cush.), 205–206.
20. Ibid., 206.

circumstances they were to be enforced "in the infinite variety of circumstance by which they are surrounded in society . . . must depend on laws adapted to their respective relations and conditions."[21] Since the petitioners were able to attend schools which, for all practical purposes, were equal to the all-white public schools—especially once renovations were complete in 1849—the only issue for Shaw was whether or not the Boston School Committee had the authority to assign pupils according to the Committee's discretion. As Shaw put it in the opinion:

> The power of general superintendence vests a plenary authority in the committee to arrange, classify, and distribute pupils, in such a manner as they think best adapted to their general proficiency and welfare. . . . The [school] committee, apparently under great deliberation, have come to the conclusion, that the good of both classes of schools will be best promoted, by maintaining the separate primary schools for colored and for white children. . . ."[22]

The fact that the School Committee had failed to follow its own rule regarding assignment to the most proximate neighborhood school did not figure at all in Shaw's reasoning. Concluding that Sarah Roberts's legal action could not be maintained because she had not been "excluded" within the meaning of the law, Shaw observed:

> It is urged, that this maintenance of separate schools tends to deepen and perpetuate the odious distinction of caste, founded in a deep-rooted prejudice in public opinion. *This prejudice, if it exists, is not created by law, and probably cannot be changed by law*. . . . [A]t all events, it is a fair and proper question for the committee to consider and decide upon, having in view the best interest of both classes of children placed under their superintendence, and we cannot say, that their decision upon it is not founded on just grounds of reason and experience, and in the results of a discriminating and honest judgment.[23]

---

21. Ibid.
22. Ibid., 208.
23. Ibid., 209–210 (emphasis added).

The importance of the Shaw decision in *Roberts* cannot be overestimated. It was undoubtedly one of the most significant decisions of the antebellum period. *Roberts* was an example—in this case, an unfortunate one—of the great influence that state constitutional decisions have had in shaping the doctrinal underpinnings of federal constitutional law. Professor Derrick Bell has documented the subsequent use of the *Roberts* precedent by state and federal courts in rejecting challenges to racially segregated schools, particularly in the north, in the decades following the decision.[24]

By 1896, when *Plessy* v. *Ferguson*[25] was decided by the Supreme Court of the United States, legal ratification of racial segregation in the public schools was already settled doctrine in many states. *Plessy* was not a school case, but an extension of the principle of segregation to railroad cars. However, the language used by Justice Henry Brown in the majority opinion in *Plessy* echoed the words Lemuel Shaw had written nearly a half century before. As Justice Brown would put it in *Plessy*:

> Legislation is powerless to eradicate racial instincts or to abolish distinctions based upon physical differences, and the attempt to do so can only result in accentuating the difficulties of the present situation.[26]

The Supreme Court of the United States ratified the application of the "separate but equal" doctrine to public schools in *Cumming* v. *Board of Education*[27] and *Gong Lum* v. *Rice.*[28] In all three cases, the high court referred to the *Roberts* precendent.

There is little that can be said to justify the Shaw decision, although some historians have certainly tried. For example, a 1962 book sponsored by the Massachusetts Bar Association declared that the doctrine of "separate but Equal" was not Shaw's decision but that of the Boston School Committee to

---

24. See Derrick A. Bell, Jr., *Race, Racism and American Law* (Aspen, CO: Aspen Publishers, 1973), 442–443 (discussing cases). Courts that refused to follow the *Roberts* precedent were very much in the minority prior to the overturn of "Separate But Equal" doctrine in 1954. Ibid., 444.

25. *Plessy v. Ferguson*, 163 U.S. 537 (1896).

26. Ibid., 552.

27. *Cumming v. Richmond County Board of Education*, 175 U.S. 528 (1899).

28. *Gong Lum v. Rice*, 275 U.S. 78 (1927).

which the Chief Justice merely deferred. "To Chief Justice Shaw the decision, under the facts, was administrative and not legal. It was [a] problem to be solved either by the legislature or the School Committee and not by the court."[29]

A more substantial defense of Shaw was made by Professor Earl Maltz, a state constitutional law scholar. Matlz argued that the *Roberts* decision rested on a limited theory of equality to which Shaw subscribed. When natural rights were involved—for example, in cases like *Commonwealth* v. *Aves,*[30] where the issue was slavery versus freedom—Shaw took a strong equality position and upheld the claims of the natural right to personal liberty. However, since education was not a natural right but a benefit conferred by the legislature through positive law, absolute equality under the Massachusetts Declaration of Rights was not mandated. The issue for Shaw in *Roberts* was not equality of rights but the lower standard of equal protection, which the School Committee satisfied by completing the improvement to the Smith School in the very year the lawsuit was brought.[31]

---

29. Elijah Adlow, *The Genius of Lemuel Shaw: Expounder of the Common Law* (Boston, MA: Massachusetts Bar Association, 1962), 320.

30. *Commonwealth v. Aves*, 35 Mass. (18 Pick.) 193 (1836). Was Shaw bothered by this decision? Shaw was opposed to the institution of slavery, and in earlier cases he had established that slavery could not be maintained on the free soil of Massachusetts. The cases that bothered him were the fugitive slave cases—cases where Shaw had to reconcile his aversion to human bondage and his duty to uphold the Federal Fugitive Slave Act.

31. Earl A. Maltz, "The Concept of Equal Protection of the Laws—A Historical Inquiry," *San Diego Law Review* 22 (1985): 499, 513. ("The standard analysis of the *Roberts* case describes Sumner as a hero whose argument presaged the conceptions of racial equality later embodied in the fourteenth amendment and Shaw as a villain whose retrograde views on the nature of equality were to haunt American jurisprudence for one hundred years. But in structure, Shaw's opinion simply reflects the dichotomy between the concepts of equality of rights and equality of protection respectively, which appears in antebellum arguments. All men—black or white—are equally entitled to protection of the laws to enforce their legal rights; but unless a particular interest can be classified as a natural right, the legislature may withhold that interest from any class at will. Since public education is not a natural right, the legislature would not violate the principle of limited absolute equality even if blacks were totally excluded." (footnote omitted)). See also Baltimore and Williams, "The State Constitutional Roots," 550–551.

Another attempt to rationalize Shaw's decision was offered by Professor Andrew Kull, a legal historian, who argued that *Roberts* was an example of a "colorblind" interpretation of constitutional equality and that the Shaw opinion

> unfairly shares the reactionary reputation that attaches to the majority opinion in *Plessy v. Ferguson*. *Roberts* was an innovative decision, answering new questions with an analysis that, in its broader implications, remains equally good law today. . . . Shaw effectively refuted the suggestion that classification is incompatible with legal equality, at least as that term must be understood in organized society.[32]

Kull viewed the *Roberts* decision "as a lucid introduction to the theory of equal protection. Its only flaw by present day constitutional standards, [was] its failure to anticipate our political conviction that the racial classification at issue in *Roberts* [was] not a reasonable one."[33]

But Shaw's opinion was anything but colorblind. As one critical reviewer of Kull's book observed, "Sarah Roberts lost . . . . Sarah's race [was] used to exclude her from a local school. . . . *Roberts* is not a case establishing color-blindness as a precedent."[34] Both Maltz and Kull failed to consider the historical setting of *Roberts*, a time when agitation for racial equality in Massachusetts was in high dudgeon. For many of Boston's African American citizens, separate equality was no longer an acceptable substitute for true equality.[35] By the time of the *Roberts* litigation, segregated schools had been eliminated everywhere in Massachusetts except in the public schools of Boston. In such a climate, special deference to the Boston School Committee could hardly be justified.

The sounder approach was that of the late Leonard Levy, whose 1957 biography of Lemuel Shaw remains the defining work of scholarship on the chief justice. In general, Levy's book on Shaw is appreciative and positive even though Levy himself

---

32. Andrew Kull, *The Color-Blind Constitution* (Cambridge, MA: Harvard University Press, 1992), 48, 50.
33. Ibid., 51.
34. Brian K. Fair, "The Contextual Illusion of a Color-Blind Constitution," *University of San Francisco Law Review* 28 (1994), 343, 354.
35. Levy and Jones, *Jim Crow in Boston*, xviii.

did not subscribe to many of the particular doctrines that Shaw developed on private as well as public law subjects. On the *Roberts* case itself, Levy suggested that Shaw was uncharacteristically motivated "by judicial self-restraint and a corresponding high regard for the School Committee" of which Shaw himself had once been a member.[36] That is probably the most that can be said in justification of the decision.

In all other respects, Leonard Levy was highly critical of Shaw in the *Roberts* case. As he put in the conclusion to his book on the chief justice, "[W]hen a government agency, in the face of a constitution with an equality-of-rights clause, classifies the legal rights of citizens on the basis of race, the reasonableness of its rule is questionable; and the self-restraint of the court is an abdication of judicial responsibility."[37] For Levy, the *Roberts* opinion was "unreasoned,"[38] a blemish on Shaw's record, a case that "had a noxious influence on American constitutional law for a century." "[N]o opinion by Shaw was more lacking in human spirit or more obstructive of the advancement of civilization than his opinion in the Roberts case."[39] On the central issue of constitutional equality, Levy even invoked the aphorism of George Orwell's *Animal Farm*: "ALL ANIMALS ARE EQUAL BUT SOME ANIMALS ARE MORE EQUAL THAN OTHERS."[40] In his later work on the subject, *Jim Crow in Boston,*[41]Levy went even further. "The 'separate but equal' doctrine, the legal linchpin of *Jim Crow in America*, has its origins in the cradle of liberty, Boston, Massachusetts," he wrote;

---

36. Levy, *The Law of the Commonwealth*, 328.
37. Ibid.
38. Ibid., 115.
39. Ibid., 328; Levy and Jones, *Jim Crow in Boston*, xxiii.
40. Levy and Jones, *Jim Crow in Boston.*
41. Ibid., xxxiii. Another important critical analysis of Shaw is that of the late Robert M. Cover, who in *Justice Accused: Antislavery and the Judicial Process* (1975), likened Shaw to Captain Vere in Melville's *Billy Budd* and saw Shaw in the vortex of conflict between the immorality of slavery as an institution and the requirements of his judicial office. The *Roberts* case received only minor treatment in Cover's book. Similarly, the tricentennial history of the Supreme Judicial Court only briefly notes that criticism of Shaw in the *Roberts* case would be "appropriate." See Russell K. Osgood, ed., *The History of the Law in Massachusetts: The Supreme Judicial Court, 1692–1992* (Boston, MA: Supreme Judicial Court Historical Society, 1992), 32.

"[t]hough the *Roberts* case is [now] dead law, its spirit, like the corpse of [a] mackerel, shines and stinks in the moonlight."[42]

Five years after the Supreme Judicial Court decision, following much agitation and repeated failure, the Massachusetts legislature passed a statute that abolished racial classification in the public schools of the commonwealth. The legislature simply established as a matter of law that such a method of classification was beyond the power of local school committees. Such classifications were no longer "reasonable."[43]

To the extent that the decision by the Supreme Judicial Court in the *Roberts* case served as persuasive precedent in other states and in the *Plessy v. Ferguson* case itself, we can safely conclude that the decision helped to establish racial segregation in American public education for years to come. However, in other ways the *Roberts* case was an important moment in the struggle to achieve racial equality in America. *Sarah Roberts* v. *City of Boston* was the first school integration case in American history. The litigation was part of a much larger strategy of social and legal reform that was designed to end racial caste in Massachusetts. Very much like the litigation leading to *Brown* v. *Board of Education,*[44] the case was brought, led, and supported by members of an energized African American community determined to achieve racial equality and to give real meaning to the words of the Massachusetts Declaration of Rights. The arguments of counsel, particularly that of Charles Sumner in his appeal to the Supreme Judicial Court anticipated by more than a century similar claims made by Charles Hamilton Houston, Thurgood Marshall and Jack Greenburg of the NAACP Legal Defense Fund, claims that would ultimately succeed in the Supreme Court of the United States in *Brown* v. *Board of Education.* Indeed, "the debate over the lawfulness of

---

42. Levy and Douglas, *Jim Crow in Boston*, xxxiii. Shaw's constitutional reasoning was not overturned by the legislature which is one reason why so many other state and federal courts continued to regard it as authoritative. The legislature simply determined that the powers of local school communities in Massachusetts were more limited in that they could no longer classify on the basis of race.

43. *Dred Scott v. Sanford*, 60 U.S. 393 (1857).

44. *Brown v. Board of Education*, 347 U.S. 483, decision after reargument as to relief, 349 U.S. 294 (1954).

segregation. . . [was] more closely reasoned and more eloquently expressed than anything that lawyers and judges. . . would again write on the subject"[45] and would define "for a century and more thereafter the constitutional arguments on either side of the question."[46] The *Roberts* case played a major role in bringing about the first school integration victory when the Massachusetts legislature abolished segregated schools in 1855.

But it would be misleading to suggest that the victory of equal school rights in the Commonwealth in 1855 meant that racism and Jim Crowism were dead either in Massachusetts or anywhere else in America for that matter. As one noted British observer remarked in describing the general attitude of whites toward blacks in the northern states on the eve of the Civil War: "We shall not make the black man a slave; we shall not buy him or sell him; but we shall not associate with him. He shall be free to live, and to thrive, if he can, and to pay taxes and perform duties; but he shall not be free to dine and drink at our board—to share with us the deliberations of the jury box—to sit upon the seat of judgment, however capable he may be—to plead in our courts—to represent us in the Legislature—to attend us at the bed of sickness and pain—to mingle with us in the concert-room, the lecture-room, the theater, or the church, or to marry our daughters. We are of another race, and he is inferior. Let him know his place—and keep it." This is the prevalent feeling, if not thc languaqe of the free North.[47]

Victories there were, and progress in race relations were made, even though these triumphs were incremental. The African American in the north was not in the same condition as the African American held in bondage in the south, although it should be recalled that the remnants of slavery continued to linger in many northern communities, including Massachusetts,[48] long after liberty had been proclaimed throughout the land at the time of the American Revolution. The struggle to end racial segregation in the public schools in Massachusetts showed how

---

45. Kull, *The Color-Blind Constitution,* 40.
46. Ibid.
47. Charles Mackay, *Life and Liberty in America, or, Sketches of a Tour in the United States and Canada in 1857–1858* (London: Smith, Elder, 1859).
48. Francie Latour, "New England's Hidden History," *Boston Sunday Globe* (Section K), 1–2.

Boston's black community was able to organize itself into a formidable political block, to publish political tracts that supported that cause of equality, to petition the government for a redress of grievances, to boycott the all-black Smith School, and to join with white sympathizers in the anti-slavery movement to advance the cause of racial justice in general and equal school rights in particular.

But the victory of the equal school rights forces in Boston after 1855 was far from complete. No black teachers from the Smith School were hired by the Boston School Committee for the newly integrated schools. In fact, black teachers were not hired in Boston until the 1890s. And within a generation of the struggle for equal school rights, the primary schools were becoming resegregated on a de facto basis.[49]

What is the significance of the *Roberts* case in our history? The answer is provided for us by Wendell Phillips, the great anti-slavery lawyer, agitator, and teacher who attended the 1855 celebration to honor William Cooper Nell and the victory of the equal school rights/anti-segregation forces in Massachusetts. "What has the Anti-Slavery agitation done?" asked Phillips. "It has opened the schools; for . . . without this agitation of the public mind, on the general question, the doors of the schools would never have been opened."[50]For Phillips, the equal school rights movement and the anti-slavery crusade were threads drawn from the same cloth. "The best thing learned by these struggles is, how to prepare for another. [We are] in for [a] war," he said, "the war to end slavery."[51]

The coalescence of the equal school rights movement with the forces of antislavery provides the clue to an understanding of why Jim Crow not only survived but flourished long after the legislature declared that racial segregation in the public schools was no longer legal in Massachusetts. Segregation was another form of enslavement. The abolition of legal slavery did not end the bondage of African American either in the south or in the north. Slavery did not cause racism in America. As the late Winthrop Jordan was able to show, racial slavery in early

---

49. Rushing, "Black Schools in White Boston," 27.
50. Ibid.
51. Ibid.

America was not the cause, but the result of a deep-seated and preexisting animus toward black Africans that afflicted most white European settlers of the Americas.[52] The reemergence of new forms of racial bondage after the Civil War, most especially in the form of racial segregation, pointed to the intractability of racism in American life. After all, racism and segregation have never been a purely southern problem. As Associate Justice Lewis Powell wrote in partial dissent in one of the great school desegregation case in the aftermath of *Brown* v. *Board of Education*:

> [T]he . . . root cause of segregated schools in all the biracial metropolitan areas of our country is essentially the same: one of segregated residential and migratory patterns the impact of which on the racial composition of the schools was often perpetuated and rarely ameliorated by action of public school authorities. This is a national, not a southern, phenomenon.[53]

Thus, it should come as no surprise that the first major case upholding the regime of Jim Crow, the *Sarah Roberts* decision, came in the north, in the Cradle of Liberty itself long before that regime was solidified in the south.

But while the opinion of Lemuel Shaw provided persuasive judicial authority for the establishment of the now discredited doctrine of "separate but equal," the political and intellectual forces that were successfully deployed to overturn Shaw's decision anticipated strategies that have been used in more recent times to combat racism in its many manifestations throughout the United States. In the end, then, the *Roberts* case provides a very rich history indeed, a history full with anticipation of more recent struggles and the many triumphs over racism that we have witnessed in our own time.

---

52. Winthrop D. Jordan, *White Over Black: American Attitudes Toward the Negro, 1550–1812* (Chapel Hill, NC: University of North Carolina Press, 1968); Winthrop D. Jordan, *The White Man's Burden: Historical Origins of Racism in the United States* (New York: Oxford University Press, 1974).
53. *Keyes v. School District No. 1*, 413 U.S. 189 (1973).

* * *

Benjamin Roberts died of epilepsy in 1881. Sarah Roberts married a sailor from South Scituate named John Casneau in 1867. She was twenty-three years old at the time. The marriage record entry notes that the couple was "Coloured." The couple later divorced, but Sarah seems to have married again. Unlike the rest of the Roberts family who remained in Boston, Sarah appears to have gone to New Haven under the name Sarah Dyer. There is no further trace of Sarah Roberts in the Commonwealth's vital records.

Sarah Roberts may have been obscure in life, but as William Lloyd Garrison said in 1855 in his great speech on the occasion of the legislative victory for the forces of equal rights:

> No great reform was ever projected or early espoused by any powerful organization at the outset. It begins in the heart of a solitary individual; humble men and humble women, unknown to the community, without means, without power, without station, but perceiving the thing that ought to be down, love the right above all things, and having faith in the triumph of what is just and true, engage in the work, and by and by, the little leaven leavens the whole lump; and this is the way the world is to be redeemed. . . . This is but the beginning of the end—the prophecy of the ultimate extinction of complexional caste throughout the land, and the reign of peace and liberty universally.[54]

Little four-year old Sarah Roberts had left her mark on history.

---

54. William Lloyd Garrison, *Address in Proceedings of the Presentation Committee Honoring William Cooper Nell* (*Dec. 17, 1855*), reprinted in Levy and Jones, *Jim Crow in Boston*, 285–286.

Twentieth Century Episodes

Episode 10

The Great Red Scare of 1920

> The documents and acts speak for themselves. . . . [A] mob is a mob.
>
> George Anderson, 1920

Of all the federal judges who sat on the bench in the early years of this century, none was more interesting or more controversial than George Weston Anderson. Anderson was a *summa cum laude* graduate of Boston University Law School, class of 1890, where he taught law for a time after his graduation. While practicing in Boston in the 1890s, Anderson became involved in municipal politics and was an outspoken member of the Boston School Committee from 1894 to 1900. Identified with progressive political causes in the first decade of this century, Anderson opposed the mayoral candidacy of John F. Fitzgerald ("Honey Fitz") in 1906 and again in 1909. He also served as a member of the Massachusetts Public Service Commission.

President Woodrow Wilson first appointed Anderson as United States Attorney for Massachusetts, then to the Interstate Commerce Commission, at the time the most important Federal administrative agency in the country. But Anderson achieved national recognition in 1916 when he served as "point man" for the Senate subcommittee considering the nomination of Louis Brandeis as an associate justice of the Supreme Court. Anderson had come to know Brandeis when he was on the Public Service Commission. "The people's lawyer," as Brandeis was known, had been deeply involved in the fight for lower gas rates and stricter utility regulation in Boston and Brookline, Massachusetts.[1]

---

* Source: Chapter 4 ("George Anderson and the Red Scare of 1920") in George Dargo, *A History of the United States Court of Appeals for the First Circuit*, Vol. I (1891–1960) © George Dargo (as assigned to the U.S. Court of Appeals for the First Circuit).

1. Alfred T. Mason, *Louis Brandeis: A Free Man's Life* (New York: Viking; 1946), 129, *et passim;* Melvin I. Urofsky, *Louis D. Brandeis and the Progressive*

In the course of the hearings, which were the most controversial ever held on a Supreme Court nominee (until the Robert Bork nomination in 1987 and the Clarence Thomas nomination in 1991), Anderson cross-examined hostile conservative witnesses testifying against Brandeis. Brandeis was not present and did not testify on his own behalf.[2] Hence, Anderson as stand-in directed Brandeis' defence against his numerous accusers.[3] For this and his long dedication to progressive causes, President Wilson appointed Anderson to the federal district court in Boston in 1918 to replace Frederick Dodge. He served until poor health forced his retirement in 1931.

As a judge, Anderson gained a reputation as a dissenter, particularly on immigration matters. He was especially concerned about the policies of the Immigration Service, then an arm of the Labor Department, in enforcing the Chinese Exclusion Act.[4] In one case he charged the Labor Department with having followed "grossly illegal methods" in deportation proceedings.[5] In another he questioned whether evidence "extorted from a frightened Chinese when under unlawful arrest" was credible.[6] But it was in a case arising out of the notorious Palmer Raids during the Red Scare of 1919 for which Anderson received national attention as a courageous federal judge willing to stand up to law enforcement authorities, including the Justice Department's Bureau of Investigation, the predecessor agency of the FBI.

The causes of the Red Scare of 1919 were many. American participation in World War I had fanned the flames of superpatriotism. Even during the period of American neutrality from 1914 to 1917, the Wilson Administration had been openly anti-German. After the declaration of war on April 4, 1917, the U.S. government intensified its anti-German propaganda. When hostilities ended with the armistice of November 11, 1918, wartime

---

Tradition (Boston: Little Brown; 1981), chaps. 2–3; See also, Urofsky, Louis D. *Brandeis, A Life* (New York: Pantheon Books, 2009).

2. Until Felix Frankfurter's nomination in 1939, nominees did not personally appear before the Senate Judiciary Committee.

3. Urofsky, *Brandeis and the Progressive Tradition,* 110–11.

4. Chinese Exclusion Act, ch. 1015, 25 U.S. Stat. 476 (1888).

5. *Charley Hee* v. *United States*, 19 F.2d 335, 337 (1st Cir. 1927) (Anderson, J., dissenting).

6. *Ah Lin* v. *United States*, 20 F.2d 107, 111 (1st Cir. 1927) (Anderson, J., dissenting).

emotions did not subside. Newly formed veterans' organizations such as the American Legion directed pent-up hatred toward unseen enemies at home. Legislative investigations of the "red peril" and Federal prosecutions of prominent Socialists like Victor Berger and Eugene Debs under the wartime Espionage Act added to the climate of suspicion and hate. In addition, race riots in the summer of 1919 were widespread and helped to create an atmosphere of tension in the country as well as in the government itself.[7]

Another factor contributing to the Red Scare was the Bolshevik Revolution in Russia in November 1917. The avowed purpose of the early Soviet leaders was international revolution, and in the wake of World War I, political turbulence erupted throughout Central and Eastern Europe. In the United States, labor unrest was ignited by hundreds of strikes and a growing number of violent confrontations. In 1919 alone, four million workers manned the picket lines in 3,600 separate strikes, making it a record year for labor-management confrontations.[8] The same year marked Massachusetts Governor Calvin Coolidge's suppression of the Boston Police Strike. To many Americans, the Bolshevik threat appeared to be spreading to American shores.[9]

The immediate events that gave rise to the crisis culminating in the Palmer Raids of January 1920 were a series of bombings and bomb threats against high Government officials.[10]

Indeed, it was the bombing of Attorney General A. Mitchell Palmer's home on June 2, 1919, that precipitated the Justice Department's determination to crack down on domestic radicals.[11] Beginning in the fall of 1919, the Department of Justice carried out a series of mass arrests of labor agitators and communists. Aliens were the immediate targets of these operations because they were

---

7. Cameron McWhirter, *Red Summer: The Summer of 1919 and the Awakenings of Black America* (New York: Henry Holt, 1919).
8. Michael E. Parrish, *Felix Frankfurter and His Times: The Reform Years* (New York: Harper & Row, 1982), chap. 7.
9. See generally, Robert K. Murray, *Red Scare: A Study in National Hysteria, 1919–1920* (Minneapolis: Univ. of Minnesota, 1955).
10. Ibid., chap. 15. Rather than seeing the Palmer Raids as the high point of hysteria, Murray viewed them as the ebb tide of anti-red radicalism.
11. The Government had developed the technique of the "dragnet raid" in its wartime campaign against the International Workers of the World (IWW). William Preston, Jr., *Aliens and Dissenters: Federal Suppression of Radicals, 1903–1933* (Cambridge: Harvard University Press, 1963), chap. 8.

subject to administrative rather than judicial process; therefore, they had few legal protections. Aliens caught up in nationwide sweeps were turned over to immigration authorities for deportation proceedings. Although the actions against "enemy" aliens proved to be effective, the Department planned to go after leftist American citizens as well.[12]

In November 1919, raids were carried out against members of the Union of Russian Workers. Although only 600 warrants were issued, several thousand persons were rounded up in various parts of the country. While the operation was poorly coordinated, lax supervision meant that beatings were common and local police reportedly used third-degree methods of interrogation. These November raids culminated on December 21, 1919 in the deportation of 249 persons aboard a United States Navy transport vessel, the Buford, known in the press as "the Soviet ark." Among the deportees were two nationally known radicals, Emma Goldman and Alexander Berkman, whom the government had singled out as examples to attract publicity to the operation. The destination was Hango, Finland, and then, by train, Soviet Russia.[13] However, the November action was only a trial run for more ambitious actions to come.

Supervising these operations was a 24 year old Justice Department lawyer named J. Edgar Hoover, who had only recently graduated from George Washington Law School in Washington, D.C. The future FBI director had worked his way through school as a filing clerk in the Library of Congress, where he learned the techniques organizing vast quantities of data, skills that bolstered Hoover's meteoric rise in the Justice Department hierarchy during the next few years.[14] Hoover got his first legal job during the war in the department's Alien Enemies Bureau where he reviewed the files of those whom the department, in conjunction with the Immigration Service, had selected for deportation. With the end of

---

12. The Supreme Court upheld high-handed tactics against aliens as early as *Low Wah Suey* v. *Backus,* 225 U.S. 460 (1912). The Court continues to give immigration authorities great deference and broad discretion. See, e.g., *Immigration and Naturalization Service* v. *Abudu,* 485 U.S. 94 (1988).

13. Murray, *Red Scare*, chap. 12.

14. Assistant director of the FBI in 1921, Hoover became director in 1924 at the tender age of 29. He then reorganized the Bureau and created the modern FBI. Richard G. Powers, *Secrecy and Power: The Life of J. Edgar Hoover* (New York: Free Press; 1987), 146–155.

the war and the demise of the Bureau, Hoover was transferred to the newly formed Radical Division where he was put in charge of Attorney General Palmer's ambitious plan to strike out at Communists and Communist sympathizers. By November of 1919, Hoover had compiled dossiers on more than sixty thousand "radically inclined" persons and a card catalogue with two hundred thousand entries. Hoover worked with virtual administrative autonomy.[15]

On Friday night, January 2nd, 1920, the Justice Department, which had maintained a cover of strict secrecy, carried out raids in 33 cities in 23 states in cooperation with local enforcement agencies and private vigilantes.[16] One account estimates that as many 10,000 persons may have been taken into custody nationwide.[17] The newspapers were filled with lurid details. In Boston, first reports appeared even before the appointed time for the raids (9 p.m.) had arrived. An "extra" edition of the *Boston Herald* reported on the late afternoon of January 2nd an early roundup by local police in Chicago.[18] In the next days, the local press carried banner headlines: "Smashing Blow Dealt Radicals in Every City in the Country"—"Hundreds of Radicals caught in Round-up by U.S. Agents in N.Y."—"Definite Plot to Set Up Soviets All Over the Country"—"More Than 2,000 Arrested in Great Roundups of Reds."[19] According to the *Boston Herald,* Federal officials were confident that they had "nipped the most menacing plot yet unearthed."[20]

In Massachusetts raids were conducted in the cities of Boston, Cambridge, Brockton, Norwood, Worcester, Springfield, Lawrence, Lynn, Chicopee Falls, Holyoke, Gardner, Fitchburg, Lowell, Reading, Salem, Peabody, Bridgewater, and Haverhill. Raids were also carried out in Nashua, Manchester, Derry, Portsmouth, Claremont, Lincoln, and other cities in New Hampshire, as well as

---

15. *Ibid,* chaps. 3–4.
16. A subsequent raid took place on January 6, 1920. See Preston, *Aliens and Dissenters*, 220. The first Friday evening of every month was the regular meeting night of the American Communist Party. Arrests continued for the next few weeks at the rate of 200 per week. See Geoffrey Perrett, *America in the Twenties: A History* (New York: Simon & Schuster, 1982), 61–62.
17. Preston, *Aliens and Dissenters*, 221; Parrish, *Felix Frankfurter and His Times*, 119.
18. "Chicago Officers Swoop on Nests of Reds," *Boston Herald*, January 2,1920.
19. *Boston Herald*, January 3, 1920; *Boston Globe*, January 3, 1920.
20. *Boston Herald*, January 4, 1920.

in Rhode Island and Connecticut.[21] Prior to the raids, federal authorities made every effort to avoid "leaks." In fact, local police were not informed of the action until just a few hours before its commencement. But once the arrests were made, they received spectacular publicity. The government wished to appear as if it were acting to avoid an imminent public danger of vast proportions.

Prisoners from Concord, New Hampshire, were brought to Boston's North Station where they were detrained and forced to walk handcuffed in pairs through the downtown streets for transfer to Deer Island, the holding station. From there, as the *Herald* put it, the prisoners were to be marched "up the gang plank of a new Soviet ark bound for some distant socialistic haven."[22] Federal agents ensured that press photographers had every opportunity to record the event. On January 4th, the *Boston Globe* featured a front-page picture of "Reds Arriving at Eastern Avenue" in handcuffs and wearing overcoats against the winter cold. That same Sunday, the *Herald* displayed a similar group of "Captured Reds on Way to Steamer *Monitor* for Deer Island." On an inside page, the paper carried a photo of Ime Kaplan, secretary of the Lawrence branch of the Amalgamated Textile Workers, behind bars at Deer Island prison.[23]

New England's textile and shoe towns were especially hit hard. Union organizers were a favourite target for arrest, and one report attributed the roundup in Boston to "complaints received recently from officials of the American Woollen Company which charged that efforts were being made to excite their employees. . . ." In other words, union activity—nothing more—was the crime of these men. Several were members of trade unions affiliated with the American Federation of Labor.[24]

Even family members of outspoken critics of the government were persecuted. Mrs. John Kliavo of Roxbury, the wife of the editor of a Lettish newspaper, was taken to Deer Island after detectives failed to locate her husband. She was forced to leave two small crying children in the middle of the night. The police did not

---

21. *Boston Globe*, January 3, 1920.
22. *Boston Herald*, January 4, 1920.
23. Ibid.
24. "How the Workers are Deported: An Account of the New England Raids," *The Call Magazine*, (undated), in clippings file, Lawrence G. Brooks Papers, Harvard Law School Library (hereafter "Brooks Papers"), Box 11, folder 2.

even notify Kliavo's neighbors that her children had been left alone in the kitchen. Mrs. Kliavo was held for three weeks without a warrant.[25] Uniformed police and plain clothesmen awakened another political prisoner, John Salem, a father of five, at 3:30 a.m. They commanded, "We want you, Johnny. Hurry up and get those clothes on. . . . Where are those anarchist books? Show 'em quick, or I'll dig around here till I find them." "Maybe papa will be shot," cried one of the children. While Soja languished at Deer Island for the rest of January, the entire family came down with diphtheria. The government promised to send food and medicine, but no relief ever arrived.[26]

A Lithuanian laborer caught at 10 p.m. at a meeting at 885 Washington Street in Boston was carrying $3,000 in his money belt, which represented personal savings he had accumulated after years of labor in the Boston streets. The police summarily concluded that the money constituted the cash treasury of the entire "Communist Conspiracy." It was confiscated and never returned.[27]

Suspects were sent to police stations and kept in six-by-ten foot cells, twelve people to a cell without food, water or bedding for eighteen hours. Some were held for thirty-six hours without food. Most were arrested and their homes and offices searched without search or arrest warrants. One woman, Stella Wasilewska, testified later that Government officials first showed her a warrant at her hearing in March, more than two months after she had been arrested.[28]

The New England raids were the most extensive in the country. Homes as well as meeting halls were invaded by police and Federal agents. Citizens as well as aliens were taken into custody. The official estimate of persons arrested in Boston on the night of January 2nd was 600, but the true number might have been twice that many. On Sunday, January 4th, the *Boston Herald* reported that nearly one thousand persons had been apprehended. Many of them were women. In Nashua, women sang their way to the station; the sound of their songs, both patriotic and revolutionary, was heard far into the freezing January night. Most of those arrested were not served with warrants. The Boston office of the Bureau of

---

25. Ibid.
26. Ibid.
27. Ibid.
28. Sidney Howard, *The Survey*, May 1, 1920, Brooks Papers, Box 11, folder 2.

Investigation received a total of only 463 warrants. In some cases, warrants were applied for and received by telegraphic communication only after arrests were completed. There were no allegations of probable cause—only generalized allegations of Communist Party membership and of the Party's criminal purposes.

In New England, prisoners were held at various "concentration points" until they were discharged or held for further processing at Deer Island in Boston Harbor. More than four hundred persons (410 men and fourteen women) were sent to the island and locked together en masse. Most were immigrants—Russians, Poles, Finns, Letts, French Canadians, Italians, Greeks and Jews. Some were American citizens.[29] Conditions were deplorable, chaotic, and totally inadequate to the need. Steam pipes were broken or disconnected so that cells were left unheated despite severe winter cold. There were few sanitary facilities. Inmates were held incommunicado for days, sometimes for weeks. One prisoner, Joseph Schmidt, committed suicide in full view of fellow internees. Another went mad. Several died of pneumonia. The *Boston Globe* stated that Deer Island had simply become one "big concentration camp."[30]

Deer Island had been used by the federal government during World War I as a prison for German prisoners of war and a stockade for American servicemen convicted of military offenses. Conditions were horrendous. "Everything on the island seemed to be broken up—the windows, the water and heating pipes, the cots in the cells, the toilet arrangements, everything seemed to be in pieces. . . ." In some cells, water was ankle-deep; prisoners had to stand on inverted pails to keep their frozen feet dry. Cots gave way in the middle of the night, sinking their occupants into the icy muck. Many of the prisoners had been rushed to the police stations without adequate clothing. Despite the fact that the Commissioner of Immigration in Boston, H.G. Skeffington, knew of the raids weeks in advance, he made no preparations to receive the hordes of prisoners. The head guard· reported that he had only eight hours notice. The state commissioner of penal institutions received $1.50 per day for each prisoner from the federal government, but the prisoners' committee, formed during the first week and dubbed the

---

29. Background information on the detainees and the circumstances of their arrests was compiled by Lawrence Brooks, the principal attorney in the *Colyer v. Skeffington* case. See Brooks Papers, Box 10, folder 14.
30. *Boston Globe*, January 4, 1920.

"Deer Island Soviet" by the press, estimated the daily amount spent for each prisoner to be only 13 cents.

Loan sharks, impostors, and government informers preyed upon the families of these victims of Justice Department zeal. Parcels of food and clothing sent to prisoners simply disappeared. Citizenship papers were confiscated or vanished. Hearings were delayed and visitation passes withheld. The food was a "nameless and inedible paste." "The meat served is strongly reminiscent of dog meat," reported one prisoner, while the coffee was prepared from "pulverized burnt vegetables of some kind." The Deer Island physician said that the bread was the worst in any prison in the country.

Eventually the prison guards let the "Reds" run the place, and the prisoners' committee made Deer Island minimally habitable for the weeks of incarceration that lay ahead. Many internees were held for the entire month of January. When it was over, these workers often returned to their jobs to find that they had been permanently replaced by "scabs." Even if they were able to find job openings, they could not explain why they were unemployed. Those who received their old jobs back invariably discovered that they had lost accumulated wages, seniority, and benefits. Aliens scheduled for deportation faced prospects even more grim. Only a few were fortunate enough to attract the attention of a growing number of civil liberties activists.[31]

---

31. Lawrence Brooks made the following vivid summary of the facts from which this discussion is gleaned:

> The facts in essence are as follows: Rules of Immigration Service requiring that officers of service make thorough investigation of each case must be submitted to nearest Immigration, Sta., were ignored. Reports instead went directly to D. of J. in Wash. which requested warrants from D. of L. which issued them—presumably without further investigation or even consideration of D.J. evidence. Warrants were then sent to Boston. Generally speaking D.J. men arrested without warrant either at hand or in existence. Took in aliens & citizens, communists & others. Seized property without search warrant or permission. Persons were arrested as suspects and telegraphic warrants applied for— meanwhile they were detained without warrant. Prisoners were questioned without opportunity to have counsel in police sta. in presence of officers. Later hearings at Deer Isl. were held without permission to have atty. Interpreters were bad. Inspectors weren't on to their job. Seized papers introduced in evidence. Prisoners were chained, went, many of them, 22 hours without food—were forced to face camera—underwent terrible experience at Deer Isl. because of lack of preparation for their arrival. Bail was ridiculous. Some waited 4 weeks for hearing. No evidence of bombs or violence or that aliens contemplated any violence. Most of them automatically

The reaction of lawyers in the developing civil liberties community was intense. They wanted a nation-wide investigation of the raids, full publicity, Congressional legislation, court challenges and civil damages against offending government officials. Organizations such as the National Popular Government League and the recently formed American Civil Liberties Union (formerly the National Civil Liberties Bureau), as well as major labor unions like the Amalgamated Textile Workers of America, immediately began to develop strategies to test the government's conduct in the "Red raids" and to come to the defense of the detainees. Roger Baldwin of the ACLU supported Congressional legislation that would hold officials to account by imposing civil damages on any public official who, under color of law, deprived a person of civil liberties or committed an assault.

However, an immediate court challenge seemed to be the most direct approach.

The initiative emanated from the government itself. Lawrence G. Brooks, the attorney who was to play a principal role in the Boston cases, received an anonymous telephone call from a Labor Department official urging Brooks to contact Zechariah Chafee and Felix Frankfurter of the Harvard Law School.[32] Brooks was not in his office when the call came, so the caller dictated a message to Brooks's secretary over the phone.[33] The leak revealed the depth of inter-departmental rivalry between the Labor Department and the

---

> and without knowing how went over to the Communist Party with Socialist Party when latter was expelled.
>
> Brooks Papers, Box 10, folder 15

32. Brooks was legal counsel for the Boston Elevated Railway from 1906 to 1909. Active in various good-government organizations in the first decades of this century, Brooks pursued a distinguished career as an early civil libertarian, and advocate for arms control, and American membership in the World Court. In 1964 at age 86 he went to Selma, Alabama, to march for civil rights. Appointed to the Massachusetts federal district court in 1928, Brooks served with distinction until his retirement in 1970. He died in 1981 at the age of 100 and remains one of the major legal figures in Boston history. See, Lawrence G. Brooks, *The Memoirs of Lawrence Graham Brooks* (Private Printing, 1981), in Brooks Papers, Box 15, folder 1.

33. Peter H. Irons, "'Fighting Fair': Zechariah Chafee, Jr., The Department of Justice and the 'Trial at the Harvard Club,'" *Harvard Law Review* 94 (1981): 1205, 1219–1220. The memorandum illustrates why oral history is a necessary, albeit inadequate, substitute for contemporaneous documents. Had Brooks been in his office, we would probably not have this important record. The memorandum, dated 21 March 1920, appears in the Brooks Papers, Box 6, folder 13.

Justice Department over the wisdom and legality of the detentions and the projected deportations. Secretary of Labor William B. Wilson had been under tremendous pressure from the Justice Department; he apparently hoped the courts would relieve this pressure by declaring that the government had acted unlawfully.

The first paragraph of the memorandum read as follows:

> It is very greatly desired by the Department of Labor, though this statement is made without the authorization or knowledge of either the Secretary or the Asst. Secretary, though on most excellent information from the inside, that a test case as to deportation of aliens for membership only, in the Communist Party or other organization declaring for the abolition or destruction of our government by force, be brought at the earliest possible opportunity before a friendly judge. There is a move on foot in another department to have such a test brought before an unfriendly judge; at least such test would be presumably made before a judge who would be likely to sustain the extreme position of the Atty. General, and for this reason, speed is of great moment.

The caller explained that he was revealing the information "because it was hardly possible or safe for an official in the Dept. of Labor to take the step." The caller indicated that an ideal test case could be brought on behalf of Amy and William Colyer, English immigrants, professed Communists, and residents of Wellesley, whose offense was membership in the Communist Party:

> It happens that there is a case in Boston now which the Dpt. considers ideal for a test case, for reasons which the memorandum which I enclose may make clear to you. The couple held for deportation do not come under any of the exceptions contained in the statement of principles to be followed in such cases, which I also enclose. But they are people of a high type, intelligent, do not advocate violence, much less attempted to use it, but they are bona fide members of the Communist Party.[34]

Brooks was urged to get the case before a friendly federal judge as quickly as possible. The caller suggested federal district Judge George Anderson: "It is thought very important that this case should be brought to trial before Judge George Anderson, and that

---

34. Ibid.

the best possible counsel be secured for the prisoners."[35] Brooks was told that Secretary of Labor Wilson did not believe that membership, either in the Communist Party or the Communist Labor Party, should alone be grounds for deportation as the Justice Department insisted. The Colyers could test this Justice Department edict because it was clear that they had been detained because of their party membership, not for advocating violence. "It is vital that the membership question be raised in [a] friendly jurisdiction first, as there is an attempt on foot to raise it in less friendly courts."[36]

Several days later Judson King of the National Popular Government League urged Brooks to get a favorable decision in the deportation cases "from a liberal minded judge, not afflicted with the Bolshevik hysteria, and who represents the institutions of justice."[37] King was critical of the lawyers who were representing the detainees; he found them "not of a very high order of legal ability."[38] And he was not alone in criticizing the Colyers' legal counsel. Another correspondent, Lee Somers, wrote: "They have a Jew named Katzeff for a lawyer. Katzeff, their lawyer, I understand is no good. . . ."[39] But Sidney Howard, the progressive editor of *The Survey* magazine, observed Morris Katzeff in action at the trial in late April. Howard thought Katzeff was "alive, foreign, and clever."[40] In any case, Somers recommended Chafee and Roscoe Pound rather than Chafee and Felix Frankfurter (who also just happened to be Jewish) for the Colyers' case.[41]

---

35. Anderson's name had already appeared in the press when he ordered the release of one prisoner on January 7, 1920. See *Boston Herald*, January 8, 1920.
36. Ibid.
37. King to Brooks, 22 March 1920, Brooks Papers, Box 6, folder 13.
38. Ibid.
39. Lee Somers to Porter E. Sargent, (undated), Brooks Papers, Box 6, folder 13.
40. See "The Colyer Trial Opens," *The Survey*, April 17, 1920, Brooks Papers, Box 11, folder 2. As Jerold S. Auerbach has pointed out, the bar was deeply divided during this period between the ABA corporate elites from Harvard, Yale and Columbia and the unscrubbed immigrant lawyers who represented working people, trade unionists, and political radicals. See Jerold S.Auerbach, *Unequal Justice: Lawyers and Social Change in Modern America* (New York: Oxford University Press, 1976).
41. Frankfurter had already developed a reputation as "the symbol of the Jew, the red, the alien." Leonard Baker, *Brandeis and Frankfurter: A Dual Biography* (New York: Harper and Row, 1984), 179. Frankfurter was raised in an Orthodox Jewish family, and he remained religiously observant until he started attending The City College of New York. As another biographer has written, "Frankfurter

King suggested that Anderson was the right judge to hear the case. "It would be of the highest value if the case be brought before Judge Anderson," he wrote. King's own involvement grew out of his deep progressive commitments that he summarized this way:

> My interest in the matter lies in the fact that I consider the whole conduct of the government toward Communists and Socialists as unworthy of the spirit of American institutions, as extremely bad public policy, calculated to inflame and augment the evils which they are claimed to irradicate [sic]; that we are at a parting of the ways in which we are to set precedents of tremendous importance for the future, that the precedents so set will quickly be used against. . .progressivism in America which seeks to reform present conditions in a perfectly constitutional manner.[42]

Brooks was also informed that there were only three federal judges in the entire country who "have some sense." One was in Montana, another "somewhere in the Middle West," and "the third is Anderson."[43] This observer reported the situation to Brooks as follows:

> I have reason to think that if Amy and W.T. Colyer could be brought before Judge Anderson a judicial ruling might be obtained which at least would not go any farther than the Secretary's view that membership in the Communist Party is unlawful. I also suspect that the Secretary would not care very much if his ruling were picked full of holes and membership in the Communist Party was found not grounds for deportation, though the law apparently would indicate that it is.
>
> I suggest this to you because I understand that Prof. Chafee and other members of the Liberal Club have been working against the deportation policy and there might be a chance to accomplish something in the case of the Colyers. Almost any day now the Secretary's ruling is likely to be brought into the

---

never denied that he was a Jew; he was quite pointed throughout his life in identifying himself as such." Robert A. Burt, *Two Jewish Justices: Outcasts in the Promised Land* (Berkeley: Univ. of Calif., 1988), 38. The youthful Eleanor Roosevelt's first impression was that Frankfurter was "an interesting little man but very jew." Quoted in Ibid. 142. This statement reveals a prevailing social prejudice not only at the higher levels of American aristocracy, but also from a woman later noted for her humane liberalism and pro-Jewish causes.

42. King to Brooks, 22 March 1920, Brooks Papers, Box 6, folder 13.

43. Somers to Sargent, (undated), Brooks Papers, Box 6, folder 13.

> courts, before an unfriendly judge who will rule that even the mildest heresy is a warrant for deportation. That is particularly likely if some friendless Russian is brought before them.
>
> The Colyers, however, have social position, an excellent background, a record of opposition to violence, English nativity, and a lot in their favor that most of them do not have.
>
> If Prof. Chafee thought it a wise thing to do, it might be possible to get them into court on a habeas corpus before Judge Anderson, who would at least give them a square deal. And in doing so he would set a precedent that would mean a square deal for the others.
>
> Prof. Chafee and Roscoe Pound could build up a very good case in behalf of the Colyers, I should think. Quick action is imperative, I understand, because some other judge may act on another case and establish a very dangerous precedent. In any event, I don't see that the Colyers could be any worse off for getting a day in court.[44]

Brooks filed the case and Anderson agreed to hear it.[45] Anderson sat "by designation" as a district judge and held fifteen days of hearings. He personally requested Frankfurter and Chafee of Harvard to serve as "friends of the court." Chafee did most of the legal research while Frankfurter conducted the cross-examination of the government's key witnesses, particularly George E. Kelleher, chief of the Bureau of Investigation's Boston office.[46] Morris Katzeff and Lawrence Brooks developed the basic facts.

While Frankfurter and Chafee were technically *amici curiae*, in fact they represented the Colyers and the other habeas corpus petitioners, originally twenty in all, as part of the plaintiffs' legal team. Anderson would later write that Frankfurter and Chafee "as *amici curiae*, have appeared in association with counsel for the

---

44. Ibid.

45. The Massachusetts Federal District Court did not adopt the rule requiring random assignments of cases until November 13, 1948. This rule formalized a practice that had been in effect for some time. But in 1920 the practice had been quite different. According to Lawrence Brooks, Anderson "rather engineered the case so it would come into his court." Interview with Lawrence Brooks, May 20, 1973, cited in Donald L. Smith, Zechariah *Chafee, Jr.: Defender of Liberty and Law* (Cambridge: Harvard University Press, 1986), 46. The author is grateful to Vincent Flanagan, the former Circuit Executive for the First Circuit, for information on the random assignment rule.

46. Irons, "Fighting Fair," 1221; Smith, *Zechariah Chafee*, 45–46.

petitioners, and assisted both in the presentation of the evidence and in the argument of controlling questions of law."[47]

The hearings took place in late April and early May of 1920. Lawrence Brooks gave a dramatic opening statement attacking the Attorney General of the United States, A. Mitchell Palmer, for organizing the raids. He asked the court to find "that the Attorney General who so conducts himself as the present incumbent is more of a menace to the country than any of the aliens whom he seeks to deport." "The nation and the world looks [sic] to this court for a revival of its belief in the underlying privileges of this Government."[48] Morris Katzeff then followed Brooks. He charged that government officials had made no effort to get at the truth. "All [they] were after was to get something on these men, and, of course, that was an easy matter." Anderson was determined "to make here an adequate record upon the supposition that some court, some time, may settle these issues consistently with the Constitution and laws of the United States and . . . with the principles of human liberty. . . ."[49]

But George Anderson was the dominant figure in the courtroom. "He played a very active role in the examination of witnesses and in 'thinking aloud.'" As one observer put it, "The liberal, wise, humorous, and humane judge dominated all."[50]

In the course of the hearings, Anderson excoriated the government for its illegal conduct. He viewed the raids with "horror," calling them an example of "that modern theory of statesmanship that you hang first and try afterwards. . . . A more lawless proceeding it is hard to conceive," he said.[51] Focusing upon the infiltration of radical groups by Justice Department agents, Judge Anderson

---

47. *Colyer v. Skeffington*, 265 F. 17, 22 (D. Mass. 1920). Anderson also seems to have used Chafee and Frankfurter also to help him prepare his final opinion, which came to sixty pages in the Federal Reporter. See Irons, "Fighting Fair," 1126.
48. Newspaper clipping (undated), Brooks Papers, Box 10, folder 15.
49. *The Survey*, 17 April 1920, Brooks Papers, Box 11, folder 2. A lengthy account of U.S. Attorney Louis Goldberg's closing argument appears in a newspaper clipping (undated) also in the Brooks Papers, Box 11, folder 2.
50. Ibid., Sidney Howard, the editor of *The Survey*, called the testimony "the most remarkable social testimony I have ever heard." Howard to Brooks (undated), Brooks Papers, Box 10, folder 15.
51. National Popular Government League, *Report Upon the Illegal Practice of the United States Department of Justice* (Wash, 1920), 43 (hereinafter *Report Upon Illegal Practice*).

declared: "the Government owns and operates some part of the Communist Party."[52] He also commented upon the public hysteria. "It is difficult to give aliens their rights when the people see nothing but red," he declared.[53] His statement elicited an editorial from *The New York Times* rebuking the judge for lecturing the American people.[54]

J. Edgar Hoover, newly appointed head of the General Intelligence Division of the Justice Department, made a dramatic appearance in Boston during the hearing, but he did not testify. In comments to the press, however, Hoover referred to Anderson's remarks from the bench as "an unjustifiable misconception of facts . . . which the most perverted mind could not put upon the evidence." In the words of Hoover's biographer, "this was strong language for a twenty-five year-old attorney to use in reference to a Federal judge."[55]

While the court hearing was proceeding, the police continued to act against radicals. Two leading members of the Communist Labor Party were arrested and jailed in Nashua, New Hampshire, after a mass meeting called to protest the January 2nd raid and to raise funds to pay legal expenses for all those challenging the deportation proceedings.[56]

After two weeks of hearings and a thorough examination of the documentary evidence including pamphlets, writings and papers of the Socialist Party, the Communist Party, and the Communist Labor Party, Anderson issued a ruling on June 23rd, 1920. He ordered the discharge of the prisoners.[57] The decision was one of the most extensive ever rendered by a federal district court in Massachusetts "and one of the harshest indictments of government misconduct ever made by an American jurist."[58] Anderson's picture appeared on the front page of the *Boston Herald* on June 24th

---

52. *New York Times*, Apri l 21, 1920.
53. Ibid., April 27, 1920.
54. Ibid., April 28,1920.
55. Powers, *Secrecy and Power*, 117.
56. *New York Times*, May 3, 1920.
57. "Anderson orders 14 'Reds' Freed—Communist Membership Not Cause for Deportation—Judge Scores Federal 'Spies' and Officials' Lawless Action." *Boston Globe*, June 24, 1920.
58. Parrish, *Felix Frankfurter and His Times*, 126.

under the headline: "Communist Party of America Lawful, Anderson Decides."[59]

Anderson had at least one recent precedent to work with. Earlier in the year, a federal district judge in Montana, George M. Bourquin, had released a member of the Industrial Workers of the World who had been held for deportation following a raid conducted by federal agents in February, 1919. Bourquin found that the government's agents in Butte, Montana, "perpetrated a reign of terror, violence and crime against citizen and alien alike. . . ."[60] Finding violations of the Fourth and Fifth Amendments of the Constitution, Judge Bourquin concluded in a striking parallel to Lawrence Brooks's condemnation of Attorney General Palmer that the petitioner was "less a danger to America than are those who indorse [sic] or use the methods that brought him to deportation. Those latter are the mob and the spirit of violence and intolerance incarnate, the most alarming manifestation in America today."[61] For Bourquin this was "government by hysteria," and these redbaiters "were more to be feared than all the miserable, baited, bedeviled Reds that are their ostensible occasion." Bourquin grounded his decision in the fundamentals of the Constitution, "the inalienable rights of personal security and safety, orderly and due process of law. . . . "[62] The *New Republic* featured Bourquin's decision in its March 31st edition, a copy of which appears in the Brooks Papers.[63] Judge Anderson did not cite the case in his opinion, but he undoubtedly had heard or read about the Montana ruling by the time he decided *Colyer* v. *Skeffington*. In language and tone, the two decisions are remarkably alike.

Anderson's opinion is laced with vigorous condemnations of the government:

> I refrain from any extended comment on the lawlessness of these proceedings by our supposedly law-enforcing officials. The documents and acts speak for themselves. It may, however, fitly be observed that a mob is a mob, whether made up of govern-

---

59. *Boston Herald*, June 24,1920.
60. *Ex parte Jackson*, 263 F 110, 112 (D. Mont. 1920).
61. Ibid., 113.
62. Ibid.
63. See, Brooks Papers, Box 11, folder 2.

> ment officials acting under instructions from the Department of Justice, or of criminals, loafers and the vicious classes.[64]

Anderson's sympathies for oppressed aliens who were caught up in a whipsaw of police-state tactics by federal and local law enforcement agents, and persecuted by local "volunteers," are evident from the rest of his opinion:

> The picture of a non-English-speaking Russian peasant arrested under circumstances such as described above, held for days in jail, then for weeks in the city prison at Deer Island, and then summoned for a so-called "trial" before an inspector, assisted by the Department of Justice agent under stringent instructions emanating from the Department of Justice in Washington to make every possible effort to obtain evidence of the alien's membership in one of the proscribed parties, is not a picture of [a] sober, dispassionate 'due process of law' attempt to ascertain and report the true facts. . . .
>
> . . . Deliberately to plan to cut these aliens off from the advice and assistance of counsel until they were involved in apparent admissions that they were members of or affiliated with an organization teaching the overthrow of this government by force and violence, the practical equivalent of a charge of treason if against citizens, is utterly inconsistent with every notion involved in the conception of 'due process of law.'[65]

Anderson grounded his decision to discharge the petitioners from custody on the absence of even "a scintilla of evidence that any alien thus set at liberty was committed in any way to acts of force or violence against persons or property."[66] After analyzing the documentary evidence of Communist subversion including the *Communist Manifesto* and the manifesto and program of the American Communist Party, Anderson concluded that "[v]iolence is no part of their Program."[67] The literature upon which the prisoners were being held was "nothing but idle words."[68] Anderson reasoned that "both religious and political crusaders commonly

---

64. *Colyer* v. *Skeffington*, 265 F at 43.
65. Ibid., 47, 48.
66. Ibid., 21.
67. Ibid., 58.
68. Ibid., 59.

use the nomenclature of warfare" and that in some parts of the non-Christian world, "Onward, Christian Soldiers" could be said to be "an alien, seditious war song."[69]

He also found that the evidence before the immigration authorities had been manipulated by government spies and informers who had infiltrated the Communist Party and arranged for party meetings to take place on the night of the planned raid. Government spies were no more trustworthy than industrial spies, he declared. "The evil wrought by the spy system in industry," Anderson stated, "has for decades, been incalculable. Until it is eliminated, decent human relations cannot exist between employers and employees. . . . It destroys trust and confidence; it kills human kindliness; it propagates hate."[70]

Anderson contended that the evidence upon which orders of deportation had been issued was vitiated by the total absence of due process of law. The records sent to the Secretary of Labor for final disposition "originated in hearings conducted by inspectors in an atmosphere and under conditions which . . . I am constrained to believe prevented the aliens from having a fair, legal, due process of law consideration of their real status."[71] This was deemed to be true for all but four of the petitioners; three British citizens cognizant of their rights were not unfairly treated and one Russian named Lew Bonder, a man of "considerable intelligence" had, in Anderson's view, been able to assert rights adequately.

Anderson's decision was grounded in due process—arrests without wholesale roundups, terrorism, brutality, the use of "telegraphic warrants" obtained after the fact, and, finally, violation of the Justice Department's own rules of procedure. In fact, *Colyer* v. *Skeffington* became the basis for a legal doctrine that was subsequently adopted by the Supreme Court and has since become a mainstay of fair administrative procedure. In April 1919, prior to the Palmer Raids, the Labor Department had promulgated a change in an Immigration Service rule governing the examination of aliens. The modification of the regulation, Rule 22, was designed to afford

69. Ibid.
70. Ibid., 69. Labor spies were among a number of weapons used by management against organized labor in the 1920s. See Sidney Howard, *The Labor Spy* (New York: Republic, 1924).
71. Ibid., 71.

aliens greater procedural protections. Specifically, Rule 22 provided that:

> At the beginning of the hearing under the warrant of arrest the alien shall be allowed to inspect the warrant of arrest and all the evidence on which it was issued, and shall be apprised that he may be represented by counsel. If the counsel be selected he shall be permitted to be present during the conduct of the hearing.[72]

But on December 31, 1919, while Labor Secretary Wilson was ill, the acting secretary directed the immigration commissioner to circulate the following amendment to Rule 22:

> Preferably at the beginning of the hearing under the warrant of arrest, or at any rate as soon as such hearing has proceeded sufficiently in the development of the facts to protect the Government's interests, the alien shall be allowed to inspect the warrant of arrest and all the evidence on which it was issued and shall be apprised that thereafter he may be represented by counsel.

In effect, the amendment changed the rule back to what it had been prior to the Secretary's earlier modification.[73]

In his argument to the court, Frankfurter had focused on this rule change. He argued that aliens had a right to the "protection that rule 22 afforded them as it stood before the ad hoc repeal of that rule for the purpose of these cases." Frankfurter continued:

> Now, if there is one thing that is established in the law of administration, I take it that it is that a rule cannot be repealed specifically to affect a case under consideration by the administrative authorities; that is, if there is an existing rule which protects

---

72. Immigration Rules, Rule 22, Subdivision 5(b). Cited in, *Colyer* v. *Skeffington*, 265 F at 46. The Brooks Papers, Box 10, folder 14, contain the full text of the rules and the changes hereinafter described.

73. Ibid. While there is no documentary evidence implicating him directly, Hoover's biographer concludes that Hoover was responsible for the modification of Rule 22 to coincide with the raids of January 2nd, 1920. Unlike ordinary indigents, some radicals had organizational support and legal counsel to take advantage of the previously revised rule. Hoover had complained about the obstructionism of defense lawyers during the November 1919 raids and wanted to avoid that problem in 1920. See Powers, *Secrecy and Power*, 102–103.

> certain rights, it violates every sense of decency, which is the very heart of due process, to repeal that protection, just for the purpose of accomplishing the ends of the case which comes before the administrative authority.[74]

In his final opinion, Judge Anderson characterized the government's changing the rules after the fact as nothing less than "extraordinary." Years later, Frankfurter recalled the *Colyer* case as the progenitor for a Supreme Court holding that "regulations validly prescribed by a government administrator are biding upon him as well as the citizen, and that this principle hold even when the administrative action under review is discretionary in nature."[75] This basic principle of modern administrative law, in which origin Felix Frankfurter played such an important role back in 1920, was reaffirmed most dramatically in 1974, when the Supreme Court ordered President Richard Nixon to surrender the Watergate tapes to the special prosecutor.[76]

The government chose not to appeal the discharge of most prisoners released by Anderson in the *Colyer* case. Its due process violations had simply been too egregious.[77] But with respect to four of the principal petitioners, the Labor Department did appeal to the Court of Appeals and won. A First Circuit panel reversed Anderson's decision holding that there had been no abuse of administrative discretion with respect to the Labor Secretary's findings of fact; that there was "substantial evidence" from which a reasonable administrator could have concluded that the Communist Party taught and advocated violent measures and finally, that members of the party could be deported.[78]

---

74. Quoted in *Colyer* v. *Skeffington*, 265 F at 48. Rule 22 was subsequently revised again by Secretary Wilson to guarantee the presence of legal counsel for defendants. U.S. Department of Labor to All Commissioners of Immigration, January 27, 1920, in Brooks Papers, Box 10, folder 14. On the other side, Assistant U.S. Attorney Lewis Goldberg argued that the December 31st modification of Rule 22 simply restored the rule to what it had been prior to April, 1919. See Preston, *Aliens and Dissenters*, 217.
75. The Supreme Court case is *Service* v. *Dulles*, 354 U.S. 363 (1957). Frankfurter's conclusions appear in H. B. Phillips, *Felix Frankfurter's Reminiscences* (New York: Reynal, 1960), 170–171.
76. *U.S.* v. *Nixon*, 418 U.S. 683, 695–696 (1974).
77. The Labor Department, however, determined that it would be bound by the Anderson decision only within Massachusetts. *New York Times*, June 25, 1920.
78. *Skeffington* v. *Katzeff*, 277 F. 129 (1st Cir. 1922).

Zachariah Chafee later wrote that this reversal of Anderson was of no consequence. What was important was that Judge Anderson had "placed the facts of those outrages before the public, and as a result they never recurred. . . ."[79] However, Anderson did have the last word with respect to one of the four petitioners, Lou Bonder. Anderson released Bonder on his second habeas petition after the government attempted to hold him indefinitely pending deportation to the Soviet Union. The government argued that American recognition of the U.S.S.R. was imminent and that deportation proceedings would soon be able to go forward. (In fact, nearly a decade would pass before President Franklin Roosevelt extended official recognition to the Soviet state in 1933.[80]) Said Anderson, "[I]t is very plain that on the record now before the court any further detention by the immigration authorities or control of Bonder's freedom is illegal."[81] Lawrence Brooks represented Bonder in this proceeding also.[82]

By the time Judge George Anderson rendered his decision in *Colyer* v. *Skeffington*, the Red Scare had subsided. Early in May 1920, Labor Secretary Wilson declared that membership in the Communist Labor Party, as distinguished from the Communist Party itself, would not be considered grounds for deportation, a ruling that caused some consternation in the Department of Justice.[83] New Assistant Secretary of Labor Louis F. Post restored due process to deportation proceedings at the Immigration Service. To the dismay of Justice Department zealots, detainees were released en masse.[84] Post's enemies in Congress called for his impeachment, but the attacks backfired. Post retaliated. His lawyer, Jackson Ralston, launched an investigation of the Justice Department. The ACLU and the National Popular Government League published a report documenting government excesses. Compiled by a group of prominent liberal lawyers and academicians including Roscoe Pound, Felix Frankfurter, Zachariah Chafee, Ernst Freund, and

---

79. Quoted in Smith, *Zechariah Chafee*, 47.
80. See *Bonder* v. *Johnson*, 5 F.2d 238 (1st Cir. 1925).
81. Ibid., 240.
82. See Brooks Papers, Box 10, folder 16; *New York Times*, June 25, 1920.
83. While *The New York Times* editorialized in favor of Wilson's decision, it still worried about the policy divisions between Justice and Labor and about "dangerous" aliens outside the reach of the law. See *New York Times*, May 6, 7, 1920.
84. Smith, *Zechariah Chafee*, 45.

Frank Walsh, the report condemned the Justice Department for its "illegal practices" and concluded that "no organizations of radicals acting through propaganda over the last six months could have created as much revolutionary sentiment in America as has been created by the acts of the Department of Justice itself."[85] The publication of the report in May 1920 not only documented the outrages committed by the government but helped to redirect public opinion from "red radicalism" to the radicalism of the Justice Department itself. Coming one month later, Anderson's decision contributed mightily to the turn in the tide because it completely undercut the government's legal position.

But the raids still had ardent supporters. A. Mitchell Palmer, whose name would be forever linked with the Red Scare, in his campaign for the Democratic Presidential nomination declared that the Anderson decision was the only jarring note in an otherwise clear record of convictions of Communists and communist sympathizers by other courts.[86] The Red Scare also had more long-term effects. The first major restrictive immigration law, enacted in June

---

85. *Report Upon Illegal Practice*, 7. Here are excerpts from the introductory portion of the report:

> Punishments of the utmost cruelty, and heretofore unthinkable in America, have become usual. Great numbers of persons arrested, both aliens and citizens, have been threatened, beaten with blackjacks, struck with fists, jailed under abominable conditions, or actually tortured . . . . Many hundreds of citizens and aliens alike have been arrested in wholesale raids, without warrants or pretense of warrants. They have then either been released, or have been detained in police stations or jails for indefinite lengths of time while warrants were being applied for. This practice of making mass raids and mass arrests without warrant has resulted directly from the instructions, both written and oral, issued by the Department of Justice at Washington . . . . We do not question the right of the Department of Justice to use its agents in the Bureau of Investigation to ascertain when the law is being violated. But the American people has [sic] never tolerated the use of undercover provocative agents or 'agent provocateurs,' such as have been familiar in old Russia or Spain. Such agents have been introduced by the Department of Justice into the radical movements, have reached positions of influence therein, have occupied themselves with informing upon or instigating acts which might be declared criminal, and at the express direction of Washington have brought about meetings of radicals in order to make possible wholesale arrests at such meetings."
>
> In Rawlston's words, the purpose of this report was "to give to the country . . . . . . some idea of the ruthless manner in which individual rights have been trampled upon by . . . the Department of Justice.

Rawlston to Brooks, April 16, 1920, Brooks Papers, Box 10, folder 15.

86. *New York Times*, June 26, 1920.

1920, was a direct result of the fear stirred up by the hysteria. Membership in leftist parties declined dramatically and never fully recovered, even during the Great Depression, a decade later. Sympathy with communism or socialism continued to be extremely dangerous. For example, in 1924, Rule 22 was again revised in order to permit interrogation of aliens without the presence of legal counsel. And persecution of radicals continued, albeit on a case-by-case basis.[87]

The decision of Judge Anderson in the *Colyer* case achieved three important civil liberties goals. First, it sustained the claims of a group of unpopular aliens that they were entitled to fair treatment under the laws and the Constitution of the United States. Second, the decision established that the federal courts would not simply rubber-stamp decisions of the Labor or the Justice Department in deportation cases. Such decisions would be subject to meaningful judicial review. Third, the Anderson decision, based upon a voluminous record transcript, detailed at length the government's illegal conduct. By calling the responsible officials "a mob," Anderson held the Justice Department up to scorn and ridicule. The Anderson decision also substituted a tone of reason for the panic and hysteria which the government had cultivated in matters pertaining to the Communist Party, communist sympathizers and the "Communist menace."[88] In short, *Colyer v. Skeffington* was a great moment in the history of the federal courts.

But the decision was a pyrrhic victory for American liberalism. The Red Scare, which opened the Jazz Age, played a significant role in bringing progressivism to an end. It helped to transform wartime fears into the pervasive conservatism of the 1920s. Despite the fact that most of the victims of the Palmer Raids were eventually released, some were not so lucky. In June of 1920, 591 persons were still awaiting deportation nationwide.[89] According to one estimate, 547 persons among those detained were eventually deported from the United States.[90]

---

87. Preston, *Aliens and Dissenters*, 235–37.
88. These points were made by Sidney Howard in *The Survey*, May 1, 1920, Brooks Papers, Box 11, folder 2.
89. Murray, *Red Scare*, 251.
90. "The Communist Prosecutions" (flyer), American Civil Liberties Union, March, 1921 (available in Widener Library, Harvard University).

There is a sequel regarding the four appellees who lost their petitions for release on appeal. Lou Bonder was freed in 1925. The fate of Frank Mack, "the Lenin of the Deer Island Soviet," is unknown. As for William and Amy Colyer—they were deported from New York City aboard the *S.S. Aquitania* on April 11th,1922.[91]

---

91. Letter from Commissioner of Immigration to Edward DeBoskey (Justice Dept.), 20 July 1932, in *Colyer v. Skeffington* file, RG 21 Federal Records Center, Waltham, Mass.

Episode 11

Sunday Blue Laws and the Kosher Supermarket

> Orthodox Jews are thus put to the dilemma of choosing between their religion and their business.
>
> Calvert Magruder, 1961

In the 1950s, Sunday "blue laws" were alive and well in Massachusetts, as they were in most parts of the United States.[1] These laws originated in colonial times in a society that was profoundly religious and deeply Protestant. The Sunday laws were part of a political and social regime that supported single church religious establishments. Laws requiring church attendance and prohibiting worldly activities on the Sabbath were common. In the words of one early provincial statute:

> [W]hereas it is the duty of all persons, upon the Lord's day, carefully to apply themselves, publicly and privately, to religion and piety, the profanation of the Lord's day is highly offensive to

---

* Source: Chapter 10 ("First Circuit Judges and the Sunday Blue Law") George Dargo, *A History of the United States Court of Appeals for the First Circuit*, Vol. I (1891–1960) © George Dargo (as assigned to the U.S. Court of Appeals for the First Circuit).

1. A leading scholar called the Massachusetts statute one of "the most stringent" in the nation. See Leo Pfeffer, *Church, State, and Freedom* (Boston: Beacon Press, 1953), 230. For a review of state Sunday closing laws in the 1950s, see "Validity of Discrimination by Sunday Law Between Different Kinds of Stores or Commodities," 57 ALR 3d 975 1974. The origin of the use of the color "blue" to describe these laws is somewhat obscure. Perhaps it derived from the blue color Puritans favored in opposition to the English preference for royal red. Another theory suggests that because the volumes of colonial laws that applied religious standards to civil conduct were bound in blue, the laws themselves were called "blue laws."

> Almighty God, of evil example, and tends to the grief and disturbance of all pious and religiously disposed persons. . . .[2]

In the aftermath of the American Revolution, most states terminated their formal religious establishments. But Sunday closing laws remained in effect, although they were no longer justified on religious grounds alone. The new theory was that Sabbath rest was wholesome and socially beneficial. On this basis blue laws survived the anti-clericalism of the late eighteenth century. Thus, the Massachusetts Supreme Judicial Court would declare in the middle of the nineteenth century that the Sunday law "is essentially a civil regulation, proving for a fixed day of rest in the business, the ordinary avocations and amusements of the community."[3] While later cases occasionally reasserted their religious origins and character[4], the central rationale for Sunday closing laws in the new secular age was the general public welfare as controlled and controlled under the state's police powers. In time, most state legislatures developed numerous exemptions to the strict prohibitions against Sunday secular activity. Selected recreational functions, some forms of professional and commercial business, and "work of necessity or charity" fell outside the proscriptions of the law. But those who observed Saturday as their day of rest, such as Jews and Seventh Day Adventists, were simply unable to take advantage of these exemptions.[5] Consequently, when Harold Chernock, the manager, part owner and corporate president of Springfield's Crown Kosher Supermarket, decided to keep the door of his kosher market open on Sundays, he challenged a time-honored American tradition and one of the most deeply rooted statutory regimes in Massachusetts.[6]

---

2. Prov. St. 1760–61, c. 20 s.1, quoted in "A General Survey of the Sunday and Holiday Laws in New England," 39 *Boston Univ. L. Rev.* 553 (1959). For a comprehensive treatment of Sunday closing laws, their history, and status circa 1950, see Pfeffer, *Church, State, and Freedom,* 227–241.

3. *Commonweath* v. *Has*, 122 Mass. 40, 42 (1877).

4. See, e.g., *Davis* v. *Somerville*, 128 Mass. 594, 596 (1880) (declaring Sunday to be "a day devoted to public and private worship and to religious meditation and repose, undisturbed by secular cares or amusements"); *Commonwealth* v. *White*, 190 Mass. 578, 580 (1906) ("It is one of a series of statutory provisions enacted to secure the proper observance of the Lord's day, as understood by our forefathers.").

5. M.G.L. c.136, §6(23); formerly, M.G.L. c.136, §6.

6. Chernock first checked with the city solicitor. "He said, if you do not open Saturday night you can open Sunday with no problem." With this assurance,

In the 1950s, the Crown Kosher Supermarket was the only store of its kind in western Massachusetts. Located on Sumner Street in Springfield, the market catered to the unique needs and food requirements of the Orthodox Jewish community. While there were other kosher butcher shops and kosher delicatessens in Springfield, Crown Kosher was the only kosher supermarket in that part of the state. The store sold kosher meats and a variety of other kosher foods. Ninety-five percent of its packaged foods were sold under an approved kosher label. Customers traveled many miles in order to buy Crown Kosher products, some coming from as far as Brattleboro, Vermont, sixty miles from Springfield. One customer came all the way from White River Junction, a distance of 140 miles. Forty percent of Crown Kosher's weekly gross sales occurred on Sunday.[7] In fact, the market had been doing business on Sundays since its opening in August, 1953.

Chernock's challenge did not go unanswered. On three separate Sundays in May and June, 1954, officers from the Springfield police department walked into Crown Kosher ostensibly to buy meat and groceries.[8] A few days later Chernock was served with a summons for having been open on three successive Sundays, the day of the week when the law said he had to be closed. On June 15, 1954, after a brief trial, the Springfield district court found Chernock guilty and fined him $15 dollars for each offense, one for each Sunday, for a total of $45. Chernock appealed the conviction to the Superior Court of Hampden County and then to the Supreme Judicial Court of Massachusetts on the grounds that the Sunday closing laws violated various provisions of the Massachusetts Constitution. These appeals failed.[9]

Caught in the intolerable dilemma of either having to close on Sunday all together or suffer continuing prosecution and fines, Chernock decided to challenge the Sunday law in federal district

---

Chernock opened for Sunday business in August, 1953. Author's interview with Harold Chernock, July 25, 1991, Forest Park, Springfield, Massachusetts.

7. "Sunday was the big day," reported Chernock. He even had to hire someone to park customers' cars, so heavy was the volume. At one point, Chernock employed as many as six butchers to do his meat-cutting. Ibid.

8. Complaint, *Crown Kosher Supermarket of Mass., Inc.* v. *Gallaher*, 176 F. Supp. 466 (D. Mass. 1959), appendix, 495.

9. *Commonwealth* v. *Chernock*, 336 Mass. 384 (1957). Chernock never paid the fine. Chernock Interview, July 25, 1991.

court in Boston on constitutional grounds. The named plaintiffs were the Crown Kosher Corporation itself, three Jewish customers of the store, and the Chief Rabbi of Springfield's Orthodox Jewish congregations. Chernock sought a declaration that the Sunday closing law was unconstitutional and an injunction barring the police from again attempting to enforce the Sunday law against him. Subsequently, several Seventh Day Adventist groups filed an *amicus* brief on behalf of the plaintiffs.[10] A brief was also filed by the Lord's Day League of New England and the Archdiocesan Council of Catholic Men in support of the Massachusetts blue law.[11]

In order to understand the problem faced by Harold Chernock and the Crown Kosher Supermarket, the federal district court had to have a rudimentary understanding of *halacha* (Jewish law), particularly as it applied to the Jewish dietary code and the laws of the Sabbath. The court also had to know something about Orthodox Jews, a community noted for its strict observance of Jewish law and the tenets, practices, and customs of traditional Judaism. With this in mind, the parties agreed to a set of stipulations that reduced a complex body of religious regulations to a simple and readily understandable list of rules. These stipulations covered the dietary laws as well as the laws governing conduct on the Sabbath and Jewish holidays.[12]

Jewish dietary restrictions, the laws of *kashrut*, are uniquely intricate. This is especially true with respect to the slaughter of meat and fowl and the preparation, sale, and consumption of all meat, meat products, and meat derivatives. Orthodox Jews may eat

---

10. Seventh Day Adventists were among Chernock's best customers.
11. The fact that these "friends of the court" were religious organizations undercut the argument later advanced by a majority of the justices of the United States Supreme Court that the purposes of Sunday closing legislation were secular and not religious. As stated in their petition to intervene, the Archdiocesan Council had "a substantial interest in the instant litigation, to wit, the preservation of the sanctity of the Lord's day. . . ." Petition for Leave to Intervene, Archdiocesan Council of Catholic Men, filed with *Crown Kosher Supermarket* v. *Gallagher* material, in Calvert Magruder Papers [hereinafter CMP], Treasure Room, Harvard Law School Library, Box 29, folder 5.
12. See, Stipulation as to Facts, filed November 13, 1958, appearing in the Record Transcript filed with the U.S. Supreme Court, November 17, 1959. In substance, these stipulations are reproduced in Judge Magruder's opinion. *Crown Kosher*, 176 F. Supp. 469–471. Rabbi Moses D. Sheinkopf of the Massachusetts Council of Rabbis, a co-plaintiff in the case, prepared these stipulations for the court.

only meat, fish, and certain kinds of fowl. Meat and fowl must be ritually slaughtered under close rabbinical supervision. Dairy products cannot be mingled or eaten with meat or meat products, nor can dairy dishes or utensils be mixed together. In addition, no packaged food containing such a mixture, or that utilize pork products or derivatives of any non-kosher meat, may be consumed.

According to Jewish law, the Sabbath begins before sundown on Friday and ends after nightfall on Saturday. *Halachic* requirements with respect to the observance of the Sabbath and the Jewish holidays are especially demanding. Commerce and most forms of ordinary work are forbidden. Orthodox Jews cannot travel on the Sabbath or on religious holidays. On the Sabbath, nothing can be carried in the public domain, and shopping is strictly forbidden. Foods must be prepared in advance, so observant Jews customarily devote much of Friday (and any day preceding a holiday) to marketing, cooking, baking, and cleaning. The Sabbath itself is marked by religious services, study, and family observances.

Since the *Crown Kosher* plaintiffs had raised the question of the validity of a state statute (the Massachusetts Sunday closing law) and sought to enjoin its enforcement under the federal Constitution, Calvert Magruder, as Chief Justice of the First Circuit, was required to appoint a three-judge panel to hear the suit.[13] Magruder designated Circuit Judge Peter Woodbury and District Judge William T. McCarthy to sit with him to decide the case. The hearing before the three-judge panel took place on November 13, 1958. The panel received testimony from Harold Chernock, the manager of Crown Kosher, and heard legal arguments on disputed points of law. The chief counsel for Crown Kosher was Herbert B. Ehrmann, then-president of the American Jewish Committee, and a distinguished Boston lawyer who had represented Sacco and Vanzetti back in the 1920s.

---

13. The use of three-judge courts in this class of cases, with direct appeal to the U.S. Supreme Court, began in 1910. See Boskey and Gressman, "Recent Reforms in the Federal Judicial Structure—Three-Judge District Courts and Appellate Review," 67 F.R.D. 135 (1975); Charles Alan Wright, *The Law of Federal Courts* (4th ed.; West Publishers; Eagan, Minn., 1983), §50. Congress believed that the panel of three instead of a single federal judge would reduce local resentment caused by federal interference in state matters. See 36 Stat. 539, 557, later codified as 28 U.S.C. Secs. 2281, 2284. This practice ended in 1976. See Pub. L. No. 94–381; 90 Stat. 1119.

In a colloquy between Ehrmann and Judge McCarthy over the issue of whether the Sunday laws represented an establishment of religion, McCarthy asked: "Well, what freedom do they [the Jews] give up? They can go to the synagogue [on Sunday] can't they? . . . Many of the Jewish synagogues are open on Sundays, aren't they? I mean those of the Reform synagogues."[14] In his reply Ehrmann politely reminded the judge that the people involved were strict observers of the Sabbath. He noted that the pressures on Orthodox Jews to give up their faith were enormous. Ehrmann added:

> Along comes the Commonwealth of Massachusetts and then adds a criminal penalty if they do anything on Sundays; and I suggest to this court as strongly as I can, that to pressure people to give up their faith by making their business suffer a great loss, as the Crown Kosher Supermarket would if it had to close on Saturday and Sunday also, and render it inconvenient and difficult to observe their duties if they want to buy food on Sunday that is ritualistically proper—that there has been added a terrific pressure, backed by the criminal machinery of Massachusetts, to observe some other day than their Sabbath.[15]

McCarthy took a jurisprudential approach. He argued that this was a legislative rather than a judicial matter. "[D]id the Crown Kosher Supermarket . . . at any time ask for relief in the General Court?" McCarthy asked.[16] Ehrmann replied that it had but that this would not resolve the constitutional issues before the court. Ehrmann also pointed out that Chernock had tried to get a special exemption through the General Court to relieve Crown Kosher's situation. But McCarthy was convinced that the supermarket was looking for commercial advantage, pure and simple:

> Isn't the gist of your complaint here that the religious liberties granted under the First Amendment of the Constitution should be extended so as to protect the business interest of those who are in a minority, that is, so far as observance of Sunday as the Lord's Day is concerned? . . . Saturday he has to do his shopping; Sun-

---

14. Transcript of Record, Supreme Court of the United States, October Term, 1960, No. 11 (*Gallagher* v. *Crown Kosher Supermarket. et. al.*), 68–69. Located in the Herbert B. Ehrmann Papers, Harvard Law School Library, Box 20, folder 4.
15. Ibid., 70.
16. Ibid., 80.

> day he has a chance if he cares to, to go to his church or synagogue. . . . Don't you think the men who gave us this country of ours . . . were wonderful men . . . that came over here from persecuted lands and obviously set up a government such as we have, set up a law a hundred years before the union of a nation, the union of the thirteen states and of the United States. . . . They couldn't satisfy everybody trying to fix a day; and so well was that fixed, Mr. Ehrmann, that you can't make a contract on Sunday. . . . I didn't like what you said about the family or the founders of the republic, and that's why I said it. I don't agree with you.[17]

McCarthy's little "speech"[18] showed how little he comprehended the problem facing the court or the peculiar predicament of the observant Jewish minority whom Harold Chernock represented. He asked if Ehrmann was aware of the fact that "the signers of the Declaration of Independence were Jews, Protestants and Catholics?" Ehrmann answered by recounting a well-known tale from Jewish history. When Rabbi Hillel, the great sage from Talmudic times, was asked to explain the essence of Jewish law while standing on one foot, it is said that he replied: "Do not do unto others that which you would not have them do unto you. That is the Law. All the rest is commentary." Ehrmann concluded: "I didn't intend to talk like this but your Honor inspired me to do it. . . ." Ehrmann then applied Rabbi Hillel's comment to the Constitution: "So I feel that the First and Fourteenth Amendments are there to translate into the basic law of our country the concept, that just because you have a majority you don't take advantage of or you don't push a minority; and the way we live together in a democracy is, we all to have to respect one another."[19]

Ehrmann ended by offering to supply the court with a pamphlet prepared by the Union of Orthodox Jewish Congregations that would further explain the complexities of the Jewish dietary code. He concluded with an eloquent appeal: "To many of us [these laws] seem very simple. Why can't you do this? Why can't you do that? How these Orthodox co-religionists of mine can cling to their devotion and all the difficulties that they have in their diet, as well

---

17. Ibid., 71, 74.
18. Lloyd Starrett, then Judge Magruder's law clerk, was present at the hearing and kept handwritten of the proceedings. Starrett characterized this long and turgid commentary from the bench as a "speech." CMP, Box 30, folder 3.
19. Transcript of Record, 77.

as the difficulties engendered by Sunday, is beyond me because it just expresses a devotion to their faith which is superhuman. . . ."[20]

On May 18, 1959, the three-judge district court struck down the Massachusetts Sunday closing law as applied to the Crown Kosher Supermarket by a two-to-one majority. In his opinion for the court, Calvert Magruder dismissed as insubstantial various procedural defenses advanced by the defendants.[21] Then, with his customary lucidity, Magruder went to the core issues presented by the case. He traced the history of Massachusetts Sunday closing legislation from 1653 to the present and noted the existence of more than seventy amendments enacted by the legislature in response to pressure groups seeking exemptions from blue-law enforcement. He dismissed the contention that the Sunday law was merely a secular day-of-rest statute, noting that a wholly separate statute imposed an obligation on employers to provide one day of relief from work each week.[22] Magruder argued that the law put an economic penalty, in effect, an unconstitutional burden upon plaintiffs' observance of Saturday as their Sabbath. "What Massachusetts has done," he declared, "is to furnish special protection to dominant Christian sects which celebrate Sunday as the Lord's day, without furnishing such protection . . . to those Christian sects and to Orthodox and Conservative Jews who observe Saturday as the Sabbath . . . to the prejudice of the latter group."[23] Magruder declared the law to be one that supported an establishment of religion for some while denying its free exercise to others. It violated the Equal Protection clause of the Fourteenth Amendment because the system of exceptions that made some activities exempt but others not was totally illogical and irrational—"and almost unbelievable hodgepodge."[24] The decision was a stunning victory

---

20. Ibid., 131.
21. Defendants raised issues of *res judicata*, standing, and the equitable jurisdiction of a three-judge federal court to enjoin the enforcement of a state statute. For Magruder's discussion of these points, see 176 F. Supp. 466 at 470–472. Professor Arthur E. Sutherland, Magruder's Harvard Law School colleague, believed that issues of standing and state action had merit, however. Sutherland to Paul Blanchard, January 12, 1961, Arthur E. Sutherland Papers, Harvard Law School Library (hereinafter "AESP"), Box 4, folder 3.
22. 176 F. Supp., 473. (See M.G.L. c. 149 S. 47, et seq.)
23. Ibid., 475.
24. Ibid., 472.

for Crown Kosher and other Sabbatarians who did not regard Sunday as a sacred day of rest.[25]

In a long dissenting opinion, Judge McCarthy disputed *Crown Kosher*'s factual allegations. He suggested that the grocery and baked goods sold at Crown Kosher were not kosher products at all but ordinary food and that Crown Kosher's primary motivation was commercial rather than religious. Commenting on the standing of the plaintiffs to bring the suit, McCarthy declared:

> I believe that the individual plaintiffs are before the court as "window dressing" to enable the corporate plaintiff to rely upon arguments that freedom of religion has been infringed and thereby help the corporate plaintiff to gain a commercial competitive advantage.[26]

What would prevent someone "from forming or joining a religious body which observes its Sabbath the day of the week on which his business is lowest?" McCarthy queried.[27] "He would then have the constitutional right to remain open on Sunday and do business with any and all customers." "But,"said McCarthy, "the law of Orthodox Judaism . . . is not part of the jurisprudence controlling this court."[28]

McCarthy held to the position he had taken at the hearing—namely, that his was a matter for a political majority in the state legislature to resolve. "[O]ur's is a government of laws predicated upon majority rule," he wrote. And if the majority agreed that Sunday should be a day set aside for comfort, safety, rest, and spiritual reflection, who was Harold Chernock to question it? McCarthy continued with an even more extraordinary comment:

> We cannot become prisoners of a false philosophy, which is truly dialectical materialisms and which in plain language represents the philosophy of Marx, Engel [sic] and Lenin, neither can we deny the right of others to disagree with our point of view. But is the person promoting this suit actuated by the spirit of the

---

25. Of the four cases coming from Federal courts that would receive full review by the U.S. Supreme Court, Magruder's court was the only one to find in favor of those petitioners seeking constitutional relief.
26. Ibid., 479.
27. Ibid., 488.
28. Ibid.

> early founders of this great country, is he safeguarding the rights and privileges of our American society or is he using this as a medium by which to destroy these spiritual and economic values, the inevitable result of which might well be complete destruction of our way of life.[29]

McCarthy had not finished. Referring to Crown Kosher's daily cashbook, he noted that substantial profits were taken in on Labor Day and the Fourth of July as well as on Sundays, evidence to him of "the commercial point of view in contradistinction to the spiritual and patriotic background, of a day dedicated to the courage and Americanism of our Founding Fathers . . . and the Crown Kosher meat market so-called remained open."[30]

Not only did McCarthy question plaintiffs' motives—their "alleged religious belief," he called it[31] —but he linked their grievance to leftist ideology. "Until very recently," he wrote, "there was scarcely a voice raised against what has become a traditional part of our way of life." McCarthy foresaw evil consequences if the Magruder decision were allowed to stand. Rather than advancing the cause of religious freedom, "its inevitable effect will be to disunite and divide the people of this Commonwealth, to dislocate our economic set-up, and to lay the foundation for the growth and development of cancer 'isms." . . .[32] After all, Orthodox Jews were "but a small percentage of the population," and it was for the Massachusetts General court to determine whether or not the rights they claimed should be recognized in view of their decidedly minority status.

Although the jurisprudential approach was later vindicated when the United States Supreme Court reversed the three-judge panel's decision in *Gallagher* v. *Crown Kosher Supermarket,*[33] McCarthy was unable to understand the genuine and deeply-felt religious convictions that had pushed the petitioners to bring their lawsuit. Otherwise, McCarthy could never have concluded that "under

---

29. Ibid., 490.
30. Ibid., 491.
31. Ibid., 490.
32. Ibid., 491–492.
33. 366 U.S. 617 (1961).

the cloak of religion a one-man corporation [is] using a spiritual garment as a medium by which unjustly to enrich himself."[34]

The Jewish community hailed the *Crown Kosher* decisions as a great victory. An editorial in the *Jewish Advocate*, New England's largest English language Jewish newspaper, said that the court "had breathed new life into the Equal Protection and Due Process clauses of the Fourteenth Amendment. . . . The court, by removing this slight to the Constitution, has answered another healthy challenge [to] our great experiment in democratic living and . . . justice in the American system."[35] Soon after the Magruder decision, the American Jewish Congress, a leader in the fight for fair Sabbath laws throughout the country, declared that the court had been able to examine the Orthodox position dispassionately. The AJC called it a "patently rational and just decision."[36] Jewish groups were not the only ones who applauded the outcome of the case. The International Religious Liberty Association, a Seventh Day Adventist group based in Washington, D.C., and dedicated "to secur[ing] worldwide recognition of and respect for the basic human right to freedom of conscience and belief," invited Judge Magruder to prepare an article on the subject of the unconstitutionality of Sunday closing laws for *Liberty Magazine*, an invitation that Judge Magruder cordially declined.[37]

Public reaction to the decision came by mail from persons known and unknown. Judge John Spalding of the Massachusetts Supreme Judicial Court expressed approval, as did Alex Lincoln, a Magruder acquaintance from Meredith, New Hampshire.[38] Lincoln explained that some of the Founding Fathers "were not Christians in the strict sense but the earlier immigrants were and the more vociferous among more modern Christians are."[39] And from Mermaid Avenue in the Coney Island section of Brooklyn, one

34. Ibid., 492.
35. *Jewish Advocate*, May 21, 1959, 10.
36. *Congress Bi-Weekly: A Review of Jewish Interests*, June 15, 1959, Vol. 26, no. 11.
37. Lemuel E. Esteb to Calvert Magruder, June 1, 1959: J.A. Buckwalter to Calvert Magruder, May 25, June 1, 1959; Calvert Magruder to J.A. Buckwalter, June 9, 1959, CMP, Box 29, folder 5.
38. Magruder to Judge John V. Spalding, July 14, 1959, CMP, Box 29, Folder 5. Spalding had been a member of the SJC panel in *Commonwealth* v. *Chernock*, 336 Mass. 384 (1957), but had not dissented from that decision, which upheld the constitutionality of the Sunday law under the Massachusetts Constitution.
39. Alexander Lincoln to Calvert Magruder, June 26, 1959, CMP, Box 29, folder 5.

Irving Friedman, an Orthodox Jewish shopkeeper, wrote that he had received a summons for opening on Sundays and that he wished to fight it out in the courts. Enclosing a stamped self-addressed envelope, Friedman invited Magruder's reply to the question, "as to what law in the Constititon of the United States [sic] . . . you base your ruling that the Sunday Sabbath laws are discriminatory and unconstitutional as Saturday is my Sabbath day, not Sunday."[40] Magruder replied that the opinion would have to speak for itself and politely suggested that "whether what I said applied to the statute in New York I do not undertake to say, and certainly you couldn't expect me to issue you any legal advice."[41]

Not all of the reactions to the decision were complimentary, however. A resident of East Natick, Massachusetts, wrote: "It is quite depressing to realize that the wise restraints which the early Christian settlers of Massachusetts placed on themselves—may be so easily set aside in the Twentieth Century." The writer applauded Magruder's decision to move to California after his retirement. "I think your choice of California as your future home is wise—believing as you do—that offices and all types of stores are open for business on Sunday in that state—and purchases of any item may be made."[42]

The initial reaction of the Catholic hierarchy was hostile. Richard Cardinal Cushing, the leader of the Boston Archdiocese, declared that Sunday had apparently lost its religious significance in the minds of many modern statesmen and jurists. The Cardinal said that "once we allow business as usual on Sunday, it is but a short step to the complete secularization of the day that was once known as the Lord's day."[43] Cushing feared that religious activities such as Sunday observance had been abandoned in favor of amusements and diversion. "Let us react strongly to the danger before it is too late," he said. "We must prove that it is the wish of the greater majority that the traditional observance of Sunday be

---

40. Irving Friedman to Calvert Magruder, June 4, 1959, CMP Box 30, folder 2. As far as can be determined, there is no relationship between this Friedman and the Sam Friedman who was prosecuted by New York in an earlier test of the New York Sunday Blue Law; *People* v. *Friedman,* 302 N.Y. 75 (1950); *app. Dism'd., Friedman* v. *New York,* 341 U.S. 907 (1951).

41. Calvert Magruder to Irving Friedman, June 5, 1959, CMP, Box 30, folder 2.

42. Mary H. O'Neill to Calvert Magruder, June 26, 1959, CMP, Box 29, folder 8.

43. *Boston Daily Globe*, June 24, 1959.

retained and safeguarded from attack by those who would destroy religion in the name of democracy."[44]

The *Pilot*, the official newspaper organ of the Archdiocese, declared, "It would be hard to imagine a Federal court issuing a decision more confusing and fatuous."[45] Professing its concern for civil and religious liberty, the *Pilot* took the position that Sunday closing laws protected the welfare of the entire community by setting aside a single day on which only "necessary business activities are continued and normal business matters are suspended." The paper observed that "the decision is one subversive of the good order of the community and itself discriminatory in favor of those whose religious commitments are observed on some day other than Sunday." Sunday laws, declared the *Pilot*, supported the spiritual fiber of the citizenry. It urged "religious Christians [to] see to it that the day of rest established by law is not so debased as to discourage Christian worship and to distract from Christian observance."[46] The *Pilot* called upon the Attorney General of the Commonwealth to appeal the decision to the United States Supreme Court.

The *Pilot* editorial elicited spirited replies. One letter writer said that since "no single day will satisfy all citizens, the democratic thing to do seems to be to satisfy the wishes of the majority."[47] Another saw the court's decision as likely to evoke "a cacophonous chorus from the faith-healers, religious anarchists, snake-worshippers, vegetarians, and a horde of other crackpots."[48] This writer compared Crown Kosher's situation to the economic inconvenience suffered by Catholics forced to support a public school system that, as a community, Catholics did not use. He concluded that, "the same groups that have fought against economic oppression through a common day of rest are usually those fighting for economic oppression when we want Catholic school

---

44. *Boston Traveler*, June 24, 1959.
45. The *Pilot*, May 23, 1959.
46. Paul Blanchard, counsel to Protestants and Other Americans United for Separation of Church and State, predicted that "a Jewish victory" in this case would lead to increased Catholic demands for "fair" treatment in the distribution of public funds for parochial schools. In general, Blanchard was surprised by the "vehemence with which Catholic leaders are defending the present Massachusetts Law." Blanchard to Arthur E. Sutherland, January 9, 1961, AESP, Box 4, folder 3.
47. The *Pilot*, May 30, 1959 (letter by J.P. O'Neil).
48. Ibid., (letter of K.L.).

children to enjoy their full rights as citizens on bus transportation and other matters. . . ."[49] Still another question "whether these people with ultra-delicate religious sensitivities are going to respect the feelings of others when they have the law twisted to their ends"—specifically, whether employees who observed the Sabbath on Sunday would be allowed to do this if their employers could do business on that day."[50] The *Pilot* reprinted only one letter that challenged the paper's editorial policy, a letter that questioned why, if Sunday closing laws were essentially civic and not religious in character, "most of the groups filing *amicus curiae* briefs on both sides of the issue are religious groups?"[51]

On June 2nd, the *Boston Globe* ran a debate between two eminent legal authorities, Father Robert F. Drinan, S.J., then dean of the Boston College Law School, and Professor Mark De Wolfe Howe, the distinguished Harvard legal historian. Drinan criticized the decision on two grounds: first, that it was costly to the state, and second, that it led to the violation of the religious liberty of other groups. He predicted that there would be added expense in "ferreting out the inevitable racketeer who practices unabashed commercialism on Sunday." Drinan also wondered whether Christians would be able to refuse work on Sundays for employers who observed the Sabbath on Saturday. "One can only hope that the demands of a militant minority, confronted with the settled customs of three centuries, will not unwittingly bring about unfortunate results for any individual group or for the moral health of America's society."[52] Mark De Wolfe Howe vigorously defended the Magruder opinion. He called the opinion a "victory of good sense and intellectual honesty" and urged the Massachusetts legislature to face up to a question that it had long debated. Howe found it difficult to believe that such a decision could possibly mark the "downfall of spiritual values."[53]

Given the excitement that the *Crown Kosher* decision engendered and the anomalous fact of a lower federal court declaring unconstitutional a state statute that had been repeatedly upheld by

---

49. Ibid.
50. Ibid., (letter of F.X.O'M.).
51. Ibid., (letter of R.S.).
52. *Boston Globe*, June 2, 1959. Father Drinan later published a more considered and less strident article on the subject. See *America* (August 19, 1961), 627–630.
53. Ibid.

the state's own highest court, it is not surprising that two weeks after the decision came down, a Springfield district court found the proprietor's of two West Springfield plant nurseries guilty of violating the Sunday closing laws and fined them each $50 dollars. The judge simply held that the *Crown Kosher* ruling was not applicable to the case before him and that the judgment of the three-judge panel in *Crown Kosher* applied only to the petitioners and those similarly situated.[54]

Even though the state courts were not bound by the federal court's ruling,[55] the Commonwealth was determined to have the decision overturned. But when a petition for a rehearing was filed, Magruder and Woodbury denied it in a short *per curiam* opinion.[56] McCarthy again dissented, arguing that the assistant attorney general had not prepared the case adequately. McCarthy adhered to his view that the entire lawsuit was an unfair competition case rather than a First Amendment case.[57] But appeal to the Supreme Court was inevitable. Magruder expected a thorough hearing and a full opinion from the high court.[58] On September 19th, 1959, Massachusetts Attorney General Edward J. McCormack filed a notice of appeal in the U.S. Supreme Court.[59] The Court ordered oral arguments in four cases coming from Pennsylvania, Maryland,

---

54. *Boston Globe*, June 2, 1959.

55. Even if the decision had had general application, state courts are not bound by decisions of the lower Federal courts but only by decisions of the U.S. Supreme Court. This doctrine was well established in Massachusetts. See *Brown* v. *Palmer Clay Prod. Co.*, 290 Mass. 108, 110 (1935) ("[State courts] are not concluded by decisions of other Federal Courts"); *Lapp Insulator Co., Inc.* v. *Boston & Maine Railroad,* 330 Mass. 205, 209 (1953) ("[State courts give] such consideration to the decisions of lower Federal courts as we think they are entitled."). The *Brown* and *Insulator Company* cases were in force at the time *Crown Kosher* was decided. The Supreme Judicial Court recently reaffirmed this principle in *Commonwealth* v. *Montanez*, 388 Mass. 603, 604 (1983). As the Supreme Court has held, state courts are the ultimate expositors of state law, and lower Federal court decisions are not binding. *Mulaney* v. *Wilbur*, 421 U.S. 684 (1975).

56. 176 F. Supp. 492.

57. 178 F. Supp. 336.

58. Lloyd Starrett to Magruder, February 18, 1960; Magruder to Starrett, February 24, 1960, CMP, Box 41, folder 14.

59. *New York Times*, September 20, 1959.

and Massachusetts on April 25th, 1960.[60] The cases were heard on December 7th and 8th.[61]

Two years after the *Crown Kosher* case was decided by the federal district court, the United States Supreme Court reversed. The high court upheld the constitutionality of Sunday closing laws against a variety of constitutional challenges.[62] Eight of the nine justices held that Sunday closing laws did not violate the Establishment Clause of the First Amendment. Chief Justice Earl Warren wrote the principal opinion; while Felix Frankfurter wrote a lengthy concurrence.[63] Only Justice William O. Douglas dissented. How-

---

60. *New York Times*, April 26, 1960.
61. *New York Times*, Dec. 8, 1960. The Supreme Court decided to make a major pronouncement on the question in order to resolve a division among the circuits, specifically the anomaly of a Federal District Court in Pennsylvania upholding Sunday laws against a challenge by an Orthodox Jew while another federal court in Massachusetts was overturning similar legislation. In addition, the whole question was receiving increasing attention throughout the country. The volumes of the *America Jewish Year Book* for the years 1959, 1960, 1961, and 1962 show increasing public attention to the problem and increasing litigation.
62. *McGowan* v. *State of Maryland*, 366 U.S. 420; *Gallagher* v. *Crown Kosher Super Mkt. of Mass.*, 366 U.S. 617; *Two Guys From Harrison-Allentown* v. *McGinley*, 366 U.S. 582; *Braundfield* v. *Brown*, 366 U.S. 599 (1961). See 29 U.S.L.W. 3173 (Dec. 13, 1960) for an account of the oral argument before the Supreme Court in the *Crown Kosher* appeal. The weight of judicial opinion was clearly on the side of the appellants. Arthur E. Sutherland of Harvard, the principal author of the Commonwealth's brief to the high court, noted this in a message to the assistant attorney general who was in charge of the Commonwealth's appeal. "At no place in [appellees'] brief do they meet the point that the vast weight of adjudication is against them, and this, it seems to me, is our biggest point." Sutherland to Joseph H. Elcock, Jr., November 7, 1960, AESP, Box 4, folder 2. In general, Sutherland orchestrated a highly coordinated research and writing effort that produced an extremely effective brief. In effect, one Harvard Law professor (Sutherland) was trying to persuade another Harvard Law professor (Frankfurter) to overturn a third Harvard Law professor (Magruder). Sutherland felt honored by the role the Massachusetts Attorney General asked him to play in the *Crown Kosher* Appeal. Congratulating the AG on his re-election to another term of office, he wrote: "I have been trying to think up an appropriate title for myself so that I can boast to my grandchildren of my official connection. Thus far I have been calling myself Deputy Assistant Acting Temporary Ad Hoc Attorney-General for Purposes of *Crown Kosher* cases." Sutherland to Edward J. McCormack, Jr., November 14, 1960, AESP, Box 4, folder 2.
63. Herbert Ehrmann later concluded that the decision was "influenced by Felix's philosophy that a state statute should never be upset if the Justices can possibly find some rational basis for its existence." During oral argument Ehrmann "managed to win what is probably the biggest laugh in Supreme Court history"

ever, only six of the justices could agree that Sunday laws did not deprive Orthodox Jews of their First Amendment right of "free exercise." On this issue Justice Douglas was joined in dissent by Potter Stewart and William Brennan. Stewart's decision was particularly forceful. He called the choice between religious faith and economic survival a "cruel" one that no state should be permitted to require. Justice Douglas observed that Sunday laws "serve and satisfy the religious predispositions of our Christian communities." Douglas could not understand "how a state can make protesting citizens refrain from doing innocent acts on Sunday because the doing of those acts offends the sentiments of their Christian neighbors."

In a plurality opinion, the Chief Justice rejected Magruder's characterization of the Sunday laws as an "unbelievable hodge-podge." Warren simply stated that they were "reasonably explainable on their face,"[64] and, therefore that they did not violate the Equal Protection Clause of the Fourteenth Amendment. On the main thrust of *Crown Kosher*'s complaint—that the Massachusetts Sunday closing statute went against the religion clauses of the First Amendment—Warren took the position that "for the most part [Sunday closing laws] have been divorced from the religious orientation of their predecessors."[65] Having found that neither in purpose nor in effect were these laws primarily religious in character, the Court declared that they did not establish a religion.[66] As to *Crown Kosher*'s claim that the plaintiffs were denied the right of free exercise of religion, Warren distinguished between *religious beliefs* which were entitled to absolute protection under the Free Exercise Clause, and *actions* motivated by religious belief which

---

when, in probing some of the inconsistencies in the Massachusetts Sunday Closing Law that permitted dredging for oysters but not for clams, Frankfurter queried: "Is there, Mr. Ehrmann, any religious difference between a clam and an oyster?" To which Ehrmann responded, after the laughter subsided, "Not for Orthodox Jews, Mr. Justice Frankfurter." See Herbert M. Ehrmann, "Felix," in Wallace Mendelson (ed.), *Felix Frankfurter: A Tribute,* (New York: Reynal, 1964). 119–120. Harold Chernock remembers this exchange but insists that no one in the audience found it amusing because no one laughed. Chernock Interview, July 25, 1991.

64. 366 U.S 623.

65. Ibid., 626.

66. Ibid., 630.

were not.[67] The fact that the Sunday law made the practice of religion more expensive to the believer was not a direct burden on religious freedom and, therefore, did not constitute a violation of the Free Exercise Clause. According to the Chief Justice, state legislatures had the power to determine that exemptions for Orthodox observers might lead to commercial activity that would deprive Sunday of its special character. In addition, the competitive advantages created by the exemption might create economic pressures on others to do business on Sunday.[68] This would force the state to inquire into the good faith of those claiming exemption on religious grounds. Exemptions might also encourage violations of anti-discrimination statutes because exempted employers would tend to hire only their co-religionists as employees.

Soon after the Supreme Court decision came down, Magruder wrote to Peter Woodbury: "I am sorry that I led you astray in the *Kosher* case. No doubt you would have done better to have followed your friend Bill McCarthy."[69] Woodbury replied: "You do not need to feel sorry that you [led] me astray in the *Crown Kosher* case. As an aider and abettor I am as guilty as you. . . . At least a majority of the [Supreme] Court could not find common ground on which to say we were wrong. I still think we were right."[70]

---

67. In drawing the distinction between *belief* and *actions*, a distinction particularly inappropriate when applied to Jewish Orthodoxy, Warren invoked a line of decisions going back to the nineteenth century, particularly the Mormon polygamy cases. *Reynolds* v. *U.S.*, 98 U.S. 145 (1878). Two years after the Supreme Court's decision in *Crown Kosher*, however, the High Court recognized that some conduct was protected under the Free Exercise Clause even from state legislation that only indirectly burdened religious practices. In *Sherbert* v. *Verner*, 374 U.S. 411 (1963), a divided Court held that a state could not withhold unemployment compensation benefits from a Sabbatarian who refused to accept employment that requited work on Saturdays. In general, see "Developments-Religion and the State," 100 *Harvard Law Review* 1601–1781, 1707 (1987).

68. On this point, the Chief Justice cited several extracts from debates in Parliament, one of which reads as follows: "It is true that the orthodox Jew will only be allowed to trade until two o'clock on Sunday, but during that time he will have a monopoly. That is a tremendous advantage." 101 Parliamentary Debates (Lords) 430, (cited at) 366 U.S. 599, 609 n6.

69. Magruder to Woodbury, June 2, 1961, CMP, Box 29, folder 5.

70. Woodbury to Magruder. June 5, 1961, CMP, Box 29, folder 9.

Magruder was never comfortable with the publicity surrounding the case.[71] Supreme Court reversals always pained him deeply. He was particularly hurt by Felix Frankfurter's scholarly concurring opinion. Anticipating his friend's dismay at the reversal, Frankfurter had written Magruder a short note:

> Now that it's all over, let me say that at the end of my heavy labors in the Sunday laws cases I felt as I did when I first read your Kosher opinion, namely great admiration for one of the best opinions it fell to me to study. It really was first rate. You know me well enough to know, as also you know my professional attitudes, that disagreement in result has nothing to do with any professional appreciation.[72]

Magruder was not mollified. In a lengthy and detailed letter, he ventilated his feeling on "the Kosher cases." "As I said to you once," Magruder wrote Frankfurter, "you have your job to do, and I have mine, and the most that either of us can hope for is that each of us will do his respective job conscientiously and competently."[73] Magruder explained that it seemed to him that the opinions in which he put the most effort were the ones least appealing to a majority of the high court. He reminded Frankfurter that Justice Hugo Black's memo to Frankfurter on *Crown Kosher* written soon after the District Court's decision, was a good example of this: "In the Kosher case, you sent a copy of my opinion to Hugo Black, who responded in a carefully phrased statement that left him uncommitted as to the ultimate disposition of the particular case, as my law clerk

---

71. Magruder's son Michael remembers the *Crown Kosher* case and his father's reaction to the newspaper publicity: "I don't think he enjoyed the public exposure that came out of that. He just wasn't the type to cultivate it. It was actively written about for several days after it came out. I don't think he particularly enjoyed that aspect of it." Author's interview with Mrs. Calvert Magruder and Michael Magruder, July 10, 1986.

72. The note is published in the 26 *Harvard Law School Bulletin* 26 (1974) 9. A year earlier Frankfurter had admonished Magruder "What matters—and what ought to matter to you—is the impressive quality of your opinion and not the inadequacy of a majority in reversing it." Frankfurter to Magruder, May 26, 1960, CMP, Box 29, folder 6.

73. Magruder to Frankfurter, June 27, 1961, CMP, Box 29, folder 6.

[Lloyd Starrett] was quick to observe."[74] Magruder then went on to express his deepest convictions about the case:

> With references to the Kosher case, while I was impressed by the amount of research that went into your opinion, I was disappointed particularly that you lined up with the Chief on the religious issue. The truth is that you fellows act like a bunch of Christians, and you do not take too seriously the bold assertions of separation of church and state which appear in other connections. . . .The Supreme Court is content to sustain legislation which buttresses the observances of 'Sunday' as it is celebrated by the dominant Christian sect. I don't know why the judges should be the one group of persons who fail to recognize that. Why do you think that the Archdiocesan Council of Catholic Men joined with the Lord's Day League of New England in filing a brief amicus curiae having the purpose of "preventing the further secularization and commercialization of the Lord's day?"[75]

With respect to Judge McCarthy's position, which had now been vindicated by the Supreme Court, Magruder wrote:

> I could never quite understand the feelings of my colleague Bill McCarthy. He seemed to recognize the hardship of the Sunday law on Orthodox Jews who are thus put to the dilemma of choosing between their religion and their business. He seemed to feel that the Massachusetts legislature should specifically pass an exemption for stores like Crown Kosher Super Market. I thought that the legislature had done this, but *Commonwealth* v. *Has* . . . said not, and of course that is the sort of question in which the Massachusetts court says the final word.[76]

Magruder ended with strong criticism of the Supreme Court's decision on the religious question. The district court had viewed this as central, but the Chief Justice made a "shabby pretense of sustaining the Sunday laws as a mere secular day-of-rest statute."

---

74. The memo from Hugo Black read as follows: "The opinion will last, I think, whatever may turn out to be the fate of the holding."
75. Since 1940 Magruder himself had been a junior warden in Christ Church, Cambridge. See Gardener M. Day, *The Biography of a Church: A Brief History of Christ Church, Cambridge, Massachusetts* (Cambridge, [n.p.],1951) 137.
76. Magruder to Frankfurter, *supra* note 74.

Public opinion was predictably divided. A grandmother from Natick, Massachusetts lamented the fact that "our Sunday is no longer considered a day of worship and rest but a day of big business. I . . . have seen Sundays lose meaning since I was a little girl."[77] Obviously, the writer supported the High Court's decision. But a Chicopee father complained that because of the Sunday law, he could not go for a pleasure ride with his son in their pick-up truck because this would violate the restrictions on travel which still existed in Massachusetts as late as 1961. He thought the law was "old-fashioned, unfair to the modern world and completely ridiculous."[78] The writer's Northhampton friend had received a ten dollar fine for attempting to go fishing with his wife and children. "Now I ask you, as one person to another, is this right? I don't think so, not in a free Society."[79]

The Jewish community received the news of the Supreme Court's decision with "great disappointment."[80] On a national level there was widespread agitation for reform of Sunday legislation. In Baltimore, Moses I. Feuerstein, president of the Union of Orthodox Jewish Congregations of America, called for "speedy action to correct a serious injustice in the American economic system. . . ."[81] At its bicentennial convention at the Waldorf-Astoria Hotel in New York City, the American Jewish Congress adopted a resolution charging that Sunday closing laws were discriminating and unequal in their operation.[82] Alvin C. Tamkin, president of the New England region of the AJC, took some comfort in the fact that the Court was deeply divided on the religious issue, evidence to him of growing awareness and sensitivity to the needs of religious minorities, Jews and non-Jews alike. Tamkin pledged renewed efforts to seek legislative relief for Sabbath observers and, if necessary, continued litigation. Tamkin singled out the opinions of Justices Douglas, Brennan, and Stewart as thin rays of hope in an otherwise gloomy atmosphere. A resolution of the National Community

---

77. Edith L. Ware to Arthur E. Sutherland, June 28, 1961, AESP, Box 55, folder 13.
78. John S. Zermny to Arthur E. Sutherland [June 1961], Ibid. These representative letters were written to the Sutherland Commission appointed by Governor Volpe soon after the Supreme Court decision.
79. Ibid.
80. *Jewish Advocate*, June 1, 1961.
81. *New York Times*, March 18, 1962, April 16, 1962.
82. *New York Times*, June 26, 1961.

Relations Advisory Council called for legislation action to exempt Sabbatarians from all Sunday closing laws.[83]

In Boston, the *Jewish Advocate* predicted that the effect of the Supreme Court's ruling would be to strengthen the hand of officials in many states seeking to uphold the blue laws. The AJC predicated that there would be "a spurt of legislative and administrative action to enact new Sunday laws, strengthen those on the books and institute more vigorous enforcement."[84] This is precisely what happened. There was a general crackdown. Orthodox businesses now faced vigorous Sunday closing enforcement. In Massachusetts, the statute provided that an exemption from the law could be obtained in any town by permission of the chief of police, but this required repeated applications and prior approval for each and every Sunday.[85] Not only did this put unusual discretionary power into the hands of local officials, always vulnerable to local pressure groups, but it also caused great uncertainly for local business people who would not know from week to week whether they could stay open on Sunday.[86] Prosecution became commonplace. Even minor infractions of the Sunday law were penalized.[87] A law

83. American Jewish Congress (Commission on Law and Social Action), Report (June 8, 1961) 8 (located at American Jewish Historical Society, Brandeis University).

84. M.G.L.c. 136 §7, formerly c. 136 §9.

85. Peter Woodbury observed "that a tangled situation developed in Massachusetts . . . in that in some towns the law was enforced and in others it was not. Perhaps all this will lead to a general overhaul of the Massachusetts Blue Laws to bring some semblance of order out of the present chaos." Woodbury to Magruder, June 5, 1961, CMP, Box 29, folder 9.

86. The local newspapers began reporting a multitude of cases involving blue law violations. See clippings file, AESP, Box 32, folder 2.

87. The *American Jewish Year Book* reported that in 1962 "the Lord's Day Law in Massachusetts was so strictly enforced that resort and home-building interests clamored for relief." *AJYB:* 64 (1963), 132. A well-publicized case was that of Charles S. Weinstein, the operator of Trans-American Spinning Mills in Fall River, Massachusetts. In August, 1961, Weinstein, an Orthodox Jew, sought a Superior Court order directing the Fall River police chief to issue a Sunday work permit. Weinstein had been granted exemptions fairly routinely until June, 1961, when the chief of police in Fall River began to follow a stricter policy of blue law enforcement. Weinstein was represented by Edward J. Barshak, regional counsel for the American Jewish Congress and Howard Whiteside of the Massachusetts Civil Liberties Union. Weinstein alleged that the refusal of the police to grant him a permit represented discrimination on the basis of religion. In view of the Supreme Court's recent decision in *Crown Kosher*, Barshak decided to approach

that had been largely forgotten—except for isolated cases, such as the case of the Crown Kosher market itself—suddenly became a basis for energetic enforcement.[88] The long-standing statement of principle of the Synagogue Council of America opposing the enactment or expansion of compulsory Sunday laws and urging exemption for persons observing another day as a religious day of rest had become an urgent call to action.[89]

While most of the public's attention focused upon church-state aspects of Sunday laws, supporters of reform proposals emphasized the millions of dollars of lost wages, business, and tourism that resulted from rigid adherence to the blue-law code.[90] An increasing amount of the nation's business was now also being conducted at "highway stores," the forerunners of today's shopping malls, which did their biggest trade on Sunday.[91]

But even at this late date there were voices of opposition from traditional Christian circles. The Reverend Dr. Melvin M. Forney, executive director of the Lord's Day Alliance, speaking at its annual meeting in the Madison Avenue Baptist Church in New York City declared: "It is suggested that we give up the observance of the Lord's Day because there may be others who do not observe

---

the problem not by attacking the constitutionality of the blue law head-on but by challenging the arbitrary and discriminatory manner of its administration. The corporation counsel argued that the Supreme Court had upheld the Massachusetts Sunday blue law as essentially a labor law and that there were no provisions in the operative statutory section dealing with religion or religious considerations. The complaint was dismissed, and the SJC affirmed the dismissal on appeal. *Weinstein* v. *Chief of Police of Fall River*, 182 N.E. 2d 525 (Mass. 1962). Weinstein was ultimately fined $100 by the Fall River District Court. This account is based upon the following newspaper reports: *Fall River Herald News*, August 24, 30, 31, 1961; September 27, 1961; October 11, 1961; *Jewish Advocate*, August 24, October 26, 1961; *New Bedford Standard Times*, September 1, 1961, October 18, 1961, as well as undated clippings and other documents furnished by Mr. and Mrs. Charles S. Weinstein of Brookline, Massachusetts.

88. "Safeguarding Religious Liberty: Statements of Policy and Position on Religious and Public Education and Other Aspects of Church-State Relationships," Synagogue Council of American and National Community Relations Advisory Council (December, 1957), located in American Jewish Historical Society, Brandeis University.

89. *New York Times*, June 10, 1962.

90. "Highway Stores Wanted Relaxation of the Sunday Laws, but Downtown Stores were Pressing for Tougher Enforcement." *New York Times*, April 26, 1960.

91. *New York Times*, Jan. 24, 1961.

Sunday as a holy day. . . . It is easy to see how deadly this concept can be to vitality of the Christian Movement. . . ."[92]

As a result of the growing public outcry over the Sunday law, Governor John A. Volpe appointed a special twenty-one person commission in June 1961 to study the Massachusetts closing law and to make specific recommendations for reform. Volpe selected Professor Arthur E. Sutherland of the Harvard Law School to serve as chairman. Sutherland had authored the Commonwealth's brief to the Supreme Court in the *Crown Kosher* case. The committee members represented a wide spectrum of interest and opinion from across the state. The Sutherland Committee, known officially as the Sunday Law Advisory Committee, met for five months, held a full day of public hearings, and collected data from a variety of sources. In its final report, a conservative majority favored keeping the Sunday virtually unchanged except for modernization as to form. The liberal minority, led by Sutherland, favored substantial changes in the law, including an exception for Sabbatarians (Seventh Day Sabbath observers).[93] But the majority and the minority agreed that some overhaul of the Massachusetts Sunday Law was needed, although no one on the committee recommended complete abolition of the law.

One year later, the Massachusetts legislature enacted a general revision of the Sunday closing law, which incorporated many of the Sutherland Committee's recommendations.[94] The revision did not provide for comprehensive Sabbatarian protection, however, and Jewish organizations as well as individuals began to press for further legislative relief to protect Orthodox interests. In Massachusetts, bills to exempt Sabbath observers and to reform the Sunday law had been filed even before the Supreme Court decided to grant *certiorari* in the *Crown Kosher* case,[95] and lobbying efforts to

---

92. Extensive manuscript material on the Sutherland Committee inquiry can be found in AESP, Box 55. The final report of the committee appears as [Massachusetts] Senate Document, No. 404 (January 1962). An analysis of the report is contained in an article by Wilfred E. Gardner, Jr., "Never On Sunday," *Harvard Law Record*, (February 14, 1962), 10–13. Ironically, Sutherland had changed sides. As a matter of Federal Constitutional law, he had argued to uphold the Sunday law, but now, as a matter of the state's social policy, he advocated substantial reform.
93. Mass. Acts & Resolves, chapter 616 (1962).
94. Lloyd Starrett to Magruder, February 18, 1960, CMP, Box 41, folder 14.
95. From the point of view of the Jewish community, one of the most significant aspects of the battle over the Sunday closing law was the unusual unanimity of

reform the law intensified early in 1962 when the Massachusetts House considered a bill to exempt Sabbatarians from the blue law. The bill had the support of the entire Jewish community, Orthodox and non-Orthodox alike.[96] Others supporting the measure included well-known liberal organizations such as the Americans for Democratic Action and the Massachusetts Civil Liberties Union.[97] In the House itself the fight was led by Representatives Fryda Koplow and Michael Dukakis of Brookline.

In 1962 the Massachusetts Senate actually approved an amendment to the blue law that would give Sabbatarians the exemption they had long desired. They vote was 21 to 14.[98] The National Social Action Commission of the Union of Orthodox Sisterhoods and the Massachusetts Council of Rabbis hailed the proposed exemption and praised those Senators who had voted for it. But the *Pilot* called the Senate action a "shocking assault" on the Sunday law.[99] The paper attacked senators who voted with the majority, saying that they had "responded to pressures that will destroy the Sunday observance in favor of those—principally Jews and Adventists—who worship on Saturday." The *Pilot* printed the names of all of those who had voted in favor of "the assault on the traditional Sunday observance," noting that "we will leave it to others to say how a careful, organized minority had done its work

---

sentiment from religious and secular groups on the issue. A long list of Jewish organizations "on record for a fair Sabbath law" was attached to court papers filed in the federal district court. These included the United Synagogue of America (Conservative), the Rabbinical Assembly of America (Conservative), the Rabbinical Council of America (Orthodox), the Union of American Hebrew Congregations (Reformed), the Union of Orthodox Jewish Congregations, the Jewish War Veterans, the Jewish Labor Committee, the Labor Zionist Organizations of America, the Zionist Organization of America, as well as B'nai B'rith, the American Jewish Congress, the American Jewish Committee, and a diverse assortment of other organizations. Not one of these organizations helped to defray any of Chernock's legal costs, however, which came to about one hundred thousand dollars. Chernock was never told that he had this kind of organizational support. Early on, an official from B'nai B'rith had told him that they would not touch the case because it was a religious issue and Bnai B'rith "didn't get involved in that." Chernock Interview, July 25, 1991.

96. The liberal community was deeply split by the question. Paul Blanchard to Arthur E. Sutherland, January 9, 1961, AESP, Box 4, folder 3.

97. *Boston Globe,* June 6, 1962.

98. The *Herald* supported the proposed exemption. See *Boston Herald,* June 21, 1962.

99. The *Pilot*, June 9, 1962.

to destroy the Sunday." *Pilot* editorials were read in parish churches along with the names of senators who had voted for measure. A few days later, a new Senate majority reconsidered the exemption and voted it down by a large margin of 31 to 8.[100] The *Pilot* commended the Senate's "prompt and intelligent action" and printed "the names of those Senators who threw out the unhappy amendment which would have destroyed Sunday as the day of rest."[101]

The Boston Jewish Community Council observed that a majority of Massachusetts senators were convinced of the reasonableness of an exemption for strict Sabbath observers, but that they had succumbed to strong pressure from the Archdiocese. The *Jewish Advocate* denounced the *Pilot* for restoring what it called "a naked display of pressure, heretofore unrevealed in this Commonwealth." The *Advocate* said that the Senate reversal was a "stinging blow . . . to democracy and freedom of conscience."[102] Rabbi Samuel J. Fox, chairman of the Social Action Committee of the Massachusetts Council of Rabbis (Orthodox), charged the *Pilot* with "striking panic in the hearts of the legislators, with most vicious results still being felt on Beacon Hill. To this day Senators are receiving threatening letters and anti-Sabbatarian insults from those who were stirred up by this propaganda." The Jewish Community Council called for a full investigation of the pressure tactics employed by the *Pilot*.[103]

But the position of the Roman Catholic Church began to soften. In April 1963, *America*, the Jesuit weekly, came out in favor of a fair-Sabbath law for New York City. An editorial on April 20th acknowledged the need to "relieve conscientious Jews of . . . an inequity" and observed that a modification of the Sunday law would be "a pragmatic adjustment of the law to meet one of the realities of pluralistic society."[104]

In Massachusetts, lobbying efforts to reform the law continued for the next several years. William Schwartz, then a young practicing attorney, prepared a new proposal for legislative consideration.

---

100. *Boston Record American*, June 12, 1962; *Boston Herald*, June 12, 1962.
101. The *Pilot*, June 16, 1962; *New York Times*, June 13, 1962.
102. *Jewish Advocate*, June 14, 1962.
103. This account is based upon the report in the *American Jewish Year Book* 64 (1963), 132–133 (1963), located at the American Jewish Historical Society, Brandeis University. See also *New York Times*, June 10 1962.
104. *America*, April 20, 1963.

Schwartz deliberately modeled his draft on the Sunday closing law that had been adopted in the neighboring state of Vermont in August 1961 and which contained an exemption for Sabbath observers.[105] This gave the proponents of the measure a tactical and psychological advantage. If conservative Vermont could have such an exemption then certainly Massachusetts, the flagship state of New England, could afford to adopt such a reform without feat of imminent social upheaval.

Schwartz met with Henry M. Leen, then counsel for the Archdiocese, in Leen's law offices on Milk Street in Boston in an attempt to reach a negotiated settlement. Leen had been a member of the conservative majority on the Sutherland Committee in 1961. When Leen asked Schwartz, "What is to stop Zayre's from opening its store on Sunday [if the proposed exemption went into effect]," Schwartz quickly replied, "Nothing, if they close on Saturday." Leen went to the phone and called Cardinal Cushing. Satisfied that the reform proposed would not cause a mass desecration of the Sunday Sabbath but was needed for genuine religious purposes by an ancient and honored religious minority, the Archdiocese changed its position. Opposition to the exemption evaporated, and the measure sailed through a third reading in the legislature without further delay.[106] Cardinal Cushing, who had denounced the Magruder decision back in 1959, was now prepared to recognize that significant religious issues were at stake, and the Sunday law had put religious Jews into an impossible position.

On March 24, 1964, the problem was finally resolved when the Massachusetts General Court enacted a special exemption for Sabbatarians with small businesses.[107] The bill was signed by Governor Endicott Peabody, who said, "I am very happy that I am signing this bill on the eve of the Jewish holiday of Passover."[108] This time the bill had the support of the Roman Catholic hierarchy and the Massachusetts Council of Churches as well as local Jewish

---

105. The Sutherland Committee had circulated draft legislation modeled on the Vermont statute in the fall of 1961. See, e.g., correspondence between Sutherland and Bishop Mills of the Southern New England Conference of Seventh-Day Adventists, September 1961, AESP, Box 55, folder 14.
106. This account is based upon the author's interview with William Schwartz, then dean of the Boston University Law School, August 4, 1986.
107. M.G. L. c. 136, § 6(8).
108. *Jewish Advocate*, March 26, 1964.

and rabbinical organizations.[109] The change in the position of the Archdiocese brought about the long-awaited change in the law.[110]

More than a half a century has been passed since *Crown Kosher* was in the news. Clearly the Supreme Court had written a section, but not the final chapter, in the long history of Sunday closing legislation. Today, Sunday closing laws no longer contain the explosive mixture they once did. Separation of church and state and the free exercise of religion still ignite passionate feelings, but the factual setting in which these issues arise have changed dramatically. The blue laws themselves have become something of a curiosity. Sunday is a day much like any other day of the week. Just about anything can be bought or sold. Sunday regulations are felt more as an inconvenience than as an absolute prohibition on particular social practices. The department store will be open, but only after the noon hour. The package store will be closed, so be sure to get what you need on Saturday night. Sunday is different, but the differences show up as changes in routine rather than as a change in atmosphere, spirit, or character. As the *New York Times* reported in 1986, after ten years of retail store openings on Sunday "life has never been quite the same. . . . Sundays have become a

---

109. *American Jewish Year Book*: 66 (1965), 228.

110. While in Massachusetts it was the Catholic Church that led the fight in behalf of Sunday closing legislation, other groups were more prominent elsewhere. In Pennsylvania, for example, city merchants and trade unions were outspoken supporters of the blue law. Local 1390 of the Retail Clerks International Association, with 25% Jewish membership, filed an *amicus* brief on the side of the state in the *Braunfield* case. See *American Jewish Year Book*, 62 (1961) 98. And in Massachusetts, the Labor Federation did petition to intervene on the side of the defendant in *Crown Kosher*. CMP, Box 29, folder 6. The new law had immediate benefits for Charles Weinstein of Trans-American Spinning Mills in Fall River. On Sunday, June 20, 1965, Weinstein kept his plant open. As before, he was charged with a criminal violation of the blue law in the Fall River District Court. This time Weinstein based his defense on the 1964 amendment to the Sunday closing law. The charges were dismissed. Freyda P. Koplow, the state representative who had introduced the measure in the House, certified "that it was the unquestionable intent of the members of the General Court to have this legislation apply to all types of business including [that] engaged in by Trans-American Spinning Mills of Fall River, Massachusetts." Memorandum in Charles S. Weinstein Files. Harold Chernock and the Crown Kosher Supermarket never really recovered financially from the defeat in the Supreme Court. Chernock sold his business in 1979 to the Friendly's Corporation, which now occupies the former site of the Crown Kosher Supermarket.

day to combine shopping, eating out and entertainment. . . . Similar changes are being felt . . . in most parts of the nation."[111]

The Supreme Court's decision in the Sunday closing cases was widely supported by the same groups who in the early 1960s were denouncing that institution as atheistic and un-American. Religious groups viewed the Court's decision as "pro-religious" because it upheld the power of the states to retain Sunday closing legislation. From the Court's perspective, however, there was no inconsistency between its decision to eliminate prayer in the public schools and allowing states to regulate Sunday as they pleased. One involved the secular school and the other the secular day of rest. Yet, Leo Pfeiffer's comment on an early Sunday closing case—"the decision is another of the many examples of the use by courts of fictions (in this case that Sunday laws are health rather than religious measures) to avoid deciding against a dominant religion"[112]—was surely right when applied to the Supreme Court's decision in *Crown Kosher*.

In contrast, the three-judge panel that decided in favor of the Crown Kosher Supermarket recognized that while Sunday had become secularized in practice, its religious underpinnings continued to work a serious disadvantage upon a particular minority that also had substantial claims upon the American Constitution. Moreover, as the American Jewish Congress predicted, "Sunday laws [were] becoming deadletter laws. . . ."[113] The Supreme Court's decision retarded this development, but it would not be able to deflect it altogether. Sunday laws in their traditional form had become "archaic." In truth, the federal district court panel had struck a far better balance between religion and the secular world, a balance that lies at the very core of the religion clauses of the First Amendment. The tension between the Magruder opinion and the Supreme Court was the tension between the future and the past, between an emerging social order and an *ancient regime*. "Somewhere between worship of the past and exaltation of the present the

---

111. "Sunday Shopping: A Way of Life for Millions," *New York Times*, October 19, 1986. In 1986 Canada was wrestling with the problem of Sunday closing laws. The Supreme Court of Canada ruled in favor of the Ontario law requiring most retailers to close on Sundays. See *New York Times*, December 21, 1986.

112. Pfeffer, *Church, State, and Religion*, 241.

113. American Jewish Congress, Report, Commission on Law and Social Action (June 8, 1961), 19.

path of safety will be found," Benjamin Cardozo once wrote.[114] It is that "path of safety" that Magruder and Peter Woodbury were seeking. The Magruder court attempted to clear away the historical underbrush, the accumulated detritus of history, in response to the claims of the present.

Crown Kosher is more than a historical curiosity. The case symbolized the special sensitivity that Calvert Magruder and Peter Woodbury had for a diverse and complex social order. The decision of Magruder and Woodbury, two federal district judges, vindicated the rights of a minority group with strong and genuine religious convictions. Thus, when Justice Hugo Black penned a short memorandum on "the Kosher case" to his colleague, Justice Felix Frankfurter—"the opinion will last . . . whatever may turn out to be the fate of the holding"[115]—he implicitly recognized the inevitability of social change that these two judges were willing not merely to recognize but to honor and salute. Indeed, the trial of Chernock's constitutional claims in the district court vindicated the vision of the framers of Article III of the Constitution who recognized the need to have federal courts decide federal issues because state courts might be too bound by prejudice and local politics. In that historic sense, the Magruder court provided Harold Chernock with a more objective forum than was available to him either in the state courts or even in the Supreme Court, where *Crown Kosher*'s legitimate constitutional arguments were blurred by competing issues and the Supreme Court's own political agenda.

* * *

Less than a month after he released the opinion in the *Crown Kosher* case, Calvert Magruder retired from active service on the bench. At the time, it had not yet become common for federal judges to step down at age sixty-five. It was Magruder and Albert Maris of the Third Circuit who established the practice, which has since become common among federal judges except for the justices of the Supreme Court.

---

114. Benjamin Cardozo, *The Nature of the Judicial Process* (New Haven: Yale University Press, 1921), 160.
115. Black to Frankfurter, June 2, 1959, CMP, Box 29, folder 9.

It happened this way: Magruder, Maris, and Peter Woodbury used to sit on cases together while on semi-vacation in San Juan where, quite naturally, they discussed retirement. According to Judge Baily Aldrich, the three agreed that when the time came, they would each retire in accordance with the Congressional retirement statute first enacted in 1948. Maris, who was exactly one week older than Magruder, led the way. In a letter to President Dwight S. Eisenhower written on December 19, 1958, his sixty-fifth birthday, Maris offered his reasons for assuming "senior status." It would increase the number of judges available to hear cases without the need to secure additional authorizations from Congress. Moreover, as a "senior judge," Maris's judicial responsibilities would be performed under specific assignment from the Third Circuit's Chief Justice. As he delicately phrased it in his letter to the President, "It will be for others than myself to decide when my physical or mental powers have failed to the point where I should no longer undertake judicial service."[116] Ten days later, in his own retirement letter to the President, Magruder embraced Maris's sentiments, adding only that Congress's generous retirement policy "will be frustrated unless judges who attain eligibility to retire are disposed to utilize these beneficent provisions of law."[117]

With the news of his retirement, Magruder received well-wishes from across the nation. Joseph Welch, of the Boston law firm of Hale and Dorr, thought that the idea of retirement at age sixty-five was a good one. Welch only wished that every judge would do the same. He did not think wisdom came with age. "Something quite the opposite to wisdom is more apt to arrive," he wrote. Welch himself had resolved "that I would not be seen in a courtroom after age sixty-five."[118] In another letter of congratulations, Justice William O. Douglas summed up the feelings of the entire legal profession when he wrote Magruder, "You have written yourself a wonderful record."[119]

After his formal retirement, Magruder moved to San Francisco, where he continued to teach torts at the Hastings College of Law. He occasionally sat on appellate panels in other federal circuits, but

---

116. Maris to President Dwight D. Eisenhower, December 19, 1958, CMP, MS Box 36, folder 6.
117. Magruder to Eisenhower, December 29, 1958, ibid.
118. Welch to Magruder, March 19, 1959, Ibid.
119. Justice William O. Douglas to Magruder, April 30, 1959, ibid.

his most important service came soon after John F. Kennedy's inauguration in 1961. On January 22nd, Kennedy announced the appointment of a three-person panel on conflict of interest and ethics.[120] He invited Magruder to serve as chairman. "No administration can hope to retain the confidence of the people nor its own self-respect unless all of its officials maintain the highest standard of ethical conduct," Kennedy wrote.[121] Magruder's report, issued two months later, was a thorough analysis and compendium of laws, regulations, reports, findings, and standards on ethical conduct in government. Although it was never actually published, the report established a set of internal guidelines for the executive branch during the remainder of the Kennedy administration and formed the basis for a presidential message to Congress on the subject.

Calvert Magruder was never a household name. But when he died in 1968, the legal profession would mark the passing of one of its legendary figures. Magruder set a standard of intelligence, fairness, integrity, and realism. His commitment to teaching, to public service, to community, and to a host of personal and family relationships showed an activism reminiscent of other great federal and state jurists of an earlier era.

As for the First Circuit, the Magruder years (1939 to 1959) were an era of transition to the modern age of the federal courts. Despite the pressures of the Second World War, the uncertainties of the post-war period, and the growing complexity and novelty of the issues that the court had to address, the Magruder era remained a more relaxed and casual time in which to serve as a federal appeals court judge, especially on this, the smallest of the federal circuits. The great surge of cases that revolutionized the business of the court did not occur until a decade after Magruder had retired. Magruder himself was a member of a generation of remarkable lawyers and judges who, in many parts of the country, made the federal courts into citadels of enlightenment, progressivism, competence, and reason. In the twenty years of Magruder's inspired leadership, the Court of Appeals for the First Circuit achieved an identity and a reputation as one of the premier courts in the nation.

---

120. *New York Times*, January 23, 1961.

121. President John F. Kennedy to Magruder, February 10, 1961, CMP, Box 40, folder 9.

In Felix Frankfurter's words, the Court had achieved "a great history."[122]

---

122. Frankfurter to Magruder, June 16, 1947, FFP, Box 186, folder 13.

Episode 12

The "Commonwealth" of Puerto Rico in American Law

> The effect of the treaty was to put the United States into possession of Puerto Rico . . . We understand . . . that we have a right to legislate to them as we may see fit.
>
> Senator Joseph Foraker,
> March 2, 1900

In 1987 few celebrants of the bicentennial of the federal Constitution were aware of the paradox that America, the oldest independent republic in the world, was the possessor of the oldest colony in the world. The people of Puerto Rico had lived under Spanish rule for 400 years, and they have lived under American rule for a century. Yet, even though they have been United States citizens since 1917, Puerto Ricans, when in Puerto Rico, lack many of the rights other Americans take for granted. A distinguished attorney of Puerto Rican descent, now a federal appeals court judge, describes the situation as follows:

> The creation of a second-class citizenship for a community of persons that was given no expectation of equality under the American system had the effect of perpetuating the colonial status of Puerto Rico. . . . [F]or the first time in history, citizenship was granted to a people without the promise of eventual statehood and without the full panoply of rights guaranteed by the United States Constitution. . . . A Congress writing laws for a compliant colonial people in 1917 extended to the Puerto Ricans a citizenship 'of the second class' perpetuating their colonial status . . .[1]

---

* Source: Chapter 9 ("The First Circuit and Puerto Rico") in George Dargo, *A History of the United States Court of Appeals for the First Circuit*, Vol. I (1891–1960) © George Dargo (as assigned to the U.S. Court of Appeals for the First Circuit).

1. Jose A. Cabranes, *Citizenship and the American Empire: Notes on the Legislative History of the United States Citizenship of Puerto Ricans* (New Haven: Yale University Press, 1979), 7, 99, 101.

The people of Puerto Rico continue to receive separate and what some critics see as unequal treatment because, in 1901, the Supreme Court of the United States ruled that Puerto Rico "belongs to but is not part of the United States."[2]

The legal and political history of Puerto Rico after its acquisition as an American colony can be briefly stated. Spain ceded the Island of Puerto Rico to the United States in the Treaty of Paris of 1898, the treaty that ended the Spanish-American War. Exercising its delegated power under the Territorial Clause of the United States Constitution.[3] Congress passed the Foraker Act in 1900,[4] creating a civil government for the island to replace the temporary military government that had been put in place during the war. The Foraker Act established a true colonial regime. As Senator Joseph Foraker, the author of the Act, put it:

> The effect of the treaty was to put the United States into possession of Puerto Rico . . . We understand . . . that we have a right to legislate to them as we may see fit.[5]

The President of the United States appointed the governor of Puerto Rico as well as the governor's council, which also served as the upper house of the local legislature. Only the lower house was popularly elected. The Jones Act of 1917,[6] Puerto Rico's second organic law, liberalized the legal structure to a limited extent by granting United States citizenship to the islanders and by making the upper house of the Puerto Rican legislature elective. The act also extended to Puerto Rico virtually all of the civil rights prescribed by the U.S. Constitution. However, the governor, members of the Supreme Court of Puerto Rico and most executive department heads were to be chosen by the President. During the Depression of the 1930s there was much agitation for change, and in the aftermath of World War II the movement for political reform intensified. In 1946 President Harry Truman named Jesus T. Pinero

---

2. *Downes* v. *Bidwell*, 182 U.S. 244, 287 (1901).
3. U.S. Const., Art. IV, §3.
4. 31 Stat. 77.
5. *Congressional Record*, Senate, March 2, 1900, 46–47, quoted in Ronald Fernandez, *The Disenchanted Island: Puerto Rico and the Limited States in the Twentieth Century* (Westport, CT: Praeger, 1992), 9.
6. 39 Stat. 951.

as governor, the first native Puerto Rican to serve in that office. In 1948, under a change in the Organic Law providing for popular election of the governor, Luiz Munoz Marin was elected on a platform advocating the establishment of a "commonwealth" as an alternative to independence or statehood. Finally, in 1950, Congress set in motion a series of events that transformed the constitutional status of Puerto Rico and established the "commonwealth," known more accurately as *estado libre asociado* (associated free state).

Five years after the 1896 decision that established the constitutional doctrine of 'separate but equal,"[7] the Supreme Court determined that Puerto Rico and its people could be treated differently because "this country may acquire territories anywhere upon the earth, by conquest or treaty, and hold them as mere colonies or provinces the people inhabiting them to enjoy only such rights as Congress chooses to accord them" despite the historical fact that such a constitutional doctrine was—according to the dissent—"wholly inconsistent with the spirit and genius as well as with the words of the Constitution."[8] In 1954 the Supreme Court overturned the doctrine of "separate but equal,"[9] but as recently as 1980 it reaffirmed the separate status of the citizens of Puerto Rico when it held that "Congress . . . may treat Puerto Rico differently. . . ."[10] This juridical fact, according to the First Circuit Court of Appeals' first Puerto Rican judge, Juan R. Torruella, "makes no sense and cannot today be sustained on legal, moral or logical grounds."[11]

The history of the First Circuit's involvement with Puerto Rico began in 1915 when Congress gave to that court appellate jurisdiction over the new United States district court for Puerto Rico, and, in certain cases, over appeals from Puerto Rico's own Supreme Court.[12] The reasons for choosing the First Circuit are clear from the legislative history of the 1915 enactment. Congress wished to

---

7. *Plessy* v. *Ferguson*, 163 U.S. 537 (1896).
8. *Downes* v. *Bidwell*, 182 U.S. at 380 (Harlan, dissenting).
9. *Brown* v. *Board of Education*, 347 U.S. 483 (1954).
10. *Harris* v. *Rosario*, 446 U.S. 651 (1980) (*per curium*).
11. Juan R. Torruella, *The Supreme Court and Puerto Rico: The Doctrine of Separate and Unequal* (Rio Piedras, P.R: La Editorial Universidad de Puerto Rico, 1985), 268.
12. 38 Stat. 803, 804.

relieve the U.S. Supreme Court from having to hear appeals from the island on issues of local law.[13] It selected the First Circuit because there was "less business pending there than in any other circuit court of appeals, and because there are established lines of communication between Puerto Rico and our North American seaports."[14]

As a consequence of the existence of this jurisdictional power, the First Circuit has been a weighty presence in the legal and political life of Puerto Rico during most of the near century following the acquisition of that colony. The award of jurisdiction thrust the court into the vortex of a sometimes turbulent political atmosphere.[15] By virtue of its jurisdiction over the U.S. district court, the First Circuit would have to interpret and apply the law governing Puerto Rico's evolving status in the American constitutional structure as that status was defined by Congress and interpreted by the U.S. Supreme Court. By giving the court direct power over decisions of the Supreme Court of Puerto Rico on matters of local law—a jurisdiction that lasted until 1961—the court would have to accommodate its own common law orientation to the deep civil law traditions which lie at the root of Puerto Rican law.

But the First Circuit has not been the dominant judicial institution on the island of Puerto Rico. Since 1901 the Supreme Court of the United States has played that unenviable role. In that year the high court decided a series of cases pertaining to the legal status of the island.[16] Barely remembered today and, at most, relegated to

---

13. E.g., *Garrozi* v. *Dastas*, 204 U.S. 64 (1907) (appeal from U.S. District Court of Puerto Rico in case involving civil law community property).
14. 63rd Congress, Third Session, Sen. Rep. No. 847 (December 21, 1914). In 1917, when the United States acquired the Virgin Islands from Denmark, the Third Circuit was given jurisdiction over the islands for much the same reasons. Author's interview with Senior Judge Albert B. Maris, Philadelphia, September 26, 1986.
15. The best example of the sensitive position which the First Circuit occupies in Puerto Rican political affairs is the recent case of *U.S.* v. *Moreno Morales*, 815 F.2d 725 (1st Cir. 1987), wherein the court upheld the convictions of police officials convicted of various Federal criminal charges stemming from the Cerro Maravilla affair, the most celebrated political event in modern Puerto Rican history.
16. *DeLima* v. *Bidwell*, 182 U.S. 1; *Goetze* v. *United States*, 182 U.S. 221; *Armstrong* v. *United States*, 182 U.S. 243; *Downes* v. *Bidwell*, 182 U.S. 244; *Huus* v. *New York and Porto Rico Steamship Co.*, 182 U.S. 392 (1901).

obscure footnotes in a few constitutional law casebooks, these *Insular Cases* were hotly debated in their time. Reportedly, then President Teddy Roosevelt did not appoint Oliver Wendell Holmes, Jr., the distinguished legal historian and jurist, to the Supreme Court in 1902 until T.R. had checked with Massachusetts Senator Henry Cabot Lodge on whether or not Holmes was "sound" on the "insular question."

The great issue raised by the insular controversy was whether the Constitution's powers and protections extended to the territories acquired from Spain as a result of the Spanish-American War. In the public debate, the question was put more simply: "Did the Constitution follow the flag?" In *Downes* v. *Bidwell*, the most important of the *Insular Cases*, a sharply divided Supreme Court gave its answer: "Whilst in an international sense Porto [sic] Rico [is] not a foreign country, since it [is] subject to the sovereignty of and owned by the United States, it [is] foreign to the United States in a domestic sense, because the island [has] not been *incorporated* into the United States, but [is] merely appurtenant thereto as a possession."[17] Barely comprehensible, this abstract formulation gave rise to one of the most famous aphorisms concerning the Supreme Court. The renowned Mr. Dooley explained it this way:

> "An' there ye have th' decision, Hinnissy, that's shaken th' intellicts iv th' nation to their very foundations, or will if they thry to read it. 'T'is all right. Look it over sometime. 'T'is all fine spoort if ye don't care f'r checkers. Some say it laves th' flag up in th' air an' some say that's where it laves th' constitution. Anyhow, something's in th' air. But there's wan think I'm sure about.'
>
> "What's that?" asked Mr. Hennessy.
>
> "That is," said Mr. Dooley, "no matter whether th' constitution follows th' flag or not, th' supreme coort follows th' illection returns.'"[18]

---

17. *Downes* v. *Bidwell*, 182 U.S. at 341–342 (emphasis added). In the *Insular Cases*, "the Supreme Court found colonialism constitutionally tolerable." Cabranes, *Citizenship and the American Empire*, 12.
18. Finley Peter Dunne, *Mr. Dooley's Opinions* (New York: Harper, 1901), 26.

Twenty years after the *Insular Cases* were decided, the Supreme Court reconfirmed the "unincorporated territory" doctrine by a unanimous vote. Said the Court in 1922, "The *Insular Cases* revealed much diversity of opinion in this court as to the constitutional status of the territory acquired by the Treaty of Peace ending the Spanish War, but the opinion . . . of the majority, in *Downes* v. *Bidwell*, has become the settled law of the court."[19] The doctrine of the "unincorporated territory" has remained the law of the land until today controlling all of the federal courts, including the First Circuit, as well as local courts in Puerto Rico.[20] But if the legal doctrine is settled as far as the Supreme Court is concerned, the political life of Puerto Rico remains anything but settled as the "status" issue continues to cause manifold legal, social, and political problems for the island and its people.[21]

The year 1950 was the mid-point of the "Magruder era" of the U.S. Court of Appeals in Boston. It was also a critical year in American life, in the history of Puerto Rico, and in the First Circuit's relationship to that island. In 1950 the Cold War reached new intensity as American military forces engaged Communist armies in Korea. Soviet and Chinese propaganda denounced American imperialism particularly where America's ideological commitment to freedom and democracy was most vulnerable—in the Caribbean Basin, an American sphere of influence since the early nineteenth century. Partly in response to that propaganda but mostly as a result of ever-increasing agitation for greater autonomy by Puerto Ricans, in 1950 Congress enacted Public Law 600 which "fully recogniz[ed] the principle of government by consent" and authorized the people of Puerto Rico to "organize a government

---

19. *Balzac* v. *Porto* [sic] Rico, 258 U.S. 298, 305 (1922).
20. See *Harris* v. *Rosario*, 446 U.S. 651 (1980), the last major pronouncement by the Supreme Court on the status of Puerto Rico.
21. The most compelling critique of the Supreme Court's management of the Puerto Rican "status" problem from a legal perspective is Juan R. Torruella, *The Supreme Court and Puerto Rico,* supra note 10. Judge Torruella was the first Puerto Rican to be appointed to the First Circuit. Perhaps the time has come for the Supreme Court to re-examine the issue of territorial status. As Associate Justice Thurgood Marshall said in dissent in *Harris* v. *Rosario*: "While some early opinions of this Court suggested that various protections of the Constitution do not apply to Puerto Rico . . . , the present validity of those decisions is questionable." 446 U.S. at 653.

pursuant to a constitution of their own adoption."[22] Public law 600 was, in its terms, "in the nature of a compact" subject to a referendum vote by the people. The act authorized the legislature to call for a convention to draft a constitution. It also provided for automatic repeal of many sections of the Organic Act of 1917, the main federal statute governing Puerto Rico[23]. The remaining sections of that act were to continue in force but were now called the "Puerto Rican Federal Relations Act." In 1952 the people of Puerto Rico elected a convention which drafted a Constitution subsequently ratified by popular vote and approved, with amendments, by the United States Congress. The Constitution of Puerto Rico governs local affairs. The Federal Relations Act governs relations between Puerto Rico and the United States. At the time of the inauguration of the new regime in July, 1952, Governor Luiz Munoz Marin, the principal architect of the Commonwealth, gave credit to his people for their heroic struggle in achieving self-government:

> Today's victory is . . . the culmination of a long historical evolution. In the last hundred and fifty years, the Puerto Rican people have exercised all their patience, all their tenacity, all their firmness of spirit in the effort to obtain freedom in the true sense. . . .Thus it has been since the beginning of this struggle for freedom in Puerto Rico.[24]

On July 25, 1952, the new regime was inaugurated in San Juan. For Calvert Magruder and other champions of Puerto Rico's unique position in the American territorial system, the Cold War implications of the events of 1950 and 1952 could not have been clearer. As Magruder said in an address defending Puerto Rico's new status in the American territorial system delivered on April 30, 1953 at the University of Pittsburgh:

> The outcome of the present "cold-war" struggle for the good opinion and support of mankind will be of profound consequence to us all. It is important to have an informed answer to the glib propaganda charges of imperialism and colonialism, which the Kremlin and its satellites, day in and day out, direct at

---

22. 64 Stat. 319.
23. See supra, note 10.
24. Speech of Governor Munoz Marin, July 4, 1952 (in typescript), CMP, Box 35, folder 5.

> the Western Powers, including the United States. Actions speak louder than words. The record of our dealings with the people of Puerto Rico affords an eloquent and favorable contrast to the rough treatment which Soviet Russia has given to helpless peoples within its power and grasp—a contrast which will not be lost upon the rest of the world, particularly upon our Latin-American neighbors in Central and South America, if they but learn the facts.[25]

Governor Munoz Marin wrote at the time that *estado libre asociad* frees the Puerto Rican spirit of a corroding sense of colonialism while it freed the United States of one element, at least, of Communist propaganda."[26]

On still anther level, 1950 was an important year in the developing relationship between the First Circuit and Puerto Rico. For the first time in history, the First Circuit court held a winter session in San Juan. The idea originated in the early 1930's when members of the Puerto Rican bar wrote to Judge John Morton "suggesting that Puerto Rico and the bar would probably be gratified if the First Circuit would hold a sifting . . . there."[27] R. Ammi Cutter, later a justice of the Massachusetts Supreme Judicial Court, was in Puerto Rico at the time and transmitted the letter to Morton whom he knew fairly well. Morton liked the idea, but he could not convince the court to go along with the idea. After the war, Calvert Magruder, then the Chief Judge of the First Circuit, revived the notion at the urging of Luis Munoz Marin and Ammi Cutter.[28] Magruder and Associate Judge Peter Woodbury had attended Munoz Marin's inauguration as Puerto Rico's first popularly elected governor on January 2, 1949. The governor suggested that an annual court session in San Juan might be worthy of consideration.[29] Magruder took to the idea immediately. He wrote to the governor soon after

---

25. Calvert Magruder, "The Commonwealth Status of Puerto Rico," 15 *University of Pittsburgh Law Review* 1, 2 (1953).
26. Munoz Marin to Calvert Magruder, August 29, 1952, CMP, Box 35, folder 5.
27. Author's interview with R. Ammi Cutter, retired justice of the Massachusetts Supreme Judicial Court, June 1, 1988, Boston, Massachusetts. Judge Benjamin Kaplan, another retired SJC justice, has the same recollection. Author's interview with Benjamin Kaplan, June 1988, Cambridge, Massachusetts.
28. Ibid., Cutter Interview.
29. Author's interview with Michael Magruder and Mrs. Calvert Magruder, July 10, 1986.

his return to Boston, "I came away with the firm resolution to hold a session of the . . . Court of Appeals in San Juan next year, perhaps in January or February. We hope this will afford us a sufficient opportunity to see something more of the island and to observe the interesting program of social and economic welfare which your administration is pursuing."[30] As he later explained, Magruder considered it "a constructive thing to do, and an altogether proper manifestation of respect for the people of Puerto Rico and their local bar."[31]

The initiative clearly had its special benefits and became "one of the agreeable perquisites of membership on the Court of Appeals."[32] Magruder established a close personal relationship with Munoz Marin. When the governor came to Harvard in 1950 to give the Godkin Lectures, the Magruders invited him to be their house guest.[33] In 1959 the governor was again invited to Harvard, and Magruder hosted a party in his honor.[34] When other members of the First Circuit, district court judges, or Harvard Law professors visited San Juan, they were, in turn, welcomed as guests at La Fortaleza, the governor's official residence. In fact, the personal connection between the First Circuit and the ruling establishment in San Juan sometimes caused friction with elements of the Puerto Rican bar who challenged the impartiality of the court in cases in which the government of the Commonwealth was an interested party. But Magruder refused to change the court's practice. He

---

30. Magruder to Munoz Marin, March 14, 1949, CMP, Box 35, folder 5.
31. Magruder, supra, note 24, at 1. In order to save expenses, in the first ten years after 1950, only two judges from the circuit sat in San Juan. To make a panel of three, the court borrowed one of the judges from the Third Circuit sitting simultaneously (by design) in St. Thomas. The First Circuit reciprocated by sending one of their number to help out with Virgin Island cases. This practice lasted until the volume of cases began to grow dramatically in the 1960s. Interview with Senior Judge Albert B. Maris, September 26, 1986.
32. Magruder, supra, note 24, at 1. The Magruders themselves were always treated like visiting royalty in San Juan. Mrs. Magruder recalls that "every time we moved we had an orchid on the door....We were greeted with the red carpet." It was the court's annual "junket". Michael Magruder, the judge's youngest son, often "joked with [his] father about the fact that they always did it in February." (Magruder Interview . . .)
33. Magruder to Munoz Marin, December 15, 1950; Munoz Marin to Magruder, December 26, 1950, CMP, Box 35, folder 5.
34. Magruder to Munoz Marin, December 9, 22, 1958; Munoz Marin to Magruder, December 18, 28, 1959, Ibid.

simply denied any "improper influence" on the court's deliberation of impending cases. In a memo he drafted in San Juan in February 1958 Magruder explained:

> It is true that in recent years we have developed the practice of staying at La Fortaleza while we were in San Juan. I suppose that has come about because we have become friends of the Governor and Mrs. Munoz. That friendship would of course continue to exist, whether or not we stayed at La Fortaleza. It might as well be suggested that we are disqualified to sit in cases in which the United States is a party because our salaries are paid by the United States.[35]

But the personal rapport between the Governor of Puerto Rico and the Chief Judge of the First Circuit was nourished by deeper sources than occasional visits and pleasant mid-winter meetings in San Juan. Magruder followed political events on the island with keen interest. He often asked for the English translation of speeches which Munoz Marin delivered either to the Puerto Rican legislature or to others on special occasions.[36] The two men were in basic agreement as to the meaning of Puerto Rico's unique position in the American constitutional system. Magruder was an enthusiastic supporter of the Commonwealth. Within a year of the commencement of the new regime, he had occasion to comment upon its meaning and significance in one of the cases coming from the U.S. district court in San Juan.

In *Mora* v. *Meiias,* the federal district court for Puerto Rico denied an application for a temporary injunction against the Secretary of Agriculture and Commerce of Puerto Rico, a Puerto Rican rather than a U.S. federal officer. The petitioners sought to block enforcement of a maximum price restriction on the sale of Puerto Rican rice. As a member of the Emergency Court of

---

35. [Memo] written by Calvert Magruder, February, 1958, CMP, Box 35, folder 5. Mrs. Magruder recalls: "I remember a lot of people criticized us for staying in the Forteleza. They thought the judges shouldn't stay in the governor's house. The governor kept saying that this was everybody's house." (Magruder Interview.) When Bailey Aldrich became Chief Judge in 1960, he put a stop to the practice of having the judges stay at the governor's residence during the winter session.
36. The Magruder Papers at the Harvard Law School contain numerous speeches by Governor Munoz Marin in English translation, some printed and some in typescript. See CMP, Box 35, folder 6.

Appeals, Magruder had become quite accustomed to hearing cases of this kind and deferring to the decisions of a price administrator. In a unanimous decision, the First Circuit upheld the denial of the injunction. But, on his own initiative, *sua sponte*, Magruder raised the issue of whether Puerto Rico was a "state" for purposes of applying the Three-Judge Court Act since this was a proceeding challenging the enforcement of a local statute on federal constitutional grounds.[37] In an elaborate examination of the "status issue, the District Court had concluded that under Public Law 600, the Federal Relations Act, and the Constitution of Puerto Rico 'a compact has been established between the government of the United States and the people of Puerto Rico [and] . . . neither . . . can unilaterally amend Public Law 600 nor the Puerto Rican Federal Relations Act without the consent and approval of the other party to the compact.'"[38] However, the district court had continued, if Puerto Rico was no longer a "territory" subject to unilateral Congressional power but a self-governing community, neither was it a federated state subject to the due process requirements of the Fourteenth Amendment. On this point, Magruder parted company with the lower court and held, in *dictum*, that since *estado libre asociado* "organized . . . a body politic by the people of Puerto Rico under their own constitution, . . . it is a state . . . within a common and accepted meaning of the word," at least for purposes of the Three-Judge Court Act.[39]

Magruder looked at the issue of status from a practical perspective. Was the Constitution of the Commonwealth of Puerto Rico *really* a constitution or was it "subject to recall or overriding by a power external to the people of Puerto Rico, namely, the Congress

37. 28 U.S.C. Sec. 2281.

38. *Mora* v. *Torres*, 113 F. Supp. 309, 313 (D.P.R. 1953).

39. *Mora* v. *Mejias*, 206 F.2d 377, 387 (1st Cir. 1953). Subsequently, the District Court decided in the third of the *Mora* cases that the matter should be heard by a three-judge panel because Puerto Rico had attained a sufficient degree of "state sovereignty" to distinguish it from other U.S. territories. *Mora* v. *Mejias*, 115 F. Supp. 610, 611 (D.P.R. 1953). The U.S. Supreme Court ultimately adopted the view taken by Magruder in *Mora* and held that, for purposes of the Three-Judge Court Act, Puerto Rico was a "state." *Calero-Toledo* v. *Pearson Yacht Leasing Co.*, 416 U.S. 663 (1974). It is worth noting that prior to the establishment of *estado libre asociado*, the First Circuit had held that Puerto Rico was not a state for purposes of the act. *Benedicto* v. *West India & Panama Telegraph Co.*, 256 F. 417 (1st Cir. 1919).

of the United States?"[40] This was a question that could be, and indeed, had been debated for decades without resolution. But as early as 1953 Magruder saw that the legal dilemma of constitutional status was "really of subordinate importance." As he put it in his Pittsburgh address: "The significant thing is the substance of freedom, and the feeling of freedom, which the people of Puerto Rico evidently possess as a result of having achieved their new constitutional status."[41]

A year later, in early 1954, while the court was holding its now routine annual session in San Juan, Magruder reflected further on the status question. He took issue with Governor Marin who, at the time, appeared to be giving in to increased pressure from the Popular Independence Party (PIP)[42] which advocated complete independence for the island. Magruder urged Munoz to remain steadfast in his adherence to the Commonwealth idea not just as "a mid-way between independence on the one side and statehood on the other" but as "a third alternative status which [was] of such dignity as to satisfy the justified aspirations of the people of Puerto Rico."[43] He reminded the governor that the Popular Democratic Party (PDP), the governor's centrist party, had pushed for *estado libre asociado* in order to release popular energies "in the execution of various programs of self-development . . . uninhibited by the preoccupation with what they regarded as their inferior 'colonial' status under the American flag." Once that had been achieved it was time to get on with "self-development" rather than squander the island's energies in fruitless and continuous agitation over the political question.

For Magruder, "Commonwealth status under the terms of the compact was intended to have some degree of permanence and stability and not to be used as a transitory jumping-off place for

40. Magruder, *supra*, note 24, at. 15.
41. Ibid., 16.
42. The three main political parties representing the three main positions on the status question are *Partido Popular Democratico* (PPD) (pro-Commonwealth), *Partido Nuevo Progresista* (PNP) (pro-Statehood), and *Partido Independentista Puertorriqueno* (PIP) (pro-Independence). Another non-binding referendum on the status question was scheduled to take place in 1993. See *New York Times*, August 8, 1993.
43. Draft of a letter from Magruder to Munoz Marin, February 12, 1954, CMP, Box 35, folder 5.

seeking further major concessions from Congress."[44] Magruder did suggest that there was room for clarification of the terms of the compact, however. For example, Puerto Ricans ought to be afforded a procedure for formal manifestation of consent to any changes in the Federal Relations Act so that Congress would not be able to act unilaterally in any future attempt to modify the island's special status. Magruder further suggested that Congress should abolish the First Circuit's jurisdiction over final decisions of Puerto Rico's highest court on matters of local law—a jurisdiction that had become purely "theoretical." Furthermore, Puerto Rico should be given greater control over tariff duties on foreign goods intended for local consumption.

But aside from these relatively minor modifications, Calvert Magruder was convinced that the Commonwealth idea was a good one and that it "ought to remain undisturbed for a decade or two at least. Then, from the standpoint of an adequate experience, we would be in a better position to determine whether any major changes in the status of Puerto Rico are desirable."[45] For Magruder, the spirit of the Puerto Rican people "[has] not been freed for concentration on the great tasks ahead in improving the standard of living on the island."[46] The main thrust of Magruder's reflections on status was "the plane of practical politics," a perspective that would allow the question of status to go unanswered until *estado libre asociado* had time to realize its potential.

Decades have passed since the events of the early 1950s, but the "status question" remains "the most intractable constitutional and political problem in the history of American territories."[47] If anything, it has become even more aggravated. The Supreme Court

---

44. Ibid.
45. Magruder to Munoz Marin (draft), *op. cit*, February 12, 1954. As one historian of the Commonwealth has written: "[Puerto Ricans] permitted Munoz Marin to channel the quest [for self-identity] in a constructive manner away for the time being from independence and statehood. Repose in the Commonwealth status, he told them, so that they might search fruitfully for a permanent solution and at the same time apply themselves to the important tasks that face them." Surendra Bhana, *The United States and the Development of the Puerto Rican Status Question, 1936–1968* (Lawrence, Kansas: University of Kansas, 1975), 207.
46. Magruder to Munoz Marin (draft). February 12, 1954.
47. Cabranes, "Puerto Rico and the Constitution," 110 F.R.D., at 475. "Eighty years after the acquisition of the island from Spain, Puerto Rico's relationship with the United States remains a controversial subject. . . ." Cabranes, supra, note 1, at 8.

recognizes Puerto Rico as an independent "state" like the other fifty states for some purposes but not others.[48] The court has held that federal due process protections apply to acts of the Puerto Rican legislature, but it has declined to specify whether the requirement is rooted in the Fifth or the Fourteenth Amendment of the U.S. Constitution.[49] The result of the continuing tensions caused by the doctrinal uncertainties set by the *Insular Cases* has been inconsistency in lower federal court interpretations of the meaning of Puerto Rico's "status." Thus, while the First Circuit has, since Calvert Magruder's time, frequently come down on the liberal side of the debate,[50] there is also evidence of an adherence to a more limited view of the constitutional implications of the events of the early 1950s.[51]

In more recent years, the legal assault on the doctrine of the *Insular* Cases has intensified. The critics view those cases as anomalous in the aftermath of the creation of *estado libre asociado.* Judge Juan Torruella of the First Circuit concluded his attack on the legal doctrine this way:

> The *Insular Cases* have had, and continue to have, a profound impact on the lives of the United States citizens of Puerto Rico and other territories. Their influence has permeated every facet

---

48. For an unpersuasive explanation of the Court's inconsistency in treating Puerto Rico as a "state," see *Calero* v. *Pearson Yacht*, 416 U.S. at 675–77, n. 11.
49. To ground the Due Process requirement in the Fifth Amendment might suggest that Puerto Rico was simply a federal territory and, therefore, governed by powers and limitations of the federal government. To ground it in the Fourteenth Amendment would imply that Puerto Rico is like a state because the Fourteenth Amendment embodies limitations of state power. See David M. Helfeld, "How Much of the United States Constitution and Statutes Are Applicable to the Commonwealth of Puerto Rico," 110 F.R.D. 435, 456 (1986).
50. "[I]n 1952, Puerto Rico ceased being a territory of the United States subject to the plenary powers of Congress. . . . Under the compact between the people of Puerto Rico and the United States, Congress cannot amend the Puerto Rican Constitution unilaterally, and the government of Puerto Rico is no longer a Federal government agency exercising delegated power." *United States v. Quinones*, 758 F.2d 40, 42 (1st Cir. 1985) (Bownes, J.).
51. "[W]hatever the actual status of the Commonwealth of Puerto Rico may be in all its details, its present status is certainly not that of a state of the United States. Nor is it even that of a territory incorporated into the union preparatory to statehood.... As such the Government of Puerto Rico has such powers as Congress from time to time has seen fit to give it." *Fonseca v. Prann*, 282 F.2d 153, 155 (1st Cir. 1960) (Woodbury, J.), *cert. denied*, 365 U.S. 860 (1961).

> of their affairs since they were decided. The archaic notion which they propound, that the United States can have a class of several million of its citizens in a subservient condition *ad infinitum*, with less rights than even aliens who reside in the United States, makes no sense. . . .[52]

The only certain fact is that the "status question" promises not to go away anytime soon.

The focus upon legal doctrine may be misplaced, however. The joint United States-Puerto Rico Commission on the Status of Puerto Rico concluded in 1966 "that there has been an excess of legalistic, somewhat academic, controversy" on the status issue.[53] Regardless of the winds of doctrine, the future of Puerto Rico's relationship with the mainland will be determined by political realities and social forces rather than the opinions of even the highest appellate courts. As Professor David Helfeld, a well-known authority and long-time student of Puerto Rico's modern legal history has put it:

> Constitutional relations between Puerto Rico and the United States are not based on a system of logically consistent principles. In the final analysis, Puerto Rico cannot escape political reality. It must recognize that the constitutional system of the United States includes a powerful dimension of partisan politics, and it must act on that recognition. . . .[54]

Calvert Magruder had made this point about as well as anyone could when he warned against disproportionate emphasis upon "the

---

52. Torruella, supra, note 7, at 268. It is natural for lawyers and judges to give great weight to legal doctrines and decided cases and to attribute to them cause and effect importance in social relations and historical change. This is particularly true in a common law system. Judge Torruella is aware of the problem and cautions against attributing a direct causal relationship between the *Insular Cases* and social and economic conditions in Puerto Rico. See Ibid, 117–118. *See also*, Raymond Carr, *Puerto Rico: A Colonial Experiment* (New York: New York University Press, 1984), 384–385, et passim.
53. Commission Report, House Document 464, 89th Cong., 2nd Session, 12. As one San Juan attorney put it in testimony before the Commission: "[W]e cannot rely on the courts to define . . . status for us. This is a legislative and an executive function." Statement of Stanley Feldstein, May 17, 1965, in Hearings Before the United States-Puerto Rico Commission on the Status of Puerto Rico, Senate Document No. 108, 89th Congress, 2nd Session, vol., 397.
54. Helfeld, "How Much of the Constitution," 110 F.R.D. 473, 475.

question of legal power." To be sure, under the doctrine of the *Insular Cases*, Congress retained ultimate legal authority over Puerto Rico. Still, Magruder observed:

> In the realm of practical affairs, certain political acts are by their nature irreversible—such, for example, as the passage by the British Parliament of the North-America Act with reference to the Dominion of Canada. The Congress, even if it has the power, could not afford by unilateral act to pass a new Organic [Law] for the internal government of Puerto Rico, supplanting the existing constitution of the commonwealth. That would be an act resting on naked power alone, without any basis of moral justification.[55]

Still, the importance of constitutional law in a democratic state cannot be minimized. In a society governed by laws, the power of the fundamental law over the destiny of the people within its jurisdiction is profound and far-reaching.[56]

Judge Levin Campbell of the First Circuit has stated that "Puerto Rico's long-term political future will be shaped by forces over which the Federal courts have little control. We work within the existing political framework, whatever it may be at the time."[57] Clearly the Supreme Court needs to be excluded from that broad generalization because the high court has much to say about the

---

55. Magruder, supra note 24, at 16. Judge Torruella concurs with Magruder to this extent: Congress would probably not revoke U.S. citizenship or the popular election of the island's governor. However, on other levels, Congress can and does exercise plenary power, particularly on fiscal matters, with profound and often disruptive effects on the lives of Puerto Ricans. Author's interview with Judge Juan R. Torruella, July 28, 1987.
56. "Part of the reality of freedom is feeling free. Indeed, man's history chronicles innumerable occasions when the symbol of freedom outweighed all practical considerations. Since men live by and for symbols, a substantial degree of self-determination may not compensate for a badge of an inferior status. Nor is the badge merely symbolic, since Puerto Rico is permitted no politically effective role in the making of national policy—even with respect of Federal policy which affects the island deeply and directly. A people with democratic convictions can hardly continue government without representation at the national level as a permanent political condition. . . ." David M. Helfeld, "Congressional Intent and Attitude Toward Public Law 600 and the Constitution of the Commonwealth of Puerto Rico," *Revista Juridica U.P.R.* (v. 21), 135.
57. Judge Levin H. Campbell, Speech at First Circuit Judicial Conference, November 4, 1985, San Juan, Puerto Rico.

future of Puerto Rico in its relationship to the United States. The lower federal courts, on the other hand, have little control over ultimate issues of status and power. They do have a great deal to say, however, about how much deference and respect American courts are prepared to give to the unique legal traditions and institutions of Puerto Rico. It is in that area where the First Circuit does have independent authority to contribute to Puerto Rico's progress toward genuine autonomy, dignity, and political integrity. The historical record indicates that the court has begun to do so.

In the early years of the First Circuit's special appellate jurisdiction over decisions of the Supreme Court of Puerto Rico on matters of local law, the court often found itself at loggerheads with the Puerto Rican court. This can be accounted for, in part, by the court's lack of familiarity with the Spanish sources of Puerto Rican law and the different approach to finding and applying the law in a civil law system in contrast to the Anglo-American common law traditions to which members of the First Circuit were attached by training and experience. A pattern developed where the First Circuit would reverse the Puerto Rican courts on interpretations of local law only to find itself reversed, in turn, by the Supreme Court of the United States. In one such case, Associate Justice Holmes curtly admonished the court this way: "Our appellate jurisdiction is not given for the purpose of remodeling the Spanish American law according to common law conceptions except so far as the law has to bend to the express will of the United States."[58] The pattern continued and eventually the Supreme Court decided on a standard so demanding that it virtually ended any meaningful appellate review by the First Circuit on issues of local law. In *Bonet v. Texas*, the Supreme Court held that in order to justify First Circuit reversal of the Puerto Rico Supreme Court for error in its interpretation of local law, "the error must be clear or manifest; the interpretation must be inescapably wrong; the decision must be patently erroneous."[59] While the First Circuit continued to try to "correct" the

---

58. *Diaz* v. *Gonzalez*, 261 U.S. 102, 105–106 (1923).
59. 308 U.S. 463, 471 (1940). This was a period of constitutional history when the Supreme Court adopted a much more deferential posture toward state legislation in general, a reaction to its own activist interventionism on social and economic questions before 1937. See e.g., *South Carolina* v. *Barnwell Bros.*, 303 U.S. 177 (1938).

Supreme Court of Puerto Rico even under this most exacting standard, in time the jurisdiction became a dead letter as the First Circuit increasingly deferred to lower court decisions on issues of Puerto Rican law.

Under Calvert Magruder's leadership, the First Circuit showed an increasing inclination to respect the decisions of the Puerto Rico Supreme Court on matters of local law. "We [are] reticent about setting ourselves up as experts in esoteric points of Spanish law in opposition to the views of the territorial courts," Magruder wrote in a 1939 case.[60] He believed that such appeals should be discouraged because, even under the "clearly wrong" standard established earlier, such appeals were "likely to be futile and merely to cause needless delay and expense."[61] But after the *Bonet* case was decided, Magruder was convinced that First Circuit jurisdiction over the Supreme Court of Puerto Rico should be withdrawn. He reasoned that, "[i]t is a bit humiliating to this court to be obliged to sit practically as a rubber stamp, or else to be reversed by the Supreme Court of the United States."[62] Magruder hoped that either the Supreme Court would modify the "inescapably wrong" test or that Congress would take away that particular branch of appellate cases.[63]

---

60. *De La Torre* v. *National City Bank of New York*, 110 F.2d 381, 383 (1st Cir. 1939).

61. Ibid. In a second appeal growing out of the same litigation, and just after the *Bonet* decision came down, Magruder declared that "it would require a touch of arrogance for us to say that the judgment appealed from is 'inescapably wrong'" even though, in Magruder's opinion, the Puerto Rico Supreme Court had been "too literal in its interpretation of its own Civil Code." *De La Torre* v. *National City Bank of New York*, 110 F.2d 976, 983 (1st Cir. 1940).

62. *De Castro* v. *Board of Commissioners of San Juan*, 136 F.2d 419, 425 (1st Cir. 1943), *aff'd* 322 U.S. 451 (1944). Magruder was quite correct to identify this judicial "Catch 22." The Supreme Court granted *certiorari* in *De Castro* because "some observations in the opinion of the [First] Circuit have raised serious questions with respect to the appropriate rule governing decision of cases involving local laws. . . ." *De Castro* v. *Board of Commissioners,* 322 U.S. 451, 453 (1944). The Supreme Court went on to declare that the "inescapably wrong" rule "is not a mere mechanical device which requires or admits . . . summary disposition of appeals. . . . Nor does it minimize the importance or dignity of the appellate function in such cases." Ibid. at 458. The Court admonished the First Circuit that appeals from the Federal District Court in Puerto Rico should be guided by principles of deference under *Erie* v. *Tompkins*. Ibid., 459.

63. Magruder to Mahoney, March 21, 1940, CMP, MS Box 35, folder 2.

Thus Magruder became one of the first to advocate the abolition of this special appellate jurisdiction. Especially after 1952, he considered it "one of those loose ends left unprovided for" when *estado libre asociado* was created. He predicted that it was a situation "which the Congress will tidy up in due time by further legislation."[64] The prediction proved to be accurate. In 1961 Congress abolished First Circuit jurisdiction to review decisions of the Puerto Rican courts.[65] The Administrative Office of the U.S. Courts had reported that the year before only seven appeals of the kind at issue had come before the First Circuit.[66] The jurisdiction had been created back in 1915 in order to relieve the Supreme Court of a burden, and now that reason appeared to be gone. Final decisions of the highest court of Puerto Rico were now reviewable only by the U.S. Supreme Court "in the same manner as judgments from the highest courts of the several States of the Union are now reviewed by that Court."[67] This made Puerto Rico's situation analogous to each of the fifty states. Only decisions of its highest court on issues of federal law were reviewable by the Supreme Court of the United States. Thus the act of 1961 eliminating the First Circuit's appellate jurisdiction over the Supreme Court of Puerto Rico made the decisions of that court final on matters of local law.

However, the termination of appellate jurisdiction over the Puerto Rican courts did not mean that the First Circuit no longer had to worry about issues of local law. Cases arising out of the federal district court of Puerto Rico on diversity of citizenship grounds, as well as so-called *pendent* jurisdictional claims, continued to raise local-law questions which the First Circuit would have

---

64. *Figueroa* v. *People of Puerto Rico*, 232 F.2d 615, 618 (1st Cir. 1956). The final withdrawal of the jurisdiction was also due, in large measure, to agitation and pressure from the Puerto Rican bar. See e.g., S.M. Beresford, "Commonwealth Status and the Federal District Court of Puerto Rico," *Revista Del Colegio de Abogados de Puerto Rico,* 10 (1958), 19–51.
65. 75 Stat. 417. The primary reason given was the change in status. The "[p]roposal appears to be appropriate in view of the change in the status of Puerto Rico from that of a territory to that of an associated commonwealth under the Act of Compact." 87th Congress, 1st Session, House Report No. 683; Senate Report No. 735 (1961).
66. Ibid.
67. Senate Report No. 735 (August 14, 1961), 87th Cong., 1st Sess., U.S. Code & Adm. News, Vol. 2, at 2449.

to decide. And after *Erie* v. *Tompkins*—the landmark Supreme Court case decided in 1938 that in diversity cases, the federal courts had to apply state common law—the attitude of any federal court had to be one of deference and respect to the law of the place in which the Federal court sat.[68] Applied to Puerto Rico, this meant that both the federal district court and the First Circuit on appeal had to "try to make the same decision the Commonwealth Supreme Court would make in the circumstances."[69] But if the change in jurisdiction triggered a change in posture from "correction" to "replication,"[70] then the First Circuit would have to become more knowledgeable in the civil law sources of Puerto Rican law.

Here again Calvert Magruder led the way. He never pretended to be expert in Spanish law. "My acquaintance with the local law of Puerto Rico is most fragmentary and episodic," Magruder once confessed to Felix Frankfurter.[71] But as a willing and eager student, he familiarized himself with the growing literature on "mixed legal systems." In his very first year on the bench Magruder decided a community property problem involving the application of the Puerto Rican Civil Code. The Supreme Court of Puerto Rico had ruled that real estate that formed part of a marital community (i.e., property held jointly by husband and wife) could be attached to secure a judgment against the husband on a promissory note he had executed independently of his wife. Guided by decisions of the U.S. Supreme Court and courts in a number of community property states, Magruder concluded that the trend in community property law was toward greater protection for the wife. Magruder made confident use of several Spanish commentators, and he performed an independent analysis of the Civil Code of Puerto Rico.[72] Nevertheless, because of the "inescapably wrong" standard imposed by the U.S. Supreme Court, Magruder affirmed the

---

68. *DeCastro* v. *Board of Comm'rs,* 322 U.S. at 459 (citing *Erie* v. *Tompkins*).
69. Stephen Breyer, "The Relationship Between the Federal Courts and the Puerto Rico Legal System." *Revista Juridica de la Universidad de Puerto Rico*, 53 (1984), 307–316, at 309.
70. Ibid.
71. Magruder to Frankfurter, January 6, 1956, FFP, Box 186, folder 14. In his letter to Frankfurter, Magruder cited articles by Joseph Dainow, a leading Louisiana legal scholar, and Max Rheinstein, a noted legal historian with a strong interest in comparative law issues.
72. Manres (*Comentarios al Codigo Civil Espanol*) and Scaevola (*Codigo Civil*). See *De La Torre, supra*, 110 F.2d at 978, et passim.

decision of the Puerto Rico Supreme Court in holding that the real estate was attachable. In recent years an increasing number of First Circuit decisions reflect growing sensitivity toward Puerto Rican local law. These decisions demonstrate deference and respect for the civil law tradition particularly as that tradition has been followed in the Spanish- speaking world.[73] These decisions show that the court is learning to use Spanish texts, the Puerto Rican codes and civil law commentators. The appointment of Judge Juan R. Torruella to the court in 1985[74], the increasing use by the court of Spanish-speaking law clerks, and the growing awareness of the importance of using civil law materials is undoubtedly having an impact.[75] The trend is evidenced by a series of strategies or approaches to Puerto Rican law identified by Judge Stephen Breyer, the former Chief Judge of the First Circuit and now an Associate Justice of the Supreme Court, as well as other commentators. One approach is to seek solutions to legal questions that are common to both Puerto Rican civil law and American common law. Another is to certify difficult questions of local law to the Supreme Court of Puerto Rico. A third way is for the court to rely upon its own ability to interpret the civil law authorities. As a fourth approach, the court may look to decisions of the federal district court in Puerto Rico for guidance. Whereas the first two strategies merely require the court

---

73. See e.g., *Stella* v. *Government Development Bank of Puerto Rico*, 663 F.2d 326 (1st Cir. 1981) (meaning of partnership under Puerto Rican civil law); *Ayuso-Morales* v. *Secretary of Health and Human Services*, 677 F.2d 146 (1st Cir. 1982) (qualification as a "widow" under Puerto Rican law); *Republic Security Corp.* v. *Puerto Rico Aqueduct and Sewer Authority*, 674 F.2d 952 (1st Cir. 1982) (limitations question); *Reyes-Cardona* v. *J.C. Penny Co., Inc*., 694 F.2d 894, 898 (1st Cir.1982) (wrongful prosecution) (Appendix A of this case lists a wide variety of Spanish civil law source materials used in constructing the opinion).

74. Judge Torruella believes that his appointment represents a political recognition of the injustice to Puerto Rico of having been within First Circuit jurisdiction for so long without having a First Circuit judge appointed from there. Interview with Judge Juan R. Torruella, July 28, 1987.

75. Breyer, "Relationship Between Federal Courts and Puerto Rico," supra note 68, 311. Judge Breyer's enthusiastic assessment of the situation may be overstated, however. For example, he viewed the opinion in *In Re Morales Travel Agency*, 667 F.2d 1069 (1st Cir. 1981), in positive terms. In that case, he writes, "we discovered that the common law and civil systems had reached similar results" in interpreting the literal terms of a contract. However, *In Re Morales* made reference to no relevant Spanish commentator or to Puerto Rican case law and cited only Professor Corbin's well-known treatise on contracts.

to lean on other authority—common law principles in the first approach and the Puerto Rican Supreme Court in the second —the third strategy puts upon the court the self-imposed discipline to deal with Spanish and Puerto Rican sources directly.[76] The fourth strategy relies upon the authority of the federal district court of Puerto Rico because the judges there are trained civil lawyers with access to the relevant civil law authorities in the Spanish language.[77]

---

76. In this regard, several First Circuit judges have had law clerks from Puerto Rico. Of course, since 1984, Judge Juan Torruella, who was a leading practitioner in Puerto Rico and who teaches at the University of Puerto Rico Law School, has been on the court. There are historical examples of common-law lawyers who became respected authorities in continental civil law. The best American example comes from the Louisiana experience where Edward Livingston, a native of New York and the son of an established colonial family, became an internationally recognized authority on the civil law of Spain and France. See William B. Hatcher, *Edward Livingston: Jeffersonian Republic and Jacksonian Democrat* (Baton Rouge: Louisiana State University Press, 1940), chapter 8, et passim.

77. The Federal District Court in Puerto Rico has been a source of controversy from the beginning. In the early years, all of the judges were from the mainland, and not until 1948 was the first Puerto Rican appointed to that court. Many of the judges thought of themselves as instruments of Americanization and acculturation. One early Federal District Court judge once commented that "the public schools and the Federal Court are the two educational forces for Americanization on the island." Quoted in Morales, "Two Roads to Justice," *Revista Derecho*, v. 26, at 303. Some Puerto Rican "legal nationalists" would prefer to have the District Court eliminated altogether, a sentiment that recalls the resentment of eighteenth century American "Anti-Federalists" who resisted the creation of inferior Federal courts because of fears of federal encroachment on the states. Similarly, in more recent years, Southern conservative resistance to Federal civil rights laws took the form of political attacks upon the role of Federal District Courts. Current critics of the Federal District Court in Puerto Rico have taken a more indirect approach by challenging the use of English as a denial of due process. See Roberto Tschudin, "The United States District Court for the District of Puerto Rico: Can an English Language Court Serve the Interest of Justice in a Spanish Language Society?" *Revista Del Colegio de Abogados de Puerto Rico,* 37 (1976), 41–86. Tensions between the District Court and the Supreme Court of Puerto Rico on the one hand and with the First Circuit on the other are highlighted by Richard Graffam, "The Federal Courts' Interpretation of Puerto Rican Law: Whose Law Is It, Anyway?" *Revista Colegio de Abogados de Puerto Rico,* 47 (1986), 111–142. A number of cases illustrate the problem as seen by Graffam. See *Thompson* v. *Ramirez,* 597 F. Supp. 727 (D.P.R. 1984) (refusal of Supreme Court of Puerto Rico to answer certified question from Federal District Court); *Hernandez Agosto* v. *Romero Barcelo,* 594 F. Supp. 1390 (D.P.R. 1984), vacated, 748 F.2d 1 (1st Cir. 1984); *Schneider* v. *Colegio de Abogados de Puerto Rico*, 565 F. Supp. 963 (D.P.R. 1983), *vacated*, 742 F.2d 32 (1st Cir. 1984) (tensions between District Court and First Circuit). Judge Torruella likens these "tensions" to the normal friction

Puerto Rico desires to preserve its cultural integrity despite its close constitutional bonds with the larger American nation. One major component of that integrity is the legal system whose roots are deep in Puerto Rico's Spanish heritage and whose branches affect the lives of Puerto Ricans in fundamental ways. Because of its social and political connections with the United States, however, and because of its exposure to the institutions, procedures, authority, and personnel of American common law, Puerto Rico has become an example of what is sometimes referred to as a "mixed" or "hybrid" legal system.[78] However, since the adoption of *estado libre asociado,* the clear tendency of Puerto Rican law has been in the direction of preserving "a strictly indigenous [system] which will continue to evolve in its own way."[79]

The "crisis of Puerto Rican law" is unique, but it is not without precedent in American experience. Early in the nineteenth century, Lower Louisiana,[80] acquired as part of the Louisiana Purchase in 1803, brought within American jurisdiction a legal culture totally foreign to American common law traditions. The problems encountered by American territorial administrators in Louisiana, and the frustrations felt there by the local inhabitants, were not unlike the experiences of Puerto Ricans in the early part of this century—the use of strange legal procedures such as jury trials in civil and criminal cases, the conduct of proceedings in English rather than in

---

between Federal and state courts and trial and appellate courts which can be found on the mainland. In general, Judge Torruella avers that the average Puerto Rican firmly believes in the high quality of justice he will receive in the Federal District Court in Puerto Rico.

78. J.A. Morales, "Puerto Rico: Two Roads to Justice," *Revista de Derecho Puertorriqueno*, 20 (1981), 293–342.

79. Joseph Dainow, "The Method of Legal Development Through Judicial Interpretation in Louisiana and Puerto Rico," 22 *Revista Juridica de la Universidad de Puerto Rico* 22 (1952)108, 153. The turning point toward a greater assertion of Puerto Rico's own legal tradition was the publication of an article in 1948 by a noted Puerto Rican legal scholar who identified "the crisis of Puerto Rican law" as the increasing assimilation of common law elements particularly in the area of procedure. Manuel Rodriguez Ramos, "Interaction of Civil and Anglo-American Law in the Legal Method of Puerto Rico," *Tulane Law Review*. 23 (1948–49), 1–37, 345–367. In more recent years, the influence of Judge Jose Trias Monge of the Puerto Rican Supreme Court has been marked. Judge Torruella attributes much of this agitation to academics who tend to prefer "pure" to "mixed" systems and who emphasize differences rather than the common approaches of all advanced legal systems to shared problems.

80. I.e., the Territory of Orleans; see 2 Stat. 283 (Act of March 26, 1804).

Spanish, the adoption of English and American texts as authoritative sources of law, the arrival of lawyers from the mainland who threatened to displace local practitioners, and the imposition of an American national court (i.e., the Federal District Court) upon the local judicial hierarchy.[81] The policy of the national government was to make Louisiana part of the Anglo-American common law world largely because Americans considered civil law not only inferior but less friendly to republican liberties and forms of government. President Thomas Jefferson expressed this policy on a number of occasions, including a letter to his Treasury Secretary, Albert Gallatin. Our plan, he said, was "to draw their laws and organization to the mold of ours by degrees . . . without exciting too much discontent."[82] In short, America's stated policy was to supplant Louisiana civil law with Anglo-American common law. But as a result of geographical circumstances, a complex political process, and a series of unforeseen historical events, the people of Louisiana succeeded in warding off this deliberate national attempt to make Louisiana part of the common law "family." Jefferson's policy failed. Subsequently, the Louisiana legislature enacted its

---

81. Examples of the parallels from Louisiana's history are many. One Louisiana planter reported in 1807: "There is no country in the world, perhaps, where the science of jurisprudence abounds with such various, complex and contradictory principles, as in Louisiana. As a system it is composed of the most heterogeneous materials. In civil concerns, rules of right are sought from a thousand sources, often enveloped in the mysteries of unknown languages, and the unwritten customs and usages of the descendants of European nations who have successively occupied the country. To these may be added the whole system of the English precedents—and the general and local regulations, that grow out of the powers of the new sovereignty." *A Letter from Allan B. Magruder of Opelousas* (New Orleans, 1808), 20. Native Louisianians mounted a protest to Congress in 1804 which highlighted their confusion over the strange new legal system: "[The errors committed by judges] uncertain of what codes they are to decide, wavering between the civil and the common law, between the forms of French, Spanish, and American jurisprudence, and with the best intentions unable to expound laws of which they are ignorant . . . [evidenced the need for] reducing this chaos to order, and calling a system of harmony from the depths of this confused, discordant mass." *Remonstrance of the People of Louisiana,* in U.S. Congress, Debates and Proceedings (42 Vols. Washington, D.C. 1834–1856), 8th Congress, 2nd Session (Dec. 31, 1807), 1597–1608 (appendix), 1607.

82. Jefferson to Gallatin, November 9, 1803, Albert Gallatin Papers, New York Historical Society.

own unique Civil Code, and Louisiana has managed to remain a civil law state in a common law country ever since.[83]

The Louisiana experience is instructive. It demonstrates the commitment of Louisianans to their own identity and their resourcefulness in protecting and promoting their unique legal heritage. It also demonstrated that America was capable of accommodating a different legal tradition despite deep national and cultural prejudices favoring Anglo-American common law. To be sure, the "crisis of Puerto Rican law" is more difficult and more intractable than the crisis that faced nineteenth century Louisiana. Louisiana became a state within a decade of its acquisition by the United States, but Puerto Rico has been an "unincorporated territory" for nearly a century. Consequently, Louisiana was able to become self-governing soon after its direct exposure to American legal institutions, whereas Puerto Rico has remained in a position of colonial subservience subject to the control of Federal authorities, particularly the federal courts, that for many years were agents of "Americanization," "territorialism," and "transculturation." Nevertheless, when compared with Louisiana, Puerto Rico enjoys certain decided advantages which may enable it to develop "an effective Puerto Rican legal ethos."[84] Unlike Louisiana, where French and Spanish are no longer spoken by the general population and where the language of the law schools is English, Puerto Rico is still Spanish-speaking, its law students receive training in the Spanish civil law, and its practitioners work with the sources of Puerto Rican law in their original forms. Moreover, the fact that Puerto Rico is physically separate from the mainland gives it a geographic insularity in which its legal integrity can be more securely grounded.

Jose Trias Monge, the former Chief Justice of the Supreme Court of Puerto Rico, diagnosed the Puerto Rican legal system this way:

> The health of a system of law depends on the nature of its relationship with the national language and culture; on its sense of identity; on its . . . relationship with other juridical systems; on

---

83. For a more detailed discussion, see George Dargo, *Jefferson's Louisiana: Politics and the Clash of Legal Traditions* (Cambridge: Harvard University Press, 1975; rev'd ed. Clark, N.J: Lawbook Exchange, 2009).

84. Graffen, "The Federal Courts," *Revista Colegio*, (47), 1323.

> its fidelity to the essential values of the country and on its capacity to contribute to the construction of a more just society. From this point of view our system of law finds itself in an extremely poor condition of health.[85]

As Puerto Rico strives to achieve a healthier accommodation of its legal heritage to American law, it must draw upon its own internal resources and insist upon greater recognition of its own legal traditions realizing always that the "crisis of Puerto Rican law" is intimately connected to the continuing crisis of Puerto Rico's "status." One cannot be resolved in isolation from the other. Through all of this the First Circuit can continue to make a special contribution. As Judge Levin Campbell, the former chief judge of the First Circuit, once advised, the court must work within a given political framework. But to the extent that it can help to build a Puerto Rican "legal ethos," the court may pave the way toward an ultimate resolution. It can do so by honoring the sources and methods of Puerto Rican law and by treating Puerto Rico's law with equality just as it would toward the courts of Massachusetts or any of the other fifty states. The First Circuit cannot end the "crisis of Puerto Rican law," but by continuing to honor that law and to work with it, the court can improve the health of the island's legal system and with it the political vitality of its people.

* * *

"Commonwealth"—the word connotes constitutional equality. Four of the states in the United States (Virginia, Massachusetts, Pennsylvania, and Kentucky) are "commonwealths." And in the age of post-colonialism, "commonwealth" is the term used to describe the completely self-governing members of the British Commonwealth of Nations. "Commonwealth" when applied to Puerto Rico, strikes a reassuring note. But the reality is somewhat different. The effects of one hundred years of colonialism have proven to be unsatisfactory from the point of view of Puerto Ricans as well as from the perspective of the United States. "[D]ecades of sporadic debate in Congress over bills to determine Puerto Rico's

---

85. J. Trias Monge, *Historia Constitucional de Puerto Rico* (4 vols., Rio Piedras, 1984), I,. 234; quoted in Graffen, "The Federal Courts", *Revista Colegio*, (47) 1413.

final status has accomplished very little."[86] The choices have been clear—independence, statehood, or a continuation of the present commonwealth in the form of a so-called "enhanced commonwealth" idea.[87] In recent years, there even has been talk of a fourth alternative—*republica asociada* (associated republic) patterned after the Pacific Trust Territories of the United States and equivalent to the United Nations' decolonization definition known as the "free associated state."[88] *Republica asociada* has been defined in the proposed Puerto Rico Democracy Act of 2010 as a "close and mutually beneficial relationship in a voluntary association."

But none of this is likely to happen anytime soon. One hundred years of colonial rule is probably going to continue given the fact that the Puerto Rican "status question" is not on the radar screen of any of the major political parties in the United States. With the current sclerotic condition of the U.S. Congress, it is difficult to imagine that Puerto Rico's political, legal and constitutional status, with all of its complex ramifications, can be expected to change in the near future. "[W]e can continue to live with a terrible contradiction. The United States of America, the oldest representative democracy on eath, over Puerto Rico, the oldest colony on earth."[89]

Consequently, the result is more likely to be a continuation of the present situation which Judge Jose Cabranes (whose words were cited earlier in this essay) has summarized this way: "The key point about Puerto Rico's place in the American constitutional system is that no word other than 'colonialism' adequately describes the relationship between a powerful metropolitan state and an impoverished overseas dependency disenfranchised from the formal lawmaking processes that shape its people's daily lives. We do well to speak plainly and accurately—and (in my view) without embarrassment—about the facts as they are."[90] Accordingly, while the time may have come for the status of Puerto Rico to be reexamined and even readjusted in the light of political realities in the world today, the Island of Puerto Rico is more likely to remain a

---

86. Juan Gonzalez, *Harvest of Empire: A History of Latinos in America* Rev. Ed., New York: Penguin Books, 2011), 279.
87. Ibid., 296.
88. Ibid., 303–304.
89. R. Fernandez, *The Disenchanted Island*, 249.
90. Cabranes, "Puerto Rico and the Constitution," Remarks at First Circuit Judicial Conference, San Juan, P.R., November, 1985, reprinted in, 110 F.R.D. 449 (1986).

striking remnant of the Age of Colonialism—America's oldest and richest colony—for the foreseeable future.

Index

www.ingramcontent.com/pod-product-compliance
Ingram Content Group UK Ltd.
Pitfield, Milton Keynes, MK11 3LW, UK
UKHW041854031026
15587UKWH00006B/1214/J

9 781616 191443